PRODUCING
ONLINE
NEWS
DIGITAL SKILLS,
STRONGER
STORIES

CQ PRESS
A Division of SAGE
www.cqpress.com

RYAN M. THORNBURG
University of North Carolina at Chapel Hill

CQ Press
2300 N Street, NW, Suite 800
Washington, DC 20037

Phone: 202-729-1900; toll-free, 1-866-4CQ-PRESS (1-866-427-7737)

Web: www.cqpress.com

Cover design: www.myselfincluded.com
Composition: C&M Digitals (P) Ltd.

⊗ The paper used in this publication exceeds the requirements of the American National Standard for Information Sciences—Permanence of Paper for Printed Library Materials, ANSI Z39.48-1992.

Printed and bound in the United States of America

14 13 12 11 10   1 2 3 4 5

Library of Congress Cataloging-in-Publication Data

Thornburg, Ryan.
   Producing online news : digital skills, stronger stories / Ryan M. Thornburg.
     p. cm.
   Includes index.
   ISBN 978-1-60426-996-3 (alk. paper)
   1. Online journalism. 2. Journalism—Authorship. I. Title.

PN4784.O62T46 2010
070.4—dc22

2010039389

To anyone striving to shine light in dark places,
hold powerful people accountable and explain our increasingly
complex and interconnected world. Your work every day
inspires me to continue looking for new tools to tell stronger stories.

BRIEF CONTENTS ——

CONTENTS ———

SECTION 3: The Future of News

PREFACE

Long before a representative of CQ Press came to my office to talk with me about the online journalism courses I was developing at the University of North Carolina at Chapel Hill, my colleagues and I at The Washington Post and the other news organizations where I worked had struggled with the challenge of finding, hiring and then training staffers who had a strong grounding in the traditional ethics and values of 20th-century journalism as well as the technical dexterity and creative leadership required in 21st-century newsrooms.

From a résumé, it was almost impossible to determine a job applicant's actual knowledge or experience. Some had been "content producers" while others had been "multimedia developers." Some had learned how to program ActionScript while studying photojournalism, and some had taught themselves HTML while writing press releases for government or nonprofit organizations.

In some ways this was an exhilarating way to assemble a newsroom—it felt a bit like being Lee Marvin in *The Dirty Dozen*. But in other ways it was no better than the spin of a roulette wheel—unpredictable and all-too-often frustrating. What's more, audience behaviors and technology were changing so rapidly that we would often have to re-write job descriptions in the middle of vetting applicants.

In that critical first decade of online journalism, we were making up the rules as we went along. In the midst of improvisation, we often lamented that there was no textbook that could help us explain to our new hires—some fresh out of college and some making a transition to digital news after a lifetime of traditional reporting and editing—how to manage a database of content, write good homepage blurbs or use multiple media to tell a single story.

That is the lament that I shared with the folks at CQ Press during my very first year in the classroom. And this is the textbook that I had wanted all of my hires to have read.

Initially, the idea of writing a textbook for students of online journalism seemed a fool's errand. I found that existing textbooks intended for use in online journalism courses were either collections of war stories that gave students no practical guidance or technical manuals that provided no journalistic context for the tools they taught students to operate.

I began by outlining a series of characteristics that an online journalism textbook would need in order to be even remotely useful in the classroom as well as carry legitimacy in professional newsrooms. And after conferring with the editors at CQ Press, it quickly became clear that we held many of the same beliefs about what it would take to write a textbook about online journalism that instructors would actually use:

- It would have to be published as a comfortably familiar print edition as well as an online edition that could be updated more regularly than the print version.

- It would need to be comprehensive—well-suited for curricula that teach online journalism in a single course and prepare students to succeed in jobs where they are expected to be jacks of all the digital trades.

- It would need to be written in such a way that each chapter could stand alone—appropriate for curricula that integrate online journalism as a portion of traditional newswriting, editing and "broadcast" courses.

- It would need to draw a clear connection between traditional skills and values and the new applications of those skills.

- It would need to give students the opportunity to actually practice the skills and apply the concepts that they read about in the book and discussed in class.

- It would need to be written in the language and style of a digital native—someone who could speak the language of today's cutting-edge digital professionals and be able to separate the technological fads from the foundational new media concepts that are here to stay.

- Finally, it would need to be a confident and comprehensive guide for experienced journalism educators who eye the industry's rapid changes with legitimate skepticism.

Clearly, it would not suffice simply to write a textbook for journalism. In fact, we had to go a giant step further and develop a transformational experience—one that would practice what it preached about the value of multimedia, interactivity and on-demand delivery. To accomplish this, we created online learning modules that have been integrated seamlessly with the book's chapters. Essential to practicing the skills outlined in this text, the modules turn the passive text into that transformational experience—and in so doing, turn students into journalists.

TEACHING DIGITAL NEWS TO DIGITAL NATIVES

While this book was conceived over the decade that I spent in professional newsrooms, it was born only after several years of teaching journalism students at UNC. I'm old enough to have worked on a college newspaper that did not have a website, but young enough to have never had a journalism job that wasn't online. Most of my students today don't remember a world without the Internet; the result is that many of them take for granted the technology and aspirations that led to the digital media revolution.

For students who have grown up using the Web for research as well as for sharing digital photos and videos with friends, this book may be their first behind-the-scenes look at how—and why—common digital networked communication tools work they way they do.

When I introduce a specific tool or technology, I do so primarily to underscore concepts that illustrate how tools and technology affect news reporting and editing. For example, students learn HTML not only so they can build and repair Web pages, but also so that they will understand the concept of separating content from its display. This concept appears again and again throughout the book and helps students think critically about how and why the audience is separating pieces of content from their original locations and re-aggregating them with other pieces of content in other locations.

TRADITIONAL JOURNALISM AND NEW MEDIA

Journalists today still must hold powerful people accountable, give voice to the voiceless and explain a complex world to their audience. But with revolutionary changes in the way that audiences consume, engage and even create journalism, professional reporters and editors have to know how to use the right digital media tools at the right time.

The book begins not with an introduction to writing for search engine optimization or with a tutorial about computer code. It starts instead at the place where all journalism instruction should start: with a discussion about the central role that journalism plays in the functioning of modern democracy and free markets. If there is value in training a new generation of journalists, it is not in teaching them to save newspapers, or save newsrooms, but to preserve and extend freedom and justice to all people.

ORGANIZATION AND FEATURES

What is it about the Internet that makes it more than just an inexpensive distribution tool? It is the three pillars of online journalism—multimedia, interactivity and on-demand delivery. This book helps students begin thinking about the opportunities and challenges of online news.

Foundations of online news—Section One—opens with Chapter 1, which demonstrates through specific examples how the three pillars of online journalism, and the tools they employ, can be used to tell stronger stories, supported by historical context from traditional media.

In Chapter 2, students meet, or are reacquainted with, the values that make news "news"—for example, magnitude, prominence and proximity, among others—as well as the core elements that every news story should have regardless of medium: Who? What? When? Where? Why? and How? With all the tools available to journalists today, these traditional news values and elements provide the essential framework that ensures that we're building real stories—not just adding bells and whistles.

The first section wraps up with Chapter 3, which features recent research that shows how the behavior of news consumers, and not just the creative desires of journalists, is driving a rising demand for journalists who can use technology to effectively report the news. The chapter describes who is using online news, as well as when, where and why they are using it.

A strong grounding in journalistic traditions and an emphasis on discovering and meeting the needs of a specific audience give students a bright beacon that will help them navigate a sea of constant change.

The second section—and the bulk of the book—takes students through the skills and strategies they need to be good journalists. These "how-to" chapters cover everything from which buttons to push in digital video editing programs to which actions to avoid when moderating online discussions about the news. Helpful "TOOLS" sections in these chapters walk students through the latest technologies—Twitter, Wordpress, Audacity, Caspio and more—to lend immediacy to their researching and reporting.

The section begins with the most widely used and most infrequently taught tool of online newsrooms—the content management system (CMS). Chapter 4 explains how this important tool works, introduces students to the vocabulary of content management and highlights how the way journalists think about content affects the editorial decisions they make and the manner in which citizens get their information. The online learning modules are built upon the Wordpress CMS to gives students hands-on experience and prepare them for the content management systems they'll encounter in the newsroom.

Chapter 5 covers another element of online journalism that is widely consumed and infrequently taught—text. Journalism students who are familiar with print journalism's traditional inverted pyramid style of writing will be in good stead. However, this chapter goes further by introducing students to the unique challenges of online text—for example, writing online headlines, the ever-changing art of search engine optimization and, perhaps the most common type of original online journalism, the construction of the homepage summary.

The traditions of journalistic verification are featured throughout Chapter 6, a guide to the use of search engines and social networks for reporting. While today's students have come of age using Facebook, Wikipedia and YouTube, they do not use them with the same discernment that professional online news producers use. Building trust in the community and judging the trustworthiness of others are skills that come up time and again throughout the book.

The vetting of online resources is nowhere more important than in the practice of building links for news stories. Chapter 7 teaches students how to choose good link destinations as well as select and write clear and effective departure text. Links should be used to increase transparency, build trust and improve the relevance of news stories. The chapter emphasizes that journalists have always been linkers and that the culture of linking that is central to online communication affects how journalists approach attribution and collaboration.

Students move away from text and into audio-visual reporting and editing in Chapter 8. The chapter shows how multiple media are being used to tell stronger stories and introduces students to the basics of reporting and editing with digital photography, audio and video. For students who have no experience with these storytelling techniques, the chapter provides a clear and efficient overview. For students who have used a camera or audio recorder, the chapter emphasizes the concepts of digital presentation.

While audio-visual online journalism has led much of the innovation in online news—especially at print-centric newspapers—perhaps the biggest gap between the supply and demand of online journalism skills today is in the field of data-driven journalism. The ability to think of information as collections of fielded data is important for journalists working in content management systems, infographics and social media. Chapter 9 gives students hands-on experience with the type of basic fielded datasets they will see in professional news settings as well as techniques for thinking about how to collect, organize and present data online. As with Chapter 8, for some students Chapter 9 will serve as a launch pad into further specialization. But also like Chapter 8, this chapter gives all students the common vocabulary and conceptual framework they need to tell stronger stories and work in modern newsrooms.

The last section of the book looks at how the culture of news is changing. It is the section that educators and students are most likely to approach with very different perspectives. Here I describe the uses of social media and computer algorithms in today's newsrooms; at the same time, I aim to inspire students to innovate and take responsibility for building their own civic and cultural norms.

Chapter 10 brings us to the worst sounding and most maligned word in digital journalism—blog. This chapter helps students and instructors step back, take a collective deep breath and accept that a blog is defined by its format, not by its content or creator. More important than teaching students about the specific writing style required of blogs, I demonstrate how blogs and the emphasis on the news value of recency establish online journalism as a service rather than a good, a process rather than a product.

The opening of the reporting process to the audience is happening hand in hand with the evolution of journalism from a lecture to a conversation. Chapter 11 teaches the journalistic techniques that are used when working with social media, crowdsourcing, distributed reporting and user-generated content. It shows digital natives that responsible and meaningful audience engagement requires thoughtful intent rather than haphazard banter.

Wrapping up the book is a chapter that introduces students to the basics of remixing news from a variety of sources and using two or more online tools to create journalistic mashups. Chapter 12 also introduces students to basic computer programming vocabulary and concepts. As much as a concluding chapter, it also serves as an introduction to a new way of training journalists to use algorithmic thinking—the bridge between computer science and the journalistic values of precision, brevity and verification.

Features throughout the text aim to develop the editorial and ethical judgment that is required of all responsible reporters, as well as introduce students to the technology that will bolster their stories. They include

- News Judgment boxes that explore journalistic choices—how to tell the right story, at the right time, in the right environment.

- View Source boxes that place the spotlight on the technology behind specific news projects—like how five editors at Yahoo News can publish more than 2,000 stories a day.

- Real-word examples from both traditional outlets and news-style sites, including ProPublica, PolitiFact, BeliefNet and Global Voices, that showcase journalists connecting with their audiences.

ONLINE LEARNING MODULES

We knew as we were developing this book that it would quickly become irrelevant if it were merely a print paperback updated once every few years. Much like online journalism, the value of this textbook is in the ongoing conversations I have with students and instructors as well as the transparent process of working on the text edition.

You will find me on my blog—www.producingonlinenews.com—and other major social media platforms, frequently posting website critiques, links to new tutorials and new tools and updates or corrections to information in the book if they're needed. These platforms are places where I host conversations with the book's audience—clarifying and answering questions and introducing the next generation of online journalists to each other and to professionals already working in online news.

CQ Press has also published 12 online learning modules—one module to correspond with each chapter in the book. These modules are sold separately from the book, or they can be purchased with the book as a package. Go to journalism.cqpress.com to register and buy or activate the modules.

When students log in to the Web-based learning modules, they will be connected to online exercises and teaching resources and will be automatically set up with their own Wordpress blog that they will use to complete the exercises. Students will be gaining experience with one of the most widely used online publishing platforms simply as a byproduct of working on the modules.

Instructors who incorporate the online modules into their classes will be able to track the progress of each student, collect exercises for grading and provide feedback directly to students.

As students work through the modules, their blogs will become what amounts to a digital portfolio that they can use to demonstrate their ability to prospective employers. Students will have complete control over the privacy of their blogs, as the Wordpress platform gives bloggers the option to make their posts public or keep them private.

Those students will also be taught the full array of Wordpress options on how to manage comments on their blogs. These choices demonstrate not only that students can use the tool, but also that they can apply the editorial judgment that is the single most valuable skill of the professional journalist.

Students who do good work will have a strong incentive to make their blogs public. Many of the exercises on which they will work involve critiques of professional stories and news websites as well as proposals for new features and discussions about current case studies in online journalism.

When the course is complete, students who choose to may export the content of their blogs and take it with them to their own domains or websites.

The exercises for each module closely re-create a real newsroom experience. When students learn about digital audio-video editing in Chapter 8, they are given actual audio and visual files to download and then edit and submit for instructor feedback. When they learn about Twitter, they spend a week in a contest with other students that has them earning points for performing different actions on Twitter. When they learn about data-driven journalism, they download real campaign finance records and manipulate them.

Many of the exercises are completed online, either right within the modules themselves or with freely available Web applications. Some of the exercises, however, require software applications on students' computers. For these exercises, the modules link—when possible—to free and open source software that students can use. Of course, students can also use any appropriate commercial software applications, from Adobe's Photoshop and Premiere to Microsoft's Excel and Access. None of the exercises require students to purchase additional commercial software.

Learning by doing is critical to journalism education. That's why the online modules also provide students with video tutorials that walk them step by step through a variety of tools. These screencasts emphasize journalistic uses for the wide range of software and Web applications to which students are introduced in the text. In addition to the introductory screencasts that are custom-made to pair with the book, the learning modules also have frequently updated links to the best free online text and video tutorials that can take the most enterprising students into more advanced topics, such as database programming and Cascading Style Sheets.

Every module also has

- a digital version of the chapter's text,
- a glossary of key terms in the chapter and interactive flashcards that use these terms,
- a printable PDF tipsheet that becomes a useful reference tool for students working on projects, and
- a multiple-choice quiz to test students' mastery of material in the chapter.

As the tools change, these online modules will quickly change as well.

ACKNOWLEDGMENTS

As you must be aware just by reading this preface, this project became a reality only because fortune brought into my life a wealth of kind, creative and hard-working people. Some are dear and lifelong friends while others are almost complete strangers. I'm truly thankful for the blessings that have connected me to them and for all of the wonderful opportunities that have ensued. I could not have purchased them at any price.

The exhilaration and anxiety I shared with my colleagues at The Washington Post, Congressional Quarterly and U.S. News & World Report during 10 years in their newsrooms gave me a true north that I could always use to test the journalistic integrity and practical application of each and every sentence in this book. I reconnected with many of them during the writing process to make sure that I still had a true picture of how online newsrooms operate after I left them for the classroom.

As much as I needed to have experienced online journalism first-hand to write this book, I also needed to leave the daily rush of online journalism. Returning to my alma mater at UNC, I found the same support and freedom that encouraged my first forays into online journalism. Jean Folkerts, dean of the School of Journalism and Mass Communication, as well as my colleagues on the faculty have kindly guided me as I came to understand that the challenges of engaging in online journalism are dwarfed by the challenges of teaching other people to engage in it too. Probably the best way to tell you who helped me would be simply to link to the staff directory at the school, but I would like especially to acknowledge Chad Stevens, who helped me more clearly explain video compression; Cathy Packer, who set me straight about the current disposition of legal issues; Bill Cloud and Andy Bechtel, who looked at early drafts of the editing chapters; former director of information technology and services Fred Thomsen for his suggestions on screencasting tools; library director Stephanie Willen Brown for her speedy research help; David Cupp for his conversations with me about Edward R. Murrow; Director of Research Administration Jennifer Klimas Gallina for her help writing grants; Paul Jones and the good people at Ibiblio.org for hosting my blog and giving me a playground to test new tools going back to 1996; Laura Ruel, whose research is cited throughout the book; and Jan Yopp, who let me first test my textbook writing skills by bravely inviting me to be a co-author on her own introductory newswriting textbook. I also kindly thank Executive Vice Chancellor and Provost Bruce Carney and the rest of the Committee on Faculty Research and Study Leaves, which provided financial support for the development of the online modules through a Junior Faculty Development Grant.

My students at UNC were the guinea pigs whose (occasional) looks of confusion and honest feedback on early drafts of the text helped me better understand my audience. Their body language in the classroom spoke volumes and made me both sad and relieved that I couldn't see the faces of the audience during my decade in online news. I would especially like to thank Alex Kowalski, whose last-minute interviewing help was invaluable. And Nick Weidenmiller, who jumped into this project at the last minute with the energy that would make you think his name was on the cover.

The path of my life does seem to keep turning me back to old friends, so perhaps I shouldn't have been surprised that this book allowed me to work with CQ again. The entire staff at CQ Press has equal parts good humor and dedication to excellence that inspired me to keep going when I sometimes returned to my original thought that writing a textbook for online journalism was a fool's errand. If there is an industry more tied to tradition and more in need of creative destruction than journalism it must be the textbook business. So it was inspiring to find editorial director Charisse Kiino enthusiastically championing my project, requiring compromise on my ideas only when I had bad ideas. Development editor Jane Harrigan taught me the difference between talking about something and teaching it. Both Jane and copyeditor Tracy Villano took my words and carefully showed me what I really meant to say. Working with assistant editor Christina Mueller was a teacher's dream come true. I first met Christina when I was a guest speaker in a class she was taking as an undergraduate at The George Washington University. We crossed paths again during her internship at U.S. News. During this third encounter, I have been happy to play the role of pupil to her excellent mastery of the book development process. Dwain Smith, online product development editor, and the rest of the crew in the online production department followed a long line of user-interface designers and Web application developers who somehow managed to take my doodles and bullet points and make them into a product with which I am so proud to be associated. Finally, I must acknowledge the careful work of production editor Allyson Rudolph and proofreader Talia Greenberg, who helped fine-tune and proof this book so that it is as accessible and accurate as possible. Allyson in particular patiently untangled the labyrinthine layout I put before her and conscientiously attended to the smallest formatting details in an effort to satisfy even the most discriminating reader.

As I was writing this book, I found myself returning time and again to previously published books and blogs. I want to acknowledge them here as a sort of virtual bookshelf:

- Dan Gillmor, whose book "We the Media" has been required reading in almost all my classes.

- Mark Briggs, whose free online pamphlet "Journalism 2.0" and CQ Press book "Journalism Next" have also been used by most of my students.

- Mindy McAdams, whose blog "Teaching Online Journalism" and all its associated resources are a treasure of thoughtful and straightforward insight.

- A trio of sites funded by the John S. & James L. Knight Foundation—knightdigital mediacenter.org, kcnn.org and j-learning.org.

- A variety of resources funded by the Poynter Institute for Media Studies—NewsU .org, its EyeTracking studies and its excellent column E-Media Tidbits, which was the source of several quotes throughout the book.

- Lynda.com and W3Schools.com—the resources to which I turn when I need to bone up on a new piece of software or computer language.

- The Pew Research Center for the People & the Press and the Pew Research Center's Internet and American Life Project, without which I would have written a skeleton of Chapter 4.

- The Project for Excellence in Journalism's State of the News Media series provided an invaluable collection of information about the industry.

- Amy Webb's knowledgewebb.net, which advised "don't sweat the tech" and gave me the opportunity to try out my training skills on professional journalists in New York and Cairo.

- Steve Krug, author of "Don't Make Me Think"—a smart book about Web design that even a visually illiterate person like me can understand.

- Jakob Nielsen, whose Alertbox columns at UseIt.org have for years helped me turn discussions about Web writing and layout from religion to science.

- Joseph Pine II and James H. Gilmore, whose book "The Experience Economy" guided much of my thinking about the rationale and format of the online learning modules.

- Lawrence Snyder, whose book "Fluency With Information Technology" inspired my thinking about how to incorporate the teaching of hard skills with the broader concepts those skills illustrate.

- Jay Hamilton, whose book "All the News That's Fit to Sell" introduced me to the theories of political economist Anthony Downs and always helps me keep the audience's motivations in mind.

- Brooks Jackson and Kathleen Hall Jamieson, whose book "UnSpun" should be required reading for young people as they face a life of nearly unlimited choices of news media and also an unprecedented responsibility to choose the right ones.

- And finally, William Strunk Jr. and E.B. White, whose "Elements of Style" never goes out of style.

One of the most enjoyable aspects of writing this book has been the opportunity it gave me to talk with people I respect about their experiences in online newsrooms. Some of our conversations were informal chats over Twitter or at conferences; others were long and wide-ranging phone interviews. Some conversations are highlighted in the book, and some gave me ideas that are dispersed throughout. Here I would like to acknowledge the people who took time out of their very busy schedules to help me:

Melanie Asmar, Denver Westword
Christopher Ave, St. Louis Post Dispatch
David Banks, CNN
Ryan Teague Beckwith, Congress.org
Joshua Benton, Nieman Journalism Lab at Harvard University
Steve Buttry, TBD, Washington, D.C.
Sarah Cohen, Duke University
John Conway, CBC New Media
Bill Dedman, MSNBC
Joellen Easton, American Public Media
Tom Embrey, The Pilot, Southern Pines, N.C.
Jesper Frank, Saxotech

Virgil Griffith, WikiScanner
Vaughn Hagerty, The Star-News, Wilmington, N.C.
Tom Kennedy, Syracuse University
Brian Krebs, krebsonsecurity.com
Tammi Marcoullier, Publish2
Jeffrey Marcus, The New York Times
Sarah McBride, freelance correspondent for NPR and former reporter at The Wall Street Journal
Brian Palmer, Slate
Christina Pino-Marina, University of Maryland

Peter Roybal, ABC News
Julie Rutherford, BeliefNet
Ryan Sholin, Publish2
Mark Stencel, NPR
Gretchen Teichgraeber, Leadership
    Directories and Forrester Research
Robyn Tomlin, The Star-News,
    Wilmington, N.C.

Daniel Victor, TBD, Washington, D.C.
Paul Volpe, TBD, Washington, D.C.
Russ Walker, Yahoo
John Walsh, ESPN
Paige West, MSNBC
Derek Willis, The New York Times
Chris Wilson, Slate
Steve Yelvington, Morris Communications.

I would also like to thank the proposal and manuscript reviewers, who made this book a reality and offered beneficial suggestions throughout the process: Jennifer Adams, Auburn University; Brett Atwood, Washington State University; Lawrence Baden, Webster University; Robert Dardenne, University of South Florida St. Petersburg; Judy Hopkins, University of Pittsburgh at Bradford; Jeremy Lipschultz, University of Nebraska at Omaha; Paula Maggio, University of Akron; Mike McKean, University of Missouri; Thomas Nelson, Elon University; Mark Raduziner, Johnson County Community College; Michelle Weldon, Northwestern University.

Finally, my deepest love and thanks go to my family. My wife, Bronwyn, was an uncredited editor and sounding board on this project—and she kept all of our family projects on track while I too often buried my head in writing. My kids, Collin and Shea, will probably forever have some Pavlovian reaction to the phrase, "Daddy needs to work on his book." But with my writing done (for now) I look forward to working on an even bigger instructional goal—teaching them to read.

1 ONLINE NEWS IS DIFFERENT

In this chapter, you will learn:

- What makes online journalism different.
- How to identify different kinds of multimedia formats.
- The role of interactivity in journalism.
- Why on-demand delivery is putting the audience in control.

It is March 21, 2010, a little after 10:30 p.m. Eastern time. The place is any living room in America. Mike, an avid college basketball fan, is watching highlights of the day's NCAA Tournament games on television. At a break for commercial, he picks up the laptop sitting on the couch next to him and sees this update from Jessica, one of his friends on Facebook: "We did it, teddy. The house passed it and health care for every American is on its way to becoming reality. #hcr."

The U.S. House of Representatives had just approved a bill that many were calling the most sweeping piece of social legislation in 40 years. It was the cornerstone of President Barack Obama's domestic agenda, widely opposed by Republicans and an uncertain prospect among Democrats until moments before its passage. The conclusion of a year-long national public debate was a real cliffhanger. And while it may not have been as popular a news story as Michael Jackson's death or the H1N1 flu, "health care" was one of 2009's most widely covered stories. It was also one of the most searched terms on Google News and one of the most discussed topics on blogs.

A generation earlier, millions of Americans might have learned about the late-breaking House vote from a network TV anchor like Tom Brokaw. But on this night, millions of Americans each played the role of Brokaw—breaking the news to their own online friends and followers. How did amateur anchors like Jessica know what had happened? Before the message reached Mike, where did it come from? The answer to this question is the story of how news is created and distributed for, by and among the more than 225 million Americans who are part of a digital, networked world. Let's trace the sources and see how we experience news a little more than 15 years into the digital revolution.

Like millions of news junkies, Jessica subscribes to e-mail news alerts from The New York Times. Less than a minute before she updated her Facebook status, she had received

From: **NYTimes.com News Alert** <nytdirect@nytimes.com>
Date: Sun, Mar 21, 2010 at 10:49 PM
Subject: News Alert: House Approves Landmark Bill to Extend Health Care to Millions

Breaking News Alert
The New York Times
Sun, March 21, 2010 -- 10:49 PM ET

House Approves Landmark Bill to Extend Health Care to Millions

Congress gave final approval on Sunday to legislation that
would provide medical coverage to tens of millions of
uninsured Americans and remake the nation's health care
system along the lines proposed by President Obama.

For Consumers, Some Clarity on Health Care Changes
http://nyti.ms/927aP5
11:46 PM Mar 21st via web

Health Care Bill Approved: A timeline -- nearly 100 years of
legislative milestones and defeats - http://nyti.ms/HJJ7k
11:23 PM Mar 21st via TweetDeck

Health care bill results: An interactive map of the U.S. that
shows where and how your Representative voted.
http://nyti.ms/aO6YlH
11:10 PM Mar 21st via TweetDeck

Health Care Bill Passes House by 219 to 212. Complete story
and coverage here: http://nyti.ms/d78YT0
11:05 PM Mar 21st via TweetDeck

Health Care Bill approved with what looks like 219 votes to
extend health care for millions. #hcr http://nyti.ms/b3cWXf
10:52 PM Mar 21st via TweetDeck

NYT NEWS ALERT: House Approves Landmark Bill to Extend
Health Care to Millions
10:50 PM Mar 21st via API

Health Care Vote Approved by House of Representatives. #hcr
261 votes in favor. Full coverage - http://nyti.ms/b3cWXf
10:45 PM Mar 21st via TweetDeck

The House of Representatives is voting now on health care
legislation. #hcr. Live blogging. http://nyti.ms/9iWfdU
10:36 PM Mar 21st via TweetDeck

News Analysis: Obama's Health Care Victory Carries a Cost
http://nyti.ms/cRKzJo
10:20 PM Mar 21st via web

Thousands Call for Immigration Reform in Capital
http://nyti.ms/9PG2Dn

Producers at nytimes.com write a headline
once and send it to many places. The convenience comes with a caveat: The headline must work well in all contexts—for
example, as an email subject (top) and a
Twitter update (bottom).

an alert on the mobile device she affection-
ately calls her "Crackberry." But where did
this alert come from? Who wrote it? Who
decided that this news was big enough that it
was worth causing mobile phones around the
world to start vibrating?

As soon as the Times' reporters on Capi-
tol Hill confirmed that Democrats had the
votes needed to pass the bill, an online producer in the newsroom began crafting the
message in the content management system.
She carefully worded a short, snappy headline
designed to catch the audience's attention in
all the places it would instantly appear as soon
as she was ready to release it. These places
included a story on NYTimes.com, a Twitter
feed and the subject line of the e-mail alert.

While cable news networks have been in
the 24-hour news business for decades, the
breaking news operations at newspapers are
still teenagers. Until the late 1990s, Monday
morning papers on the East Coast wouldn't
have included a story that broke at 10:30 on
a Sunday night. Print reporters and editors
would have had 24 hours to engage in deeper
reporting. But no more. Newspapers are now
part of the 24/7 news cycle; today, editors
must use their judgment to make minute-by-
minute decisions about how to cover breaking news and where to play it on the Web.

As the editors and producers at The New
York Times were exercising their news judgment, Google News and Yahoo News were
turning decisions about what to publish over
to a machine. Still others were letting the
crowd determine what should be published:
both the 5-year-old online liberal news and
commentary site The Huffington Post and the
online site of the 133-year-old newspaper The
Washington Post automatically published
comments about the health care debate posted
by users of Twitter.

Jessica's post would have appeared on both of these sites. At the same time she broke the news to her Facebook friends, she also sent the post to Twitter, a microblogging service that in just three years has become a news source for more than 14 million Americans. And because the post included the health care reform hashtag "#hcr," it was automatically picked up on washingtonpost.com and huffingtonpost.com.

Support for publishing readers' comments, untouched by journalists, isn't something you'd have found in the newsrooms of your parents' generation. Neither are the skills and tools that it took to get those comments up on the site. Today, computer programmers and journalists work in tandem. After journalists decided what keywords to grab from Twitter and place automatically on their news sites, programmers pulled data either directly from Twitter's application programming interface or from an RSS feed published by Twitter. To make sure that the words posted to Twitter appeared on The Washington Post's site in the right font and location, the computer programmers used cascading stylesheets, or CSS, and HyperText Markup Language, or HTML.

Newsroom Web developers were part of the coverage of the health care debate from the start. Over at The New York Times, programmers had created a database of congressional votes and built an interface on the Web so that users could search and sort information on demand. The database of the health care vote wasn't a resource only for visitors to NYTimes.com; it was also a resource for Times reporters. On its Prescriptions blog, dedicated to the narrow topic of the health care debate, reporters at NYTimes.com were able to post the final vote at 10:44 p.m. ET, almost as soon as it was tallied. The Times' reporters had been blogging fast and furiously all day, posting each detail as it happened. Within 23 minutes of the vote, the site's

Live health-care vote updates from Twitter

Scroll for streaming news on the House health-care reform debate happening now. A vote is expected to happen tonight.

slackadjuster - 12:48 a.m.
RT @FreedomofLies: glenn beck lie: #hcr is about reparations. yes he did say that. YES.

panndder - 12:48 a.m.
RT @UMN_Health_Talk: Join Senator @alfranken for Public Health Week at #UMN School of Public Health for talk on #hcr impact on Minnesota http://ow.ly/1vEFJ

KEder - 12:48 a.m.
RT @Mattphilbin: Ha! Wonder if woman who thought BHO would pay her mortgage & gas is 1of the dopes asking where they get their free hcr

FoxNewsMom - 12:48 a.m.
"Private Health Insurance Death Spiral Begins Sept 23" (@NCPA) http://bit.ly/c7jRzl #hcr #tcot #tlot #teaparty #sgp /via @ucbook

mmaction - 12:48 a.m.
.@RepJoeBarton: "We're Not Gonna Repeal Everything" In The Affordable Care Act http://bit.ly/amwn1N #p2 #tcot #hcr

RNCResearch - 12:48 a.m.
#HCRFallout: FL medical device firm CEO says Obama's #hcr taxes will lead to "layoffs and less investment" http://bit.ly/a3R8LP #tcot

alaskan - 12:48 a.m.
#HCRFallout: FL medical device firm CEO says Obama's #hcr taxes will lead to "layoffs and less investment" http://bit.ly/a3R8LP #tcot

hudsonryan - 12:48 a.m.
@arthurwerry People in favor of HCR have done their research - we know where the $ comes from. No need to speculate. Facts are out there.

marclaitin - 12:48 a.m.
@judicialabuse i'm sure your rates haven't ever gone up before, right? /snark #hcr

alaskan - 12:47 a.m.
#HCRFallout: ObamaCare victimizing job creators and care providers. http://bit.ly/9VkYXR #tcot #hcr #handsoff #firepelosi

real time twitter by: monitter.com

By Rachel Weiner | March 21, 2010; 2:49 PM ET
Categories: 44 The Obama Presidency

The Washington Post used JavaScript, CSS, HTML and code that is freely available from monitter.com to create this live feed of comments related to health care legislation that were posted on Twitter.

readers knew that the bill had passed. Times staffers then updated the news with a link to the site's database of the vote. The brief post at 11:07 p.m. ET read as follows: "Here's our breakdown of the first vote on the Senate bill, known as HR 3590. This will show you by party, by region, who voted how." The link to the database also appeared in the full story that was posted on The New York Times' site. Reporters Robert Pear and David M. Herszenhorn wrote the words, "With the 219-to-212 vote, the House gave final approval to legislation passed by the Senate on Christmas Eve." Web producers decided to link the words "the 219-to-212 vote" to the congressional votes database on their site.

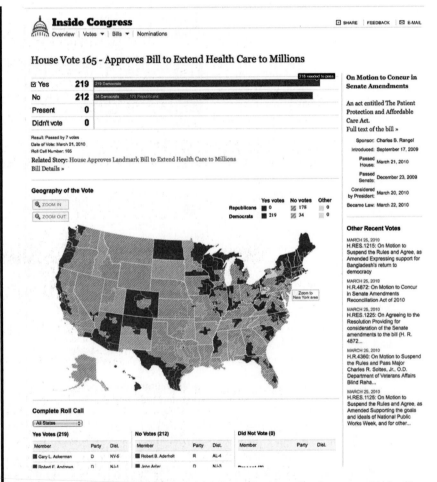

Users of The New York Times' database of congressional votes could identify supporters and opponents of the bill by district, read the full text of the legislation and follow all major actions as the bill moved toward the president's desk.

Analysis of the political fallout of votes on the bill began almost as soon as it was passed. There were 431 votes, but many Americans cared about only one—the vote cast by their district representative. Visitors to NYTimes.com could read the story, click on the link to the database and quickly answer the question that mattered most to them. The stenographic information about where each representative stood on the bill was readily accessible at The New York Times' site; context from which to draw wider conclusions, however, might be sought elsewhere. People who chose to could seek context from the array of partisan blogs that had sprung to life over the past decade. Most Americans—even those who

On the Web, news sites can make their reporting more transparent by showing readers the documents and other sources on which their stories are based. ProPublica created a service that helped readers compare two versions of health care reform legislation.

look only online for their news—rely primarily on traditional news companies for information. Yet Americans remain suspicious of these sources. To balance the perceived bias in the mainstream media, many news consumers—ironically—turn to partisan blogs on both the left and right. These partisan bloggers, with a simple link back to a story on The New York Times' site, CNN site or thousands of other news sites, can quickly and effortlessly direct their readers to a news story before spending the bulk of their effort on commentary.

And that takes us back to those Twitter links on The Washington Post's site. It wasn't just bloggers who were posting their opinions about "#hcr" to Twitter. Journalists were posting comments as well. A few days earlier, "DevnaCNN"—Devna Shukla, a 22-year-old assistant producer on CNN's "AC 360°" show—had posted a link to ProPublica.org, an online nonprofit reporting organization that was launched in June 2008 to help fill a perceived gap in in-depth reporting following the layoffs of thousands of journalists amid shrinking revenues in the late 2000s. DevnaCNN wrote: "Pro Publica's side by side of the health care bills—really cool! http://hcr.propublica.org/document/show/1.html #HCR."

ProPublica had obtained copies of the House and Senate versions of the bills and compared them side by side, providing depth and transparency to the site's coverage of the health care debate. Visitors to the site could read ProPublica's analysis, but they could also see the original source documents for themselves. Mainstream news sites as well as partisan blogs on both the left and right linked to ProPublica's comparison. Armed with the same set of facts, journalists, advocates and citizens were equally able to come to their own conclusions about what the facts meant.

#AC360
11:43 PM Mar 19th via UberTwitter

Approaching my 14th hour with #AC360 aka POWER HOUR!!!
10:45 PM Mar 19th via UberTwitter

@joneilcnn @newsjunkie365 I'll do it! I was trying to get Joneil to take a video this evening...#keepingthemhonest
9:24 PM Mar 19th via UberTwitter in reply to joneilcnn

Pro Publica's side by side of the health care bills - really cool! http://hcr.propublica.org/document/show/1.html #HCR
4:41 PM Mar 19th via web

#TGIF fashion tip: wearing @toryburch always puts a pep in my step!
3:26 PM Mar 19th via UberTwitter

Thank you #AC360 viewers for your feedback! TGIF!
1:01 PM Mar 19th via UberTwitter

This story about the homeless family in Georgia is heartbreaking. What do you think? #AC360

DevnaCNN wrote posts on Twitter about health care reform legislation as well as her thoughts about television comedies, Beltway socializing and messages back to her followers, including: "Thank you #AC360 viewers for your feedback! TGIF!" Journalism was becoming a conversation, but many consumers wondered if that was making news any better.

While Jessica and Mike may have been among the millions of Americans to receive the breaking news on Sunday night, many millions more first became aware of the news when they woke up Monday morning and heard TV and radio anchors talking about the dramatic conclusion. What was everyone talking about? Cameras had caught a bit of incivility on the House floor. As Michigan Democrat Bart Stupak addressed his peers, a voice called out, "Baby Killer!" It was the kind of dramatic video that everyone wants to see. The most common search term on Google that day was "baby killer." While many of Monday morning's newspapers included a description of the scene, and video of the outburst played repeatedly on Monday morning's television news shows, it was on the Web that audiences could experience the event in its entirety. There, where television

On the Web, journalists can mix multiple media to tell stronger stories. This video allowed visitors to Politico to see and hear the events on the House floor; the accompanying text provided context.

news and newspaper sites vie with each other in multiple media, visitors could see, hear and read all about it. Television sites were able to present text alongside the video to put events into context while newspaper sites were able to include with their text video that allowed visitors to experience the scene for themselves.

If you've grown up with the Internet, you probably recognize some of your own news consumption patterns in our example about the health care bill. Other patterns might surprise you. News in a networked world is challenging and exciting. Audiences have unprecedented choices and control over what news they receive and when, where and how they receive it. As you read this book, you will be moving from news consumer to news producer, but you will also come to understand that the distinction between the two is blurring.

In a world where anyone can publish, what does it mean to be a journalist? Today, as always, it means understanding what news is and why it matters. It means understanding what the audience wants and needs to know, figuring out where to get the facts and sorting through all the options for presenting a story so that the audience feels its impact. Online journalism is more than a montage of existing media. The technology that forms its backbone is different. The time, manner and place that people use it are different. Its capabilities to make stories more relevant and more memorable to its audience are different.

As an online journalist, you'll still work with the traditional elements and values of news. But you'll also take advantage of the three attributes of online communication that make reporting, producing and distributing your stories via the Internet fundamentally different from working in any other medium. It is these three pillars of online journalism that have taken "the news" from something that people passively consume to something that people actively experience:

- Multimedia. Journalists have a variety of choices about how to combine storytelling techniques to tell different elements of a single story.

- Interactive. Sources, journalists and members of the audience all take part in the creation of a common story.

- On-demand. The audience has unprecedented control over the time, place and subject matter of the news it consumes.

Identify the 3 pillars in news stories

Jaron Lanier, one of the founders of virtual reality technology, characterized information as "alienated experience." No medium can perfectly replicate the experiences that it describes, but for millennia humans have tried their best to make their stories as rich as possible. This is what it means to "show, not tell."

It is no longer enough for journalists to "show" their audience the news. Journalists now have the tools to help the audience create its own experiences with and around current events. In their book "The Experience Economy," Joseph Pine II and James H. Gilmore argue that experiences must be three things: engaging, personal and memorable. Your audience isn't turning to online news just to watch TV on another kind of screen. The audience wants to climb inside, look around, jump into action and better understand both themselves and the world we all share. When used together in the appropriate settings, the three pillars of online journalism—multimedia, interactivity and on-demand delivery—help journalists create a better news experience, one that is engaging, personal and memorable.

Perform comprehensive site review

MULTIMEDIA

In the context of this book, **multimedia** means the use of more than one technique (text, audio, still images, moving images) to tell a single story. A multimedia news story, then, is any piece that uses two or more media to tell it.

What's "**media**"? It's the plural of "**medium**." What's a "medium"? It's the substance through which information is stored and transmitted. Paper is a medium. Computer screens are a medium. DVDs are a medium. Even cave walls have served as a medium.

In the context of journalism we think of a medium as a storytelling technique rather than the actual substance on which a story is conveyed. We think of newspapers and magazines as "print" media because they are printed on paper. Books, pamphlets and fliers are also print media, although they are rarely used for journalism. Print media uses text and static images to convey information. Paper, of course, cannot transmit moving visual information or audio. There are many styles of telling stories in print media with text and pictures. A nonfiction book is written in a different style than a news story, which is written in a different style than an instruction manual or a greeting card.

Video and audio are also examples of media. Moving pictures and audio can be broadcast over the air, via satellite or through cables. They can be sent over the Internet or stored on a DVD or CD-ROM. There is a wide combination of computer code, physical media and delivery channels that can be used for audio and video. Like text, video and audio have a variety of styles. A 90-second story about crime in your city uses a different style than a 90-minute documentary about penguins, which has a different style than a call-in sports talk radio show or a segment about natural sounds on public radio. And all of these are different from an animated political cartoon on JibJab.com.

There are degrees of multimedia integration. The degree of multimedia integration is called **convergence**. When journalists use one medium to tell one aspect of the story and other media to tell other aspects of the same story, they are achieving high levels of media convergence. For example, a story about the local high school football game might use text to summarize the game stats, videos and photos to show the top plays and audio for a post-game interview with the coach. These components combine to form the story's core. The story wouldn't be complete without each element, and no one element would make much sense without the context provided by the others.

When CBS and other broadcasters transmit the same programs over the Internet as they do over cable, satellite and airwaves, they are delivering the same product via multiple channels rather than telling a single story with multiple media.

THE SWAN PROJECT

The girls had grown up poor, lost their parents to drugs and jail and God knows what. They emerged from childhood uncouth and unrefined. Most had never eaten at a nice restaurant, set a table or put on makeup.

Not one of them had ever walked in heels.

Now teenagers, they were all classmates at a school for troubled girls. When a counselor told them they had to take an etiquette class, they protested.

Why would someone who was always hungry want to know how to throw a dinner party? If you weren't sure you wanted to go on living, why would you care about being a lady?

In this special report, writer Lane DeGregory and photographer Kathleen Flynn show what happened when an idealistic teacher tried to make diamonds out of coal.

Can knowing which fork to use change a girl's life?

READ THE STORY

captions | credits

Story by Lane DeGregory | Photography by Kathleen Flynn

The story

☒ The swan project
For teenagers at a school for troubled girls, etiquette classes open another world

☒ Etiquette 101:
Tips for table manners
Excerpts from handouts Miss Kedine passed out in class

☒ More special reports

⧉ ShareThis

ETIQUETTE (et'i kit; *also*, -ket') n. (Fr *étiquette*, lit, TICKET) 1. the forms, manners and ceremonies established by convention as acceptable or required in social relations, in a profession, or in official life

-- *Webster's New World College Dictionary*

How to help

Most students at the PACE Center for Girls struggle with poverty. They need everything from clothes and shoes to deodorant and magic markers. You can send a check to any of the schools, or send supplies including:

Clothes and shoes for teenage girls
Personal hygiene items including shampoo, deodorant, body lotion
Hair accessories and hair dryers, curling irons
Art supplies
School supplies, journals, paper, pens and pencils
Gift cards
Computers or electronic equipment

School locations include:

☒ Pasco
5462 Grand Boulevard
New Port Richey, FL 34652
727-849-1901
chris.lemon@pacecenter.org

☒ Pinellas
5540 Park Boulevard
Pinellas Park, FL 33781
727-456-1566
Sally.Zeh@pacecenter.org

☒ Polk (where the story is set)
440 South Florida Ave.
Lakeland, FL 33801
863-688-5596
Michele.DeLoach@pacecenter.org

☒ Hillsborough
1933 E. Hillsborough Ave, Ste. 300
Tampa, FL 33610-8253
813-739-0410
Chantel.Griffin-Stampfer@pacecenter.org

☒ Manatee
3508 26th Street West
Bradenton, FL 34205
941-751-4566
Amy.WickMavis@pacecenter.org

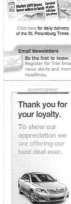

Kedine Johns -- Miss Kedine to her girls -- instructs Savannah Kowalski, left, and Lindsey Kennedy on how to eat soup properly. "Scoop the spoon away from you; don't slurp," she said.

ABOUT THIS SPECIAL REPORT: Last fall, a counselor at the PACE Center for Girls in Lakeland, Fla., came up with an idea for a class in etiquette.

At PACE, counselor Kedine Johns worked with disadvantaged girls who knew nothing about manners and social etiquette. Many of the teenagers didn't own dresses, had never worn makeup, had never been to a sit-down restaurant, and didn't know anything about table manners, phone etiquette, or how to behave in a social situation. Johns believed the girls would be better prepared for work and social life if they learned basic rules of etiquette.

Johns' etiquette class lasted eight weeks. Two *St. Petersburg Times* journalists, Lane DeGregory and Kathleen Flynn, observed the classes, where the girls studied dinner etiquette, proper grooming, table manners and first date etiquette. The etiquette class culminated with a sit-down luncheon at a fancy restaurant, which served as the girls' final exam.

DeGregory, winner of the 2009 Pulitzer Prize for feature writing, joined the St. Petersburg Times in 2000. She can be reached at degregory@sptimes.com. Flynn joined the St. Petersburg Times in 2002 and can be reached at kflynn@sptimes.com.

The Swan Project: Girls, please meet social etiquette and good manners

By Lane DeGregory, Times Staff Writer
In Print: Sunday, March 28, 2010

Counselor Kedine Johns — Miss Kedine to her girls — instructs Savannah Kowalski, left, and Lindsey Kennedy on how to eat soup properly. "Scoop the spoon away from you; don't slurp," she said.

[Kathleen Flynn | Times]

LAKELAND

They had just finished lunch, were just crumpling paper napkins into trash bins, when the call came through the school speakers:

"Will the following girls please report to the conference room . . . "

The teenagers looked at each other. What was going on?

"Lindsey," said the voice coming through the speaker. A girl with green bangs hung her head.

"Spring," the voice continued. In the corner of the lunchroom, a 15-year-old huddled behind her black curtain of hair. Dark liner smudged her eyes. She looked as if she had been crying.

The voice called several other names. Finally it said: "Chayna." A girl with a short ponytail cringed. The look on her face said: What did I do now?

They trudged into the conference room, 10 girls wearing a kind of slacker uniform — jeans and flip-flops and baggy school T-shirts. They dropped into swivel chairs

Story Tools

- ✉ Email Article
- 🖨 Print this story
- ✉ Email Newsletters
- 👤 Contact the editor
- ✏ Comment on this story
- 🖼 Purchase reprints

Social Bookmarking [b] Buzz up!   ⊲ ShareThis

St. Petersburg Times reporter Lane DeGregory, a Pulitzer Prize–winning feature story writer, teamed up with photographer Kathleen Flynn, photo editor Ted McLaren, video assignment editor Catriona Stuart and senior online designer Desiree Perry to tell in audio, photos and text the story of an etiquette school for girls who "had grown up poor, lost their parents to drugs and jail and God knows what."

It is important to distinguish what is *not* multimedia journalism. Sometimes news organizations will have one reporter write a story about a local protest against income taxes at the same time another reporter produces a video story about the same protest. The text story might be sent to a print publication and the video story might be sent to a broadcast television news outlet. Perhaps both end up on a website that is a partnership between a paper and a TV station. While the story in this case is being told in multiple media, the two stories are being distributed via different channels to different audiences. Even on the website they are not intended to be used together. One of the stories is for an audience that prefers video and the other is for an audience that prefers text. The two media have nothing to do with each other aside from the common subject. The journalists who created these stories considered the best way to tell the story in each of their given media, but they didn't start with the story and pick one media to tell each aspect of the story. This is an example of **parallel reporting and presentation**, but not multimedia convergence.

Another example of multichannel delivery that is not multimedia journalism is a video news story that is both transmitted over the air and posted to a news website. Multichannel delivery often has nothing to do with storytelling. It has to do with the economics of aggregating the largest possible audience with the smallest possible effort.

When Philly.com covered the Pennsylvania state football championships in 2009, a writer wrote a game summary story and a photographer put together a photo story that also told the story of the game. Although they were linked to each other, each story could stand alone. They offered the same information, but through different media.

The Illustrated London News was the world's first illustrated newspaper. It was first printed as a weekly in 1842.

Multimedia Then . . .

Newspapers and print magazines have been telling stories with words and pictures for a long time. In fact, even before the advent of photography, newspapers printed drawings or illustrations of newsworthy events. In the 19th century, the combination of text and photos was so innovative that the newspapers used it as a selling point; P. T. Barnum called his publication the "Illustrated News." Today, designating news as "illustrated" seems silly; we take it for granted that newspapers will include pictures with the words. Perhaps one day the designation "online" in referring to news will seem as silly.

Television news also contains examples of multimedia. While video and audio most obviously tell the story, consider how television news uses text on the screen. Often words and numbers are displayed to help viewers remember specific information, such as telephone numbers, dates and addresses, or to clarify the spelling of a word, such as a name, or to make clear distinctions between two similar-sounding words, such as "million" and "billion" in a piece about the state budget. Text is good for conveying some kinds of information while video is good for conveying other kinds.

. . . and Multimedia Now

Journalists can choose from any of the following multimedia categories when deciding how to best present the news:

C-SPAN offers three channels of live online video as well as a stream of live audio. It also offers a deep library of video related to politics and government.

Graeme Smith, a reporter for The Globe & Mail, in Toronto, led the production of a documentary based on video interviews with Taliban fighters in Afghanistan. The entire project included more than 45 minutes of video.

- Live audio/video. Audio and video can convey information as it happens. Typically, news sites use this technique to cover events of great significance, especially those that occur during the workday, when many people are away from televisions or radios. Some news sites also transmit online live events that perhaps do not have a broad enough audience to justify their transmission via mass media such as television or radio.

- Archived audio/video. News organizations post audio or video that was previously recorded. The material may have been recorded hours before, or perhaps years before. It is posted on the site and stored there for audiences to recall at their leisure. Examples of this type of multimedia include full interviews; clips that highlight the most important moments in a speech, game or meeting; or even information conveyed by a reporter in the field.

- **Feature story.** As in print, a feature story in news audio and video tends to be lengthy and **evergreen**—that is, it retains its relevance to the audience for longer than the week or so that is typical of an event-based story. Feature multimedia presentations—sometimes called documentaries—give the audience a chance to spend more time with a subject and achieve a deeper understanding of an issue. Feature stories often strive for emotional impact, putting an emphasis on the news values of who, where, why or how.

Editors of The Root, an online magazine published by The Washington Post Company, discuss issues in the news every week and distribute audio of the conversation as a podcast.

- **Podcast/vodcast.** A podcast and its video counterpart, the vodcast, is a series of recorded presentations available through subscription. New episodes are delivered upon request. The fundamental element of these forms of multimedia is their episodic nature—the content unfolds in a specific order with common elements that connect each episode to the next.

- **Photo gallery.** A photo gallery is a collection of photos that tells a story. There are several different subcategories of photo galleries. Some include audio to which the display of the photos is timed. Some have a narrative arc. Amateur photographers may be familiar with the concept of a photo-gallery if they have created an album on a photo-sharing website.

- Animated graphics. Often produced with a program called Flash, animated graphics can be used to explain a process or can provide simple navigation among several multimedia elements. Many animated graphics also allow the user to manipulate and control the narrative, a technique that we will discuss in more detail in Chapter 7.

INTERACTIVITY

The history of media is dominated by the one-way flow of information. Going back to the days when early humans wrote on the walls of caves, the process of reporting news has been basically the same: event happens, person observes event, person relates the observation to

Green Inc.

Energy, the Environment and the Bottom Line

April 5, 2010, 10:55 AM

Q.&A.: Transportation Secretary on Biking, Walking and 'What Americans Want'

By LEORA BROYDO VESTEL

Agence France-Presse/Getty Images

"It's what Americans want to do," said Transportation Secretary Ray LaHood, of his emphasis on the role of bicycles and walking in good transportation policy.

The United States transportation secretary, Ray LaHood, recently caused a stir when he proclaimed that bicycling and walking should be given the same consideration as motorized transport in state and local transit projects.

Supporters, who continue to post notes of adulation and thanks on Mr. LaHood's Facebook page, say the acknowledgment of biking and walking as legitimate modes of transportation is long overdue.

Critics, conversely, believe the secretary is taking the country in the wrong direction.

Mr. LaHood, formerly a Republican congressman from Illinois, spoke with Green Inc. about his reasons for introducing the new policy, the impact it will have on transportation financing, and why bike paths are a good bang for the buck.

Q. Bicycling and walking advocates had a very positive reaction to the policy change. But here at Green Inc., we heard mostly from critics who said it showed you were "delusional" or reflective of some sort of "Maoist" bent. What's your response to the response?

A. My response is that this is what Americans want. Americans want alternatives. People are always going to drive cars. We're always going to have highways. We've made a huge investment in our interstate highway system. We'll always continue to make sure that those investments in the highways are maintained.

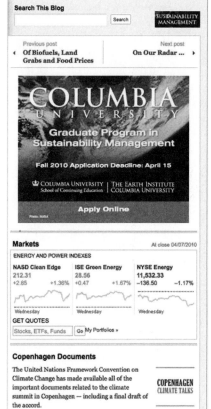
Markets At close 04/07/2010

ENERGY AND POWER INDEXES

NASD Clean Edge	ISE Green Energy	NYSE Energy
212.31	28.56	11,532.33
+2.85 +1.36%	+0.47 +1.67%	−136.50 −1.17%
Wednesday	Wednesday	Wednesday

GET QUOTES

[Stocks, ETFs, Funds] [Go] My Portfolios »

Copenhagen Documents

The United Nations Framework Convention on Climate Change has made available all of the important documents related to the climate summit in Copenhagen — including a final draft of the accord.

COPENHAGEN CLIMATE TALKS

· Visit the U.N. Web Site
· The Final Accord (PDF Format)

TIPS & SUGGESTIONS
Talk to Green Inc.
Got a hot tip on breaking green news, or a suggestion for areas of coverage? Email us directly at greeninc@nytimes.com.

On the Web: Energy & Environment

AUTOBLOGGREEN
BMW Megacity EV makes carbon fiber jobs in America

THE OIL DRUM
The Mining Disaster in West Virginia

ALTERNATIVE ENERGY STOCKS FROM SEEKING ALPHA
Will Rising Oil Prices Make the Solar Industry Shine?

IT'S GETTING HOT IN HERE

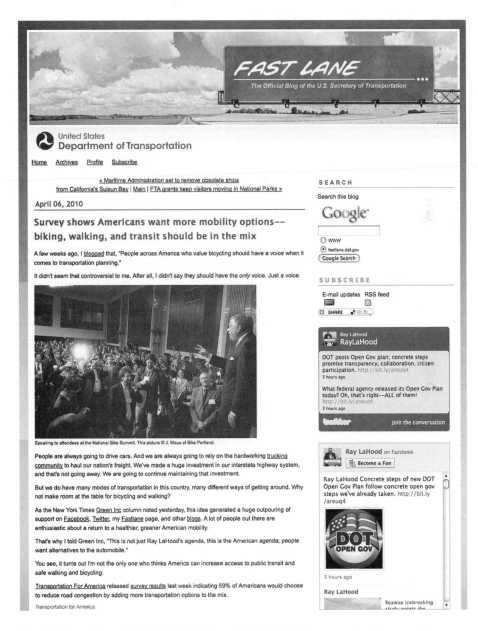

After his interview with The New York Times in April 2010, Transportation Secretary Ray LaHood used his own blog to expand on remarks he made to the journalists. A few months earlier, LaHood had used his blog to criticize—but also link to—Wall Street Journal stories.

another person. The medium through which news was related stood between reporter and audience.

The invention of printed words allowed the separation of the story from the storyteller, making it possible to spread information across great distances and even across time. These chasms of space and time made it difficult for the audience to interact with the reporter. The best that many of our ancestors could do was write a response and have that response carried back to the original sender by foot, horse or boat.

Today, **interactivity**, or the multidirectional flow of information, has changed the media game once again. With the rise of the Internet as a news medium, the possibilities for creating instant interaction between the subject of a news story, the reporter and the audience have risen so dramatically that some media critics no longer draw a distinction between the three. In most cases, posting a firsthand account of a news event online is as easy as reading or watching the firsthand account of someone else. CNN, the White House press office and a political blogger in Alaska can all publish to the same platform. Their reports, sitting side by side, are equally accessible, both to one another and to everyone else with Internet access.

News is becoming less of a lecture and more of a conversation. The use of e-mail, links between websites and comments on articles means that the reporting of news is done by journalists, sources and the audience alike. Interactivity is about more than getting a television to respond to a viewer's remote control. It is about creating connections between people in pursuit of a more complete and accurate view of the world.

To understand how interactive journalism works, think about what happens when you tell a story to a friend. The friend might add details or a different perspective. Then you likely ask questions of each other. You respond to the questions raised by the other person. This sequence of questions and responses might slowly change the focus or direction of the conversation. While one of you probably plays a greater role in guiding the conversation than the other, both you and your friend are actively playing a role in the process.

Now imagine that same conversation occurring in front of 20 people, some of whom you know and some of whom you don't know. Now imagine it happening in front of 20 million people, as it might on Twitter or Facebook. Here is both an opportunity and a challenge for interactive journalists. At its best, interactive journalism gives a voice to the voiceless. At its worst, interactive journalism is littered with ignorance, lies and hatred. It is up to you to sort it out.

Interactivity Then . . .

The idea of composing letters intended for a mass audience can be traced back through the roots of the American Revolution to as long ago as the writing of the New Testament of the Bible. If letter writers seek to sway the opinion or behavior of their audience, then broad distribution is a prerequisite for success. For centuries of letter writers, paper was scarce and costly, and broad dissemination required both time and money. With the advent of the Internet, letter publishers are now able to avoid the incremental costs of each copy. In fact, letter writers themselves can be their own publishers for almost no cost.

In broadcast media, interaction with the audience has become a staple of talk radio. Common topics for talk radio are politics and sports—subjects about which many people can voice an opinion, sometimes informed and sometimes not. Political conservatives especially have taken advantage of this technique to circumvent what they regard as a liberal bias in the so-called mainstream media originating in the big cities of New York and Los Angeles. Radio station owners have found too that they can fill airtime at a very low cost by allowing the audience to provide much of the content of a radio program. In online media, this is referred to as **user-generated content.**

...and Interactivity Now

Researchers for decades have been trying to describe, classify and order different levels of interactivity in settings ranging from digital video to classroom instruction. To summarize their findings very simply, levels of interactivity are based on three things: (1) how much people control the content they consume; (2) how easy it is for people to create, publish and share their own content; and (3) the degree to which content creation is shared.

Following, from least to most interactive, are some examples of what you will find online:

- **Tip line.** Reporters sometimes use the Internet to find sources who have firsthand knowledge of specific topics that the reporters want to cover. Many news websites allow visitors to send a message via a tip line to each of the journalists on staff. Such messages, however, are not published on the website.

The Center for Public Integrity celebrated Sunshine Week in 2010 by asking readers to send in tips about their experiences accessing public documents.

Comments: Displaying 1 - 5 of 5

beaglemom said on April 7, 2010 at 1:30 PM

MODOT has done alot for Hwy 44 and that stretch of road. If your familiar with the area, you will see the hwy is straight were the accident acurred. If you read the statement above you will see it says the driver lost control of his vehicle. If you also look at the pics. The gentleman was driving a pickup truck. He had to be going really fast to hit a tree that hard and do the damage he did to the truck. Its a shame to lose a young man like that and also for the driver to lose a friend and to live with the death of a friend. We should all pray for the family.

missyriver said on April 7, 2010 at 1:00 PM

I-44 at Eureka has taken so many lives, I think the D.O.T. should do something about that scretch of the highway.

larson0357 said on April 6, 2010 at 4:44 PM

the one killed is named merrill. he went to eureka high school. he will be missed greatly

nonamesleft said on April 6, 2010 at 4:27 PM

Arched means that the patient was air lifted by helicopter to the hospital. ARCH Air Medical Services is the name of the company.

freemb62 said on April 6, 2010 at 3:29 PM

"The Driver Was Arched to St Johns"....What does this mean ? and NO one know's a F'ing Thing ?.........Weird !!!

Like many news sites, KMOV in St. Louis allows registered site visitors to comment on stories. And just like the comments on many news sites, the quality of comments on KMOV.com varies widely.

- Article **comments.** Some news sites allow visitors to post comments about individual stories. Sites have different standards of verification for these comments, but all comments are intended for publication. Each comment often stands as its own piece of content, much as a letter to the editor.

- **Discussion board.** On a discussion board, also sometimes called a forum, readers engage with each other to create a common conversation, sometimes unprompted and untied from a specific article created by the site's staff.

- **Live chat.** Newsmakers and journalists in live chat rooms directly answer questions from the audience. Because these chats are often limited in time, the collaboration effort gets compressed and is usually more focused than in formats that are not restrained by time.

forums

Welcome to the Mom2Mom forums! All registered members can post comments and start new discussions in this section. Log in or create an account to get started.

Click here to start a new discussion

A few ground rules: We love a good debate, but as you chat with others, please be respectful and considerate. Please remember that we all love the kids in our lives and are doing the best we can. No personal attacks or profanity, please. And, if you'd like to list your business or service, please be sure your post meet Mom2Mom's rules, then go to our "offers and deals" forum or contact our advertising staff. *Happy posting!* Log in or create an account to get started.

Login to post a new forum topic.

Forum	Topics	Posts	Last post
Welcome			
New member introductions	107	344	2 days 5 hours ago by Patinchapelhill
Questions about the site	12	26	6 weeks 5 days ago by tleonard
Offers and deals	51	65	3 days 14 hours ago by discoverycdcenter
Becoming a mom			
Trying	14	56	1 week 7 hours ago by brickpuzzle
Pregnant	53	290	6 days 13 hours ago by dineer526

The News & Observer in Raleigh has created a site on which moms living in the area can share their experiences and exchange advice.

- **User-generated content.** Some websites allow visitors to tell their own stories in text, photographs, video or audio. In many cases, this user-generated content has little connection to the content created by the site's staff. The user-generated stories are meant to augment but not necessarily complement staff-generated stories.

- **Distributed reporting** and **crowdsourcing.** In addition to using the Internet to find a source, some reporters assign reporting tasks to the audience. These journalists are hoping to distribute the work across a broad group of people in order to compose a story that is either more complete or produced more quickly than if just one person were working on it alone.

- **Third-party social site.** Rather than waiting for the audience to come to them, some journalists actively seek out conversations by posting comments to stories on other sites or by joining online social networks that are not controlled by the publishers of the sites for which they work.

HTO LIVE DISCUSSIONS »   » Return to HTO live discussion page

Steve Kain, Richland-Bean Blossom Community School
Corp. superintendent

Monday, August 10, 2009 at 11:00 AM

QUESTION: *MODERATOR: Good morning everyone, thanks for joining us. Richland-Bean Blossom school superintendent Steve Kain is here to answer your R-BB and back-to-school questions. Feel free to ask to Steve now.*

Steve, thanks for visiting. Are you ready to get started?

STEVE KAIN: I am ready with the brave new world of on line media. Thanks for involving RBB in this process.

QUESTION: *Is it too late to consolidate with Monroe County. It is obvious that the town of Ellettsville does not want to cough up the cash to support and build a good school system so I say lets consolidate so we have a bigger tax basis.*

Leslie

STEVE KAIN: It would be legally possible but it is unlikely that RBB or the MCCSC boards would ever entertain such a proposition. Indiana law does allow such a consolidation. The school corporation includes much more than the town of Ellettsville. The population of the school district is about 16,000 and only about 6,000 live in the town of Ellettsville. Our tax base includes GE and Cook and everything north and west of the intersection of Third Street and Smith Pike. Our student population includes about 2,800 students compared to MCCSC's 11,000.

About once a week, The Herald-Times in Bloomington, Ind., moderates a live online discussion with a newsmaker.

Visitors to Cincinnati.com can upload their own news stories, photos and event listings to the website of The Enquirer.

As part of The Huffington Post's coverage of the 2008 Democratic presidential primary, 214 people wrote up individual profiles of influential superdelegates to the party's national political convention.

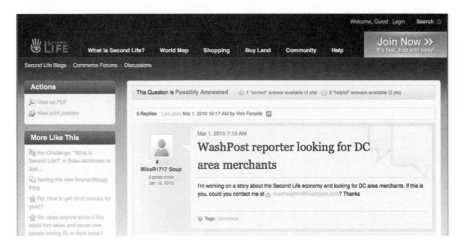

Washington Post reporter Michael Rosenwald utilized a blog hosted by Second Life to hunt for sources.

ON-DEMAND DELIVERY

One of the jobs of a journalist is to get the right information to the right people at the right time. If news is information that is meant to be useful, then it is important to get news to people at the moment they can most effectively use it. The Internet, with its 24/7 capabilities, is uniquely suited to help them do just that. **On-demand delivery** allows an audience to control the time, place and subject matter of the news it consumes.

For example, voters tend to place greater emphasis on political information they receive as Election Day draws nearer than on information received earlier in a race. In the final week or two of a race, attention to political news jumps markedly. And the Internet, via on-demand delivery, is always ready to provide it. Likewise, when people are looking for news and information online, there are some kinds of content they seek only when they need it. Traffic to dining and entertainment sections of news sites spikes on Friday afternoon. Most people tend to seek information about the latest medical research only when they or someone they love is faced with a specific disease or condition.

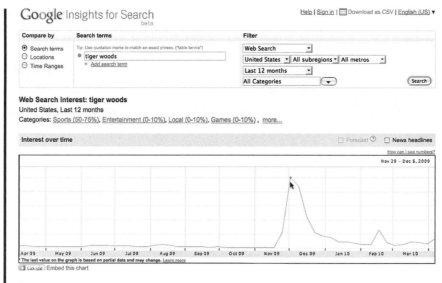

News of Tiger Woods' car crash and marital troubles in late 2009 generated sudden interest in the golfer and an accompanying jump in searches on his name.

On-Demand Delivery Then . . .

The idea that people can turn on a box and get instant news at any hour of the day or night didn't begin with the Internet, but with the birth of the Cable News Network on television in 1980. For the first time, Americans didn't have to wait until the anchors of the three major television networks were ready to tell them about the events of the day during a nightly news broadcast. But on-demand delivery is more than just being able to always access the information that someone else is sending you. It's about having the ability to seek out the information you want in the time and place you want it.

The invention of writing and the subsequent spread of literacy made it easier to convey information reliably across space and time. Information could be delivered to its audience, rather than forcing the audience to go to the source. You can read a book—even one written thousands of years ago—in any place and at any time you want. As technological innovation progressed, the factors of time and distance became less and less relevant for audio and video communication. The telephone, radio, television and satellite all allowed the audience to be in one place while experiencing the sights or sounds that were being created in another place at exactly the same time. Today, you can watch a riot unfolding on the other side of the globe even as you pet your dog while sitting in front of your television in your own living room. This kind of audience-controlled place-shifting is an example of on-demand delivery.

With the arrival of digital video recorders, or DVRs, people gained the ability to watch TV news whenever they wanted. Expect to be stuck in traffic when the nightly news comes on? Simply remember to program your recorder in the morning before you leave and then watch it later at a more convenient time. Some DVRs have evolved so far that they can now guess the programs each viewer is likely to want to see. Based on the patterns of a user's viewing behavior, DVRs can suggest other shows that might be of interest to the user.

Children born today into families with MP3 players in their cars, DVRs in their living rooms and search engines on their computers will never know a world in which people had to wait to get generic news. They will always be able to get exactly the news they want in exactly the place they want it at exactly the time they want it.

. . . and On-Demand Delivery Now

Audience control over the subject, time, place and format of news reception, which has been built into the foundational technology of the Internet since the Web's inception, represents the lowest level of interactivity. However, news organizations have followed the lead of other industries toward mass customization. Following are some common tools of on-demand delivery and audience control found on news websites:

- **Hyperlinks.** The technology that allows every piece of content on the Internet to be connected to every other piece of content creates the fundamental "web" of information that gives the audience a high degree of control over the order in which they encounter information. The ability of users to choose their own path results in a nonlinear experience.

Oklahoma House panel OKs changes to workers' comp

BY THE ASSOCIATED PRESS 💬 3 Comments
Published: April 7, 2010

A House panel on Wednesday approved a bill to overhaul the state's workers' compensation system, a key item on the GOP-controlled Legislature's agenda.

Meanwhile, as the state grapples with an estimated $1.2 billion hole in the budget for the upcoming fiscal year, nursing home owners rallied at the state Capitol to protest deep cuts in Medicaid reimbursement rates they say will lead to the closing of facilities across the state.

The Senate bill approved by the House Economic Development and Financial Services Committee would reduce the number of judges on the Workers' Compensation Court, limit judges to one eight-year term and require Senate confirmation of new judges.

The bill also would create a new position of medical director for the court to oversee the medical care of people making claims. It also redefines the term "objective medical evidence" to state that complaints of pain cannot be considered when determining an injured worker's impairment.

"Our workers' compensation system is broken, and we must make changes or risk driving businesses out of our state," said Rep. Dan Sullivan, House sponsor of the bill.

Nursing home owners also expressed concern about facilities closing their doors as state leaders consider budget cuts that could amount to a 10 percent reduction in Medicaid reimbursement rates, said Don Greiner, president of Grace Living Centers and a board member of the Oklahoma Association of Health Care Providers.

Reimbursement rates already were slashed 3.25 percent last week, but Greiner said lawmakers expect further reductions for the fiscal year that begins July 1.

"A lot of rural homes will close," Greiner said. "We're already losing homes right now."

Association Executive Director Rebecca Moore said Oklahoma already has lost about 6,000 nursing home beds as the number of homes has declined in the last 10 years from 435 to 315 homes.

"It's really a train wreck coming," Moore said.

Readers of a news story on NewsOK.com, the website of The Oklahoman newspaper, can follow links within the text of a story to delve deeper into a topic.

- **Complete uptime.** Online publishers don't take their websites off the air. Even newspaper sites that only update once a day remain available to visitors whenever they want them.

- Search tools. All of those Web pages out there have made organizing them in a meaningful way a lucrative business. With the ability to search online content, people can cherry-pick information.

- Archives. The incredibly low cost of storing digital information has meant that there is little financial reason ever to delete anything from the Web. Combined with search tools, every item in this vast archive is instantly available for global consumption.

- iPods. Mobile digital audio players mean that news and information are no longer tethered to one place. As wireless Internet access becomes more widely available, users will have increased control over the places where they get online news.

From any one of the hundreds of newspaper sites that have partnered with Legacy.com to publish online obituaries, visitors can search for death notices by name, date, location or source.

A massive database sits behind ESPN.com, allowing visitors to the site to view a 10-year archive of basketball scores for the University of Connecticut women's basketball team that includes every game of the team's two consecutive undefeated seasons.

VIEW SOURCE

THE PEOPLE BEHIND THE PILLARS

The three pillars of online journalism—multimedia, interactivity and on-demand delivery—have ushered in entire new categories of jobs, both inside and outside of traditional newsrooms. Meet some of the people who are making decisions today about which tools to use to tell a stronger story.

> From Text to Video
> Christina Pino-Marina, Journalism Lecturer, University of Maryland
> Video journalist, washingtonpost.com, 2003–2008
> Text reporter, washingtonpost.com, 2000–2003
> Reporter, El Paso Times, 1999–2000
> News Assistant, USA Today, 1995–1999

As the Internet grew as a news medium, so did the breadth of Christina Pino-Marina's reporting skills. When she graduated from the University of North Carolina at Wilmington in 1993, the Internet had just been born. Fluent in Spanish, Pino-Marina brought her language skills to her first encounter with a broadcast newsroom as an intern at Univision. Almost a decade passed before video journalism became her primary medium of communication. When it did, she was working for a newspaper company. Pino-Marina joined washingtonpost.com in 2000 to boost the site's speed at posting text reports, especially about local news. Soon after she began to carry and use a video camera in filing her reports; eventually, it became her medium of choice.

"A real turning point for me was, I was working on this long-term project ["A Life Lived in 4–4 Time," 2005]. I had something on the back burner for a long time, and I wasn't really sure what I wanted to do with it. . . . For a while I thought it was going to be a magazine piece, you know, something long-form. Maybe online it would have some sidebar elements, some audio from the musician's performance or some video clips of him performing. The more I thought about it, the story was very layered, there were all these elements of history and music. These layers—it didn't make sense to me to divide them up, to split that effort, and also fragment the user experience. So I was like, 'Why would I have someone read one article here and click over there for this little bit of music?' It seemed like the type of story that needed to be pulled together in a different way. So that piece, the magazine piece, became an online video documentary."

Tech Helping Text
Chris Wilson, Associate Editor, Slate.com
U.S. News & World Report, reporter and blogger, 2007
Congressional Quarterly, graphics reporter, 2006

What do you get when you cross a physics major with the editor of The Cavalier Daily at the University of Virginia? A writer and reporter who looks for ways to use computer programming to tell stronger stories. Throughout his young career, Chris Wilson has been a writer who sees the "tech stuff," as he calls it, as supplemental to his reporting. His advice for young journalists is to know HTML and Excel, at least. Why should they learn that stuff? Well, Wilson, like all good journalists, has a fierce sense of independence.

"It's so much better to be able to do that stuff because you know exactly what you want, how to write the script; you don't have to wait for someone to do it. The developer guys are always overworked, and when it breaks, you know how to fix it, and you already know the editorial mission. . . . Smart producers always do fine for themselves."

Making Links
Ryan Sholin, Director of News Innovation, Publish2.com
Director of Community Site Publishing, GateHouse Media, 2007–2009
Online Editor, Santa Cruz Sentinel, 2006–2007
Reporter, Oakland Tribune, 2006

Ryan Sholin started his career in journalism just as an upheaval of the newspaper business model forced thousands of experienced reporters and editors out of the industry. Amid the reduction of reporting power, Sholin became more and more interested in the possibilities for collaboration and cross-linking between news sites to help fill some of the void and make reporting more efficient. He now works for a company that's growing, not shrinking. Its primary goal is to help journalists save and share Web links in ways that make their stories stronger.

"The key ethic of the link is that you're not just providing fresh content for your readers, but you're showing your work. In a lot of ways, after you demonstrate to your readers that your reporting is based on real events and real facts and things you can go out there and find on the Web, it becomes much more credible and it's much easier to keep your readers interested and coming back for more."

ONLINE LEARNING MODULE 1

ACTIVATE THIS MODULE: journalism.cqpress.com

Now that you are familiar with the three pillars of online journalism, you are ready to start learning how to use them to tell stronger stories. A good first step is to begin looking more analytically at online news packages—as a journalist rather than as an audience member.

On my blog, I am facilitating an ongoing conversation about the use of the three pillars as well as writing about and linking to examples of online news organizations using multimedia, interactivity and on-demand delivery.

When you buy or activate this chapter's online learning module, you will have access to:

- A digital version of this chapter's text.
- Interactive flashcards for the terms used in this chapter.
- A printable one-page tip sheet outlining how to make a website a platform for telling strong stories rather than a pipe for delivering material from traditional media.
- A quiz to test your mastery of the material in this chapter.
- Exercises to help you identify online news pillars.

As you complete the module's online exercises, you will:

- Identify and describe the three pillars of online news as they appear on professional news sites.
- Recognize the three pillars of online journalism in award-winning professional journalism.
- Reflect on your own experiences with the three pillars of online journalism.
- Critique and discuss a professional news organization's online journalism.

2 ONLINE NEWS IS STILL NEWS

This chapter will teach you how to identify:

- The characteristics of information that give it news value.
- The elements that need to compose any news story in any medium.

Logging on to the Internet one morning, you find 14 new e-mails in your inbox. Nine are spam, two are newsletters and three are from people you know. Your mom has sent you her flight information for an upcoming visit, and a high school buddy has sent you a link to a YouTube video of his band. Your younger cousin is alerting you to federal legislation that would increase the tax on candy bars—a hoax, of course, that you already know about. Seven of the messages offer links to stories on news websites and blogs. With CNN on in the background, you've already heard most of the news headlines for the day, so you click over to Facebook, where several hundred status updates are waiting for you.

Less than 15 minutes after turning on your machine, you update your own status: "Overwhelmed."

With so much "stuff" on the Internet, what are we really talking about when we discuss "online journalism" and "news"? Journalism has never been simply about publishing and distributing facts. In reality, it is far more nuanced. Journalism is the exercise of judgment and discretion by people trained to organize information in a way that makes it meaningful to specific audiences.

While the Internet provides unlimited space to publish news and offers an exciting array of new storytelling tools and techniques, today's information overload highlights the need for journalists who understand how to turn information into news. If you hope to have your message cut through all the others that bombard the audience each day, then you have to know the characteristics of a good news story in any medium. Familiarity with traditional news values and news elements will help you decide how to use one or more of the three pillars of online journalism—multimedia, interactivity and on-demand delivery—to make your story more relevant and memorable to your audience.

The arrival of the Internet changed many things, but it did not change the role of the news in a democratic society. Freedom of the press is a right guaranteed in the very first amendment to the U.S. Constitution. With this right comes responsibility: the responsibility to report the truth. Truth—complete, precise and proven—is critical to journalism because of its role in ensuring that democracies and free markets work. Today, journalism remains what it always has been and always will be—it's true, it's new and it matters to you.

In the middle of the 19th century, Scottish writer Thomas Carlyle referred to reporters and editors as "the Fourth Estate," noting that their activities placed a check on those of the other three estates: nobility, church and commoners. In an American context, the Fourth Estate might be translated to mean that journalists act as a check on the three branches of government: executive, legislative and judicial. Journalists report on all facets of government. They want their audience to know its representatives and understand political processes so that each person in a democracy has the ability to make fully informed decisions about the government for which they share responsibility.

Journalism holds powerful people accountable. Thomas Jefferson saw journalism as a potent censor of government. He called it the "tocsin"—or alarm bell—of his new nation and noted that "those who fear the investigation of their actions" were the most likely to seek limitations on press freedom. But if journalism is an alarm bell, then it is one that people learn to ignore if it clangs on unabated with the same insistent monotony. Journalists must seek out new information—information concerned more with the threats and opportunities that lie just over the horizon than with the miscellanea of daily life.

In the 5th century B.C., when the Greek writer Herodotus traveled far from his home country and returned with tales of the people he met, he was practicing a form of journalism. Seeking neither personal fortune nor political favor, Herodotus went to parts of the world that were hidden from Greek view and illuminated them for his countrymen. His stories were probably meant to entertain as much as they were intended to inform. In telling them, the ancient Greek offered proof of just how complex and interconnected the peoples of Europe, Africa and Asia were already becoming more than 2,500 years ago.

Journalistic narratives should be rich and engaging, but entertainment and news are not the same thing. What's the difference? Consider honeybees. Upon returning to the hive after a reconnaissance mission, the bee shakes its rump amid the gathered crowd. Why does it do this? Is it a mating ritual—a seduction meant for a single other bee but not for all? Or is it just the latest honeybee dance craze—entertainment and raw self-expression? In fact, scientists have discovered that the honeybee "shake" is a form of information: the bee is conveying to the folks back home where they can find some good nectar. The bee is reporting news of the shared world.

So even bees know what news is. News is information that does something—that is, it is information that can be put to use by the person who receives it. In the crowded and sometimes frantic hive of the online world, your efforts as a journalist will stand out only if it is relevant to your audience. In Ralph Ellison's novel "The Invisible Man," the narrator notes the power of the press when he wonders who will tell the stories of African Americans in a way that will make them relevant to a society that doesn't even see them: "All things, it is said, are duly recorded—all things of importance, that is. But not quite, for actually it is only the known, the seen, the heard and only those events that the recorder regards as important that are put down, those lies his keepers keep their power by. . . . Where were the historians today? And how would they put it down?"

You, the journalist, are the historian today. You will decide which people and which events qualify as news. You are charged with writing a first draft of history. At the same time, you are a pioneer, faced with the challenges and opportunities of inventing new ways of recording and conveying the news. While this book will help you use news tools to tell stronger stories, you must first learn how to identify the stories worth telling. In this chapter, you will learn the characteristics of information that give it news value, and the traditional elements that need to be a part of every news story in every medium.

NEWS VALUE

What is it about a news story that makes you want to e-mail a link to a friend? What is it in someone's status update on Facebook that makes you sit up and say OMG? The answer is **news value**—certain characteristics that distinguish news from all other kinds of information. For example, if news is information that does something, it is more precise to say that news is information that does something *right now*. That is, it exhibits immediacy, or timeliness. Timeliness is a news value. In this section, we will examine the eight traditional news values:

1. Timeliness—How recently did the events in your story unfold?

2. Proximity—How geographically close is your audience to the setting of your story?

3. Impact—What direct effect will your story have on your audience?

4. Magnitude—How many people were involved in your story? How big was the area affected by your story?

5. Prominence—How familiar is your audience with the main people in your story?

6. Conflict—Are there disputed perceptions or desires that your reader needs to consider? Have they been resolved?

7. Novelty—How unusual is the subject of your story?

8. Emotional appeal—Aside from the information your story conveys, how does the story make your audience feel?

Knowing these eight characteristics helps you keep an eye out for news and, once you've done the reporting, helps you organize and emphasize the right information for your audience. This is true in any medium. But in online journalism the ability to identify the

Analyze news values in award-winning stories

news values in a specific story serves another important purpose: it helps you choose the best tools for telling the story. Certain storytelling techniques of online journalism are more appropriate for stories that emphasize certain news values.

Timeliness

Breaking news drives people to the Internet. News sites such as CNN and CBSNews saw their traffic jump 500 percent in the hours after news broke about the death of Michael Jackson in 2009. In 2001, many news websites went down as a global audience rushed online to find updates about terrorist attacks in the United States. On any given day, the top search terms on Google will be related to some sort of breaking news or cultural event.

Journalists have always emphasized their efforts to get the audience the most current information available. Traditionally, reporters and editors thought of the news value of timeliness in terms of their product's publication cycle. Monthly magazines would tie their stories to events that had happened during the 30 days since they had last communicated with the audience, and the stories would be written to stay as fresh as possible until the next issue. Newspapers would break a story one day and immediately start working on a "second day" story, which would be framed by the assumption that readers had seen the initial report. Television news operations might report an overnight robbery on their morning program and lead the evening broadcast with an update on the investigation.

On-demand delivery. Breaking news is a clear demonstration of the Web's ability to customize information and deliver it on demand. Unlike traditional news media, the Internet has no cycle. Websites never go off-air, so the audience expects them always to be up-to-date—even in the middle of the night. Even when people are away from their computers, they receive breaking news alerts via mobile phone.

Weather reports are the most commonly sought news stories on all devices connected to the Internet. On mobile phones, sports scores, traffic and financial information—all topics that have value only if they are current—are among the most popular types of content.

Live video. When you're reporting a story that's happening *right now,* live video or audio will convey more information more quickly than even an onsite reporter typing text. An image is worth a thousand words—but it takes an awfully long time to type a thousand words. According to a December 2009 Pew Internet and American Life Project poll, more than 60 percent of people who use the Internet watch breaking news video online.

When the president speaks, news organizations first play the live video and later write a news story. During a high school sporting event, a local news site will stream live video of the game and write up a summary afterward. Even when reporters live blog an event, the text updates appear once every several minutes while the video is updated every second—actually, up to 30 times per second.

Live text. If you do not have the ability to transmit live video of an event on your website, it will usually be quicker to write a story than to shoot and edit a video to be posted later. Most news stories break online via a single text headline or brief paragraph. A blog is another way to emphasize the news value of timeliness when your story calls for it. A blog's format places the most recent post at the top of the page.

Proximity

Ease of international travel and instant global communication notwithstanding, many of our information needs remain grounded in our geographic location at any given moment. Newspapers, long confined by the logistics of delivery, and broadcast news operations, by the reach of their signals, have historically given more coverage to the cities in which their audiences lived than to cities outside their distribution areas. Presumably, the audience in St. Paul, Minn., is more interested in the actions of the St. Paul school board than those of the Minneapolis school board.

Today, when you can sit at your computer in St. Paul, Minn., and get news from sources in St. Petersburg, Fla., and St. Petersburg, Russia, as easily as you can access the hometown paper, emphasis on local coverage among local news organizations is essential. National and international news will reach the audience from a variety of sources, but the St. Paul Pioneer Press may be the only source of news about the schools to which local residents send their children. Even as national and international news stories crowd the Internet, reporters and editors are on the lookout for unique "local angles" more than ever before.

On-demand delivery. One of the challenges facing journalists today, both online and off, is that people very often do not work, play, worship and shop all in a single city. When the news can reach anyone, anywhere, at any time, the definition of proximity becomes more dynamic. Using the news value of proximity doesn't mean only making it clear how the story is about *right here*. It really means creating information that is relevant to *right here, right now.*

Multimedia. Online news organizations use databases and maps to pinpoint information on crimes, snowfall amounts and traffic conditions that site visitors can have delivered on demand. The growing use of mobile phones with high-speed Internet access is making the news value of proximity increasingly important. People today are using tools that help them obtain information not just about the city where they live or work, but about the exact road on which they are driving at a specific moment or the precise block on which they are looking to buy a fruit smoothie. By using phones and other devices equipped with **GPS** technology, consumers expect a news organization to provide customized information— information that does not rely solely on a typed-in zip code but that changes automatically as the consumer moves around.

Impact

Creating news reports for mass media can be challenging because every person in the audience gets the same version of a story, or the same collection of stories. Traditionally, this

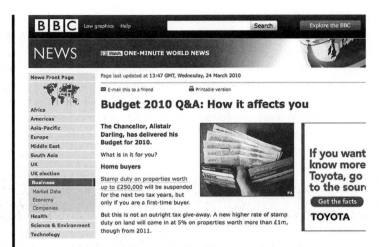

When dealing with stories that have significant impact on your audience, text will convey information better than audio or visual elements.

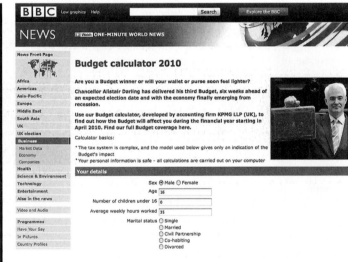

On the Web, users can take advantage of interactive tools that customize information and illustrate individual impact more directly.

fact has forced journalists to highlight information that will be relevant to the broadest possible audience. In reality, though, each person in the audience is asking just one question: "OK, but how does this affect *me?*"

When members of the audience are able to choose their own news diet and receive select information on demand, they are more likely to put a priority on the information that will have the most impact on their own lives. Journalists don't have the time to write a unique version of every story for every member of the audience. The challenge for journalists, then, is to figure out how to use technology to find an efficient way to tell stories that can be personalized.

On-demand delivery. The news value of impact often goes hand in hand with the news values of timeliness and proximity as people seek information that is tailored to a specific time and location. For example, movie times used to be one of the most popular features of a newspaper. But today it is easy for people to use the Web or a mobile phone app to find the very next showing of a given film at the theater closest to their current location. In times of war or natural disaster, journalists can save lives by helping people know where to go to avoid danger at any given moment.

Text, audio and video. Because the impact of a news event is not always obvious, text is often a better tool than audio or video for conveying impact. Carefully written words based on carefully conducted reporting can explain the context of a situation and illuminate invisible connections between the subject of the story and the reader in a way that no other medium alone can. Few images can successfully convey how a story will affect each individual; text provides ready interpretation that allows visitors to assess impact from a personal standpoint.

Interactivity. The Web's ability to foster interactivity with the audience allows the creation of a feedback loop. Individuals can share with you, the journalist, as well as with other site visitors the ways in which a general trend might be exerting an impact on specific people.

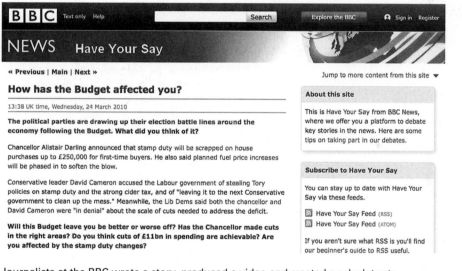

Journalists at the BBC wrote a story, produced a video and created a calculator to *tell* their visitors how the British budget would impact them. But they also created a forum to *ask* the site's visitors about the budget's impact.

Magnitude

The news value of magnitude shows up in news stories in many different ways. An 8.2 magnitude earthquake does more damage and kills more people than a 2.8 magnitude earthquake. It is bigger news because of its bigger magnitude.

Events become more important when they impact more people. The 7.0 earthquake that hit Haiti in 2010 was smaller than the 7.2 earthquake that struck near the Mexico-California border a few months later. So why was the Haiti quake bigger news? The quake in Haiti killed more than 200,000 people. The Mexico quake killed only 2.

This image shows the destruction in Port-au-Prince following the January 2010 earthquake.

SOURCE: Reuters

Photos and video. Visual elements such as photographs or video should be included with any report about an event that is news because of its magnitude. Video, with its ability to pan across large areas or zoom from the foreground to objects in the background, can help convey a sense of size and distance. Taken from the right perspective, photographs do a great job of showing the relationship between the sizes of two things—whether they be a town and a tornado or a coin and a caterpillar.

Audio. Sound is also a multimedia tool that can convey information on magnitude. From rocket launches to protest marches, if the magnitude of your story is measurable in decibels, then audio is the medium for you.

Text. Of course, the magnitude of an event may unfold over time, making it difficult to capture with audio and visual reporting. Consider stories about a sudden increase in cases of domestic violence or an all-time high in the unemployment rate in your county. In stories where the magnitude must be explained, or where things are not as they first appear, text may be the only way to ensure that your audience is not left with a false impression of the world.

Prominence

In many cases, the very definition of prominence is a well-known face. When we see the face of someone who is famous attached to a news item, we tend to pay more attention. There are entire magazines devoted to photographs of prominent people—People, UsWeekly, Sports Illustrated. In online media, as in any other, when your story is about a prominent person the audience will want to see his or her face.

Photos and video. When you have both photos and video, which do you use? Video can show nonverbal communication cues that are difficult to convey in still photography. These cues can be important to understanding the motives and mindsets of public figures. Another question to ask yourself when determining whether to use photos or video is whether your audience wants to *hear* something the person said, or whether *seeing* the person is enough.

Audio. Sometimes, audio alone carries the true power of the narrative. Hearing the voice inflections of a prominent person can create a powerful connection with the audience. Reading a transcript of Martin Luther King's "I Have a Dream" speech, or seeing a photo of him standing on the steps of the Lincoln Memorial, is interesting. But to hear King actually deliver the speech is inspiring.

Text. Not every prominent person has an instantly recognizable face or memorable voice. While frequent viewers of CNBC could perhaps identify the face of the chief executive officer of Bank of America, most Americans probably could not. Text descriptions may be necessary to tell your readers who a particular person is and why he or she is prominent.

Interactivity. Seeing, hearing or reading about a prominent person often leaves an imprint. But to actually interact with a prominent person can be an indelible experience, capable of creating deep and lasting memories. With their privileged access to powerful people and historic events, journalists have long been the gatekeepers of communication between sources and the audience. Part of the traditional job of a journalist has been to connect people with one another. In some ways, a journalist is the medium of a conversation. And even in a world where powerful people can and do talk to the masses via Twitter, Facebook and their own blogs, journalists still play the role of host by guiding the conversation. When the subject of a story is a prominent person, the audience will naturally be drawn to an opportunity to chat with him or her.

Interactivity and on-demand delivery. Today we

Journalists for the Richmond Times-Dispatch moderated a live online discussion between Virginia Gov. Tim Kaine and site visitors in 2009.

⌂ Sports

Football coach who tackled kid gets fired

Petero, 36, also faces felony child abuse charge for nailing player at game

msnbc.com news services
updated 9:36 p.m. ET Sept. 7, 2006

◄NBC VIDEO

STOCKTON, Calif. - A youth football league⊠ has fired an assistant who was caught on video charging onto the field during a game and leveling a 13-year-old player from the opposing team. Cory Petero, 36, of Riverbank, has also been banned for life from the league following the incident during a weekend game in Stockton, KCRA reported.

"This is a very serious offense. This coach won't be coaching in the league anymore," said Jim Hall of Delta Youth Football⊠.

Launch

Video of acute conflict, such as this video of a football coach attacking a 13-year-old player in 2006, helps viewers determine the context of the action.

guardian.co.uk

News | Sport | Comment | Culture | Business | Money | Life & style

News 〉 World news 〉 Democratic Republic of the Congo

FAQ: Crisis in the Congo

Chris McGreal, Africa correspondent
guardian.co.uk, Sunday 2 November 2008 16.12 GMT
Article history

Why did David Miliband go to Rwanda when the crisis is in Congo?

Rwanda has been heavily embroiled in Congo since more than one million Hutus fled there in 1994, led by extremists responsible for the genocide of around 800,000 Tutsis. The extremists used the cover of the UN-run camps to continue attacks which led Rwanda to invade in 1996, beginning a cycle of conflict that continues today with various armed groups, the Congolese army and Rwandan Hutus competing for territory and control of mining interests.

There is particular focus on Rwanda now because it is accused of backing the Tutsi rebel leader, Laurent Nkunda, who is threatening Goma and whose attacks on government forces have forced about 250,000 people from their homes in recent weeks.

Text, such as this 2008 FAQ explaining the crisis in the Congo, can more quickly summarize long-standing animosities.

can access websites such as Flickr and Facebook that are dedicated to sharing the photos of the ordinary people who are important to each of us. With apologies to Andy Warhol, today it is said that everyone is famous to 15 people. A journalist's job is to figure out which people are prominent to which part of the audience. **Hyperlocal** or community news sites are based on the understanding that people love true stories about real people they know—not just about celebrities, politicians and CEOs.

Conflict

Conflicts and their causes play an important role in all forms of storytelling, including journalism. Reporters tell stories of conflict not for dramatic effect, but to hold people accountable for their actions and to improve chances for resolution to long-standing animosities. Because conflict can take on many different forms, journalists have to consider the type of conflict before determining how to tell the story.

Videos and photos. When conflict is an acute action—whether a fist punch or a verbal joust—video does a tremendous job of capturing it. And photos can emphasize the exact moment of impact when that is important.

Text. Conflict in the news often involves multiple points of view or critical nuances that must be taken into account when considering accusations that one person or group levels against another. Rarely do visual media allow the audience to determine motivation. These details are best described with careful word choices.

Interactivity. A quick survey of online news stories will reveal that the articles that garner the most comments are those on politics and sports—two subjects in which conflict is inherent. Conflict can be heightened or resolved through interactivity, depending on how the conversation is framed and moderated.

Novelty

As the old saying goes, it isn't news when dog bites man—but when man bites dog. Perhaps a useful definition of "news" is one that highlights the unpredictable: any time the world doesn't behave as we expect.

Video. There are some things that are so unexpected that they have to be seen to be believed. When the subject of your story is an odd action, video is a great medium with which to tell it.

Photos. Photos give the audience more time to ponder the true novelty of unusual subject matter. When the thing that must be seen to be believed does not involve an unusual action, photos can tell the story better than video.

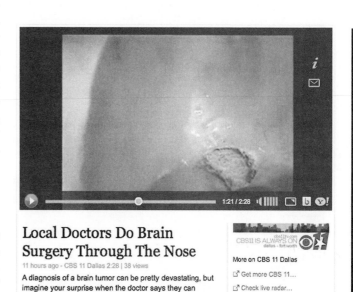

Local Doctors Do Brain Surgery Through The Nose

11 hours ago - CBS 11 Dallas 2:28 | 38 views

A diagnosis of a brain tumor can be pretty devastating, but imagine your surprise when the doctor says they can remove it through your nose! It's the most non-invasive brain surgery out there, and...

CBS11 IS ALWAYS ON

More on CBS 11 Dallas

Get more CBS 11...

Check live radar...

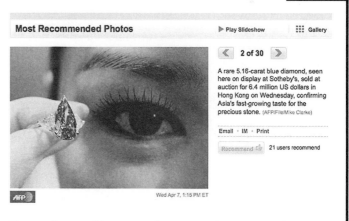

Most Recommended Photos   ▶ Play Slideshow   ⠿ Gallery

◀ 2 of 30 ▶

A rare 5.16-carat blue diamond, seen here on display at Sotheby's, sold at auction for 6.4 million US dollars in Hong Kong on Wednesday, confirming Asia's fast-growing taste for the precious stone. (AFP/File/Mike Clarke)

Email · IM · Print

Recommend   21 users recommend

Wed Apr 7, 1:15 PM ET

Photos of unusual items are often among the most popular among visitors to online news sites. This AFP photo from Yahoo News also illustrates how photos can be used to convey magnitude.

Interactivity. The more unusual the subject of a story, the more likely it is that the audience will have questions as it attempts to fit new information into old ways of thinking about the world. Journalists can use interactivity to connect the audience with experts who can field questions and help increase understanding of the story.

Emotional Appeal

In telling stories journalists look for real-world heroics and tragedies that no novelist could dream up. Stories that evoke the hopes and fears of the audience tend to be widely discussed and long remembered.

Video and photos. Many stories are driven by the emotional appeal they have on the audience. Visual journalism is an effective tool for conveying such stories. Videos can be emotionally powerful, and a photograph can be more powerful. With videos, moments of joy or tension pass in real time. With photos, however, emotions are captured and frozen. A word of caution: your audience may find some newsworthy images more disturbing in photographs than in video.

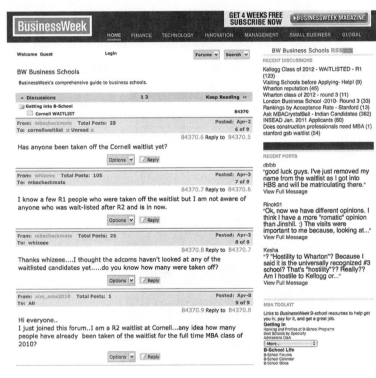

For applicants to MBA programs, the message boards on Business Week's website have become a mandatory stop for both commiseration and practical advice.

Audio. Because people tend to listen to news at times when and in places where they are alone, audio can be an intimate experience. Series such as "This I Believe" or "Story Corps" on public radio have made the voices of ordinary people so compelling that the stories told can move listeners to tears.

Phil Bronstein, the editor of the San Francisco Chronicle who came up with an idea to turn the voice messages of irate newspaper readers into a podcast, told a columnist for The Poynter Institute that emotional appeal was part of the reason he thought the idea worked. "'Because this is an audio feature, I think [you get an added] intensity and uniqueness,' Bronstein said. 'These are not things that you'll hear in the normal course of the day. . . . [They're] unpredictable. . . . In audio, you can sort of hear how people feel.'"

Interactivity. Often, the emotional appeal of a story comes only after someone shares it with a friend. Interactive online conversation can connect people on an emotional or practical level.

The eight traits that determine the news value of information do not change, even as the methods of conveying the values do. News isn't everything that happens to everyone. The mundane events of daily life become news only when they're reported in a way that communicates their news value. To put it another way, news value is the reason for telling a story.

NEWS ELEMENTS

News value provides the reason for telling a story, but how exactly should you go about creating your story? The **news element** is the basic building block of a story. Every news story has to contain the answers to six questions: *Who? What? When? Where? Why?* and *How?* Together, the answers to these questions comprise the essential elements of every news story.

In traditional newswriting, the first paragraph, or lead, of a story includes the most important news elements. If you are telling a story about a prominent person, then you must tell the audience who it is. If a story has news value because it is taking place near your audience, then you have to tell the audience exactly where. News elements and news value go hand in hand. The more accurately and precisely you provide information about the news elements, the more clearly your audience will understand the news value of your story.

Today's online news stories are no different; they too must contain the essential news elements. In fact, in the case of online news it is these very elements that are most helpful in determining which tools to use to tell the story. In print news stories, leads that attempt to answer all six questions in the first paragraph often fold under their own weight. The sentences become complicated and the paragraph gets too long. Similarly, online news stories that try to use all tools equally don't give the audience any clear place to begin. As an online news producer, it is your task to make crucial choices: Should you create a story that is told primarily as an interactive map but supplemented with photos? Should you write some text and then embed a video next to the paragraphs? Should you use a live discussion, with links to searchable databases? Journalists today have an unprecedented array of storytelling techniques from which to choose—and an unprecedented burden to choose their techniques wisely.

Who?

Reporters search high and low to put human faces on their stories. Sometimes those human faces are used to tell a story through anecdotes—the health care debate through the eyes of a family with a chronically sick child, or the financial crisis through the struggles of a woman who lost her job and retirement savings at age 58. In many cases, names alone make news. Apple CEO Steve Jobs and former president George W. Bush can make news when they do something that for the rest of us would be completely ordinary, for example, celebrating a birthday or undergoing outpatient surgery.

Audio, video, photos. Any time you have a story in which the "Who?" element is prominent, you'll certainly want to talk to the subject of your story. Interviews are the key to any personality profile. As you'll learn in the chapter on multimedia reporting, interviews are conducted differently for different media. And by using different media, journalists can emphasize different elements of the interview.

Reporters for newspapers and magazines have long faced the challenge of capturing in their writing the exact tone and body expressions of their interview subjects. With multimedia journalism, reporters can craft compelling text but also record on audio or video their subject's voice inflections and body language for their audience to hear and see.

Video journalists are subject to tight limits on the length of their stories, forcing them to pare down interviews to brief sound bites—with the bulk of an interview typically ending up on the cutting room floor. Online news, however, avoids such waste. Reporters can post the audio or video of the most compelling quotes from an interview inside a longer text story that provides the audio and visual elements with both perspective and context.

Interactivity. Stories that are driven by human drama or prominent personalities can have a deep impact on audience members and connect them with our shared humanity. Online journalists can make these connections literal by creating opportunities for interactivity. Conversation isn't about technology; it's about people. And when you have interesting or prominent people who play an important role in your story, discussion boards or live chats with the subjects of the story emphasize the "Who?" news element.

Finally, the rise of social networks has seen members of the online audience spend more and more of their time monitoring the latest news about their friends and colleagues, perhaps at the expense of learning about the lives of people who are very different from themselves. The value of professional journalists is that they seek out stories from people who don't have hundreds of followers on Twitter or friends on Facebook. Perhaps a fundamental question of journalism is changing from "Who?" to "Who else?" or "Who isn't?"

What?

Perhaps no question is uttered in newsrooms more often than "What's the story about?" Even the most prominent people in the world have to do *something* in order to make news.

Video. If the "What?" of a story is an action that takes place over a relatively short period of time, it can unfold before your audience's eyes—that is, if you're smart enough, and lucky enough, to have recorded video of the action. Think about how you feel if you walk away from the TV at a key moment in a basketball game, or out of the movie theater at a decisive moment in a thriller. At the very least, you'll want to ask someone, "What just happened?" Their recounting of the action may have to suffice. But, if you can, you'd really prefer to rewind the video and see what just happened with your own two eyes.

---

washingtonpost.com > Live Q&As

Video shows death of 2 Reuters employees in Baghdad attack

David Finkel
Washington Post Staff Writer
Tuesday, April 6, 2010; 1:30 PM

Pulitzer-winning Post staff writer David Finkel discusses newly released video of a 2007 helicopter attack on a Baghdad suburb, which led to the deaths of two Reuters employees.

Finkel wrote about the battle in his book The Good Soldiers, a chronicle of 'the surge' in Iraq 'the surge' through the experiences of a battalion of soldiers known as the 2-16.

David Finkel: Hi everyone. Thanks for joining this chat. We got to see an edited version yesterday of a

VIDEO

Saeed´s body

AP source confirms video of Baghdad firefight

A senior U.S. military official says video of a Baghdad firefight is authentic. The video shows U.S. troops firing on a group of men, some of whom were unarmed. A Reuters photographer is among those believed to have been killed in that attack.
» LAUNCH VIDEO PLAYER

In an online chat with Washington Post reporter David Finkel, the news organization embedded the video under discussion: a leaked video showing U.S. troops firing on a group of unarmed men.

The "What?" of a story isn't always the action, though. Sometimes the story is about an object—a new medical device or a strange fish. In rare cases, objects can make the news without doing much of anything. Their mere existence is interesting enough. It is easy to imagine the audience looking at a photograph of a newly discovered, and oddly configured, sea creature and exclaiming, "What is *that?*"

For stories that are published online, the "What?" of a story holds special importance because it is often the descriptor that people type into a search engine when they want on-demand delivery of information about a particular topic. In Chapter 5, on editing for searchers and scanners, you will learn how online news producers use the "What?" of a story in headlines and HTML metadata to make it easy for search engines to find their stories.

While it might be interesting to read about how the World's Ugliest Dog competition got its start—and then kept going for 21 years—this story on the Time website grabs the audience's attention by showing some examples of the contestants.

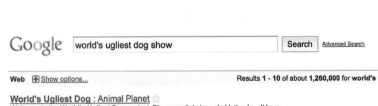

I'm sorry . . . what did you say that story was about? A contest for the world's ugliest dog? Oh yeah . . . I'm going to need to Google that.

When?

In online journalism, or any other 24/7 news medium, the answer to the question "When?" is very often "Right now!" From stock prices to medical breakthroughs, the online news audience wants the latest information.

Live video. In many cases, live video can be used to add the "When?" element to a story. Reporters in the field with no more than a

CNN has extended its branding as a source for live news from its cable television channel to its website.

mobile phone can now send live video to the Web. Letting the audience watch an event unfold before its eyes allows viewers to experience an event in a way that text never can.

On-demand delivery. In the case of crime stories or reports that hold people accountable for their decisions and actions, the "When?" news element often unfolds over time. Interactive timeline graphics put events in relationship to one another.

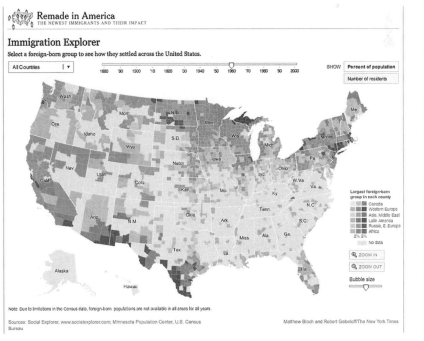

By using the timeline slider at the top of this animated graphic on The New York Times' website, visitors can watch immigration patterns change over time.

By putting events into a database, journalists allow site visitors to compare trends over a certain period of time and focus only on the desired information.

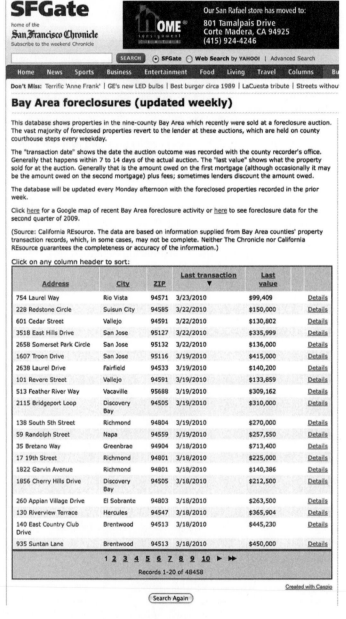

The San Francisco Chronicle's database of Bay Area foreclosures allows site visitors to search and sort by date.

Where?

A visitor to a news website is going to care much more about a robbery that occurred around the corner from his house than a robbery that occurred in a neighborhood where he neither lives nor visits. And a fire at a historic church is going to be much bigger news than an equally destructive fire at a 10-year-old office complex.

Multimedia. When you are telling a story about a place, you want to take your audience there. You can do this with maps or with video, audio and photographs. But you can do it even better when you put the sights and sounds inside the map and give users control over how they visit locations on the map.

On-demand delivery. With news consumption increasingly occurring on mobile devices, journalists are starting to use technology that determines the location of an information-seeking user to automatically deliver content that is geographically relevant.

Why?

Journalists begin to demonstrate their value as they add context, explanation and trend information to their stories. If the mayor suddenly resigns from office, a reporter should look for the causes of her departure. If stock prices suddenly

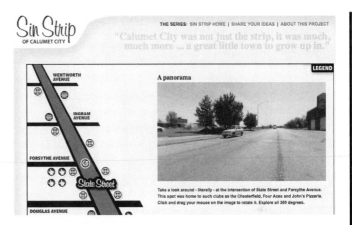

By overlaying video and photography on an interactive map of State Street in Calumet City, three staffers for The Times of Northwest Indiana created a multimedia feature that allowed visitors to explore different elements of the story in any order and at their own pace. The map puts each multimedia element in relation to the others.

Foursquare is an application for mobile devices that detects your location and the locations of your friends and provides you with different information as you move about a city.

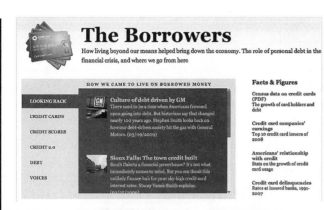

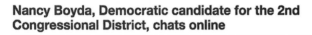

Although the package was laid out to promote non-linear, on-demand navigation, a page on the "Marketplace" radio show's website relies almost exclusively on text to explain how personal debt contributed to the financial crisis.

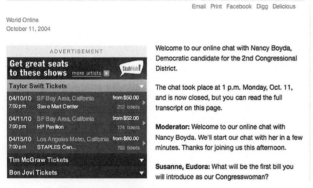

This news site, hosted by the Lawrence Journal-World, offered users the opportunity to discuss issues with political candidates and ask for information and policy explanations. While candidate Nancy Boyda lost the election in 2004, she went on to represent Kansas in the U.S. House from 2007–2009.

jump, journalists should attempt to explain which of hundreds of possible causes are most responsible for the rally.

Text. Causes and motivations are difficult to capture on camera. They rarely manifest themselves in a single moment. When the truth of a situation lies buried in the details that you are able to uncover only after a long time spent with your subject rather than in a finite moment that can be captured and reviewed, then text is really the only viable way to convey that truth.

Interactivity. Whether it is a politician explaining his or her stance on a controversial bill or a physician introducing a new medical discovery, interactivity allows explanatory news stories to efficiently answer the "Why?" questions that are of greatest interest to the audience.

How?

It is rare for a story's most important news element to rest on the "How?" question. The "How?" news element is really about process—how something happened or how something will happen. When the process is unusual, though, it can help turn an event into news. For example, when a high school football player dies from a heart attack, that's news. Every year about 180,000 Americans die from a heart attack—but their average age is 61, not 16.

Text. Unusual causes or processes are often hidden, or unfold over time in a way that is difficult to capture on camera. Stories that emphasize the "How?" news element are best told primarily with text.

The Multiple Beefs Behind the Kyrgyz Government Overthrow

by Katie Paul (/authors/katie-paul.html)   April 07, 2010

Protestors overran Kyrgyzstan (http://www.nytimes.com/2010/04/08/world/asia/08bishkek.html?ref=global-home) on Wednesday, forcing the country's president, Kurmanbek Bakiyev, to evacuate the capital city of Bishkek on his presidential plane. Police fired bullets, tear gas, and stun grenades into the crowds, killing 41 people (opposition leaders say the toll is much higher, perhaps 100). The protesters, for their part, have bloodied the cops by hurling rocks, brandishing sticks, overturning vehicles, and crashing vans through gates. The opposition succeeded in taking over national television channels, though news Web sites were being blocked (http://www.eurasianet.org/departments/insight/articles/eav040610b.shtml).

Kyrgyzstan, one of the poorest countries of the former Soviet Union and host to a strategic U.S. airbase used, isn't a regular on the international-crisis-headliner circuit. But nor is the explosion of unrest there entirely unexpected. On the surface, the protests were prompted by state-mandated hikes in the price of heating and electricity (here's a quick backgrounder (http://eurasianet.org

Newsweek's Wealth of Nations blog explained to readers some of the causes for the 2010 coup d'état in Kyrgyzstan and included links that allowed readers who were interested to dig deeper for information about specific underlying issues.

Readers of The Morning Call newspaper in Allentown, Penn., had to rely on the reporter's words to describe the sequence of events that led to a deadly shooting. But visitors to the organization's website could watch the surveillance video as well.

Multimedia. Sometimes videos, photos, animations or illustrations are the best way to explain a process to your audience. Maybe the process is how to cook a steak, or how a bill becomes a law. In either case the process involves motion, and each story could benefit from a medium that moves.

On-demand delivery. In many cases, journalists don't just report about problems. They also help people solve problems. Traditionally, journalists produce such stories whenever there is a **news peg**—that is, a newsworthy event—for them. For example, television stations will do stories about how to safely fry a turkey in the days leading up to Thanksgiving. But the online news audience wants its information on demand. Whether it is consumer news that helps people spend and save their money more wisely or news about how to get tested for the H1N1 virus, there are certain types of news that people seek only when they need to know how to solve a specific problem. In these cases, online news producers must make sure their stories can be found by search engines.

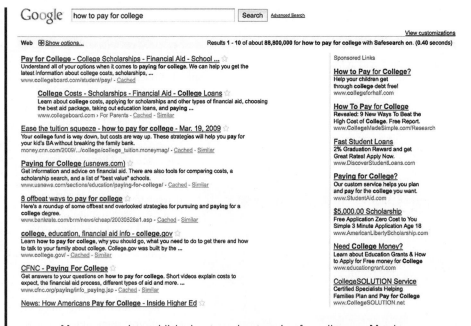

Money magazine published a story about paying for college on March 19, 2009. U.S. News published a story on September 23. But for a parent who wanted to start her college savings plan in January 2010, the two will appear side by side in a Google search.

VIEW SOURCE

PLAYING THE NEWS AT AMERICAN PUBLIC MEDIA

You call up the website, click "Play" and choose your avatar. That might sound similar to the start of a visit to the wildly popular "FarmVille" game that swept Facebook in 2009, but it is also the way that visitors to the American Public Media website kicked off a round of "Consumer Consequences" in 2007.

The game was created as part of the Marketplace radio show's coverage of sustainability issues. To play the game, you answer questions about your lifestyle: How big is your house? How far do you commute to work? As you answer these questions, the game tallies the number of Earths necessary to support your lifestyle.

The game features clever animation, humorous avatars and suspenseful theme music. But all of this rests on a

CHARACTER SELECTOR

Humorous avatars add an element of fun to a serious subject.

solid layer of serious journalism aimed at helping people understand the increasingly complex and interconnected world we share. It works as a news product not because it looks good, but because it uses the pillars of online journalism to further the traditional values and elements of news.

Like all good news stories, the game begins with a good question: "What would the world look like if everyone lived like me?" This question sets up the two news values underlying the game: impact and conflict. As players interact with the game, they receive information that directly relates to their lifestyles and circumstances. The more they interact, the more information they receive. This additional information opens the eyes of players to the conflict between their lifestyles and global sustainability.

Joellen Easton, the American Public Media producer who led the team that created the game, said that the entire narrative of the game had to lead players to the moment at which they discover the conflict. "Storyboarding helps you figure out . . . the metaphor that guides you through the reveal—the 'Aha!' moment," she said. But Easton and her team didn't want the "Aha!" moment to be the end of the story. They wanted the game to initiate discussion among players and serve as a tool for journalists to use in gathering information about the individual and aggregate choices that Americans might make about their

VIEW SOURCE

consumption habits if they were given certain pieces of information. At the end of the game, you can add your name or comments to American Public Media's Public Insight Network, a database of 84,000 people who serve as sources for the company's reporters. You can also compare your score to other players or invite your friends to play against you.

These same pillars of interactivity and multimedia storytelling were also incorporated into a game called "Budget Hero" that American Public Media launched in 2008. In that game, players attempt to balance a federal budget. Players first choose which policy goals (national security, energy independence) they want to achieve; they are then given budget decisions to play as "cards" during the game. "We wanted to explain the budgeting process—what a budget is made of and how those decisions are made," Easton said.

In this game the two news elements "What?" and "How?" are in play. And, in a sense, the game turns you, the player, into the "Who?" news element of the story. The "When?" of the game is 2009 and 20 years into the future, and the "Where?" is the United States. Easton added that these two elements were critical to the accuracy of the game. "The data has a shorter shelf life than the experience," she said. "You need to update the data for it to stay relevant." Since its launch, Budget Hero's data has been updated seven times to reflect changing national policy debates and shifts in the federal government's finances. These changes demonstrate the value of timeliness.

Easton said she was also interested to see how the game could be reused to tell the stories of state budgets as well. Why? Because news games are better when they incorporate the news value of proximity. The key to a good news game, she said, is making sure it is accurate and simple—two of the same keys to any good news story. "Sometimes it was really difficult to combine the need for simplicity and not burden it with layers and layers of new information so it can [remain simple]," she said. "You want the experience to be something you can navigate through. We had to sacrifice detail for sure."

Like the reporters at American Public Media, online producers have to know which details can be left out in order to highlight the most important news values and news elements of a story. The tools and the techniques cannot become more important than the truth. Easton said there were some choices her team would like to have given players to complete in "Consumer Consequences," but that had to be left out. "Some of it was just that the numbers for that information [weren't] solid enough," she said.

The creation of this kind of interactive explanatory journalism can happen only when reporters and editors are able to clearly articulate the traditions of journalism as well as imagine the possibilities—and appreciate the limitations—of new media.

ONLINE LEARNING MODULE 2

ACTIVATE THIS MODULE: journalism.cqpress.com

Multimedia, interactivity and on-demand delivery tools won't do a news story any good unless the reporters and editors working on it have a strong understanding of how traditional news values and news story elements are used to shape a story's structure and determine which pillars are best suited for telling the story. Use traditional news values and elements to help you decide which online storytelling tools to apply.

On my blog, I write about and link to examples of how traditional news values and elements are helping shape the future of journalism.

When you buy or activate this chapter's online learning module, you will have access to:

- A digital version of this chapter's text.
- Interactive flashcards for the terms used in this chapter.
- A printable one-page checklist to help you decide what's news and which storytelling techniques you should use.
- A quiz to test your mastery of the material in this chapter.
- Online exercises to give you experience applying online news judgment.

As you complete the module's online exercises, you will:

- Match traditional news values and news elements to the three pillars of online news in actual Pulitzer Prize–winning articles.
- Advise real reporters and editors on how to build stronger stories using the three pillars of online journalism.
- Critique and discuss professional online news sites in preparation for seeking a job or internship.

3 THE ONLINE NEWS AUDIENCE

In this chapter, you will learn the *who, what, when, where, why* and *how* of online news demographics:

- Young people and news junkies are the people *who* are most likely to go to the Web for news.
- National and international news from television sites is *what* the audience is mostly likely to consume online.
- The middle of the day is *when* online news is most popular, and people consume it in small chunks throughout the day.
- More and more news consumers are getting their news from mobile phones, using them to find news *where* they are.
- The reason *why* people turn to online news is to access breaking news updates and to share news with friends.
- Online news users differ significantly from their print and broadcast counterparts in terms of *how* they consume news.

Journalists without an audience are just diarists, solitary scribblers of their own thoughts. But journalists who know and connect with their audience can, quite simply, change the world.

Communicators have been changing the world since before the days of the Greek philosopher Aristotle, who argued that the audience was the most important element in human communication. "[O]f the three elements in speech-making—speaker, subject, and person addressed—it is the last one, the hearer, that determines the speech's end and object," he wrote in his treatise "Rhetoric." You, the journalist, are the speaker. But you can't tell a story about your subject effectively without understanding your audience. The technology you use may be new, but journalists' desire to inform and engage their audience is ancient.

As communication technology evolves, so too do audiences. The audiences for whom you write today behave in fundamentally different ways from the audiences of ancient Greece—or even from the audience for whom journalism students were trained to write a decade ago. People who get their news and information from online sources behave differently than people who read newspapers or watch television. And a person who gets his or her news from multiple media consumes and interacts with each of those media differently. While both a newspaper and a website may offer their readers the same text of an article, it is important to understand that these readers consume the text in different environments, and often for different reasons. Their actions before and after they read the text story will also differ depending on the medium.

An understanding of the changing nature of audience habits is crucial to good journalism. Awareness of your audience isn't something you get just by reading one chapter of a textbook or passing a year-end examination; audience awareness hinges on audience needs. As a journalist you must always place the audience's needs above your own—whether they involve a political agenda, financial considerations or even artistic self-expression. Perhaps more so today than ever, a journalist in a networked world is not just a storyteller on a stage or at a lectern, but a conduit for connecting ideas and people.

Without an audience, all of your hard work reporting a story—and your creativity in presenting it—will be wasted. Study after study has shown that the online news audience has different behaviors and expectations than a print or broadcast news audience.

WHO READS NEWS ONLINE?

Who reads news online? The short answer to this question, at least in the U.S., is nearly everyone. Somewhere between 75 and 80 percent of American adults use the Internet, and between 70 and 75 percent of these people have used the Internet to get news in some way. In just 10 years, the Internet overtook magazines, then radio and then newspapers as a major source for news, especially among people between the ages of 18 and 30.

A Growing Audience, Second Only to TV

In 2009, more than 170 million American adults said they used the Internet, and about 120 million said they at least occasionally used the Internet to gather news. But for most Americans, the Internet is just one of several places to turn for news. Despite the rapid growth of the Internet, television clearly remains most Americans' preferred source for national, international and local news and information. The two media may be on a collision course, however, as the popularity of television declines and its audience fragments while the popularity of the Internet continues to increase. For about 18 percent of American adults, the Internet is their number one source for news.

One of the most consistent and thorough sources of free public data about the online news audience is the Pew Research Center. Several times every year, the center surveys thousands of Americans about their news habits and attitudes. In December 2009, the Pew Research Center for the People & the Press asked American adults to name the two media from which they got most of their national and international news. Seventy percent said television was one of the two most important media, 35 percent said the Internet and

Figure 3.1 American Media Use Over Time

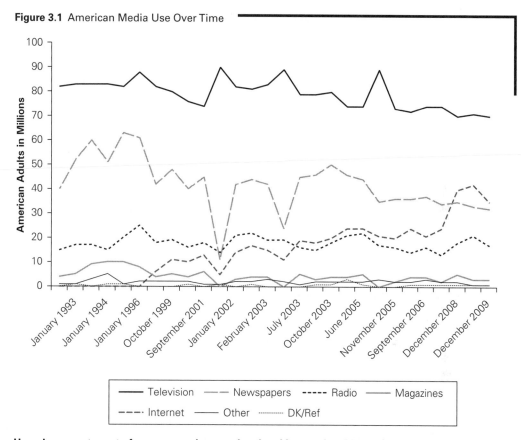

How do you get most of your news about national and international issues?

NOTE: Figures add to more than 100 percent because of multiple responses.

SOURCE: Pew Research Center for People and the Press. December 2009 Political Survey, http://people-press.org/reports/questionnaires/573.pdf.

32 percent said newspapers. It was the second consecutive year that the Internet was named more often than newspapers as a top source of news. Since 1999, when Pew first began including the Internet as a source of news, the percentage of television news viewers has dropped from 82 percent and newspaper readers from 42 percent. In 1999, only 6 percent cited the Internet as an important source for national and international news.

For local news, however, the Internet plays less of a role. In a July 2009 Pew survey, the Internet trailed all other media as a source for local news and information. Only 17 percent of respondents said that they get most of their local news from the Web, compared to 64 percent who cited television, 41 percent who named newspapers and 18 percent who preferred radio.

The period between the 2004 and 2008 presidential elections saw rapid growth of the Internet as a source for political news. By the end of the 2008 campaign, more American adults said the Internet was one of the two media from which they got most of their election news. A third of the people in a Pew poll said the Internet was one of their most important sources, while 29 percent named newspapers. Meanwhile, television was the top source, cited by 72 percent of respondents.

Big news events have tended to push more and more people to the Web for breaking news as well as in-depth reporting and a broader variety of sources. On Election Day in 1996, news websites saw traffic spike as Americans turned to the Internet for quick access to results and analysis. Much of that audience has remained, and in fact the Internet audience grows each time a new story breaks—for example, the Clinton-Lewinsky scandal in 1998–99 and the 9/11 terrorist attacks in 2001. This trend continues. During the outbreak of H1N1, or "swine flu," in May 2009, 25 percent of American adults cited the Internet as the most useful source of news about the illness; this compared to 45 percent who found television the most useful source of news and 9 percent who cited newspapers.

Despite the rapid growth of the Internet, it would be tough to make the argument that the advent of online news has made most Americans more aware of current events. If the Internet is having any effect on the overall news diet of Americans, it may be that it is merely slowing the decades-long decline in the amount of time the average person spends with the news. Between 1994 and 2004, surveys done by the Pew Research Center showed steady erosion in the amount of time that people were spending on news consumption. But in 2004, when Pew first started asking about online news consumption, there was a sudden jump in the average time spent on news—a jump that hadn't been seen before and hasn't been seen since. Time spent with traditional news media, however, continues to be replaced by time spent getting news online. In 2004, Americans spent 92 percent of their news consumption time with offline media. In 2008, that percentage had dropped to 86 percent.

A Young and Elite Audience

To the disappointment of many people who saw the rise of the Internet as a sign of a renewed interest in the news, more and more Americans are simply ignoring news from any source. Nearly 20 percent of Americans didn't see or hear any news yesterday, a five-point jump from 1998. Among adults younger than 24—the most frequent and engaged online news audience—more than one-third got no news yesterday, a nine-point jump in 10 years.

In an April 1997 article written for Wired magazine, author Jon Katz led off with idealistic optimism: "On the Net last year, I saw the rebirth of love for liberty in media. I saw a culture crowded with intelligent, educated, politically passionate people who—in jarring contrast to the offline world—line up to express their civic opinions, participate in debates, even fight for their political beliefs." Katz and others hoped that by making online publications cheap to start up and nearly free to distribute, the Internet would see a flourishing of new voices—voices that had been ignored by traditional mainstream reporters and editors.

VIEW SOURCE

FINDING AND TRACKING A SHIFTING AUDIENCE

For more than a decade, Julie Rutherford has been chasing and catching an audience that has been constantly changing its behavior. First at Washingtonpost, Newsweek Interactive and then at BeliefeNet, the nation's largest website about religion, Rutherford has worked with journalists, computer programmers and sales and marketing departments on projects aimed at reaching the shifting news audience via e-mail, search engines, social media and mobile devices.

Q: What statistics should journalists use to learn about their audience?

It depends on your goals, but for most websites that sell advertising, the **unique visitors** are the first thing you look at because they help define your reach, which is really important to Internet advertisers. That provides a volume of the number of eyeballs you're going to reach. Then you want to look at how many **visits** you get from those uniques, which is a measure of frequency, so how frequently those folks come back. So you can have 3 million uniques and 5,000 visits; your goal would be to try to find ways [to] induce readers to come back more and more frequently during the month. Then you have **page views** and the metrics associated with that, which really show the depth of reader engagement—so this is how many page views a user consumes during the visit. Those are the three big ones. For us, as well, we have a really large e-mail business so you want to see how many click through those.

Q: What relationship do you have with people who work in the newsroom?

Most editorial people use the same analytics data—[for example,] uniques … tells them [which] people [are] interested in the content [and] how do we get more people who are interested in the content. We work really close with our editorial group on [search engine optimization] because we can get a lot of data around what people are searching for. So, we may find that there are religious or inspirational or emotional health topics that we don't have a lot of content for and that users are actually asking for by the way they're searching on Google. What are people asking for that you might not have thought to cover? [Data] can really help you direct your editorial [staff].

Q: What are valuable metrics? What are not valuable?

Depends on where your business is, what part of the department you sit in. I've worked in places where there was too much of a focus on page views; you get a behavior that creates a lot of page views for the site but you might not actually be directing a lot of new people to the site. What you need to do is make sure you're using multiple metrics so you are getting more people to the site and they're also using the product a lot.

On Newsstands Now
Issue 5.04 | Apr 1997

Birth of a Digital Nation

By Jon Katz

Page 1 of 8
previous | start | next
Printing? Use this version

For some, this past election year was about the slow death of the current political system. For Jon Katz, on the other hand, it marked the rise of postpolitics and the birth of the Digital Nation.

First stirrings

On the Net last year, I saw the rebirth of love for liberty in media. I saw a culture crowded with intelligent, educated, politically passionate people who - in jarring contrast to the offline world - line up to express their civic opinions, participate in debates, even fight for their political beliefs.

I watched people learn new ways to communicate politically. I watched information travel great distances, then return home bearing imprints of engaged and committed people from all over the world. I saw positions soften and change when people were suddenly able to talk directly to one another, rather than through journalists, politicians, or ideological mercenaries.

I saw the primordial stirrings of a new kind of nation - the Digital Nation - and the formation of a new postpolitical philosophy. This nascent ideology, fuzzy and difficult to define, suggests a blend of some of the best values rescued from the tired old dogmas - the humanism of liberalism, the economic opportunity of conservatism, plus a strong sense of personal responsibility and a passion for freedom.

I came across questions, some tenuously posed: Are we living in the middle of a great revolution, or are we just members of another arrogant élite talking to ourselves? Are we a powerful new kind of community or just a mass of people hooked up to machines? Do we share goals and ideals, or are we just another hot market ready for exploitation by America's ravenous corporations?

Wired magazine's archived article from Jon Katz.

In some cases, Katz's optimism has been rewarded. New voices have emerged. Fringe social and political groups were among some of the first to use the online media to communicate with each other, find allies and tell the stories that were not being told in popular newspapers and television. In 1998, former professional wrestler Jesse "The Body" Ventura tapped into this anti-establishment energy online and used it to propel himself to the Minnesota governor's mansion.

But from the outset, the pioneers on the Internet have also been mostly educated, affluent, white city-dwellers. The people who could afford the expensive early versions of home computers and Internet access were the first to go online. Later, the same demographic was the first to buy smart phones and iPods and to set up high-speed Internet connections at home. This gap between the online haves and have-nots has been dubbed the "digital divide." In all news media except television, there is a divide between historically privileged groups and historically disenfranchised groups. Like the news audience for most other media, the Internet news audience skews white, male, affluent and educated. The gap is especially large in terms of age, education and income.

Adults between the ages of 18 and 29 years of age—the so-called Millenneals—are an overrepresented age group among the online news audience. While they account for 22 percent of the total U.S. adult population, the Millenneal age cohort makes up nearly 30 percent of the online news audience. This age group may be less likely than previous generations to be avid news consumers, but that portion of the cohort that *is* reading news is doing so in ways that differ sharply from those of older cohorts. The unique methods by which Millenneals acquire and share information about their world are worth watching; if decades of research hold true, the media patterns established at this age will remain throughout life.

Among Millenneals, the Internet has left newspapers and radio in the dust and is quickly catching up to television. Television remains the top source of news for 65 percent of 18- to 29-year-olds, but the Internet is a close second at 59 percent. Millenneals are also the group most likely to watch news video online, visit news blogs, maintain a profile on a social networking site and receive news by e-mail. Yet they are the least likely to use RSS feeds and to access news on a custom Web page.

Millenneals don't just consume online media, though. They are more likely to create it too. They're 50 percent more likely than Gen Xers—those ages 30 to 45—to create social network profiles or use Twitter. Twenty-nine percent of Millenneals check their online social networks several times a day. They are also more than three times as likely as older cohorts to have posted video of themselves online.

But Millenneals don't just differ from older generations in their digital media consumption and creation. They also differ in the times and manner they get news. It is the only age group that prefers getting news after dinner to getting news any other time of day. It is also the only group that is less likely to use a news site's homepage to find a story than to follow a link directly to the story from some other site. And it is the group most likely to just stumble across news while doing something else online.

One way in which Millenneals mirror previous generations is in the racial, educational and income divides between those who use the Internet to get news and those who do not. The gap between the percentage of college graduates who use the Internet to get news and the percentage of those with no more than a high school diploma who do so is widening rapidly. No other demographic characteristic saw the development of a wider gap between 2006 and 2008. In just two years, the percentage of college graduates who went online for news daily jumped from 32 percent to 44 percent—the fastest rate of growth among any demographic group. Meanwhile, the percentage of people with only a high school degree who accessed news online daily inched forward only 1 percentage point, to 11 percent. While there are also gaps between white and black online audiences, and between men and women, these gaps have remained flat since 2006.

It is important for journalists to remember that even the most compelling online news won't reach those people who don't get their news from the Web. Nor are these people contributing comments and sharing photos with the online community. Different patterns in media consumption can lead to differences of perception that are based solely on the chance circumstances of birth. As long as there is a digital divide, journalists will need to realize that engaging the audience is going to mean finding ways of connecting people across media platforms.

WHAT NEWS DO PEOPLE GET ONLINE?

While the Internet has meant more people are getting their local news from a new medium, most are getting it from the same news organizations that were popular before the establishment of the Internet. Blogs and social media are contributing new stories to the mix, but for the most part social media is functioning as a new distribution tool for legacy media stories.

Much From the Same Old Sources

Among the 199 most popular news sites in the U.S., two-thirds are sites for news organizations that were in business before the Internet existed. And two-thirds of the traffic to the top 199 sites goes to legacy news sites, or sites that are run by companies that produced news before the arrival of the Internet.

While Yahoo News is the most popular online source of news in America, most of its content comes from traditional news sources, especially the Associated Press. The websites of two national cable TV channels, MSNBC and CNN, vie most months for the second largest online news audience. Among the online news audience, 56 percent, or 66 million people, say they get their news from news aggregators such as Yahoo or Google News, and 46 percent say they get their news from a site connected with a television station.

The New York Times has the most popular newspaper website in the U.S., which makes it the fifth or sixth most popular news site overall most months. Even so, the number of people who visit The New York Times' site every month is less than half the number who visit Yahoo News. USA Today and The Washington Post are neck and neck for the second spot among U.S. newspaper sites; according to Web analytics company Nielsen, they each have less than half the audience of The New York Times' site.

The first story on this screencapture of the Yahoo News homepage features both an AP wire story and photo.

There are plenty of indications that the people who read newspaper websites are not augmenting readership of the print product. In 2008, only 5 percent of all Americans said they read a newspaper both in print and online. Nine percent of Americans read newspaper stories only online, and 25 percent said they read newspaper stories only in print. People who grew up with traditional media seem to prefer it in its native form.

While blogs and social networks such as Facebook are growing in popularity as news sources, most of these platforms rely heavily on traditional journalism, especially newspapers. According to a 2009 analysis of outgoing links from social media sites done by the Project for Excellence in Journalism (PEJ), about 80 percent of the links go to traditional media sites. The list of destinations to which bloggers send their readers is dominated by just three news sources: The New York Times, CNN and the BBC. Interestingly, the pattern at Twitter looks a bit different. Newspapers account for less than 3 percent of links from Twitter posts. All legacy media accounted for just less than a third of outbound Twitter links, according to the same PEJ study.

Looking at the way that traditional national news outlets dominate the list of the top news sites in the U.S., it is not surprising that the type of news that most people seek online is national and international news. Weather, sports scores, financial news, entertainment news and health information round out the remaining top categories of online news.

Local news still seems to reach Americans mostly from local television, though journalists should keep a close eye on the local news consumption patterns of young people. Young people today say that they are interested in local news much less than other topics, but according to a survey of college undergrads done by Kevin Kiley at the University of North Carolina at Chapel Hill, Millenneals may be using Facebook as one of their primary sources of news about local events.

Some Different Stories, in a Different Way

Overall, social media is growing as a source for news distribution—though not necessarily news creation. On one hand, about 42 million Americans say they get news from their friends on social networks. This is just 3 million fewer than say they get news from newspapers. On the other, bloggers not associated with a mainstream media outlet are a source of news for only 13 million Americans, and fewer than 8 million Americans say they get news from a friend on Twitter, according to a December 2009 telephone poll done by the Pew Research Center.

People use Facebook and other social sites primarily as a social filtering device rather than as a way of staying connected to specific journalists or news outlets. On both Facebook and Twitter, people are much more likely to say that they get news on these platforms from a friend than from a journalist or news organization.

Perhaps the biggest role for social media sites is as a distribution tool because of the way they link back to original source sites. Journalists need to be aware of which stories are being discussed on social media—and which are not. The Project for Excellence in Journalism's 2009 study of the topics covered on blog and mainstream news sites found that blogs and the mainstream media both had the same most-popular story in only 13 of 47 weeks.

On-demand delivery offers the online audience much more control over which stories it sees via social media as well as news aggregators such as Google News. Because they are reading headlines on social networking sites, many people may be getting as much news as they want without ever actually visiting a news site. According to a 2009 study done by the research firm Outsell, 44 percent of people who read headlines on Google News never click through to the site where the story originated.

On the upside, the use of search and social filtering means that for many people their news diet is becoming more balanced—68 percent of the online news audience regularly relies on more than one source for news every day, and 11 percent regularly uses at least six sites every day. Much of this diversity is coming from increasing use of partisan news sources such as political blogs. On both the right and left, political bloggers and news aggregation sites enjoy loyal audiences that visit more often and stay longer than do the audiences of most mainstream news sites. And nearly a third of Americans say that they prefer to get news from a source that shares their point of view. These audiences aren't necessarily small, either. Conservative blogger Andrew Breitbart, for example, has more monthly visitors to his website than do major metro newspaper sites such as the Philadelphia Inquirer, Miami Herald and Houston Chronicle.

Figure 3.2 American On-Demand Media Use

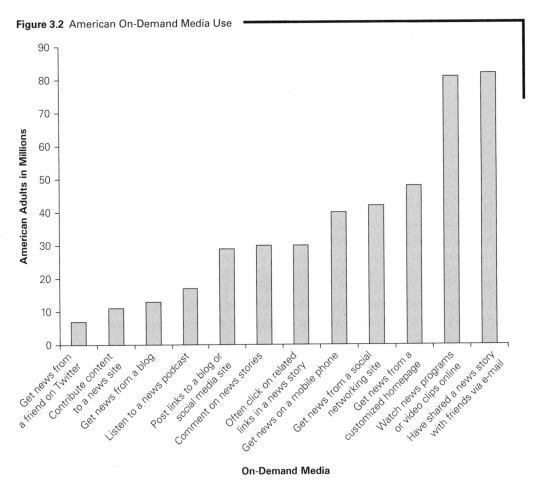

SOURCE: Data compiled from the U.S. Census Bureau, December 2009, National Estimate of Postcensal Civilian Noninstitutionalized Population; and Pew Research Center's Internet & American Life Project, Online News Survey, December 28, 2009–January 19, 2010, http://www.pewinternet.org/Reports/2010/Online-News.aspx.

WHEN DO PEOPLE READ NEWS ONLINE?

If you've ever asked your grandparents about how they got their news, you might have heard a story that was common when they were young adults. Every morning the newspaper boy—and it was almost always a boy—would ride his bike by the house a little before dawn and toss the morning paper on the doorstep or driveway. With a cup of coffee in hand, your grandfather or grandmother went out and retrieved the paper and brought it back to the breakfast table, where it was divided up among the family. Every morning, the family had an appointment with the newspaper, and it was the same paper delivered at about the same time to nearly every house in the city.

Your parents might tell a similar story of an appointment they had with the nightly network news. Every evening at about dinner time, a man—and it was always a man—would appear on whichever of the three national broadcast television networks your parents preferred and spend 30 or maybe 60 minutes telling them about what he and his editors and producers thought was the most important news of the day, or at least the most important news for which they had video.

Fast forward to your generation. If either your parents or grandparents asked you the same question, after thinking about it for just a few minutes you'd tell them that the days of appointment news consumption are over. You and your friends get news when you want it, where you want it and how you want it. You choose the stories you find interesting, and your friends may recommend some of the stories you see. A number of these stories may in fact have been written by journalists whose primary audience is the residents of a city on the other side of the country. Today's audience—the online news audience—doesn't eat three square meals at about the same time as everyone else every day. It snacks throughout the day, a nibble at a time.

During the Workday

One of the reasons that the Web has grown as an online news source is that it is often the only medium that reaches office workers during the day. Sixty-four percent of Americans say they check news during work hours. The middle of the day is second only to the morning as the time when Americans are most likely to be looking at news.

Of the people who check news during the day, a third say that they use the Internet to do it. Although television is the most

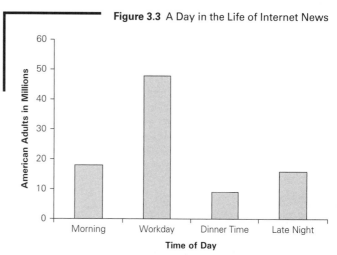

Figure 3.3 A Day in the Life of Internet News

SOURCE: Pew Research Center Biennial News Consumption Survey, April 30-June 1, 2008, http://people-press.org/reports/pdf/444.pdf.

popular source of news during the workday, providing 44 percent of the daytime news audience with its information, for Americans under 50 the Internet is by far the most popular daytime source of news. Ten years ago, only 5 percent of the daytime news audience used the Internet.

Among people who prefer to get their news online, 82 percent check news during the day. Only 61 percent of people who prefer to get their news from a traditional source check news (from any source) during the day. Ninety-two percent of the heaviest users of online news sites—a group Pew has dubbed the "Net Newsers"—access the Internet to get news during the day. Only 4 percent of people who get their news from traditional media outlets check for news on the Internet during the day.

Throughout the Day

In 2008, according to a survey by the Pew Research Center, 51 percent of American adults said they check in on the news from time to time during the day, rather than get the news at regular times. This marked the first time that a majority of Americans considered themselves "news grazers." For news grazers, the Internet is a popular source of news—9 percent of them say they turn to the Internet for news at least three days a week, compared to the 39 percent of people who get their news by appointment. The appointment news audience is more likely to rely on television, newspapers and radio for its news than the Internet. Net Newsers are the people most likely to be grazers. Seventy-eight percent of Net Newsers say they check news from time to time, compared to 41 percent of people who are traditional news consumers.

While online news consumers dip their toes into the stream of information more often than people who rely on traditional sources, online users spend less of their time engaging with the news than do people who get their news from traditional media. Online users average just 35 minutes a day looking at news from all websites. This is less than the 39 minutes the average newspaper reader spends with his or her newsprint, and far less than the 54 minutes spent on television news by the average television news viewer. Not everyone uses the same sources of news in the same proportion, but an average American adult spends 66 minutes consuming news from all sources each day.

The online news audience—always "on" and always "snacking"—relies on short bursts of information and interactivity. Journalists have taken note. The challenge today is figuring out how to produce in-depth investigative and explanatory news in a way that suits audience behavior.

Tool: Google Analytics

For a large number of Web publishers, the online news audience remains a mystery. Getting detailed information about the traffic to your site can require purchasing analytics server software, such as **Omniture's SiteCatalyst,** while getting information about traffic to other sites in a way that allows for easy comparison requires the purchase of reports and data from analytics companies. Thankfully for small publishers, Google offers a free tool called Analytics. By placing a small piece of code within the HTML of your Web pages, you can use **Google Analytics** to track the visits, unique visitors and page views to your site.

Screencast on applying Google Analytics to your blog or website

Tutorials on using Google Analytics

HOW DO PEOPLE READ NEWS ONLINE?

If we know anything about the 121 million people who regularly go online for news, it is that they are fickle. They flit from site to site, spending an average of only three minutes on each one. Many people who visit online news sites don't even know or care which site they are on. They simply get news when they want it, where they want it and how they want it; choose the stories they find interesting—or those their friends have found interesting and recommended; and not infrequently access stories written by journalists whose primary audience is the residents of a city on the other side of the country.

Searching and Scanning

It would be tough to overstate the role of search engines on online news consumption. Searches empower people to find news on exactly the topic they want at exactly the time they want. Search engines such as Google drive massive amounts of traffic to news websites, and the search function within a website is one of the most common ways for people to navigate a site. Seventy-one percent of Americans who use the Internet to get news say they use search engines to find news at least once every few weeks. A third say they use a search engine to find news at least three times a week. In fact, search engines may be one reason why the news consumer is so fickle: oftentimes users don't even know the names of the sources they're hooking up with. Forty-eight percent of online news users say their searches for news take them to websites with which they are not familiar.

The prominence of search engines as a starting point for online news consumption means that journalists have to consider not just how humans will read their stories, but how computers will read them as well. As you will learn in Chapter 5, on writing for searchers and scanners, the manner in which content is placed on a Web page and the words in a headline can affect whether or not searchers find your news stories.

Search engines are one of the primary reasons that so many people begin their visit to a news site directly on a specific article rather than first going to a site's homepage. Only 41 percent of the online news audience reads news by going directly to the homepages of news organizations. Half of the people who visit online news sites typically start on an article page. A 2007 report in Advertising Age magazine noted that 57 percent of all visits to websites began at a page other than the site's homepage. The editor of one of the largest online newspaper sites in the U.S. told the Project for Excellence in Journalism that only a third of the traffic to his site came through the homepage.

Even though the homepage is, for most websites, the single most-visited page on the site—and the page on which most people begin their visit—its influence pales in comparison to the power of a broadcast's lead story or the stories on the front page of a newspaper. Change in audience behavior is forcing today's journalists to think differently about the traditional elements of news judgment and editorial control.

On the Go

The online news audience isn't just sitting in one place moving from site to site. A growing number of Americans are getting news while *they* are moving from site to site. Internationally, mobile phones have long been an important tool for accessing the Internet or sending short text messages. In the United States, mobile Internet use has trailed tethered desktop use, but recent years have seen a dramatic increase as more and more Americans are using Web-enabled **"smart" phones** such as the iPhone, Blackberry or Droid. Overall, 15 percent of Americans say they have a smart phone, and more than a third of those say that they look at news on these devices.

Of the 170 million American adults who use the Internet, 70 percent of them access it through some sort of wireless device—either a mobile phone or **WiFi**. Among mobile phone Web users, more people choose to pull information from the Web via searching or browsing than to have e-mail or text messaging alerts sent to their phones. Weather, sports, financial news and traffic information are some of the most popular news topics that people want to see on their phones. Many industry analysts see mobile technologies as a growth opportunity for journalists. New devices such as Apple's iPad offer companies new platforms. For example, ESPN and The New York Times were the first to provide special applications that take advantage of the features of the iPad.

Technological change brings with it challenges for journalists. For example, with each new screen dimension comes the need for a fresh design with fresh features that fit consumer habits. Most major news organizations have built stripped-down versions of their online sites so that mobile phones with slow Internet connections can more quickly download the content. For online news producers, this means fewer pictures, shorter headlines to fit a smaller screen and less Web page width in which to create links to related content.

Good mobile news operations, however, don't just retool their existing site to fit a new screen. Content for mobile devices can take advantage of geographically targeted information. The New York Times, the Financial Times and several Canadian papers have teamed up with a company called Foursquare to create content based on a user's location. According to media consultant The Kelsey Group, about a third of all Web searches conducted by mobile phone are initiated to access information on something that is situated nearby.

Podcasts are another form of mobile media that is formatted to fit the audience. Podcasts are digital audio news shows that can be downloaded and played on a mobile music device such as an iPod. Because so many of the 16 million Americans who listen to news podcasts do so during their commute, most podcasts are edited to run between 5 and 20 minutes in length—about the same amount of time it takes many people to get to work.

A Social Experience

We've already discussed the way in which the online news audience snacks on information throughout the day, so you probably won't be surprised to learn that according to a survey done in 2006 by the Pew Research Center, the most popular reason that people say they go online for news is because of its convenience and to get breaking news updates. These reasons remain the most prominent motivations for the audience's shift to online news. But the rise in social networking has become increasingly important, as its interactivity features facilitate the exchange of online news. In fact, when Pew asked in 2009 what were the most important factors in deciding where to get news online, the audience cited links to related material, aggregating news from around the Internet and the ability to easily share stories with others as their top three factors.

The importance of sharing news, though, predates the rise of Facebook and Twitter. E-mail was the first way that people shared links to online news stories, and it remains the most popular. About 104 million Americans say they have received a news story in the e-mail from a friend. And about 81 million say they've sent news to a friend via e-mail. This compares to about 30 million adults who have posted a story to a blog or social network, and only 6 million who have posted a link to a story on Twitter.

It appears that people are much more interested in reacting to or sharing news content that has been developed by someone else than in creating news content of their own. Despite having the ability, the vast majority of Americans do not make their own news content. According to several surveys done by the Pew Research Center, less than 10 percent of American adults who go online for news have ever posted photos, video or information about their communities to a news site.

Even before the Internet, talking with friends about the news is one of the most common reasons that people say they follow the news, according to survey research. Reporters have always pitched their most interesting stories as "water cooler stories"—reports that people would read and then discuss around the water cooler while on break at work.

In the field of mass communication research, the uses and gratifications theory says that people consume news and information for one of four basic reasons: (1) to be aware of dangers and opportunities in the world, (2) for entertainment, (3) to feel connected to other people, and (4) to reinforce personal feelings or opinions. Similarly, political economist Anthony Downs as far back as 1957 noted that there were four reasons people seek the news: (1) to help them make smarter consumer decisions, (2) to improve their workplace productivity, (3) to entertain themselves, and (4) to make voting decisions.

These findings create a challenge for online news producers. On the one hand, favoring timeliness above other news values and creating content that can be consumed in short bursts will match audience behavior. On the other hand, producers face the challenge of figuring out how to deliver in-depth investigative and explanatory journalism to a restless news audience. When people can easily ignore information that doesn't entertain or inform them, it is important for journalists to create news that people want to talk about.

Interactivity is one of the pillars of online news that make it fundamentally different from news in other media. A site's visitors can become its best advocates by sharing with their friends the information they find there. The audience isn't just the audience anymore. If you, the journalist, give them news that is engaging and relevant, they will share it with their friends. Your work has the opportunity not only to connect your sources with your readers, but also your readers with each other. That's how journalism builds community.

ONLINE LEARNING MODULE 3

ACTIVATE THIS MODULE: journalism.cqpress.com

The online news audience looks and behaves differently from the audience for traditional news sources in print or broadcast. Your ability to identify the characteristics of the online news audience is the first step toward building stronger stories that fit that audience's specific needs.

On my blog, I write about and link to the most recent material on the ever-changing trends of the online news audience. This blog is a resource for you regarding all the latest research on this topic.

When you buy or activate this chapter's online learning module, you will have access to:

- A digital version of this chapter's text.
- Interactive flashcards for the terms used in this chapter.
- A printable one-page guide to the who, what, when, where and why of the online news audience.
- A quiz to test your mastery of the material in this chapter.
- A video screencast that shows you how to use Google Analytics.

- Links to tools to help you track your audience and to free tutorials from across the Web that show you how to learn more about the audience for your own site.

- Online exercises that give you experience working with online news consumers.

As you complete the module's online exercises, you will:

- Identify a news site's editorial strategies to increase unique visitors, repeat visits and depth of visits.

- Track the news consumption behaviors of a real person.

- Identify how your personal preferences may differ from those of the overall news audience.

- Develop an idea for a new editorial product.

- Interview professional journalists about the online news audience.

ONLINE LEARNING

4 MANAGING CONTENT ON A NEWS SITE

This chapter will help you create a CMS mindset by showing you how to:

- Create and edit content that is stored in a CMS.
- Lay out a homepage or section front index page using CMS templates and content in a CMS database.
- Understand what happens to content as it moves through the separate components of a CMS at each stage in the content lifecycle.
- Work with programmers to explain editorial rules that automate the display of different pieces of a story and the placement of the story's pieces in various locations on a website or mobile phone application.

Every day, Yahoo News publishes more than 2,000 news articles, more than 4,000 photographs and nearly 400 news videos. The vast majority of this material originates with journalists at about 50 news outlets that have partnered with Yahoo to republish their content. Handling it all at Yahoo News—making sure all of these thousands of pieces of information get sifted, sorted, edited and organized—is a group of news editors whose number you can count on just one hand: five. They are the professionals who enable Yahoo News to get the right information to the right people at the right time.

The work is tough enough on a normal day. But consider Jan. 12, 2010. On that Tuesday, just before 2 p.m. in the site's California offices, word began coming across the wires that a devastating earthquake had struck Haiti. It was the kind of day that sends traffic to news sites skyrocketing, as information-hungry news consumers scour the Web for the freshest and most reliable updates. On such a day, millions of people turn to Yahoo for their news.

How can just five news editors channel an avalanche of news to such a massive audience? They use their journalism knowledge, and they get lots of help from Jake. Jake is Yahoo's **content management system,** or CMS. A CMS automates many of the technical publishing details that would take hours for a human to process. If the editors at Yahoo News want to control the words, photos, audio and video that appear on their site, they have to know how to control Jake.

A content management system is the essential tool of the trade for today's online news producers at organizations ranging from a simple, locally focused neighborhood newsletter to the intricate, globally focused BBC. Content management systems make it easier for online news producers without knowledge of **HTML, CSS** or **FTP** to create, organize and publish news and information to the Web and other platforms. Automating the publishing process in this way frees journalists to spend more time reporting and crafting their stories.

Here is how content management works at Yahoo. When a story arrives from one of Yahoo's content providers, it takes only about 15 seconds before it is automatically published to the live website. This kind of lightning-fast publishing can happen because editors and programmers have written rules that tell Jake how to display the various pieces of every story: headlines, 28-pixel Georgia font; bylines, 11-pixel Verdana; all photos, 135 pixels wide and flush left with the top of the first line of the article text. They've also told the system where and how to display the same article—or at least links to it—on all the pages on the site where someone might be looking for it. The editors don't have to worry about these details; Jake is taking care of them.

As each new story on the Haitian earthquake poured in, an accompanying headline was printed on the homepage, the world news section front, the Latin America news page, and each of the RSS feeds for those pages. The story automatically triggered e-mail news alerts to subscribers. In short time, the story's headline had to be printed on the lists of "Most E-mailed" and "Most Viewed" stories, and those lists then appeared on almost every page of the site. As more and more people clicked on a story, its position on the popularity lists automatically changed as well, which in turn triggered a reprint on all of the pages on which it was displayed. And when a new version of the same story arrived, Jake had to know it was new and place it at the exact same Web address as the old version. All of this happened automatically. All of it happened because in developing the CMS, journalists had teamed up with programmers to write very specific rules about how stories should be treated—not only on huge news days, but every day.

Automating all that technical work still left plenty for the editors to do. They hand-picked the photos that best illustrated the quake's destruction. These photos could then be used in the slideshows Jake would later create. They added photos to stories that didn't have them. They linked one story to another. They added video that was related to the text of stories. They edited typos, and they corrected Jake—because while Jake's computer brain will always follow the rules the way the editors and programmers have written them, it takes a human brain to recognize the times when rules should be broken. As such, the editors had to know how to tell Jake to break the rules they had written for him.

It didn't take very experienced news judgment to know that stories on the Haitian earthquake would be leading the site for several days. But editors had to use the content management system to choose which stories beyond the quake would be the four next most important on the homepage and on each section front. The front page itself called for a layout that was different from the standard layout. This was big news, and Jake adopted a different set of rules when his editors told him it was a big news day.

In many ways the job of an online news producer is similar to that of a layout editor or copy editor in a print publication or a segment producer for a television news show. A large part of these jobs in newsrooms is to decide what's worth covering, which stories appear where, how the stories should be laid out, which photos or videos or other graphics should accompany them and how the stories should be "teased" with headlines and other elements. But while news producers who work in content management systems may be freed from the need to handcode HTML and push static documents to a Web server via FTP, they have a new job: understanding how a content management system works so they can use it to get the right information to the right people at the right time.

Amy Gahran, the editor of The Poynter Institute's E-Media Tidbits blog, has said that it is important for online journalists—both editors and reporters—to get into "a CMS mindset." This was her advice to students on Poynter's website: "Think of content as modules that can be structured, mixed, mashed, and reused—rather than thinking strictly in terms of narrative stories. . . . This is a key point where hands-on experience with a CMS affects journalistic practice. When you start thinking of your end product as a series of modules that can be configured in a story but that can also be used and distributed in other ways on your site and beyond your site, that can affect how you go about doing the reporting."

EDITING AND LAYOUT

Content is the collective term for news articles, videos, animations, audio interviews, photographs, discussion forums and any other tool for transmitting information. Content has a lifecycle. First it is gathered through research and reporting. Next it is distilled and organized through the editing process. And finally it reaches an audience of news consumers. Audiences see only the final stage of the content lifecycle, as it is published to the live site and made available at a public URL.

Journalists work with content at all phases of the lifecycle, and to do so they log in to private areas of a content management system that allow them to edit and organize the content so that it shows up in the right place at the right time on the public site. This private area of a CMS is called the **administrative interface**. The administrative interface provides special tools that allow journalists to do the following:

- Search both published and unpublished content that is stored in the CMS database
- Create new content
- Edit or delete existing content
- Order different content items in a list
- Relate content items to one another

- Manage the permissions of registered visitors to the site
- Write new rules that automate frequently used patterns of content management and publishing

The fact is, you've probably already spent a lot of time in the administrative interface of a content management system, whether you knew it or not. If you're familiar with the way that your Facebook status updates get posted to your wall and then appear in the news feeds of all your Facebook friends, then you already have a pretty good idea about how a CMS uses modular components of content to enforce site-wide consistency. Your status updates are processed through the administrative interface of the Facebook CMS, which automatically links content together as people move it around the site and allows multiple users to change the site's content simultaneously.

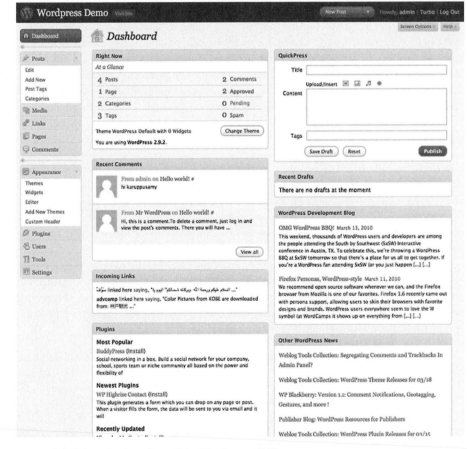

Administrative interface of the Wordpress CMS.

Administrative interface of the Drupal CMS.

Tool: Drupal

The website CMSReview.com has cataloged more than 350 content management systems. Content management systems range from blogging tools like Wordpress to **MediaWiki,** the software package that supports Wikipedia. Many of the largest news organizations build their own CMS or create highly customized versions of either proprietary or open-sourced publishing tools. Some have invested in CMS companies. Many of the most popular content management systems were developed by a community of programmers and are available free of charge under open-source distribution.

In 2009, the John S. and James L. Knight Foundation provided nearly half a million dollars to support the development of an open-source CMS project called **Drupal.** Drupal was designed to suit the unique needs of online news publishers and is already used by a wide variety of news organizations, including geographically based news provider the Savannah Morning News, the participatory news network Now Public and even the satirical news site The Onion. It is also the content management system that runs whitehouse .gov, the official government website of the Obama administration.

If you're interested in getting your first taste of using a content management system, the first CMS you may want to test out is Wordpress, probably the most popular blogging tool in the United States. (At wordpress.com, you can sign up for a free blog with limited functionality.) But if you're interested in exploring more advanced concepts, Drupal is a tool that you can get up and running quickly; it is also one that is almost unlimited in its complexity and tolerance for customization.

Screencast introduction to using Wordpress and Drupal

Annotated lists of free CMS resources and tutorials

To use Drupal, you must have your own version of the CMS that has been installed on a Web server that is dedicated to your site. The easiest way to do this is to visit http://drupal.org/hosting and select one of the hosting companies recommended by the Drupal project. You will pay about $10 a month to rent some server space from a hosting company. Many of them allow you to install Drupal on your rented space with the click of a button, which sure beats configuring databases and Web servers.

Get Started With Drupal

Try it out and see what you think:

1. Go to http://php.opensourcecms.com/scripts/details.php?scriptid=191.

2. Select a host by going to http://drupal.org/hosting.

3. Start learning at http://drupal.org/getting-started/before.

4. Find and install a new theme to give your site a unique style by typing in http://themegarden.org/drupal6/

5. Add new tools to your site by installing additional modules at http://drupal.org/node/340271.

Adding Content to a CMS

The first stage in the lifecycle is the collection of content and its entry into the CMS. Traditionally in a news organization, information is collected by a reporter and brought back to the newsroom in whatever format best suits the story. Sometimes that is text; other times it is photographs, videos, audio or **PDF** documents. A CMS must have a way for all of these different types of content to be entered and stored in its database.

At its core, a content management system is essentially two things: (1) a database that defines the structure of the content, and (2) a collection of rules and design templates that determines how and when different pieces of the data should be displayed. Most often the content enters the database through a Web-based facilitator. The content is first written and edited on a word processor or some other multimedia editing tool. Editors then save the piece of content somewhere outside the CMS. Finally, either an automated process transfers the content into the CMS or a news producer copies and pastes it into the system.

As content is added, the CMS keeps track of all sorts of information that describes the piece of content. This is metadata—essentially, data about the data. Metadata can include the date the content was created, its subject, its source or author and even the location at which it was created. Every day, for example, the Associated Press (AP) sends thousands of pieces of text, photography, videography and animated graphics to the news organizations that are its subscribers. Many of the AP's clients receive this information in a format called **eXtensible Markup Language,** or **XML.** XML contains not just the content, but also its structure—that is, details about how the metadata is associated with each piece of content and how the content should be divided into fields.

Computer programmers at news organizations write rules that translate the structure of the content as it is sent by the AP into the correct corresponding fields in the news organization's CMS. This is called **parsing.** Incorrect parsing of data causes all sorts of problems: bylines show up where headlines are supposed to be, photographs are matched to the wrong stories or entire articles fail to appear. Accurate parsing, then, is essential. Once content is successfully parsed and entered into the CMS data, it is either published automatically to the live website or it sits in the database awaiting further work by editors and producers.

An external news sources like the AP isn't the only way that news organizations add content to their CMS. Many news organizations also automatically feed the news stories originally created in their print or broadcast editing system into the Web CMS. The audience, too, is becoming an increasingly important source of content, so newsroom content management systems must have a way for site visitors to add their own content to the CMS, either for direct publication or for later vetting and publication by professional journalists. This type of user-generated content can include restaurant reviews, photos of a youth baseball game, community events or comments in response to an article.

Whenever content is added to a CMS from an outside source—whether from an external news provider like the AP, a legacy newsroom print editing system or the audience—online news producers have to be careful that all of the text characters and all of the text formatting make the journey without being corrupted. Unusual text characters such as smart or "curly" quotes often get translated into gibberish when they move from the original source of content into the database. This can also happen with question marks, dashes and other punctuation. Common symptoms of corrupted formatting can include missing paragraph breaks or the removal of bulleted lists. Solving these problems is the job of programmers, but spotting these problems is the job of news producers. If the content doesn't get into the CMS in the right way, it won't come out the right way. As the old computer programmer saying goes, "garbage in, garbage out" (also known as **GIGO**).

Organizing Content in a CMS

Once content has been gathered and stored inside the CMS database, news editors and producers have to figure out when, where and how it should appear on the site. They also have to figure out how different pieces of content should be related to one another.

As content in a CMS is organized, it begins to collect metadata. Metadata doesn't necessarily ever get published, but it follows the piece of content wherever it goes and helps describe important information about the content to the CMS as well as to the editors using it. You can think of the process of organizing content in a CMS as the process of adding metadata to the content.

```
<title>How Health Care Costs and Goals Came Out Right for Obama -
NYTimes.com</title>
<meta http-equiv="Content-Type" content="text/html; charset=utf-8" />
<meta name="description" content="Building the health care legislation
was not a shopping spree, but more like a trip to the local fruit stand
with a set amount of money in hand and every item clearly marked." />
<meta name="keywords" content="Reform and Reorganization,Health Insurance
and Managed Care,Law and Legislation,Budgets and Budgeting,Prices (Fares
Fees and Rates),Medicare,National Debt (US),Obama  Barack,House of
Representatives" />
<meta name="ROBOTS" content="NOARCHIVE" />
<meta name="DISPLAYDATE" content="March 18, 2010" />
<meta name="hdl" content="Fine-Tuning Led to Health Bill's $940 Billion
Price Tag" />
<meta name="byl" content="By DAVID M. HERSZENHORN" />
<meta name="lp" content="Building the health care legislation was not a
shopping spree, but more like a trip to the local fruit stand with a set
amount of money in hand and every item clearly marked." />
<meta name="cre" content="The New York Times" />
<meta name="edt" content="NewYork" />
<meta name="pdate" content="20100318" />
<meta name="ttl" content="" />
<meta name="virtloc" content="" />
<meta name="des" content="Reform and Reorganization;Health Insurance and
Managed Care;Law and Legislation;Budgets and Budgeting;Prices (Fares,
Fees and Rates);Medicare;National Debt (US)" />
<meta name="per" content="Obama, Barack" />
<meta name="org" content="House of Representatives" />
<meta name="geo" content="" />
<meta name="misspelling" content="" />
<meta name="dat" content="March 18, 2010" />
<meta name="tom" content="News" />
<meta name="cat" content="" />
<meta name="col" content="" />
<meta name="dsk" content="U.S." />
<meta name="articleid" content="1247467386283" />
<meta name="ARTICLE_TEMPLATE_VERSION" CONTENT="700">
<meta  name="hdr_img" content="" />
<meta  name="thumbnail" content="" />
<meta  name="thumbnail_height" content="" />
<meta  name="thumbnail_width" content="" />
<meta  name="xlarge" content="" />
<meta  name="xlarge_height" content="" />
<meta  name="xlarge_width" content="" />
<meta name="CG" content="us">
<meta name="SCG" content="">
<meta name="PT" content="Article">
<meta name="PST" content="News">
<link rel="canonical"
href="http://www.nytimes.com/2010/03/19/us/19score.html" />
```

On every article on NYTimes.com, you can view the source of the HTML document in your browser and see some of the metadata. This example shows the 37 different pieces of metadata that are visible in the HTML code. And this is just some of the metadata The New York Times stores about its articles in its CMS.

The New York Times has an unusually robust set of metadata associated with its stories. Metadata for an article might consist of various versions of its headline—one to use on the homepage, one to use on the article page itself and one to use on a mobile phone version of the story, for example. Metadata might also include several versions of an article's date—the date the article was first published, the date it appeared in print or on air, and the times at which it was updated. At the Times, metadata also includes the lists of people and organizations mentioned in the story. Each of these pieces of metadata allows the CMS at the Times to readily organize all of the content.

The staff of The New York Times applies news judgment and computer programming skills to write content management rules that use metadata to place each piece of content in the right places on the website. The metadata for the story in the example here allows the CMS to automatically place a link to the story on pages where it might be of most interest to the site's visitors: the health section front (http://www.nytimes.com/pages/health/index.html), the Times Topics page on Barack Obama (http://topics.nytimes.com/top/reference/timestopics/people/o/barack_obama/index.html) and the politics section front (http://www.nytimes.com/pages/politics/index.html).

The metadata does more than tell the CMS on which page to display a link to the story; it also uses the date of the article to order the headlines on each page. On most sites, the default ordering of articles on a page is to put the most recent stories at the top. This is an example of how the news value of timeliness determines which articles get the most prominent display on a news website. Producers can override this default article placement and ordering, however. They can override the default order of article headlines, for example, if a new, minor news update gets posted above a major investigative report that may have already been on the site for a few hours. In this case, the journalists would be deciding that the news value of impact trumps the default news value of timeliness.

Journalists also usually determine which pieces of content are featured on the site's homepage and in what relative importance. Producers use a CMS to organize content by choosing photos, video and graphics to either display inside an article or to use as link destinations from an article. As journalists create relationships between one piece of content and another—a photo and the story that goes with it, for example—they are adding metadata to the CMS and even programming the content management system's database without even realizing it. All of this automation allows journalists to perform common tasks more efficiently and spend more time on news judgment than on programming. But as you will see time and again throughout this book, journalists who want to innovate—to break the rules and produce strong stories that are uncommon in their power and impact—need to learn at least to be fluent in the language of information technology.

Publishing Content From a CMS

In the early days of online journalism, publishing a story simply meant uploading a static HTML file to a Web server—not much more technically complicated than e-mailing a Word document to a friend. But as online news began to move faster and as sites grew larger, the way that a piece of news got from a newsroom to a visitor's Web browser also became much more complex.

One of the reasons that publishing content from a CMS can become so complicated for news organizations is because the audience expects that a news website will never fail. Large news organizations in particular must be able to accommodate large amounts of content in their CMS; they must likewise be able to handle the large number of audience requests for content from the CMS. As news organizations experience spikes in traffic during big events, they have to be as close to 100 percent certain as possible that their website will not crash under the volume of users. This nerve-wracking responsibility largely falls to the technical staff and is mostly hidden from journalists—as long as everything is functioning correctly.

If a website's content management and publishing system breaks down, however, it is up to reporters and editors to help fix it. In such moments, even journalists with no technical background can become acutely aware of the importance of technical concepts such as "database **failovers**" and "misaligned **load balancing**." Journalists at any news organization, especially entry-level online news producers who are apt to start their careers working nights or weekends when there is no technical staff in the office, should spend at least some time trying to understand the basics of how the content they create leaves the CMS and ends up on the screen of a visitor. Knowing the basic vocabulary and the possible reasons that the publishing process might fail can mean the difference between getting life-saving information to your audience in a time of emergency and not getting it to your audience, forcing regular users to go elsewhere.

If your audience does not get the information it needs at the moment it needs it, the audience will not care whether the reason for the failure is technical or editorial. Maybe the reporter was having a bad day, or maybe the editor cut the story, or maybe the delivery boy tossed the paper in the gutter, or the storm interrupted the satellite signal, or the telephone company ran a backhoe over the fiber optic line in the neighborhood, or Web server number three failed to connect to the database. To your audience, the reasons don't matter. What matters is the news wasn't available. As a journalist whose aim is to affect the public discourse, you need to have some knowledge of the potential problems that could prevent your audience from receiving the news so that you can reduce the risk that these problems will stand between your story and your audience.

Every news organization is different, but the following is a common sequence of steps that moves content from inside the administrative component of a CMS to the public website:

1. The publishing process begins, triggered by a programming rule at automatic, regular intervals or triggered manually by a news producer.

2. The CMS requests specific content fields from the database, and those fields are then sent to design templates.

3. The design templates tell the data where to appear and how to look.

4. The data and templates together are sent as HTML, either generated at the moment a user requests it or as a static page that sits on a server waiting to be requested.

5. If the news organization is large, each piece of final content is copied to several Web servers. The larger the news organization, the more Web servers it will have. Each server will have a copy of all of the pages of which a site is comprised. Requests coming in from users are routed to the various servers in order to equally balance the load across all of them.

If the publishing function of the CMS is working well, these steps together take place in just a fraction of a second.

Whether to publish a story or hold it is traditionally one of the most important decisions that journalists make, one that ultimately rests in the hands of the top editors at a news organization. On the one hand, holding a story may mean that a competitor breaks the news. On the other, publishing a story when it is not yet ready—when all of the facts have yet to be confirmed—can leave organizations with the dubious honor of having a so-called permanent exclusive.

In news organizations from Yahoo News to The Washington Post, the decision to publish a story is being increasingly automated. A story automatically gets added to the CMS, it is automatically categorized and then it is automatically published. Some stories from trusted sources such as the AP are automatically published as soon as they are fully organized and formatted. Stories that are part of the daily newspaper may all be automatically pushed out to the live site at the same time every day—usually some time in the late night after the entire paper is put to bed. At some sites the need to reduce the strain on databases and Web servers means that completed stories will sit in a queue and be automatically published at regular intervals. In these automatic publish scenarios, you can think of the CMS as having stories in the pipe. When the automated publishing process is triggered, the stories queued in the pipe are flushed from the CMS's administrative interface onto the news organization's live site.

On March 22, 2007, an automated publishing process that the producers at The Washington Post didn't fully understand caused a false story to be published to the website. The story stated that presidential candidate John Edwards had withdrawn from the race. The Post's producers knew that Edwards was preparing to make an announcement of some sort, so they had prepared three versions of the story, one for each of the three likely scenarios. This is common practice for news organizations that want to be ready to get the news out fast. It is similar to the long-established practice of news organizations writing obituaries of famous people in advance, so they'll be ready when a public figure dies.

But, as the Post's producers learned, the danger in preparing three different versions of a story is that one of the two wrong versions might accidentally make it into the pipe and be automatically flushed onto the live site. That is what happened with the Edwards story. And even though the story was only on the site for 51 seconds, it became the topic of several blog posts and a story in the Post itself. It hurt the credibility of the news organization and forced the site's editor to explain and apologize in a post on his blog. It is not clear exactly how the wrong story got on the site. What is clear is that there was a miscommunication between the human judgment of the journalists and the automated judgment of the publishing tools they were using. "It was not an error of journalism," site editor Jim Brady explained to Howard Kurtz, the Post's media critic. "It was an error of production. . . . Nobody knows how it got up because nobody hit the publishing button."

VIEW SOURCE

IN CONWAY, A CMS "CANDY STORE"

On an average day at the Log Cabin Democrat in Conway, Ark., reporters are blogging and using Twitter. A photographer is shooting pictures on her Blackberry and publishing them instantly on the paper's website. Local residents are posting complaints about potholes and weighing in on the fate of their college basketball brackets. And the paper's editor, Waylon Harris, is giddy—because until recently, none of this activity was possible.

For the Democrat's first decade online, its website was created the same way every day. "The old workflow was you build the newspaper and then some guy comes in and runs some tools that pulls the stories off InDesign pages, and sometime between 7:30 and 10:30 in the morning you actually get today's newspaper up," says Steve Yelvington, the chief digital strategist at the Log Cabin Democrat's parent company, Morris Communications.

The site was static for a simple reason: the staff didn't have the tools to do anything more creative. So Yelvington helped get them a new CMS—a version of the free and open source Drupal CMS that Yelvington and his team have customized for papers in the Morris chain. Now the site is updated all day, and traffic has increased 43 percent from the same time a year earlier. For Harris, the paper's editor, it was as if "suddenly we [gave] him the keys to the kingdom," Yelvington says. "He sent me an e-mail a week after we launched his site saying that he was a kid in a candy store."

For even a small staff like that at the Log Cabin Democrat, the ability to edit, lay out and publish a site with a CMS means more time to spend on news gathering and news judgment. With an hour of training, staff gained the ability to post a breaking news alert to every page of the site—and set an automatic expiration date. When a new story is added to the site, its headline is automatically posted to the paper's new Twitter account.

But it's not the ease and efficiency of pushing out text and photographs that makes most editors giddy. Relieved? Yes. But giddy? That comes when journalists see the possibilities a CMS offers to create entirely new forms and styles of journalism. Not long after getting the keys to the CMS kingdom, the journalists in Conway used them to create a photography contest for site visitors. Elsewhere in the Morris chain, papers are practicing with geo-coding stories and delivering them on mobile devices.

According to Yelvington, the news industry desperately needs this kind of innovation, and it can't happen "unless we have some people in the system who are smart and know enough technology that they can see the possibility. So we're always looking at hiring smart recent graduates who are geeks." Yelvington urges students to think early about where they want their careers as professional journalists to take them. "If the role they want to play over time is just purely reporting the news, there's a set of skills you can get by with," he says. "But if you want to shape what we do with that content—in a role that used to be called an editor, but today requires new product envisioning and creating—then that's a whole different conversation. That's about what can you do with technology to create new stuff. You've just leapt into a much richer and complex universe."

DISPLAYING CONTENT IN TEMPLATES

Close your eyes. Try to remember the last grocery store you went into. Where were the cash registers? Probably in front. The fruits and vegetables? Most likely, just to your right as you came in the front door. The meats, milk and produce? Somewhere along the back or side wall. How could I know that? Because most grocery stores are organized according to a **template.** A template is anything that establishes a pattern—usually a visual pattern. And a key component of content management systems is their use of templates to enforce site-wide visual consistency.

Whether it is grocery stores or websites, visual consistency is important so that your customers can get what they need as quickly as possible. If your shopping list includes hot dogs and onions, you don't want to have to walk up and down every aisle of the store looking for them. You want to know that no matter which Piggly Wiggly you walk into, you can turn to the right and pick up the onions before heading to the back to get the hot dogs and then return to the front of the store to check out.

The same is true with a website. When you visit an article, you want to instantly be able to tell which text is the headline and which is the byline and which is the article text. This kind of visual consistency reduces anxiety; it means you can find what you're looking for as quickly as possible. The colors, layout and font choices of a site also help differentiate it from the billions of other sites on the Web. This is important when the online news audience jumps from site to site. When the Los Angeles Times breaks a story and bloggers link to it, the editors want to make sure that the readers coming from those blogs recognize the source as the Los Angeles Times. Building trust—and return visits—occurs only where identity has been established. Visual branding is key. Visual branding means that the stories posted on the Los Angeles Times site look the same—and that they look different from the blog pages that sent readers there.

Without templates, imagine how many different layout and design rules each online news producer at the Los Angeles Times would have to understand. What font face is the headline? Is it 28 pixels or 32? What about on the section front? Maybe 17 pixels? And that photo in the article, should it be to the left of the text or to the right? Vertically flush with the top of the headline or with the top of the first line of article body text?

Content management systems contain rules that govern all display issues. This means that journalists don't have to think about them. But it also means that producers who want to create innovative displays need to know how to break the rules without altering the entire site. With a templated site design, changes to the appearance of one article can mean that every article on the site will change the same way.

A simple website might have three templates: one for the homepage, one for perhaps five section fronts and one for the hundreds of articles. Of course, more complex websites might have dozens or even hundreds of templates. There would be at least one for each content type. But some content types might also have different templates that could be used for different circumstances. For example, one template for a homepage might feature a photograph while another might display a breaking news head-line banner.

In online newsrooms, designers and Web developers using HTML and CSS are the people who most often create display rules. Programming logic can also be a part of display rules, so it is important even for journalists who never do computer programming to be able to describe different conditions that might alter how an article is displayed. For exam-ple, an online editor might need to make it clear to a Web programmer that *if* an article has been updated *then* it would need to display both the time it was originally published and the time it was updated. Or, *if* there is breaking news *then* every article on the site should display a breaking news alert banner across the top of the page. Newsroom pro-grammers take these plain English instructions and convert them into computer code in the CMS templates. Journalists must work with programmers to create the desired display—and journalists must be sufficiently knowledgeable about programming to understand what is achievable.

One Story, Many Pieces

As you begin to understand how a content management system uses a database to store and organize content, and how it uses templates to display the pieces of informa-tion stored in the database, you're beginning to grasp one of the most important concepts of online publishing: content is separate from the rules that govern the display of content.

Journalists think in terms of the story. But the word "story" means nothing to a CMS. To a CMS, a "story" is just a collection of fields in a database that are related to one another in a specific way and displayed according to specific rules in a specific kind of template. Some content management systems have only one kind of "story"; others have dozens of different types of stories—and each of these has a different type of content, with different properties and different rules for how that content should appear on the site. For journalists and content management systems to understand one another, they need to agree that they will be working on a finite list of content types (one of which may be a "story"), and that each content type will be made up of certain fields in a database.

The first thing you need to know when you start working with a content management system is how your particular CMS defines and labels types of content. For example, is everything in a "blog" called a "post," even if it is a video report or an image? Is an "article" a different type of content than a "page"? Types of content on news websites include articles, blog posts, images, video and audio. While humans may use these words inter-changeably in conversation, to the computer that runs a Web content management system, each of these words has a specific meaning. Like all computers, content management sys-tems only know what you say. If you say something other than what you mean—even if it is similar—you're sunk. So, in a very fundamental way, the key to working successfully with a CMS is the key to reporting the news: precision. In both news writing and news programming, Mark Twain's quote holds: "The difference between the right word and the wrong word is the difference between lightning and the lightning bug."

Each type of content is really a specific collection of small pieces of information called a **field.** One field might be the subject of an article, one might be the URL of a related video, one might be the headline and one might be the actual text of the article. These fields are stored in a database. All of the fields that are part of a single piece of content make up a **record.**

Journalists have more flexibility when the fields in each content type are defined as narrowly as possible. For example, the **timestamp** of an article could be a single field that contains the day, month, year and time.

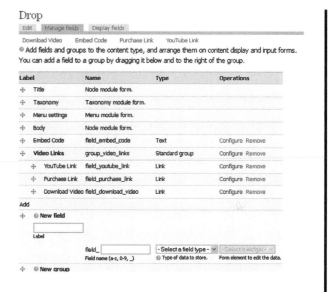

In the Drupal content management system, you can create new kinds of content by using the Content Creation Kit module, shown here from the CCK tutoral on learnbythedrop.com.

But news producers will be able to create more precise display and relationship rules where the timestamp is more granular—in this example, divided into at least four separate fields: one for day, one for month, one for year and one for time. Both ways would work in most cases, but in the first journalists wouldn't be able to tell the CMS to display all articles from a certain month because to the CMS there would be no "month," but only the more broadly defined "timestamp."

If you've been working with the online learning modules associated with this book, you're familiar with the role of the administrative interface of a content management system such as the blogging CMS Wordpress. Of course, this type of CMS is very easy to use because to do so requires only the most basic familiarity with filling out Web forms. If you've ordered a book on Amazon or updated your status on Facebook, you know how to fill out Web forms. Web forms offer our first clues about how a single piece of content is comprised of many different fields. This page in the administrative interface of the Wordpress CMS is used to create new blog posts. On it, you can see a variety of form fields. The one at the top center is for the blog post's title. The larger one in the middle of the page is the place to compose the post's body. Below that is a field to write an excerpt, or summary, of the post.

After you've added text to each of these fields, and perhaps edited several of the other fields on the page, you'll save the blog post. When you save it, the information you've put into each of those Web form fields is sent to a specific place in the CMS database.

This Web form in the Wordpress administrative interface connects with the information that is stored in the Wordpress database.

Field
ID
post_author
post_date
post_date_gmt
post_content
post_title
post_excerpt
post_status
comment_status
ping_status
post_password
post_name
to_ping
pinged
post_modified
post_modified_gmt
post_content_filtered
post_parent
guid
menu_order
post_type
post_mime_type
comment_count

To display a headline on an article the only thing the article template needs to know is: the font size, style and color for the headline; where the headline should appear on the HTML page relative to other pieces of information (like byline); and the location in the database where it can find the headline, or "post_title," for each content record in the database.

Here are the fields in the Wordpress CMS database that hold information about the post. Is it obvious which field holds the headline? The body content? The excerpt?

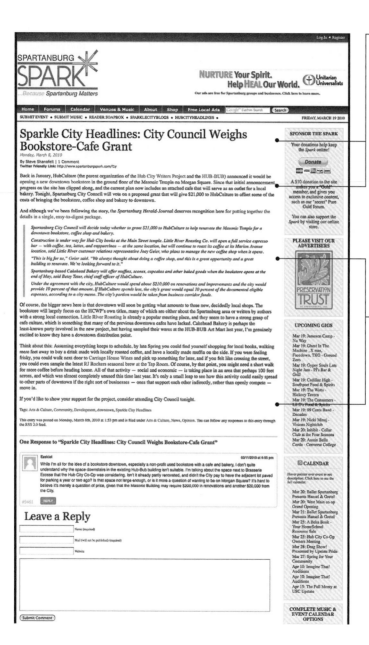

On the website of the Spartanburg Spark—started in 2008 to be "a local alternative news source" in Spartanburg, S.C.—a headline and post body that was written in the CMS administrative Web form and stored in the CMS database finally gets displayed on the live website after a post is published.

The templates used by the Spartanburg Spark ensure that each piece of information is pulled together to create what the visitor sees as a "story." And the template also ensures that every story the visitor sees on the site will have the same visual branding and navigational continuity.

ESPN Albany Great Danes page.

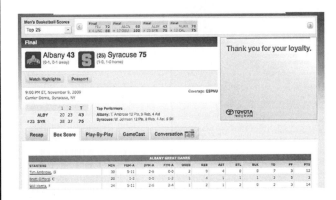

Box score of a game—Albany Great Danes.

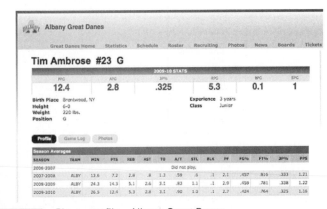

Player profile—Albany Great Danes.

The simple example of the Spartanburg Spark makes it easy to see the connections between the Web forms in a CMS's administrative interface, the fields in its database and the display of the content within a templated HTML page that is published to the live site.

But now let's take a look at ESPN.com. Here we can better appreciate the value of modular content pieces as we consider the nearly 5,000 NCAA Division 1 men's basketball players who play a total of more than 5,000 games every year. Start by looking for the name of your favorite men's college basketball team. You might begin at ESPN's page about the Albany Great Danes, at http://espn.go.com/ncb/clubhouse?teamId=399. Do you think of this page as an indivisible entity, or do you see a collection of different pieces of content—player names, opponent team abbreviations, and game scores?

From the Great Danes page, you might go to the box score of a game, which is a collection of player names and their positions and game stats. Or, you might go from the Great Danes page to the profile of junior guard Tim Ambrose at http://espn.go.com/ncb/player/profile?playerId=36699. Break this page down into its component pieces and you'll see Ambrose's number, position, height, weight and hometown, as well as the team for which he plays and his game stats.

Each of these pages—the team page, the game page and the player profile page—uses the same modular pieces of content. Each piece of content has its own little home in ESPN.com's massive database, which means that each piece can be dynamically updated as stats change. These updates can be reflected across the site. The kind of journalism that is done by ESPN requires its online news producers to think about each page not as a single, indivisible story, but as a collection of many small pieces.

One Story, Many Places

You've begun to see the advantages of how a CMS works. How, for example, it disaggregates a single story, breaking it into many component pieces that make it easier for journalists to create complex rules and relationships that help site visitors easily find content that is dynamically related. And how, by splitting up articles into pieces, a CMS allows website designers to use templates to enforce visual consistency on a site. A further advantage of the CMS is its ability to re-use content. By separating content from layout, the CMS allows already created content to be re-used in many different places all at once.

Probably the clearest example of this is an article's headline. A headline is written once in the

Here, a photo appears as the lead piece of art above a text story. Its caption: "Harold 'Rusty' Billingsley's hard hat and work boots are reminders of the job that led to the iron-worker's death Oct. 5 while working on CityCenter."

Here, the photo appears again in a photo gallery about the topic. Same photo. Same caption. Both edited once and recycled throughout the site, giving the audience the opportunity to view them in a variety of contexts.

CMS's administrative interface, then it is stored in a particular field in the CMS database. That single headline can then be used by several templates—for example, by a homepage template, a business section front template and an article template. The headline from the article might even be used in an e-mail news alert template, an RSS feed template and an iPhone app template. The ability to re-use a single piece of content creates newsroom efficiency and makes it easier to get the right information to the right people at the right time.

You can see an example of CMS efficiency in the captions used for a photo that was part of the Las Vegas Sun's 2009 Pulitzer Prize–winning series on safety conditions for construction workers in that rapidly growing city.

But having a single piece of content that is used in a variety of places also requires some thoughtful consideration. What if you don't want to use the same headline at the top of an article as you used in the link to the article from the section front? Unless there are two different fields in the database—one for article headline and one for section front headline— you're stuck writing a single set of words that must work in every template where the headline appears.

Let's examine one instance when the journalists at The Seattle Times wrote a headline for the "All You Can Eat" blog written by food reporter Nancy Leson. The writers had to know how the headline would read in each context in which it appeared. They needed to make sure that the headline contained enough information to make sense in contexts where it may have been unclear that the headline linked to a food opinion blog. But they also needed to write a headline that wasn't redundant, that is, one that did not utilize information that already appeared next to the blog post's headlines on other pages.

When the blog's headline appears in a feature box on the homepage of The Seattle Times, it often appears with a photo of food. Those photos provide context that allows the headline writer to use her words to convey additional information.

On the Living section front of the site, the headline doesn't have the photo to provide context. However, it is surrounded by other text that provides additional information. We know the content behind "El Pilon, a taste of Puerto Rico in Columbia City" links to a Living blog, and we know that it is written by Nancy Leson.

On the Food & Wine front of the site, we have the same context as on the Living front, but we know that the post is not just about "living" but about "food and wine" as well.

The headline for the blog post also appears on the front of Nancy Leson's blog. Here, the headline is supported by an excerpt of the post that appears below it. In this case, information that might have been needed in the headline when it appeared on the homepage or section front pages might now be redundant to information that is in the summary.

Because the staff at The Seattle Times is aware that visitors to the site are much more likely to enter through a specific piece of content such as a blog post than through a section front or a homepage, they've also made sure that the template for each blog post contains links in the upper right corner that direct readers to "Recent entries." In this way visitors can access additional content in which they might be interested, even if they never visit the site's homepage. The headline for the blog post about El Pilon appears in this list on every post in Leson's blog.

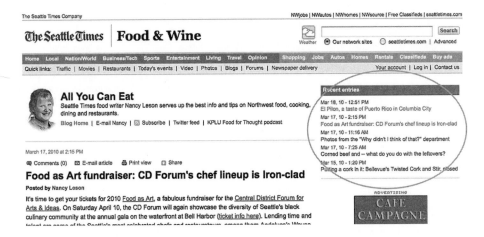

Obviously a headline needs to appear on the article itself, as it does here. But remember how the template for blog posts works? Each one contains a prominent link to the five most recent posts on the blog. Look at the upper right and you'll see that this blog entry includes a link to itself. The CMS doesn't have a rule that tells it to exclude from the list of "Recent entries" the headline of the article on which the list appears.

The headline for the blog post also appears on the front of Nancy Leson's blog. Here, the headline is supported by an excerpt of the post that appears below it. In this case, information that might have been needed in the headline when it appeared on the homepage or section front pages might now be redundant to information that is in the summary.

So what would you do if you were the producer posting this story? Well, unless you could reach a programmer who wrote the rules for the CMS, there's nothing you can do about this. And even if you could get a hold of the programmer, the change would likely take some time to implement. Changes like this shouldn't be rushed, because fixing this problem might create unintended consequences elsewhere on the site.

But let's say you are able to get in touch with a CMS developer. How would you describe this rule to her? How would you describe it in such a way that it fixed not just this one self-referencing link, but all self-referencing links on the site? Display rules put the "management" in content management systems. Rules are what allow Yahoo News to write a headline once and have it appear on dozens of pages. But rules can be frustratingly inflexible when big news breaks or when an editor wants to create a special display for a feature article. There isn't a CMS in the world that can handle every scenario that a journalist might encounter—for example, when the president gives the State of the Union address at the same time a jury in a civil action finds NFL hall-of-famer O.J. Simpson responsible for the killing of his ex-wife and her friend, or when terrorists fly airplanes into the Pentagon and World Trade Center. Online news producers must know backward and forward the rules of the CMS in which they work, because that's the only way they will be able to creatively bend those rules at a moment's notice when news breaks.

If you aren't familiar with computer programming, here are some concepts and vocabulary terms that can be useful for journalists when working with programmers:

- **Loop.** In many cases, news producers want to display several of the same type of content field for multiple records. For example, perhaps you have a database of crime reports in your CMS and you want to create a page that lists all of the different types of crime that were committed in town the previous night. For each crime report you will want to print the same piece of information, for example, the time, location and category of crime. This type of rule is called a loop. A loop rule for displaying the types of crimes that were committed might read like this: "For every crime record, display the type of crime, the address where it took place and the time it was reported."

- **Conditional statement.** There is rarely a rule that doesn't need to be broken. That's where conditional statements come in. A conditional statement is a statement that almost always includes the words "if" and "then." For example, you might want to tell a programmer that *if* a reported crime is a felony *then* its headline should be printed in bold text to make it stand out from the other crime reports.

- **Exclusion statement.** Perhaps you want to exclude from your Web page of crime reports all reports of disturbing the peace because there are so many of them, and most are not serious. You could give a computer programmer a list of which crimes to include. But in most instances, it would be easier to simply provide a list of the types of crimes you want to exclude. You would provide the programmer with an exclusion statement. Here is how such a rule might read: "For every crime record, if the type of crime is *not* disturbing the peace, *then* display the type of crime it was, the address where it took place and the time it was reported."

- **Boolean logic.** Of course, rules can get very complicated very quickly. Most rules that govern the automation of news websites include many loops with many conditional statements. Boolean logic is a form of logic that creates a nexus of dependent relationships. Statements made according to Boolean logic require the use of such words as "and" and "or" to create relationships between conditions that either reduce or increase the chances of the conditions being met. For example, if you want to create an automatically generated gallery of all the photos from last night's Giants game, you could write a rule that instructs the CMS to do the following: "For every photograph, *if* the subject field contains the word Giants *and if* the subject field contains sports *and if* the date is yesterday's date, *then* display the JPG photo file, the caption field and the name of the photographer."

At the Wisconsin State Journal, the CMS has rules that prevent the same headline from appearing twice on the homepage. Like many sites, the Wisconsin State Journal has sections on its homepage directing visitors to stories that live in various sections of the site. But doing so forces staff journalists to make some

---

User specific visibility settings

Custom visibility settings:
- ◉ Users cannot control whether or not they see this block.
- ○ Show this block by default, but let individual users hide it.
- ○ Hide this block by default but let individual users show it.

Allow individual users to customize the visibility of this block in their account settings.

Role specific visibility settings

Show block for specific roles:
- ☑ administrator
- ☐ anonymous user
- ☐ authenticated user
- ☐ Forum Moderator
- ☐ Professional News Editor
- ☐ Professor
- ☑ student-contributor
- ☐ student-editor

Show this block only for the selected role(s). If you select no roles, the block will be visible to all users.

Page specific visibility settings

Show block on specific pages:
- ○ Show on every page except the listed pages.
- ◉ Show on only the listed pages.
- ○ Show if the following PHP code returns TRUE (PHP-mode, experts only).

This example from the Drupal CMS shows how you can create rules that display certain types of content only to certain types of site visitors as well as rules that determine the pages on which different content blocks will be displayed.

choices about where to place links to stories that might be relevant to more than one category. Do you allow the headline only to be printed in one category so that there isn't repetition on the homepage? Or do you print the headline in more than one category so that it will be found by the broadest possible audience?

Recycled headlines don't just pose a writing challenge because they appear in different contexts across a news website. They can also pose layout challenges, especially when they have to fit into the tight spaces of mobile phone screens that are becoming increasingly important to the online audience. For example, traditions of visual design teach headline writers that they should avoid writing headlines that create "widows"—stray words that sit by themselves on a line below the rest of the headline. Widows are created when a headline is too long for the space in which it is being printed.

In these two screenshots from The Wall Street Journal, there are major differences between what appears on the online homepage and how news items appear on a version of the same homepage specifically for mobile devices. On the online homepage of The Wall Street Journal, the headline writer forced a line break after the word "Set" so that the compound word "Health Bill" wouldn't sit by itself on the second line. The headline appears visually compact and is easy for the site visitors to read.

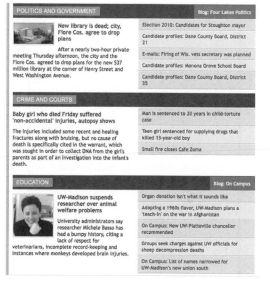

Note that the candidate profiles in the Monona Grove School Board are listed only once on the local news page of the Wisconsin State Journal. It is in the Politics and Government section, but it could also have been in the Education section.

On the homepage that is specially formatted for mobile devices, that hard break that made perfect sense on a computer screen creates a problem on a mobile phone screen. In this case, the break forces down all of the headlines below it, forcing the reader to scroll down before it would have otherwise been necessary. Remember, both of these templates are pulling the headline from the same field in the Journal's CMS database. Change it in one place, and it will change in the other.

The fact of the matter is, sometimes being an online news producer in the real world means choosing the least bad option—that is, the option that harms the user experience for the smallest portion of the audience.

Content management systems have made it easier for news organizations to efficiently publish news online. Journalists can update stories quickly and work collaboratively to

In this example from the homepage of The Wall Street Journal, look at the main headline: "Showdown Set On Health Bill." The headline writer forced a line break after the word "Set" so that the compound word "Health Bill" wouldn't sit by itself on the second line. The headline appears visually compact and is easy for the site visitors to read.

Showdown Set
On Health Bill
Democrats made a final sprint toward a weekend vote on their health-care bill, pressuring wavering lawmakers as the CBO put the cost of the legislation at $940 billion over the next decade.

March U.S. Car Sales Rise
A surge in U.S. car sales during the first half of March is lifting expectations that totals for the full month will show the auto industry's recovery is picking up speed.

Insurers Toughen Stance on Hospital Rates
Health insurers are fighting demands by hospitals for sharply higher reimbursement rates by threatening to drop the hospitals from their health-plan networks, and blaming them for higher insurance premiums.

But here's how the same headline appears on the version of The Wall Street Journal's homepage that is specially formatted for mobile devices.

publish many different stories for many different sites simultaneously. To take advantage of a CMS's efficiency, however, it is important to understand the modular nature of news content as you add it to a CMS, organize it and publish it.

ONLINE LEARNING MODULE 4

ACTIVATE THIS MODULE: journalism.cqpress.com

On my blog, you can post questions and comments to me about newsroom content management, and I will be writing about any developments related to the topics covered in this chapter.

When you buy or activate this chapter's online learning module, you will have access to:

- A digital version of this chapter's text.

- Interactive flashcards for the terms used in this chapter.

- A one-page guide to the basic components of newsroom content management systems.

- A quiz to test your mastery of the material in this chapter.

- Links you can use to test various content management systems and to free tutorials from across the Web that guide you from the most basic to the more advanced features of two popular open-source content management systems.

- Video screencasts that provide guided introductory tours of Wordpress and Drupal.

- Online exercises that give you experience working within a content management system.

You also will be able to work with a live CMS built to give you practical experience with the skills and concepts you need to manage content in a professional news environment.

CHAPTER 5 EDITING NEWS FOR SEARCHERS AND SCANNERS

This chapter will teach you how to:

- Write headlines that attract and inform fast-moving and fickle readers.
- Re-edit print stories for the Web.
- Add metadata to a news article to help search engines know what the article is about.

People don't read news online. Or rather, they don't read news online the same way they read news on paper. The online news audience searches. It scans. It surfs. It browses.

Most online newsreaders get their news the way hummingbirds eat. They flit in and out. From story to story. From site to site. Online news viewers click on a headline, skim the first part of a story, jump to a photo on the page, then go to a different spot in the text. They click on the "Back" button of their browser, scan for another headline, click on it, then start to skim the new story. Little wonder, then, that a 2007 Poynter Institute study found that the print news audience is twice as likely as the online news audience to read stories methodically from top to bottom without interruption.

As an online news producer, it is your job to "get 'em in and get 'em what they want"—and to do it as fast as possible. If coaxing readers to your site is the goal, then the reasonable question to ask is, how do readers arrive at sites? Following are statistics that answer just that:

- Fully 71 percent of online news readers in the U.S. use search engines to find news.

- Fifty percent of the heaviest online news users follow links to specific news stories from websites, search engines or e-mails.

- Sixty percent of visits to news websites start somewhere other than a site's homepage.

And if keeping readers on your site once they're there is a further goal, then the next question to ask is, how fast do readers move? A few more statistics will shed some light:

- At many news sites, visitors spend only about a minute on each page—even though online readers tend to read more of a story when they find one that interests them.

- The average visitor spends only 3 minutes, 4 seconds on a typical news site before going somewhere else, according to a 2010 analysis of Nielsen data done by the Pew Project for Excellence in Journalism.

- The online news audience spends an average of only 35 minutes looking at news online each day.

- Nearly 70 percent of the online news audience divides its time between two and six sites on a typical day.

If the online news audience can't find your story via a search engine, and if it can't quickly scan a story to find relevant information, then your work as a journalist will not realize its potential to impact the community in which you work. Simply put, for all its multimedia and interactive potential, the Web demands the same style of concise and precise writing that is valued in traditional journalism.

In 2006, U.S. News & World Report was at the start of its transition from being a weekly print newsmagazine with a website to being a website with a print magazine on the side. Its writers and editors were producing more copy for the Web than ever before, but they were still learning how to write for the Web. Page 107 shows an article that was written to appear first, and primarily, on the organization's website rather than in its print magazine.

A few hours after this story was posted on USNews.com, the organization's staff sent it over to the editors and producers at MSN Money. U.S. News provided the story to MSN Money in exchange for links back from the MSN Money website, which had more unique visitors. The only product at MSN Money is its website. Its only audience is the online audience. On page 108 is the version of the story the MSN Money producers posted.

What differences can you see between the two versions? Take a look at the following:

- Headline—Is it the same, or has it been rewritten? Why?

- Subhead—One version has one, the other does not. Why?

- Byline—How does its placement differ between the two versions?

- Paragraphs—Do they differ in length? Why?

- Section label—One version has them, the other does not. Why?

- Highlighted text—One version has it, the other does not. Why?

How were all of these differences put into place? More important, why were these changes made? Why did MSN Money invest time, and hence money, in making them? Keep these questions in mind. As you read on, you'll be able to offer some answers.

Tuesday, May 6, 2008

Nation & World | Health | Money & Business | Education | Opinion | Science | Photo | Video | Ra

Money & Business

Home > Money

Print | E-mail | Subscribe | ⊞ Share

Blockbuster Offers Netflix Customers Free Movies

By Kenneth Terrell
Posted 12/6/06

From now through December 21, Netflix customers can get free movie rentals at Blockbuster stores in exchange for the Netflix mailing labels they normally would throw away (one DVD rental per label). The promotion highlights the advantage that Blockbuster has over its Web-only competitor: physical stores for video renters' immediate gratification.

A Blockbuster store in New York City.

ANDREW H. WALKER—GETTY IMAGES

Related News

- No Pause in DVD Rental Wars
- More from Money & Business

"We want these movie fans to to experience getting the movie they want without the wait," says Blockbuster CEO John Antioco.

Derek Brown, an analyst with Cantor Fitzgerald, calls the move "an interesting approach that has the potential to do what Blockbuster wants, which is get consumers into their stores with greater frequency. But history over the last 12 months suggests that Netflix has more than held its own, despite the pricing and retail advantages Blockbuster has."

Netflix, which leads the online DVD rental market, offers overnight film delivery to the majority of its 5.7 million customers. Blockbuster has told analysts it expects to have 2 million subscribers to its online service by the end of the year. The free rental promotion could draw more subscribers to Blockbuster's program, which also recently started a "Total Access" feature that marries the benefits of Netflix's online model (pick movies on a PC, receive them by mail, keep them as long as you like) but adds the twist of being able to return the DVDs by just dropping them off at one of the company's 5,000 stores nationwide.

But by expanding its online customer base, Blockbuster could end up hurting the same stores that give it an advantage. "The more consumers use this type of service online, the less frequently they go into stores," Brown says.

Print | E-mail | Subscribe | ⊞ Share

Original article on USNews.com.

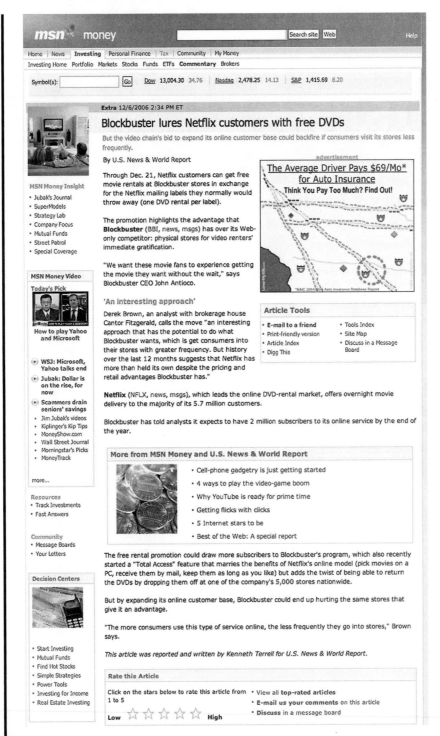

Version of article on MSN Money.

The difference between the two versions is the difference between writing for a print audience and writing for an online audience. As reporters and editors in a culture that is overloaded with entertainment and information, you are competing against everything else your audience needs and wants to do during the day. In this chapter we will look at how you, as the online producer, can improve your chances that the news audience will find your story, read it through to the end without being distracted and actually remember the news and information you want it to remember.

WRITING HEADLINES

The **headline** is perhaps the most important piece of information you will write for an online news article. It is at the top of the page and usually displayed in the biggest text. When search engine algorithms are trying to determine what a page is about, they put extra emphasis on the words in a headline. For many readers, headlines are all they'll ever see, because they are often the only taste of a story that people get when they see it on a search engine result page, an RSS reader or an e-mail inbox.

A good online headline must do three things: (1) be able to stand on its own without the benefit of other visual or design cues to help clarify it, (2) integrate as many keywords as possible and (3) work well the instant it is published and continue to work well months, even years, later.

First, online headlines must be able to stand alone because of the unpredictable ways that content management systems pull apart and rearrange stories. As you write a headline, keep in mind that the audience won't always see all of an article's elements at the same time. "When [a headline] is on a printed page, it interacts very well with the subhead that appears with the photo that appears with everything else that's on the page, including usually the lead of the actual article—you can see the headline with the actual lead," says Jeffrey Marcus, senior producer for sports at NYTimes.com. But on the Web, he notes, "there are places where you might only see the headline or you might see the headline and the photo or you might see the headline and a summary of the article."

Second, the prominent role of search engines in online news consumption means that headlines have to be packed full of keywords. A **keyword** is a text aid that automated algorithms utilize to decide whether your story is related to the search being conducted by a potential reader. "There are other times when a person might not see the headline at all, but a search engine will see the headline and that needs to be indexed. When someone searches for a particular term, you want your article to come up," Marcus says.

The last element of online news that makes headline writing unique is the Web's "always on" characteristic. When writers of headlines for a print magazine or newspaper put text on a page, they know that all copies of that page will arrive in front of readers at pretty much the same time. Sometimes the words in print won't be delivered until days or perhaps weeks after they're written, but even so the writer would know with a high degree of certainty when they will reach their audience. On the Web, you'll be writing headlines not only for readers who see your copy moments after it is written, but for readers who might not see it until years later. And if you're writing for a site with an international audience, you might be writing for a person in another time zone who sees your headline today—even though his today is your tomorrow. "You can never be quite certain how somebody is going to come to your article or blog post online," Marcus says. "They might come through the website's homepage, they might come through a search engine, they could be accessing it through an RSS feed, or it might just be a link that's been forwarded to them."

Be Brief

Because your headlines are being sent all over the Web, they should travel light. Sometimes they have to squeeze into some pretty tight spaces, so keep them as brief as they can be without losing clarity or accuracy.

One of the most important places your headlines can end up is on a search results page on Google News. Only the first 60 characters of your headline will display on Google News. Longer headlines get cut off, which can lead to misunderstanding and confusion. At the very least, truncated headlines are going to make people work harder to decide whether they want to visit your site. And with so many other options out there, making people work too hard may cause them to go elsewhere.

In many content management systems, headlines are converted into a special HTML tag called the title tag. The contents of the title tag are shown to the user in the title bar of the browser and are also used as the page name on Google Web search results pages. Here too Google displays only about the first 60 characters. We will return to this topic later in this chapter in the section on search engine optimization (SEO).

Use Keywords

Because so many of your potential readers will use search engines to look for stories, and because search engines place extra emphasis on headlines in their efforts to figure out whether your story is relevant to the query of a potential reader, it is important to use in your headlines the keywords that someone undertaking a search is likely to type in to find an article on your topic.

In some ways, it is not as important to write a headline that reflects what *you* think the story is about as it is to write a headline that you think a *potential reader* might think it is about. Journalists need to think about the story first, their audience next and themselves last.

 Tool: Google Keywords —————————————————————

If you're working on a voter's guide to mayoral candidates on this year's ballot, what keywords should you use in crafting your headline? Do people type in "voting" or "votes" or "election" or "campaign" or what when they initiate a search? Well, here is a piece of good news. You don't have to guess because Google, in an effort to increase revenue for its online advertising business, provides several free tools that can give you answers.

After you have a better idea of how keywords work, you will see that Google tools can be used to answer real-world questions. For example, if your research is on the psychological power of naughty words, should you use "swearing" or "cursing" in your press release? And if the authors of the Constitution had been seeking **search engine optimization**, would they have called the initial section of their document "Powers Granted to Congress to Make Laws" instead of "Article I"?

Screencast on how to use Google keywords to create searchable headlines

Tutorials on Google keyword and search insight tools

As you start to think about keywords for your headlines and explore the popularity of various search terms, it can be tempting to write headlines that are all about celebrity sex scandals or three-headed cats who do stunts—even if none of your stories are about these things. But it doesn't do any good to try to trick search engines into thinking your story is about something it is not. Search engines are difficult to fool, and even if you succeed you will end by losing the trust of your readers. You work hard to publish good stories. The point is to help people see what's good about them. Remember, even when you write headlines that are optimized for search engines, it is still a human being who makes the click.

Figuring out which keywords are best to include in your headlines is just the first step, however. The placement of keywords within a headline is also important, both for search engine optimization and for human readers who tend to scan online content.

The Poynter Institute's 2004 "Eyetrack" study indicated that readers tend to scan down the left one or two inches of a Web page, looking for words that might indicate whether the information there is relevant to their needs, before they go back to the top and read each line horizontally. Placing keywords at the start of your headline, rather than at the end or scattered throughout, will improve the chances that even the most rapid page scanners will see the words that are most relevant to your story. Search engines also place extra emphasis on words that appear at the start of a headline.

In print, headline writers stress active verbs. Active verbs show people doing things—and, of course, people doing important things constitutes one definition of news. Sentences written in the active voice use the subject-verb-object order, for example, "Congress approved the bill." "Congress" is the subject doing the approving. The "bill" is the object that the Congress approved.

In contrast to the active voice, a sentence written in the passive voice usually starts with the receiver of the action, for example, "The bill was passed by Congress." Here, the "bill" receives an action initiated "by Congress." Using the passive voice may be entirely appropriate if the object is the information in which people will be most interested. For example, the passive sentence "The president was shot by an unknown assailant" does a better job of putting the most important information on the left margin of a page than the active version of the sentence that reads, "An unknown assailant shot the president." Because of the way that online news consumers scan the first few words of a headline, use of the passive voice is acceptable when writing for the Web.

Sometimes the most important element of a news story is the "Who?" As we learned in Chapter 2, public figures such as politicians, athletes and actors can make news simply by doing or saying things that would not be news if the "Who?" were any one of the rest of us. In fact, the names of famous people are among the most common search terms and can be valuable keywords to include in a headline. It is especially important to include the "Who?" element at the start of a headline if attribution is important to the readers' understanding of the story. For example, writing "Obama: Congress must pass health plan" rather than "Congress must pass health plan, Obama says" will be more effective in attracting news searchers and scanners. Of course, anyone can say that Congress must pass a piece of legislation—it's just more likely to be "news" if it's the president who says it. When attribution appears at the start of a headline, searchers and scanners are more likely to quickly understand why they should care about the story.

Attribution shouldn't always go at the start of a headline, however. Sometimes the source of the information may not be widely known or appreciated by your audience. This is especially true of stories that relate news of medical breakthroughs. Most people searching the Web will be far more interested in the findings of a groundbreaking research study than in the name of the professor who conducted the study or the journal in which it was published. While attribution should still be included in such stories, it is not the kind of information that will help news searchers or scanners to quickly understand the reasons to care about a piece, and therefore should not appear at the beginning of a headline.

The separation of online headlines from the content they describe can create special challenges for sports news. It is almost always important to include either the sport name or at

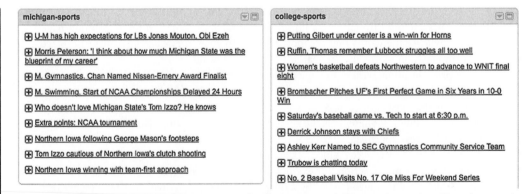

This is how a fan of Michigan sports and college sports might see relevant headlines from various news sites' RSS feeds in his personalized Google homepage. The last entry on the college sports list might leave this fan wondering just which baseball team is visiting Ole Miss.

least one team name in the headline of every story about a sporting event. It doesn't do searchers any good to know the outcome if they can't quickly establish which teams are involved.

Just as with names, locations should be put at the front of the headline if the "Where?" element is most important. Writers should make an extra effort to get the relevant location in a headline, especially when the article has a long shelf life or is similar to other articles on the site. Examples of "Where?"-focused headlines include the following: "Milwaukee Car Wreck Kills 12"; "Oklahoma Tornado Leaves Family Homeless"; and "California Budget Devastates Public Parks." In each of these examples, the location of the news is important to an understanding of the story. Use of place-name nouns provides searchers or scanners with vital information on the story's relevance to them.

Choosing Verb Tenses and Time Elements

Timeliness is one of the most important news values on the Internet. Online news readers turn to the Web during the day for breaking news. But, through the use of search engines, a story can see a substantial audience for weeks and even years after its initial publication. This makes the placement and wording of the time element in a headline very important—and tricky.

Stories that have a breaking news element and a short shelf life—for example, a traffic accident that is critical information to this afternoon's commuters but that will be cleared by tomorrow morning—are often commingled with headlines that point to feature stories, so it is important to emphasize words like "now" and "today" when the time element is important to a story. These time words become even more important in headlines that are not packaged with a timestamp.

For stories that may have very long shelf lives, it is not a good idea to include relative time references such as "this year" or "last week" in the headline. A better option is to include absolute date references such as "2010" or "July" where it makes sense to do so without distorting the meaning of the headline. Wire services that report from around the world have long operated this way, referring, for example, to the day of the week rather than "today" or "tomorrow" because their audience spans the globe's time zones.

Additional rules of thumb in choosing verb tense are as follows: Use the *simple present tense* for action recently completed ("Obama Signs Bill"), habitual action ("Summer brings savings as shops clear shelves") and general truths ("Happiness Is a Warm Puppy"). Use the *present progressive tense* for ongoing action ("Weather Hampering Commute" or "Congress Considering Budget"). Use the *simple past tense* for action that happened in the distant past but was only recently revealed ("Government Denied Benefits to Veterans"). And, finally, use the *present infinitive tense* for future action that is almost certain to occur ("President to Sign Bill Tuesday").

Writing Headlines as Labels

When it comes to search engine optimization, headlines should be thought of as a label for the content on the page. And in labels, verbs are optional. In newspapers, almost all

Only one headline on this edition of WebMD's homepage is a traditional news headline with a verb.

headlines have a verb. Magazines, with their less time-sensitive content, often use headlines without verbs. When feature stories lack a hard news peg, headlines can be less direct and more evocative. Feature headlines often work better as labels, without verbs, than as sentences, with verbs.

Verbs in online headlines are caught between a rock and a hard place. On the one hand, strong action verbs are more compelling to readers than verbs that indicate little action, such as variants of the verb "to be." On the other hand, few people use verbs—even strong action verbs—when they search for information online. What is a headline-writer to do? In general, the longer the shelf life of a piece of content—that is, the longer the information in a story stays relevant—the better off you are in writing a headline that does not include a verb. By contrast, the shorter the shelf life of a story—for example, in the case of breaking news or event-based content—the more likely your headline will need a verb.

As an example, let's take a look at the consumer health site WebMD. The site's homepage is frequently updated. But most of the stories on it are evergreen. The tips and checklists have value long after they are first posted to the site. In scanning the headlines, you will see a notable lack of verbs.

Only one headline on this edition of WebMD's homepage is a traditional news headline with a verb—"1 Million Baby Slings Recalled." The recall was breaking news on the day this screen capture was taken. One headline—"Jennifer Love Hewitt's 13 Love Lessons"—came from WebMD's print magazine. The headline as written in the magazine, however, did feature a verb—"Jennifer Love Hewitt Dishes Dating Advice in 'The Day I Shot Cupid.'"

Headlines that link to multimedia content often include a label identifying the type of medium in which the content is presented. If you have a list of headlines that includes both text stories and video stories, the media type that is the least common should include a label in the headline, for example: "Text: Transcript of the governor's budget speech";

"Video: Best plays of the game"; or "Audio: Complete interview." These media labels let readers know what kind of content they are going to get when they click on the page. The labels serve as hints that help readers decide which link will best fit their needs.

There are many ways to use words in headlines to convey the primary media type of the page, but a site needs to take care to be consistent with its labels. If a site with audio content uses the labels "Video," "Watch" and "Multimedia" interchangeably, a reader could easily expect that these different labels indicate completely different types of content. Whatever you choose, the multimedia labels on a site's headlines should be consistent.

Journalists may start their headlines with verbs such as "Watch" or "Listen" when the headlines link to audio/visual content. This helps to differentiate them from links to text content. Command verbs such as these are known as imperatives. News organizations have found that readers are more likely to click on headlines that employ the imperative than headlines that don't. Some news editors find these types of commands insulting to readers, however. They view them as an inappropriate call to action that should not be made by unbiased journalists.

Imperatives aren't used only with multimedia content. Just as with label headlines, imperative headlines are also found in magazines. For example, they commonly appear in consumer stories ("Add Instant Curb Appeal").

Imperatives can function as labels on interactive or customizable content ("Search Movie Reviews"). When giving instructions to homepage visitors, however, be sure your headlines are as explicit as possible without being verbose. Without the word "Reviews" the label "Search Movies" is unclear; while some readers might expect to find movie *reviews,* others might expect to find movie *showtimes* at local theaters. If instructions are too complicated, people will move on. No one wants to struggle to get needed information. A tool that is not immediately intuitive needs the help of a user-interface design expert, not a gifted headline writer. Online news sites must be user friendly. Visitors should "get it" without having to read instructions.

Visitors are drawn to headlines that pique their curiosity. After all, audiences in search of news are by definition in search of something they don't yet know. The use of questions to "tease" the audience has been a staple of broadcast journalism for years. Broadcasters tempt viewers to "stay tuned" through the duration of a commercial break by posing alluring questions, questions that they promise to answer "after these messages." Question headlines online work the same way. A reader's curiosity is heightened when a headline is formulated as a question—one that can be answered only if the reader clicks on the link. But take care: crafting a headline in this way requires that you deliver an answer. Failing to do so erodes reader trust.

Question headlines online have the added benefit of potentially matching the query that people type into a search engine when they're looking for an article like yours. Following are some examples of well-worded question headlines:

- "What are the most reliable cars of 2010?"
- "Where do the candidates stand on the issues?"

- "Where have all the honeybees gone?"
- "What will Obama's budget mean to you?"

Compare these to the following examples of badly worded question headlines:

- "Is Michael Jackson dead?" (even though this was actually one of the most popular search phrases on Google the day the pop singer died)
- "Are burritos yummy?"
- "Which small town was devastated by a tornado overnight?"

EDITING ARTICLES

For a century and a half, journalists have put the most important information at the top of their stories. This is called the **inverted pyramid** style of writing. Born of an earlier technological advancement—the telegraph—the inverted pyramid style of writing is the dominant format for today's news stories.

In the late 19th century, telegraph transmission was expensive; writers learned to send the most important information first in case their editors didn't have the budget to accommodate lengthier pieces. Telegraph wires also tended to be unreliable. Prudence demanded that reporters send their good stuff first in case later transmissions got cut off. Long after the telegraph left newsrooms, the inverted pyramid remained. It was particularly suited to the need of editors to quickly cut a story from the bottom up when there wasn't room in the newspaper for the whole report.

Today, the prevalence of brief stories is driven in part by technological limitations—the character limit in mobile messages, for example—and in part by budget constraints. But the biggest constraint today is neither technological nor monetary. Today's biggest constraint is time. The audience, faced with an avalanche of information from a dizzying array of online news sources, simply doesn't have time to spend on long-winded writing. And your audience's time, as they say, is money—especially when so many of your online news visitors are hitting your site from their desks at work!

The best advice for writing online news today is the same as it was in 1918, when William Strunk Jr. and E.B. White wrote "The Elements of Style." Strunk and White gave this economical advice: "Omit Needless Words." To a generation of journalists accustomed to telling their friends it was "gr8 2 c u," perhaps advice that is more obvious has not been given.

For reporters who have gone out and gathered mountains of information for a story, and who are tempted by the unlimited **news hole** that is the Web, it is harder to write short than it is to write long. Young journalists especially have a tendency to want to cram every bit of information into an article, leaving no note or quote unreported. Helping with focus is one of an editor's main tasks, whether in print or online.

There is nothing you can do with story layout or metadata that will make poor writing any better. Thoroughly reported stories that are written concisely and precisely are the best way to serve your audience, both online and off. People stop reading when they get bored or confused, regardless of the medium. Bad writing isn't just writing that is unnecessarily long. Bad writing is also writing that is riddled with grammatical and spelling errors. The worst writing is text that contains factual errors. Nothing slows people down like the confusion they experience when they have to decipher mangled spelling or question the accuracy of the information being presented. You never want your readers to stop and say, "Wait, *what?*" They will hit the "Back" button and be off to another site in a flash.

Simply stated, a good headline isn't enough. An article needs to be well constructed, with an informative (albeit brief) summary, compelling subhead and engaging lead, if it is to propel the reader along.

Article Summary

The **article summary** appears directly under the headline in a homepage package. It is a one-sentence description of the destination content. The primary job of a story summary is not to tell what the news is, but to tell why the news is interesting or important. A summary should be brief, but packed with information. It rarely takes more than three lines of text, which translates to about 150 to 200 characters (including spaces) on most news sites. Following are a few examples:

Odierno Seeks To Move Troops To Northern Iraq
Political tension between Iraq's Arabs and ethnic Kurds has resulted in a security gap in the north.

In this example, from the NPR homepage, the headline tells the reader *what* is happening while the summary explains *why*. The summary can be brief because the reader has already seen the information in the headline. The summary on its own omits the most important aspect of the story, but there is no need to repeat information that has already been stated in the headline.

This homepage package might nevertheless leave the reader with a valid question: "Who is 'Odierno'?" Summaries should fill in details that may not be appropriate for a brief headline. In this example, the identity of Odierno is important because he was the top American military commander in Iraq at the time.

Immigration official says agents will no longer have quotas
The head of ICE says he has ended quotas on a controversial program designed to go after illegal immigrants who have ignored deportation orders.

This example comes from the homepage of the Los Angeles Times. The summary here adds the *why* to the *what* stated in the headline. In this instance a big part of the reason the story is important is that it wasn't just any immigration official who made this statement, but the "head" immigration official—a crucial detail that readers get from the summary.

Bookmaker pays off early on Tiger, loses $2 million

Stunning victory by South Korean Yang Yong-eun meant Paddy Power paid off $2.12 million in bets that actually were losers.

In this example, from the USA Today homepage, we see how a headline's wording can appropriately contrast with a summary's details. The headline for this feature story uses the first name of golfer Tiger Woods, even though Woods was the second-place finisher in the 2009 PGA Championship. Woods is widely known, so using "Tiger" rather than the name of the more obscure champion ensures more clicks as the audience conducts searches and scans headlines for newsmakers. The name of the first-place finisher, Yang Yong-eun, appears instead in the summary, along with the proper noun "Paddy Power," which offers further detail to the headline's common noun, "bookmaker."

Distilling the key details of a story can sometimes be challenging. Doing so requires homepage summary writers to have an intimate knowledge of the story and the audience's potential interest in it. Take the following example from The New York Times' homepage:

Healthy One Day, Dying the Next

A medical team stretched the limits of America's transplant system to save the life of Jessa Perrin, a Cincinnati teenager with a deadly form of a rare disease.

This headline and summary appeared on a feature story that begins with a quick narrative that sets the scene for the crux of the story. The homepage summary was derived from a sentence that didn't appear in the article until the very end of the sixth paragraph: "The two medical teams on opposite sides of the Atlantic began a steady stream of e-mail and phone calls in hopes of stretching the limits of medicine and America's transplant system to save the life of a girl with a deadly form of a rare disease."

Summaries should be evocative—even promotional—in their tone. Summaries can tease with questions that are answered in the story or make allusions to details that are revealed in the story. Look at this example from a feature story in the Travel section of the msnbc.com homepage:

World's weirdest hotels

On your next trip, you could be checking into a wine cask, a salvaged 727 airplane, or a room where the furniture defies the law of gravity.

The headline has no verb. The summary uses the second-person pronoun "you"—a definite no-no in hard news stories—and it really doesn't reveal much about the story. But since people don't need to learn about weird hotels, the goal is to intrigue them so that they want to.

Healthy One Day, Dying the Next: A Medical Race

Summaries are not always the same as leads. In this feature from The New York Times, the summary is drawn from the sixth paragraph.

Béatrice de Géa for The New York Times

A RARE DISEASE Jessa Perrin, 16, at an exam last week just weeks after undergoing a liver transplant at New York-Presbyterian. With her, from left, Dr. Nadia Ovchinsky, Kara Ventura, Dr. Steven J. Lobritto and Dr. Tomoaki Kato.

By DENISE GRADY
Published: August 17, 2009

Jessa Perrin had a backpack, an iPod and an air of independence when she boarded a plane in Cincinnati on July 5, headed for Israel with a group of other high school students. She told her parents not to expect a lot of calls home; she would see them in a month.

Related

Health Guide: Wilson's Disease

🔍 Enlarge This Image

Béatrice de Géa for The New York Times

THANKFUL Jessa Perrin sharing a moment with her mother, Bonnie Ullner, at the hospital. "She was basically dying," Mrs. Ullner said, and doctors did not know why.

FACEBOOK
TWITTER
RECOMMEND
E-MAIL
SEND TO PHONE
PRINT
SINGLE PAGE
REPRINTS
SHARE

NEVER LET ME GO
WATCH THE TRAILER

About a week into the trip, she became ill, with what appeared to be a stomach virus or food poisoning. A clinic checked her, judged the illness minor and let her go.

But the next day, her skin began turning yellow, and she was taken to a hospital in northern Israel and then transferred to Hadassah Hebrew University Medical Center in Jerusalem. After that, she went into free fall. By the next day, Wednesday, July 15, her liver, kidneys and lungs were failing, and there were signs of damage to her heart. She was put on a respirator.

"She was basically dying," said her mother, Bonnie Ullner. At first, doctors did not know why.

One thing was clear: Jessa, 16, needed a liver transplant — fast. She would not live more than a week without one. But the odds of a liver's becoming available soon enough in Israel were low. She would have a much better chance in the United States, but was then too ill to be transported. Doctors in the intensive care unit struggled to stabilize her.

At the same time, they began calling transplant centers in New York, because it is reachable by nonstop flights from Israel. The first to respond was NewYork-Presbyterian Morgan Stanley Children's Hospital. The two medical teams on opposite sides of the Atlantic began a steady stream of e-mail and phone calls in hopes of stretching the limits of medicine and America's transplant system to save the life of a girl with a deadly form of a rare disease.

Kara Ventura, a nurse practitioner and transplant coordinator in New York, answered the call from Dr. Gadi Lalazar, in Hadassah's liver unit, about 3 a.m. on Thursday, July 16. Her hospital had never received an emergency call for a transplant for someone in another country, but Jessa was a child and an American citizen. They had to try to help her, Dr. Ventura said.

She alerted the rest of the transplant team, including someone who would contact insurers to make sure the bills would be paid. Doctors on the team began putting out

Subhead

The **subhead** appears underneath the headline on the page where the body of an article is found. It typically offers additional detail or specific information that would not fit in the headline. A subhead can also serve as a way to present information that mitigates, contradicts or qualifies a statement made in the headline, as is the case with the Blockbuster story on MSN Money presented at the beginning of this chapter. In that example, the editors at MSN Money added the following line of text just below the headline: "But the video chain's bid to expand its online customer base could backfire if consumers visit its stores less frequently." This is the subhead (also sometimes called a "deck" in print publications).

The Poynter Institute's 2004 Eyetrack study examined readers' behavior when confronted with an element similar to a subhead. Poynter called this element a "summary graph" in its experiment. This was a two- or three-sentence-long blurb that was set "slightly darker and larger in size than the story text type." The study found that readers will sometimes read the subhead and nothing more. Other times readers will tend to do one of three things when these "summary graphs" were included at the top of an online news story:

1. Quickly realize they didn't want to read the article, perhaps because the topic didn't interest them

2. Slowly realize they didn't want to read the article, perhaps because they received all the information they wanted from the summary paragraph

3. Continue to read the story, spending no more or less time with these stories than on stories that had no summary paragraph

So it appears that while subheads can help readers move faster, subheads may also discourage readers from staying on your site longer.

Lead

A **lead** is the first paragraph of a news story. Many of the rules for good newspaper leads apply to leads of online news stories as well. A breaking story will contain information that your audience is not likely to know. The lead should begin with one or two short, active sentences that summarize the most important information in the story.

Keeping a lead short has always been good advice for news stories, but online producers have a further reason to keep it brief: it is an online news story's lead that is typically picked up and reprinted in the search results pages on Google News. Google News shows only about the first 20 words of a lead; leads that are longer than this get cut off mid-sentence.

Online leads should emphasize the news values of time and impact. Scanning readers want to know immediately the answer to the question, "*When* and *how* is this development going to affect me?"

Leads should not be anecdotal. While they work well in print, anecdotal leads should be avoided in almost all cases when writing online news stories. An online news story that merits an anecdotal lead is one that should be told using multimedia elements. After all, the value of a good anecdotal lead is its ability to illustrate how one person has been affected by a larger issue or event. Good anecdotal leads help readers "see" an abstract problem when words are the only medium available. In online news, words are never the only medium available. Chapter 8, on multimedia reporting, offers more information on how to tell stories with audio and visual material.

Paragraph

A **paragraph** is a distinct block of one or more sentences. When thinking about the best way to structure paragraphs for an online news story, we can turn again to the ever-reliable Strunk and White. According to their "The Elements of Style," writers should "make the paragraph the unit of composition: one paragraph to each topic."

Remember that online readers tend to scan down the left side of the page rather than methodically read through each line. Writers can't dictate which words will appear at the start of every line, but they can control the words that appear at the start of each line that begins a new paragraph. When writing for searchers and scanners, pay attention to what words begin each paragraph. These are the words people are most likely to see as they scan down and across the page in a pattern that looks like a capital "F." An easy way to get in the habit of putting the most important words at the start of a paragraph without consciously contorting and re-editing your copy is to follow another long-held tenant of good news writing: use active verbs.

The Poynter Institute's 2004 Eyetrack study found that short paragraphs of one to two sentences encourage readers to continue: "The bottom line is that stories with shorter paragraphs got more than twice as many overall eye fixations than those with longer paragraphs. These data suggest that the longer-paragraph format discourages reading and that short-paragraph format overwhelmingly encourages reading."

Page Length

If Strunk and White were alive today, the latest version of their book might add that the pages, like paragraphs, should be focused. **Page length** is an important tool of any online news story. Writers should aim for just one topic per page. Text-heavy Web pages should be brief and remain focused on a single topic for two reasons. First, short pages about a single topic are "keyword dense"—that is, they have a high percentage of keywords relative to the number of total words on the page. This makes it much easier for search engine algorithms to tell what a page is about. Second, short pages about a single topic offer a more precise target for links coming in from outside pages.

Imagine, for example, that a blogger wants to link to Article II of the U.S. Constitution, or imagine that a legal researcher would like to see for herself the text of Article II because it is referenced in a news story about a Supreme Court ruling. Article II is the element in which these readers are interested—not Article I, not the Preamble, not Article III and not the amendments. If the entire Constitution—all 7,000 or so words of it—were printed on the same Web page, it would be impossible for the blogger to link directly to Article II, and it would be difficult for the researcher to find the specific text she's looking for. Break the text of the Constitution down, however, and both the blogger and the researcher are better served.

Compare the version of the Constitution at http://www.usconstitution.net/const.txt to that at http://www.law.cornell.edu/constitution/constitution.overview.html. A blogger could link directly to any article or even any section of any article of the version published by Cornell. But the version published at USConstitution.net is simply one indivisible block of text through which the reader must skim in order to find the specific section he or she wants.

Web usability expert Jakob Nielsen attempted to quantify just how few words on each Web page people actually read. He found that people read just enough to know whether they want to read more. In a typical online news article of 750 to 1,000 words, for example, the average person reads only about a quarter or a third of the words on the page. Remember, though, that averages can mask extremes at either end. If online news users find something they like, they will actually read more of it online than they will in print. The 2007 version of Poynter's Eyetrack study found that regardless of length, readers go through about 77 percent of an online news article once they commit to it.

Online news writers could learn a lot about tightening their prose from another group of people who write content that fights for the attention of a busy audience—writers of business memos. Memos are often written to convince a decision maker that a certain approach is best. Decision makers are notoriously short on time, so good memos have to be brief, clearly written and easily scanned.

Take a look at the following examples of the memo format:

- http://www.theatlantic.com/doc/200808u/clinton-memos

- http://www.nku.edu/~fordmw/memo.htm

These examples contain a few formatting elements we've already seen in online news stories. They also contain elements effective in corporate memos that could be readily adapted to online news stories. For example, boldfaced words in the body of an article and bulleted lists that set off important information encourage efficiency in reading and retention of key facts and figures.

In memos, words in boldfaced type tend to be key phrases or talking points that the memo writer would like her audience to remember. In news articles, such as the MSN Money example, boldfaced words tend to be keywords, like the names of the two primary businesses involved in the article.

Bulleted lists in memos and online news articles effectively display pieces of information that in narrative form would require awkward conjunctions; they can also be a good way to summarize several actions taken by a single subject or several characteristics of a single subject. For example, in an online article about Academy Award nominees, you might see the following:

The supporting actor nominees were:

- Matt Damon
- Woody Harrelson
- Christopher Plummer
- Stanley Tucci
- Christopher Waltz

Or, in an article about national politics, you might find this:

The House Majority Leader said the emergency legislation would provide three major benefits to Americans who had fallen behind on their mortgage payments:

- provide them with the right to free credit counseling
- automatically halt foreclosure proceedings against anyone who had lost his or her job in the last nine months
- allow banks to renegotiate loans at lower rates as long as the homeowner continued to make payments.

Articles on Wikipedia are also full of subsections, bulleted lists and boldfaced text. In fact, Chris Nodder, a Web-writing expert and user-experience specialist for the Nielsen Norman Group, told The Poynter Institute's Guillermo E. Franco that the rules for formatting online news articles are much the same as the rules for formatting encyclopedia articles or the descriptions of products on online retail sites:

Typically the user's goal is the same in every case. Find the relevant block of text, and then find the required information within this block. Content creators must avoid the vain notion that website visitors care about eloquent prose. Visitors are goal oriented, so they care much more about the ease with which they can extract information from the page. While this may not initially seem very "sexy" to aspiring writers, the difference between poor and good Web writing is so great that it can often be the factor that distinguishes a good site from a bad one.

Section Titles

When it is not possible to split a single news story into several pages, each focused on a single topic, writers can use **section titles** throughout an article to provide scanners with a visual speed bump and an efficient way to determine whether the subsections of

$400,000, according to the city attorney's office. Because the case didn't go to trial, the flaws in the NOPD probe have never been revealed.

The police story

Mitchell told detectives that he and his partner were rolling along Convention Center Boulevard in the early morning hours of Sept. 3, 2005, when Brumfield "started jogging

Fearing the huge crowd gathered at the Convention Center would attack them in anger over the shooting, the two officers drove away.

The family's version

Brumfield and his wife, Deborah, rode out the storm in their home on Port Street in the Upper 9th Ward, watching the floodwaters rise. When a rescue crew showed up, the

"He took a couple breaths, and that was it," Augustin said.

The investigation

The post-shooting investigation did little to resolve the contradictions between the competing narratives.

This story, produced jointly by Frontline, ProPublica and The Times-Picayune in New Orleans, has three strong section titles: "The police story," "The family's version" and "The investigation." There's no doubt what each is about.

an article might be interesting, even if the lead is not. According to Poynter's 2004 Eyetrack study, section titles don't necessarily encourage scanners to read more of an article. They do, however, break up a page of dense text and help scanners find the information they need. They're also useful in helping search engines identify key words and concepts.

In constructing section titles, a writer should follow the same guidelines as those established for writing headlines. Section titles are set in type that is bolder than that used for the article body. Looking back at our introductory example from MSN Money, you can see that "'An interesting approach'" is the first section title. Since section titles are written primarily to serve the scanning eyes of Web readers, there is no need for them to be much longer than three words—as long as those three words pack a punch.

ADDING SEO METADATA

Every journalist's first obligation is to tell the truth as fully, fairly and accurately as possible. Online journalists face the additional challenge of placing keywords high on a page to attract search engine algorithms and down the left side of a page to attract readers who scan. These two duties often collide, and when they do it is writing that is clear, precise, complete and accurate that must trump everything else. Journalists don't have the same luxury as advertisers and politicians who can craft their words to suit their primary obligation—that of being a strong advocate for a particular point of view.

When the text of a story does not contain some of the keywords a reader might be searching for, online producers start thinking about using a type of HTML code that is hidden from the reader but is visible to search engine programs. This type of HTML code, called metadata, allows online journalists to balance their need to draw an audience via search engines and their obligation to provide that audience with a well-written story.

What Is Metadata?

Metadata is essentially "data about the data." For example, when you listen to a song in iTunes, the audio of that song is the data. But the information about the song that you use to find it, for example, the name of the song, the name of the artist, the name of the composer, the music genre, the album name and the duration of the song, is the metadata.

For HTML documents, the metadata is stored on a part of the page that is invisible to readers. This part of the page is called the **header**. When a Web browser sees the header portion of the HTML document, it does not display it to the reader. But when a search crawler sees the header, it can read the text inside it and use that text to get the right information to the right people at the right time.

The only way for an online journalist to create and edit the metadata is to have access to the HTML code, either directly by editing it manually or through editing fields in a content management system. Once you have access to the code, the three pieces of metadata you will be editing most often as an online journalist are the title, description and keywords.

 Tool: HTML Tags

When you open a Web page in a browser, you may think you're looking at HTML, but you're not. What you're really looking at is a translation of HTML that is unique to your browser and operating system. Although Web browsers display an interpretation of HTML rather than raw code, they do provide an easy way to pop open the hood, so to speak.

HTML stands for **HyperText Markup Language.** The first step toward seeing the raw HTML of a Web page is to open it in your browser. Once you've done that, you will need to "view the source." The specific instructions for viewing the source of an HTML file differ by browser. However, regardless of which browser you use, once you arrive at the source on the HTML page you'll notice that the text you see in the browser is marked up with a lot of words and letters that sit between the angled brackets < and > . Inside these brackets are tags. An HTML tag is a keyword that tells the browser how a document is structured. Tags separate the structure of a document from the actual content of the document. Most tags are written in pairs. There is an opening tag and a closing tag.

HTML has two kinds of tags: structural tags and formatting tags. If an HTML document were a house, structural tags would be the frame. They give Web browsers the basic information needed to know which elements of a page come before and after other elements. On every well-formed HTML page, you will see three structural opening tags: <html>, <head> and <body>. You will see as well their associated end tags: </html>, </head> and </body>.

The <html> tags tell a browser where the HTML code it needs to read begins and ends. The <head> tags give the browser information that the page's author wanted to associate with the page but not have displayed to the audience. And the <body> tags denote the beginning and ending portions of the visible parts of a Web page.

You will see that the <head> tags and <body> tags appear inside the <html> tag. Putting an HTML tag inside another HTML tag is a practice known as **nesting.** You already know how nesting works because you're familiar with the concept from basic arithmetic. When you see the math problem (5+3) x 2 , you know that you first do the operation inside the parentheses—adding 5 and 3 to get 8—before you do the operation outside the parentheses—multiplying 8 by 2.

Nesting identifies the relationships that exist between tags. In effect, the <head> tag is a "child" of the <html> tag. The <body> tag is as well. The <html> tag is the "parent" tag of both the <head> tags and <body> tags. The <head> tag and <body> tag are "siblings" to one another. And just as in biology, the traits of parents are "inherited" by their child tags in HTML.

The next commonly used tag you'll see in an HTML page's source code is the <p> tag. The <p> tag gives you your first introduction to the key work of HTML—separating structure from content. The opening and closing <p> tags only tell a Web browser that the content in between is a paragraph. They do not in any way describe the information that is conveyed in that content. In fact, you could take the information out and put it between <h1> tags (the HTML tags that indicate "main headline") without changing the information in any way. In doing so, you will have simply rearranged structure—not altered content.

HTML—from viewing source code to using tags

Tutorials and resources on HTML

The Title Tag

The title tag usually contains the first pieces of true content on a Web page. Inside the <head> tags, the title tags on all sites look similar to the following example from a story on the site of The Anniston Star:

```
<title>Anniston Star—Oxford project shut down Oversight in reporting
human remains costs city thousands delays work</title>
```

For news articles, the title tag is often the same thing as the headline. Many content management systems will copy the content that a producer has typed into the headline field in a CMS's administrative interface. But there are cases in which you may want to change it if you can.

Journalists are concerned with the title tag for two reasons. First, its content appears in the browser's title bar as the name of the page that is seen by the reader.

Anniston Star - Oxford project shut down Oversight in reporting human remains costs city thousands delays work

Title bar.

Second, title tags are used by search engines, which will display the title metadata as the name of the page and as hyperlinked text on its results pages.

Anniston Star - **Oxford project shut down Oversight in reporting ...**

Search result on Google's Web search.

Google displays only 66 characters of a page's title, truncating the headline at the end of the last whole word under that limit. So, it is best to keep title tags—and headlines—at 60 characters. Here are some other guidelines on how to use the title tag to help searchers find the most relevant information on your site:

- **Make it unique.** Some news sites include boilerplate information—such as the name of the site—in each title tag. If your site does this, the boilerplate information should be placed after the unique description of the page.

- **Avoid superlatives.** Too many spammers try to pass off their products as the "best" or "most." Search engine algorithms seem to be on the lookout for extraneous superlatives and may penalize sites that use them too often.

- **Leave out prepositions, conjunctions and articles.** Search engines don't take these words into account when determining the subject of the page, but these words do count toward that precious 60-word limit.

- **Don't make them too short.** If Google's algorithm doesn't think your title tag is substantial enough to be useful to its search audience, it will try to grab other information about your page and display it as the page title in its search results. For example, Google might pick up the less-than-attention-grabbing filename of your page. Whatever it picks up is less useful to the reader than a clear and concise title tag that you have written.

The Meta Description Tag

The **meta description tag** also appears within the header of an HTML document, hidden from the audience. The content of description tags often appears as the summary of information about a page in Google's Web search results. While this is not always the case, it is wise nevertheless to craft a good description for each page on your site. A meta description tag looks like this:

```
<meta name="description" content=" ">
```

When writing a meta description for a news Web page, it is best to emphasize keywords and the "Who?" and "What?" of the page. It is also a good idea to include the reason "Why?" a person should read the page. For news articles produced in a content management system, a description might be the same as the lead. Or, it might be the same as the summary blurb you write for the homepage and other index pages. The best content management systems will use one of these options as the default, but allow producers to override it and handcraft their own description. Since Google displays only about the first 20 words in your description, leads and summary blurbs should be kept short as well.

Following are two examples of meta descriptions from news content. First, an automated description of a story about a motorcycle crash from the Arizona Republic:

> 3 dead in north Phoenix motorcycle crash, The Carefree Highway was expected to be closed for several hours after a dump truck crashed into several motorcycles.

Second, a handcrafted description of a story about the death of Michael Jackson from the Los Angeles Times:

> Michael Jackson died today at the age of 50

For index pages—the pages on your site that serve primarily as collection and navigation stations—a description should summarize the type of content that a reader might find on the listed pages. Following are two examples of handcrafted meta descriptions for index pages on news websites. First, from the Yahoo News homepage:

> Use Yahoo! News to find breaking news, current events, the latest headlines, news photos, analysis & opinion on top stories, world, business, politics, entertainment, sports, technology, and more.

Second, from the front page of a Miami Herald blog:

> Steve Rothaus' blog for and about gay, lesbian, bisexual and transgender people throughout Miami and Fort Lauderdale.

The Meta Keywords Tag

The **meta keywords tag** represents a writer's final chance to provide search engines with keywords that are relevant to the page being published. In many cases, especially on a news site, it is impossible to tweak the body of an article to include search terms that might be highly relevant and very popular. In this case, the writer uses the meta keyword tag. Like the other meta tags, the meta keywords tag lives inside an HTML's header. It looks like this:

```
<meta name="keywords" content=" ">
```

The content of the keywords tag is a set of single or multiword search terms. Good keyword tags should be brief (no more than 10 keywords or 200 characters, whichever is fewer), focused (use only keywords that are directly related to your page), and straightforward. Don't be deceptive—once again, don't put "celebrity sex scandal" as the keyword phrase in your article if the story is about an increase in sewer rates. Neither search engines nor readers like to be tricked.

VIEW SOURCE

SEO FOR ARTICLES AND INDEX PAGES

For online news producers, the new skills required for search engine optimization and the traditional skill of writing clear and concise headlines and story leads cannot be separated. The words you craft for a story show up in too many different contexts. You can't write good headlines that aren't optimized for search engines any more than you can write metadata that will remain completely hidden from your audience. Following are some examples of how headlines, leads and metadata come together to affect how pages on The New York Times' website appear to site visitors as well as searchers on Google.

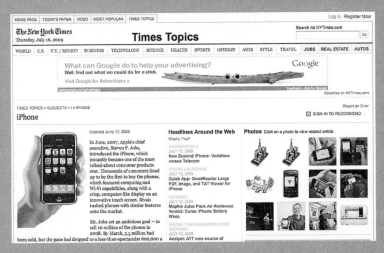

The New York Times' iPhone Topics page.

Here is the relevant section of the page's metadata:

```
<title>iPhone News—The New York Times</title>

<meta name="description" content="News about the iPhone.
Commentary and archival information about the iPhone from The
New York Times." />

<meta name="keywords" content="iPhoneiPhone" />

<h1>iPhone</h1>
```

And here is how the metadata appear as a search result on Google:

Web Images Videos Maps News Shopping Gmail more ▼

Google   times topics iphone   Search   Advanced Search
                                                  Preferences

Web   Show options...   Resul

iPhone News - The New York Times
News about the iPhone. Commentary and archival information about the iPhone from The
New York Times.
topics.nytimes.com/top/.../timestopics/.../i/iphone/index.html - Cached - Similar - ◌ 🔼 ⊠

On iPhone, Lucky Magazine Is All About Shopping - NYTimes.com
Feb 2, 2009 ... Times Topics: iPhone. The application features more than 70 shoes listed in
its March shoe guide (including those of advertisers), ...
www.nytimes.com/2009/02/02/business/media/02lucky.html - Similar - ◌ 🔼 ⊠

Booming iPhone Sales Slow Profit Decline for AT&T - NYTimes.com
iPhone Sales Push Up Apple's Profits (April 23, 2009). Times Topics: AT&T Inc. The
company, based in Dallas, reported its net income for the quarter was ...
www.nytimes.com/2009/04/23/technology/.../23phone.html - Similar - ◌ 🔼 ⊠
More results from www.nytimes.com »

Metadata as it appears as a search result on Google.

The page's "title" on Google comes from the metadata, not from any specific text on the page, including the content inside the <h1> tags. The description on Google is also being pulled from the metadata.

Now let's look at one of the articles that linked from the topic page. Here's the headline and summary:

Apple Aims for the Masses With a Cheaper iPhone
By JOHN MARKOFF

The company announced a new version of the iPhone with lots of new programs.

June 10, 2008 | TECHNOLOGY | NEWS

Headline and summary on New York Times iPhone Topics page.

VIEW SOURCE

And here are the headline and first few words of the article:

New York Times headline on article page.

Here is how the same metadata translate to Google:

Apple Aims for the Masses With a Cheaper iPhone

New York Times headline on Google.

And here is the article's metadata:

```
<title>Apple Aims for the Masses With a Cheaper iPhone—
NYTimes
.com</title>

<meta name="description" content="The company announced a
new version of the iPhone with lots of new programs.">

<meta name="keywords" content="iPhone,Wireless
Communications,Apple Inc,Jobs Steven P,Prices (Fares Fees and
Rates)">

<h1>Technology</h1>

<h1>Apple Aims for the Masses With a Cheaper iPhone</h1>
```

The title tag and headline tag content are the same, and this headline remains the same on all of the places the article appears. The summaries on the topic page and on the Google search results page are the same as the meta description tag, which was handcrafted by a producer using The New York Times' CMS. As you can see, the way you construct article headlines and metadata affects how readers view your article—both on your site and on other sites.

Other Elements That Affect SEO

Headlines, subheads, section labels and the rest of the visible words on the actual body of a page are the most important elements of search engine optimization, followed by the metadata that is hidden from the user. But other elements can also affect where your stories show up in a Google search.

Search engines take into account the number of times a specific string of characters appears on a page. Some engines also look at the words that *other* pages use to link to a target page in an effort to determine the relevance of a particular search string.

In addition to a page's relevance, Google and other search engines try to help their users figure out which pages are the most trusted. Google uses a system called "**Page Rank**" to determine the importance of your page relative to the importance of other, similar pages.

Google looks at the number of links to a Web page from other pages, as well as the "quality" of the linking sites. According to Google, "five or six high-quality links from websites such as www.cnn.com and www.nytimes.com would be valued much more highly than twice as many links from less reputable or established sites." One analogy for reputation ranking is the idea of "strength of schedule" that is sometimes used to rank college sports teams. For example, two teams with 10 wins might not be equal because one of those teams has beaten opponents with an overall better "reputation." How complex is this calculation of relevancy and reputation? Google's algorithm for returning search results has more than 500 million variables and 2 billion terms.

Additional elements can affect your page's placement in Google's search results:

- **The age of your site overall.** Sites that have been on the Web at the same address for a long time are considered more trustworthy than sites that have been recently launched.

- **The age of a particular article.** The currency of a particular news article can help it get placed above older pages.

- **The overall site size.** Bigger sites tend to gather more inbound links, which gives Google the sense that they are authoritative.

Good writing still drives good journalism—even when news judgment has been turned in part over to an algorithm. But for the online journalist, good writing simply isn't enough. Finding and linking to trusted sites will increase the prominence of your site in the automated mind of a search engine. This in turn will lead other high-quality sites to establish links with yours, creating more opportunities for your stories to find their audience—and make an impact. Now that's a good result.

As reporters and editors in a culture overloaded with entertainment and information, you are vying for time against everything else your audience needs and wants to do during the day. Improving your writing for an online audience means improving the chances that the news audience will start with your site, get to the finish line before they get distracted and remember the news and information they read.

ONLINE LEARNING MODULE 5

ACTIVATE THIS MODULE: journalism.cqpress.com

On my blog, I often discuss examples of online news writing. You also will find site critiques, interviews with journalists and reactions to your comments and questions.

When you buy or activate this chapter's online learning module, you will have access to:

- A digital version of this chapter's text.
- Interactive flashcards for the terms used in this chapter.
- A printable tip sheet covering search engine optimization for news.
- A quiz to test your mastery of the material in this chapter.
- Video screencasts that show you how to use Google's keyword tools and give you a guided tour of basic HTML tags.
- Online exercises that give you hands-on experience with writing and editing online stories, headlines and summaries.

As you complete the module's online exercises, you will:

- Edit headlines for length and keyword placement.
- Create headlines.
- Edit and write article summaries to match headlines.
- Add subheads, section titles and lists to stories written for print.
- Take facts and turn them into a text story written specifically for the Web.
- Edit metadata for text and audio-visual news content.
- Create metadata from scratch for both text and audio-visual news content.
- Debug a broken HTML document.
- Code your own basic HTML document.

6 BASICS OF WEB RESEARCH: CULTIVATING LINKS, CULTIVATING SOURCES

This chapter will teach you how to:

- Find information quickly.
- Verify the accuracy of information.
- Identify sources of information using social media.
- Monitor a wide variety of online news sources efficiently.

The Internet is littered with filth and lies. Right there, on the same screen that brings news of scientific advances and medical breakthroughs, of democracy protesters being fired on halfway around the world and evidence documenting once-secret human rights abuses, are images of Britney Spears wearing only underwear, or no underwear at all, and manufactured documents intended to make people think that Sen. Al Gore laughed off warnings about Osama bin Laden and his al-Qaida fighters.

One of the oldest cartoons about the Internet, appearing in The New Yorker magazine, shows two dogs, one typing at the computer and saying to the other, "On the Internet, nobody knows you're a dog." Fake online identities have long been part of the Internet culture, and they've been used for both good and evil. Democratic activists hide their true identities as they risk their lives to report on conditions inside totalitarian regimes to the world; at the same time, sexual predators hide their true identities to lure children into dangerous, even life-threatening situations.

The good news for journalists—professional fact-finders and truth-tellers that they are—is that the troughs of deceit are oftentimes the most effective places for them to ply their trade. A journalist's job is to ferret out lies; it is also a journalist's job to ensure that her own reporting remains accurate, complete and transparent amid all of this misinformation—and to help the audience know the difference.

In order to operate in a networked world, where business transactions and political debates are increasingly occurring online, journalists need to understand the online techniques that people use to conceal truth and spread inaccurate information. One of their major responsibilities is to cultivate links and share news through online conversation. Journalists today must understand how to use online media to search out and communicate with potential sources and verify claims.

Anyone can search for and find information online. A professional journalist must be able to discern which information is accurate and identify where there are gaps. The Internet offers a mind-boggling array of information, resources and leads. But the truth is, the cacophony that can be the Internet hasn't made it easier to be a professional reporter—in many ways, the Internet has made it harder.

FIND INFORMATION FAST

A button on the homepage of Google says "I'm Feeling Lucky." Press it and Google takes you directly to the website that it thinks is exactly what you're looking for. That button is a nice way for Google to show off its algorithmic prowess, but it is no way to conduct even basic research on the Web. For professional journalists, it is better to be good than to be lucky.

Journalists can't work with the expectation that they can simply type one search query into Google, hit a button and accept at face value the first thing that pops up. When they begin digging into a new topic, journalists conduct one search after another. Think of doing research as doing re-search.

Timeliness counts. The online news audience wants the latest information, and it wants it now. Journalists need to find accurate information, and quickly. This means that they can't afford to leisurely surf the Web in hopes that they'll catch an answer as it floats by. As a journalist, you must develop a search strategy. And that strategy will depend on your goal. When you go online to find something, you're doing one of two things. You are either trying to find general information on a topic about which you know nothing, or you are attempting to verify a specific fact. Whatever your goal, you can get started on an effective search by following some simple tips.

Start With the Right Questions

It has been said that a news story is only as good as the questions it aims to answer. It can likewise be said that a Web search is only as good as the searcher who sets it in motion. In fact, every day millions of people around the world turn to search engines with questions of their own. And while some of them find answers, many others do not. What every good journalist knows, quite simply, is how to pose a good question.

Search engines are dumb. Or, at least, they are incredibly literal. They can't infer what question you're really trying to ask. They can simply take a specific pattern of characters and see whether that pattern matches exactly a pattern on one of several billion Web pages. If you want search engines to help you quickly find relevant information, you need to learn how to speak their language. Talking to a search engine is not the same as talking to a fellow human. But in either case, you have to know how to phrase the right question in order to quickly find the right answer.

Imagine what would happen if you walked up to one of your friends and asked, "Indians big win?" He would probably give you a blank look in return, trying to figure out what in the world it was you wanted to know. If he tried to make sense of your question by recasting it in his mind as a complete sentence—"What was the score of the Indians' big win last night?"—your friend would likely fare much better. Unless, of course, you weren't asking that at all. Perhaps what you were really asking was something else entirely—"What was the name of the battle where the Lakota Indians had their big win against George Custer?"

Like people, search engines have a difficult time inducing a real question from just a few words. But unlike people, search engines also have a difficult time translating natural language questions into effective search queries. Many of the words in question sentences are so common they are useless to a search engine that is trying to determine relevance. For example, the sequence of characters, or **string,** "the" appears regularly on most Web pages. As such, it is useless in terms of search engine relevance. To effectively speak to a search engine, you must learn how to speak its language.

Look at the following plain-English questions. How might they be translated into questions that can be easily understood by search engines?

- What was the score of the Indians' big win last night?
- What was the name of the battle where the Lakota Indians had their big win against George Custer?

If we start with the assumption that natural language questions aren't—yet—the best way to talk to search engines, how then should we configure questions to best exploit a search engine's power? More simply, what should our **search query** say? Which words are most useful? Least useful? To answer these questions, you have to ask more questions:

- Which words are the most likely to appear on the pages for which you're looking?
- Which words are the least likely to appear on pages for which you're *not* looking?

You can think about the process of creating a search query as something like target practice. You want to give yourself your best chances of hitting the bull's-eye without picking off an innocent bystander. If you use words that you're pretty sure would be used on a page that would answer your question, then you'll increase the chances that your search will hit the page you're looking for. But you also may be increasing the total number of pages you hit, many of which won't be relevant to your search.

While working on a story about Los Angeles Dodgers owner Frank McCourt, you might run across pages about the writer Frank McCourt, author of the Pulitzer Prize–winning book "Angela's Ashes." To narrow your search, then, you might decide to add the term "2009" since you know that it was in that year that McCourt the Dodger owner split with his wife and business partner. However, because McCourt the author died that same year, you wouldn't be much better off. You would still bring up pages featuring both McCourts. You might write a search query that omitted the words "angela's ashes." But in so doing you would merely avoid turning up pages about the author that emphasized the title of his most famous book; you would not avoid gathering pages about the author entirely, or even pages that included the words "angela's ashes." In fact, your best strategy would be to add the word "dodgers" to your query; it is unlikely that this term would appear on pages about the author while quite likely that it would appear on pages about the Dodger owner.

When you're thinking about the right search query to use when asking a question of a search engine, you have to put yourself in the mind of the person who authored the page of information you want. (In Chapter 5, on writing pages that are easy for searchers to find, you'll see that the inverse is also true—when writing for a website, you need to think about how people conduct searches.)

Overcoming your natural propensities as a writer can be difficult. While you might know that the correct AP style to describe the indigenous people of North America is "Indian Americans" or "Native Americans," most people who write Web pages don't study AP style. A Google search for "Native Americans" and "tribe" turns up about 7 million results. A search for "Indians" and "tribe" turns up more than 10 million results. Understanding the words that other people use to describe a subject can be most helpful in determining the perspective of the source.

As you think about how to construct the right questions for search engines, keep the following tips in mind:

1. Nouns are better search terms than adjectives, verbs and other parts of speech.

2. The more specific your term, the more specific your result. For example, a search for "actors" will yield more specific results than a search for "celebrities."

3. If you get stuck, first phrase the search as a natural language question. Then create your search string by typing the exact phrase, surrounded by quotation marks, that would precede the answer to your question. For example, if you're looking for the most common names in the U.S., your search query should say, "The most common names in the U.S. are"; search engines often understand that quotation marks are a searcher's way of telling it that he wants only to find pages that have this exact string of characters in this exact order.

4. Online searches for information do a great job of helping people answer questions that begin with "Who?" "What?" "Where?" or "When?" They don't do a great job, however, with "Why?" or "How?"

It is important to remember that there are only two kinds of problems that you can encounter when initiating a search: your first search query can be either too broad or too specific. In fact, *every* first search is either too broad or too specific. As you gain confidence and improve the quality of your search queries, you will find that you have adopted the excellent habit of conducting *re*-search.

 ## Tool: Google Web Search

As the starting point for more than 60 percent of the 18 billion Web searches Americans conduct every month, there is no doubt that Google is the 800-pound gorilla of the industry. Its next closest competitor, Yahoo, generates only about 17 percent of searches each month.

Professional researchers and professional online publishers must understand the basics of how Google—and search engines in general—work. Because you, as a journalist, are both an online information seeker *and* an online information publisher, knowing how search engines like Google work is twice as important for you. When you understand how search engines work, you'll be in a better position to discern whether one search result is more reliable than another.

Google, like all search engines, uses two basic components: a crawler and a query processor. A **crawler** allows search engines to find each of the trillions of Web pages on the Internet. The biggest engines do this by "spidering" the Web, or following hyperlinks from one page to the next until they hit a dead end. In order to find newly published Web pages more efficiently, Google and other search engines allow the creators of new sites to submit the locations of their Web pages directly to the crawler. To do this they must access http://www.google.com/addurl/.

A **query processor** goes to work when a user starts a query by typing text into the search engine. The simplest of search engines attempts to match a string of text from the query to an identical string of text on all the pages it has crawled. Complex search engines like Google, however, work harder to interpret the text a searcher inputs. For example, a Google search for "CA" will return results for pages where "CA" appears, but also return results for pages that have the word "California" on them.

The strength of a search engine lies in how it determines the relative strength of all the pages that contain the same string. In fact, search engines take a page from journalism and know that people want to see the most important—or relevant—information first. Every search engine has its own way of using complex programming logic to determine page relevance for a particular search. For the most part, these programming algorithms remain a secret, both because search engine companies don't want their competitors to steal their programming and because they don't want to be manipulated by online publishers trying to trick query processors into thinking their sites are more relevant than they are.

Tutorials on advanced Google search tools and techniques

Google says it determines relevance in part by examining the "fonts, subdivisions and the precise location of each word" in a Web document. For example, boldfaced words and headlines are presumably more important than photo captions that appear in a smaller font.

Hone Your Search

Many journalists will tell you that the best part about their profession is that they're always learning something new. The best journalists exhibit a heightened curiosity about unfamiliar subjects. These days, the first place we turn when we want to learn about a new subject is the Internet. Whether it is a bartender looking for a new drink recipe, a new parent trying to learn about the latest trends in car seat safety or an adult child whose parent has just been diagnosed with cancer, the Web is a frequent first stop for people in need of information. The Web is square one.

For many people, square one is just fine. But journalists must dig deeper. They tap into their fount of curiosity and take their searches further. So, when a first search turns up millions of pages that may or may not be relevant, a journalist must pursue a specific strategy for homing in on her target.

When you are looking for information on a topic that's new to you, you'll want to start with a broad overview. Only after you have familiarized yourself with the broadest aspects of your topic can you then delve into the specifics. For this kind of search, you'll use more generic terms, or maybe even start your research by browsing a specific site you trust to see whether it has information on your topic.

A first search on an unusual topic should be perhaps no more than one single noun that most closely describes the topic about which you want information. Let's say, for example, that you're curious about the situation of Sudanese refugees in the United States. Within this topic there are really two topics—"Sudan" and "refugees in the United States." In order to write this story, you're going to need to understand the situation in Sudan as well as the legal and social issues that impact refugees in the United States. Your initial search query, then, should be simply the single word "Sudan":

| sudan | Search |

Your next search query might be "'United States' refugees":

"United States" refugees	Search

Notice how the words "United" and "States" are placed inside quotation marks. Doing this tells the search engine that you are asking for these specific words in this specific order. For terms such as "United States" Google automatically treats both words as a single search string, given that you have placed them next to each other in a specific order. Not only will Google automatically convert the two words to a single string, it will also search for pages containing "US" and "U.S."

Not all search engines will group words automatically. For example, on Yahoo the search query

"United States" refugees	Search

will yield different results from a search where the quotation marks have been omitted:

United States refugees	Search

Even Google will not always group words together in the way you intend. On Google, each of the following searches will give you slightly different results:

- United States Sudan refugees
- Sudan refugees United States
- "Sudan refugees" United States
- United States "Sudan refugees"

The point here is that it is good to get into the habit of honing your searches by placing quotation marks around words that you want to find on a page only if they're in a specific order.

Why do search engines get so confused when you have two words that aren't within quotation marks? Because they aren't smart enough to know whether you are looking for pages that have both the word "Sudan" AND the word "refugees," or if you're looking for pages that have either the word "Sudan" OR the word "refugees."

Some search engines treat words like "AND" and "OR" as a **logical operator**. Lexis-Nexis, a private subscription database that includes newspaper articles and television transcripts, is a prominent example of a search engine that requires the very specific use of logical operators to narrow a search. Google assumes that searchers always intend to search for pages that contain all of the words in the search query. With each additional term you add to a query in Google, you are narrowing your search and homing in on a specific target. In the next section of this chapter, we will look more closely at how to use the OR connector in Google to make sure you don't miss anything.

As you home in on your target, you will want each successive search to be more specific. For example, as part of your initial searches for information about Sudanese refugees in the United States, you discover that Omaha, Neb., is home to the country's largest concentration of Sudanese refugees. So you may want to focus on that information by adding the word "Omaha" to a search.

Or, maybe you find that there are quite enough stories already about the Sudanese refugees in Omaha; you decide instead to write about refugees in a less-covered city. You can narrow your search so that you exclude all pages that mention Omaha. In some search engines (Lexis-Nexis is one) this is done by using the logical operator NOT before the word you want to exclude. In Google, you place the minus sign before the word you want to exclude:

"Sudan refugees" United States -Omaha	Search

Let's consider another example of a search in which you'd want to have a good strategy for homing in on your target. Perhaps you're doing a story about property taxes in the town of Oak Grove. To get started, you type in the following:

property taxes Oak Grove	Search

This is "Googlese" for "Find me all pages that are relevant to the words 'property,' and 'taxes,' and 'Oak' and 'Grove.' Then, after you do that, rank the pages so that the ones that are most relevant and that have the best reputation are at the top of the list."

But wait. Did you want all pages about "property in Oak Grove" *and* also all pages about "taxes in Oak Grove"? Or did you want all pages about "property taxes" in "Oak

Grove"? Did you want to try to calculate the "property" "taxes" on your "grove" of "oak" trees? The only way Google will know how you want to narrow your search is for you to speak its language.

Now, which "Oak Grove" are you talking about? "Oak Grove" is one of the most common city names in America, so you'll need a way to tell Google which Oak Grove you mean. By adding to your search a word that's unlikely to be on pages you don't want, you'll be able to focus on the pages most likely to be ones you do want. In this case, if you add the postal abbreviation for the state in which your particular Oak Grove is located you will likely eliminate irrelevant search returns for pages related to all the Oak Groves you do not want. How else could you change this search to home in on your topic?

Make Sure You Haven't Missed Anything

Good reporters clearly describe what they see. But great reporters wonder what they aren't seeing. Homing in on your target will help you make sure you're getting as much detail as possible about your subject. But you're not done with your re-search until you make one last pass to ensure you haven't missed anything.

You have already been introduced to one of the easiest tools you'll use to make sure you haven't missed anything—the logical operator "OR." If you were doing a story about the spread of the H1N1 virus in South America, you might want to type in the following search query:

> "South America" H1N1 OR "swine flu"   Search

By adding the string "swine flu" to your search, you'll also find pages that use the popular but inaccurate name for the virus.

Do you notice a problem with this search? It's in English, right? But what's the dominant language of the region in which you're interested? Spanish. So, to address this aspect of your search you might want to expand your search by typing in the following:

> "South America" h1n1 OR "swine flu" OR "la influenza porcina" OR "gripe porcina"   Search

As you begin to search in languages other than English, you will become more familiar with a problem that can arise even when searching English-only sites: people don't always spell words the same way. When the leader of Cairo's Al Azhar University, the oldest and most prestigious center of learning in the Sunni Muslim world, died in 2010 most major American and European news organizations spelled his name "Mohamed Sayed Tantawi."

A search for "Tantawi" turned up 434,000 hits in Google. But some pages, including Wikipedia's, refer to him as "Tantawy." Searching for one spelling but not the other would have caused you to miss an additional 129,000 pages. But there was yet another spelling of the sheikh's name that turned up more than these two searches combined. What was it? It was "طنطاوی"—Tantawi's name in the Arabic characters of his native language. Of course, this doesn't do you any good unless you read Arabic. But at least you'll know that you might be missing quite a lot, and you'll have the power to make a decision about whether these pages are important to your story.

Foreign names aren't the only way a name query can prove challenging. Take as an example President Barack Obama. Until he was in college, he went by the name Barry Obama. Individuals can often be identified with more than one name. In the case of President Obama, you might type in the following search query:

Obama Barry OR Barack	Search

Some search engines utilize a tool known as the **"wildcard operator."** In card games, the wildcard is a card that can be used as a substitute for a card of any other value. In searches, a wildcard operator stands in for one or more words or characters. One common wildcard operator is the asterisk. If the search engine you are using employs the wildcard operator, you could modify your search query as follows:

Bar* Obama	Search

Unfortunately, the wildcard operator in Google will only replace whole words. For example, if you wanted to know Obama's middle name you might type in

Barack * Obama	Search

One last step you might want to take before declaring your re-search complete is to look for pages that are similar in some way to the most useful pages you've already found. You can do this by trying to find pages that link to the pages you've already found. With Google, this is done by typing the term "link:" in front of the Web address of a page you've found useful.

A search query that would request all pages linking to the Spanish language pages about H1N1 on the website of the Centers for Disease Control and Prevention would appear as follows:

```
link:http://espanol.cdc.gov/enes/h1n1flu/|          Search
```

One of the toughest things about conducting re-search is to know when you are done. If your re-search goal is to verify a fact, you might decide to call it quits after you find two independent and authoritative sites that confirm the fact. But what if you conduct a search—or 15 or 1,500—to confirm a fact but fail to find two good sources that agree? Can you then infer that the fact is wrong because you can't verify it on the Internet? No, you can't. As the old saying goes, just because you've never seen a black swan doesn't mean that one doesn't exist.

VIEW SOURCE

FINDING NEVERLAND—MICHAEL JACKSON ON THE DEEP WEB

It is easy to find the King of Pop on the Web. Google says there are 127 million pages about Michael Jackson. But finding information about his former home—the famed Neverland Ranch in California—is a bit more difficult.

While search engines are able to crawl through billions of documents on the Web, there are many more billions that they are not able to access. Initial estimates of the size of the **Deep Web**—also known as the Invisible Web—put it at hundreds of times larger than that part of the Web that can be accessed by search engines. The Deep Web contains two types of information: (1) information that is hidden in databases and displayed on a Web page only at the moment someone requests it, and (2) information that is intentionally kept private by its publishers.

It's not difficult to find the street address of Neverland Ranch on the public Web: 5225 Figueroa Mountain Rd., Los Olivos, CA 93441. But if you want to know how much the property is worth, you'll have to visit the Deep Web. Most counties maintain a database of the tax values of all real estate within their boundaries, but a simple search of the Neverland address doesn't turn up its property tax record.

You might think that online databases that store property tax records are analogous to stacks of 8.5-by-11 pieces of notebook paper—that is, to a collection of static documents. But in reality online records are a collection of dynamic database queries written in a programming language such as **SQL (structured query language).** Programmed queries pull information from a database only at

VIEW SOURCE

the moment it is requested. Think of an airline ticket or a hotel reservation. The prices and availability of these products change constantly, so the websites that sell them need to be able to instantly and continually update their inventories. Their pages are generated dynamically, or "on the fly." Search engine crawlers cannot reach these pages and analyze their content because the content is always changing. This kind of dynamically generated page is part of the Deep Web.

A good strategy for finding information that is generated dynamically by database queries is to do a search of the public Web for the word "database" along with the general topic you're researching. For example, to go back to the tax records of Neverland, you could type in the following:

| santa barbara county property tax assessment database | Search |

This search query results in a link to a database where you can search the property tax bills in the county: http://taxes.co.santa-barbara.ca.us/propertytax/ptcriteria.asp?Report=Tax+Bill+Search&ReturnTo=taxbillsearch.asp. A search of this database using the Neverland address leads you to the following page: http://taxes.co.santa-barbara.ca.us/propertytax/taxbill.asp?FiscalYear=2008&ParcelNumber=13312040008. There, you find that the value of the property in 2008 was $19,366,401.

Santa Barbara County also maintains a database with more detailed information about property tax bills, including information about delinquency and dates that property owners paid tax bills. It is found at https://mytaxes.sbtaxes.org/PropTax/default.aspx. Because the county stipulates that this site is available only for noncommercial use, users must register with a user name and password to access the site. These pages, then, are also hidden from the public Web. Search engine crawlers cannot automatically log onto the site, and if they could there would certainly be legal questions about what search engine companies might do with the information if they were able to retrieve it.

FIND SOURCES ON SOCIAL MEDIA

If part of a journalist's job is to distinguish newsworthy information from that being amassed online by anyone who has an axe to grind or a product to sell—and it definitely *is* part of a journalist's job—then perhaps an even bigger part of the job is to help find and ask questions of people who sometimes don't want to be found.

Using social networks to find good sources for stories is nothing new. It's the reason journalists used to hang out in the bars frequented by cops and city hall politicians. It's the reason reporters would go door-to-door in the neighborhood of a murder victim. This is good ol' fashioned shoe-leather reporting, which the rise of online social networks has made easier in some respects and more treacherous in others.

When people use services like MySpace, Facebook, LinkedIn and Twitter, they are revealing a lot about their connections to other people and to institutions. Journalists are learning to mine these connections for quick answers. After reporters at The Washington Post used Facebook to find sources for stories about the mass shooting at Virginia Tech in 2007, the newspaper's executive editor, Leonard Downie Jr., noted, "Now we know that reaching people on the Internet is like knocking on doors."

On the downside, remember our New Yorker cartoon? As major league baseball manager Tony LaRussa can tell you, it is much easier to fake an identity on the information superhighway than inside a house on a sleepy suburban cul-de-sac. LaRussa brought and later settled a lawsuit against Twitter after an imposter operated an account in LaRussa's name. More than 15 years after that prescient New Yorker cartoon, it is still true that, on the Internet at least, nobody can tell whether you're a dog—or a major league manager.

Tool: Twitter

Since its inception in 2006, Twitter has seen rapid growth as a source of news and information for Americans—particularly Americans under age 30. However, if you're one of the 66 percent of people in their late teens and 20s who hasn't yet used it, the best way to describe it might be as a platform that combines blogging with text messaging and social networking.

The election year 2008 saw a marked increase in the use of Twitter to relate information about candidates and issues to voters. Democratic contender Barack Obama's campaign was notable for its innovative use of Twitter. Globally, Twitter is packing a punch as well. In June 2009, Iranians protesting disputed election results in their country used Twitter to inform a global audience about street clashes with government forces. Twitter is even making an appearance in legislative assemblies; in Australia, during an August 2009 floor speech, Prime Minister Kevin Rudd referenced comments posted via Twitter by Sky News political editor David Speers.

Many news organizations are using Twitter as a way to distribute breaking news headlines and post links back to full stories on the news organizations' websites. A few enterprising reporters have begun to use Twitter to find, follow and engage with sources. Twitter's expanding role in news reporting means that *every* journalist should know enough about Twitter to be able to search for sources and access information.

Tutorial on finding and following potential sources on Twitter

Find a Person Who Might Know Something

Watch television news channels like ESPN or CNN for a few minutes and you are likely to encounter segments that feature quotes from blogs. These segments have their heritage in a technique that has long been a staple of traditional journalism—the "man-on-the-street" interview. Journalists have always sought to amplify voice and summarize public opinion by looking for cogent and compact quotes from people who are not in positions of power.

The Washington Post and U.S. News & World Report were among several news organizations that turned to Facebook when news of the mass shooting on the campus of Virginia Tech broke in April 2007. Post reporter Jose Antonio Vargas saw a student who had survived the attack interviewed on television. With the student's name, Vargas searched for his profile on Facebook and found it. Vargas contacted the student via Facebook and asked for an interview. Just hours after surviving the attack, the student checked his account, saw the message from the reporter and agreed to do a 20-minute interview over the phone.

At U.S. News & World Report, Chris Wilson had graduated from the University of Virginia just two years earlier. After the shooting, a friend of his conducted a search for anyone who had both "Columbine High School" and "Virginia Tech" in his or her profile. Although the Columbine shootings had occurred eight years earlier, the search came up with a match—Regina Rohde. Rohde had been in her first year at Columbine in 1999 and was a graduate student at Virginia Tech in 2007. Wilson used Facebook to send a message to Rohde and set up a telephone interview for a story he posted on the U.S. News website later that same day. "While Facebook appears to have since changed its search options somewhat, the basic lesson is the same: When information is well organized by subject, as it is on Facebook, it is tremendously easier to unearth strange connections and unlikely stories," Wilson said.

As in offline social networks, the ways that online social networks can be navigated are always changing. Meg Smith, a researcher at The Washington Post, told a group of journalists in 2008 that while she had once been able to find teenagers on social networks by searching for anyone who listed their age as 99 years old—a favorite lie of underage online denizens—she now no longer can. Social networks put a stop to the ability to search by ages greater than 68 in an effort to thwart child predators. Smith also noted that she had used a Facebook group to find the names of teenage congressional pages to interview during the scandal related to sexually explicit messages that had been sent to pages by Rep. Mark Foley. The Facebook group has since gone offline.

Some reporters monitor profiles on high school and college student pages when they receive news that a student at a particular campus has died. Names of victims are often not immediately released by the police, but reporters who watch online social networks have been able to see how news of the death makes its way around a school before information on it is released to the public. Often, people will put "RIP" and the name of the dead student in their profile or status updates on Facebook or MySpace. Immediately after the 2007 massacre at Virginia Tech, students quickly joined the group "I'm OK at VT" to let their friends know that they were safe.

Twitter is a useful tool for monitoring a breaking news story that is impacting several places at once. During weather crises, for example, news organizations and ad hoc social networks use Twitter to monitor specific road conditions or the flood status of different locations around a city. The outbreak of the H1N1 "swine flu" in 2009 saw more than 10,000 Twitter updates per hour on the topic, many of which contained inaccurate information fueled by uncertainty about the seriousness of the virus. And, as noted above, in Iran in 2009 Twitter proved invaluable as a disseminator of first-hand information about the violence that followed the contested national election. Social networks were particularly important because journalists at the time were being confined to their hotels or even kicked out of the country.

Online social networks are also a good place to monitor political movements and even legal disputes. Journalists can watch how advocates on either side of an issue seek to sway the public's perception in their favor. During the 2008 presidential campaign, Facebook was home to groups both supporting and opposing specific candidates. Prospective candidates continue to use social networks to test the waters, often engaging with groups that sponsor "draft the candidate" sites. In several cases, the sponsors of these groups can be traced back to operatives closely associated with the prospective candidates themselves.

On Twitter, organizers use keywords—known on Twitter as hashtags—to mobilize supporters. When you look at a Twitter message, a **hashtag** is the word or words preceded by the # symbol. For example, opponents to a North Carolina tax on Amazon.com affiliates in the state used the #ncaffiliatetax hashtag. On the day in 2009 that opponents to a federal stimulus bill gathered in cities around the country, they used the #teaparty hashtag on their Twitter posts, and it quickly became one of the most-searched terms on Twitter that day.

But while widely used social networks such as Twitter, Facebook and MySpace might be the first stop on your hunt for someone who might be able to shed light on a story you're reporting, they shouldn't be your last stop. Since the explosion in the last decade of blogs and sites that allow people to upload and share photos and videos, millions of Americans have used these tools to make public their personal experiences. Since some of these personal experiences can add depth and detail to your reporting, they're worth exploring. But because there are so many, you have to have an efficient strategy for quickly finding what is relevant to your story on amateur personal publishing platforms.

Before you go "blog diving," consider a preliminary search through online discussion groups hosted by popular services such as Google or Yahoo. Neighborhoods, parent-teacher organizations and political organizations often use these groups to discuss issues of common interest. Some of the groups are public and can provide journalists with background on a civic debate or crime trend. And because the primary means of interacting with these groups is through e-mail, they tend to attract a broader group of participants that may not be as tech-savvy or self-promotional as people who have the ability and inclination to launch and sustain their own blogs.

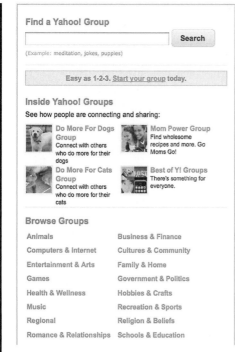

Yahoo groups.

A good place to start when searching blogs is with two search engines that specialize in finding content on blogs. Google has a blog search tool, and the website Technorati has an advanced search page at http://technorati.com/search?advanced. Technorati also offers frequently updated categories that allow you to browse by author, title of posts and general subject.

Your second stop on your hunt for sources' blogs is at one of the two most popular blog services in the United States—Blogger and Wordpress. (Keep in mind, however, that alternate blogging platforms, such as LiveJournal, Hi5 and Maktoob, may be more popular in other countries.) On Wordpress .com (though not on Blogger) you can easily search all blogs that it hosts. The easiest way to do this is to go to http://en.search.wordpress.com/ and type your search term into the form. Although comments are usually less useful to reporters who need verifiable factual information, Wordpress lets users search all comments on blog posts by selecting the "comments" radio button on the Wordpress search page.

Reporters can also browse Wordpress blogs by the subject keywords that each author chooses for his or her blog. An author-chosen keyword is known as a **tag**. The most popular tags can be found at the top of http://en.wordpress.com/tags/. Any word can be a tag, so reporters have to be sure to check synonyms. You can browse all blogs tagged with any word by going to the URL http://en.wordpress.com/tag/[tag]/, where [tag] is the keyword you're seeking. For example, Wordpress blogs about Christianity can be found at http://en.wordpress.com/tag/christianity/.

You'll also need to get used to changing variables in website addresses in order to browse the more useful features on Blogger. You can look for Blogger accounts by geographic location if you know how Blogger's website addresses are constructed. For example, at this URL you will find profiles of all the Blogger accounts registered by people who say they live in Chattanooga, Tennessee: http://www.blogger.com/profile-find.g?t=l&loc0= US&loc1=tn&loc2=Chattanooga. In this example, you can see that the end of the URL contains the variables "loc0," "loc1" and "loc2." The values for loc0 are two-letter country codes. The values for loc1 are two-digit state postal abbreviations, and the values for loc2 are city names.

If you can decipher the codes for all the variables in the URLs, you can also browse by the interests, occupations and industries of bloggers. You can even search out bloggers' favorite movies, songs and books. Following is a list of examples of how to search for a specific category of blogger:

- Interest: t=i&q=, free text search with words joined by "+," http://www.blogger.com/profile-find.g?t=i&q=Chinese+Medicine

- Industry: t=j&ind=, set list of industries, http://www.blogger.com/profile-find.g?t=j&ind=INTERNET

- Occupation: t=o&q=, http://www.blogger.com/profile-find.g?t=o&q=Program+Manager

- Favorite movies: http://www.blogger.com/profile-find.g?t=m&q=Yaoi

- Favorite songs: http://www.blogger.com/profile-find.g?t=s&q=Bring+Me+To+Life+ (Evanescence)

- Favorite books: http://www.blogger.com/profile-find.g?t=b&q=Kiyoshiro+Yumemizu

Once you've found a blogger who looks like a potentially interesting link or source for your story, you'll need to get in touch with the person if you want to conduct an interview. At the very least you'll want to confirm the identity of the blogger, if possible. In the next section of this chapter, you'll learn some techniques for verifying the information you find online. One easy place to start, however, is by looking for the profile pages on each blog you want to use as a link or a source. Blogs on both Blogger and Wordpress contain a default link to the author's profile page in the upper right of the blog's homepage.

Find a Person Who Might Have Seen Something

The growth in blogging has been accompanied by a rapid and continued growth in amateur multimedia, especially photos and videos. Sites and services that people use to share ideas and images are digital haystacks, but a quick search through them just might yield the needle you are looking for. Amateur photos and video can have incredible news value when ordinary people capture extraordinary events like a tornado touching down or a crime in progress. They can also be revealing, shedding light on a person's relationships in a community or capturing a public figure in an unguarded moment.

The most popular photo-sharing site by far is Flickr.com. **Flickr** also has the most sophisticated search features. Searching for images is much more difficult than searching for text because search crawlers can't look at a photo and automatically identify the subject of the image. Photo search depends strongly on the metadata that is attached to the images. In many cases this metadata comes in the form of tags or keywords chosen by the person who has taken the photo.

A good strategy for searching photos is first to search by tag. Then, if your search of tags does not yield sufficient results, you can repeat the query on the full text of photo or video captions. Broad terms are most useful for an initial search of photos. You will likely come up with a large number of hits that can then be browsed for relevant images. These in turn can provide you with additional words that people have used to tag the photos; a search of these may lead to more specific results.

Each photo gallery on Flickr has a link at the top of the page to the profile of its creator. On these profile pages you can find the photographer's "contacts." These are other Flickr users, either people or groups, with whom the person has a connection and who may also have posted photos related to your subject.

Other popular photo-sharing sites are **Shutterfly,** Slide and **Photobucket.** Shutterfly is a good place to search for community photos, especially photos related to schools. Effective search terms on this site would be the name of a school, town or sports league. You can also browse tags, though most of these are so generic they probably won't be of use to a reporter working on a specific story. To conduct a search you would type in http://community .shutterfly.com/gallery/ search/start.sfly; to browse by tags you would type in http://com munity.shutterfly.com/ gallery/tags/start.sfly.

Flickr.

Slide and Photobucket feed many photo elements on popular social networking sites such as MySpace and Facebook. The news value of these images, however, tends to be lower than on Flickr. Images of celebrities or young people at parties are what you typically find. Slide has a nice feature that allows you to search by user name. To do so, type in http://www.slide.com/ search?qry=[name]&safe=on&t=u, where [name] is the name of the user. At Photobucket you can conduct a search by typing in http://photobucket.com/findstuff/.

Google owns two of the biggest video sites on the Web—Google Video search and YouTube. These can be searched by topic or by source using techniques similar to those used to search photo-sharing sites. You may also want to check for amateur video sources on MySpace and **Vimeo.com.**

Find Something Out About a Person You Know

It is not only the "man on the street" who is using personal Web-publishing tools. Powerful people are also on Facebook, Twitter and other online publishing platforms. And inevitably, someone in power makes news—either intentionally, but more often unintentionally—with something they have published to the Web.

Every year, too, major local and national news stories force into the headlines people who shared information about themselves online but who never expected to become newsworthy. Whether it's the man who impregnated the daughter of a vice presidential candidate, the woman who is having a secret affair with the governor of New York or a college student who is tragically murdered, these people have often been quietly living online and building a semipublic record of relationships and thoughts that help journalists quickly build profiles when they become "news."

During the 2008 U.S. presidential campaign, news broke that the unwed daughter of Republican vice presidential candidate Sarah Palin was pregnant. Reporters quickly found the MySpace page of the baby's father, 18-year-old Levi Johnston, and discovered that he was a self-proclaimed "redneck" who didn't want kids and who wasn't shy about using profanity. It wasn't long before the profile was removed from public view. In an interview with the Associated Press a few weeks later, Johnston said the page was a "joke" and that "his friends created the page a few years ago and he had nothing to do with it."

In stark contrast, Ashley Alexandra Dupré, the prostitute whose liaisons with former New York governor Eliot Spitzer led to his resignation, retained her MySpace page online at http://www.myspace.com/ninavenetta even after news broke of Spitzer's dalliance. The New York Times quoted liberally from it in a profile of Dupré.

Simply searching social networks for the name of the person about whom you want more information can give you the pages you want. In some cases, however, people don't publish under their real names. If you can't find a person by searching for their name, you could try using an e-mail address. In a sense, a person's e-mail address is a bit like a Social Security number—a key piece of information that serves as a unique identifier.

If you don't have a person's e-mail address, there are a few places to look for it. First, try the website of the organizations for which they work or to which they belong. Many organizations have a "Contact" or "About Us" page that lists key people. Some of these pages include e-mail addresses. Another place to look would be on online discussion forums on Google Groups or Yahoo Groups. People often engage in these forums by sending e-mails to them. When they do that, they may leave a trace of their e-mail addresses. The final place to look for an e-mail address is on social networks themselves. If you're fortunate enough to have found a person's e-mail address on one page—for example, on your subject's Facebook "Info" page—then you may be able to use that e-mail address to connect to the subject's activity on other social networks.

The reason that e-mail addresses are so helpful is that social networks allow you to search for members by e-mail address. Some even automatically scour your entire list of e-mail contacts to find the online profiles of people whom you already know. Also, having a subject's e-mail address increases the likelihood that the online profile you find was actually created by that person and not by an imposter.

Once you have evidence of a person's behavior on a social network, be sure to look at the user name of the person. If you are able to find the pseudonym that your subject uses in one online social network, check other networks to see if the same handle is being used there. Unless they are really leading multiple lives, most people don't like to try and keep up with multiple login names. In 2006, the true identity of "Lonelygirl15," an actress posing as a 16-year-old girl in a series of YouTube videos, was unmasked by a teenage sleuth who conducted a Web-wide search for the pseudonym.

You also may be able to use a person's screen name to find his or her blog or to identify additional online activity related to the person. Sometimes people use a consistent online pseudonym as the names of their blogs. The Web addresses of all blogs on Blogger follow the pattern "http://[BlogName].blogger.com"; all blogs on Wordpress follow the similar pattern "http://[BlogName].wordpress.com."

Other online communities use screen names as well. **Delicious.com** is a site that people use to save links to the Web pages in which they're interested. The comments that people save along with their bookmarked Web pages often reveal your subjects' thoughts about the topics. If you know the pseudonym that someone is using on his or her Delicious account, you can find the person's public, though not private, bookmarks at http://delicious.com/[UserName].

Amazon.com does a comprehensive job of tracking its users—their preferences, activities and connections. And because many Amazon users don't make their activity on the site private, you may not even require a screen name to access information. A simple search on Google for "amazon profile [first name] [last name]" may turn up the public profile of your subject's book reviews, wish lists and other public activity on Amazon. Former House Speaker Newt Gingrich showed up in The Washington Post's gossip column in 2000 when reporters found the online gift registry for his wedding to a former House staffer 22 years his junior.

Finally, you may be able to use someone's **UID,** or unique ID, on a social network to aid in peeling back the onion of his online profile. A UID is a unique number, usually running to about nine digits, that social networks assign to each of its members in order to better organize information about them. You can often see each person's UID in the URL of any page that is related to that person on a social network. Find it once and you may be able to use the number to guess the URLs of other parts of a member profile, such as photos and groups. For example, Levi Johnston's ID on MySpace was 410187364.

Here's an example of how UIDs look in the Web addresses on three popular social networks. The UID is in bold in each:

http://www.facebook.com/profile.php?id=**692928528**;

http://www.linkedin.com/ppl/webprofile?vmi=&id=**6388496**;

http://www.myspace.com/**254959367**.

Contact Sources Using Social Media

Big stories happen in small towns all the time. Whether the story is about a Midwestern town that has been leveled by a tornado, or a mystery that surrounds an unsolved murder at a military base, reporters from national media "parachute" onto the scene and scramble to find sources at the police station, in a downtown coffee shop or around a victim's neighborhood. But the best reports about the situation—the stories with the most detail and nuance—are put together by the staffs of the local television station and newspaper. Why? Because these reporters live in the community. They already have established relationships with sources.

The same principle applies to mining social networks for sources. A journalist's access to reliable sources on social media is strengthened with every day she has spent engaging the people in her network. When a big story breaks, it is too late to parachute into a social network and expect the same kind of results that a reporter who has been living in the community can expect. One of the first rules of traditional reporting applies as well to digital social networks: cultivate your sources *before* you need them.

At the very least, you can create your own network of readers and sources just by collecting their e-mail addresses and a few bits of key information, suggests Ken Sands, an online editor at Bloomberg Government.

When you create a profile on a social network with the intention of using it as a professional reporting tool, decorate it as if it were your cubicle in the newsroom. Feel free to put up a picture of yourself and include posts about your sincere interests, whether on cooking or sports or music. These authentic messages may have little to do with the stories you're reporting, but they send a signal that you're a real person who is accessible, even trustworthy; they can also serve as conversation-starters with potential sources. Just don't post that picture of yourself at the beach!

Or your favorite dirty joke. Anything you post on a social network contributes to your professional as well as personal reputation. Readers and sources will research you the same way you research them. Comments or photos you post online become a part of your permanent personal record. Inappropriate or ill-advised posts can haunt you long after you put them up. Make an off-color remark at the top of your lungs one night in a bar and in most cases the impact of the moment passes quickly. Make an off-color remark on Facebook one night after coming home from the bar and that moment can be replayed online for years to come by people you may not even have known at the time you posted it.

The way that messages spread quickly through social networks—especially Twitter—is particularly valuable to journalists. It used to be that reporters looking for sources might post a note in the newspaper or on their website. Those notes would reach only the people who saw them in their original location. But by putting out source requests on a social network, your friends can share the request with their friends who can share it with their friends who can share it with their friends and so on—essentially, there is no limit to the number of people a request can reach.

The time will come when you are ready to use social networking to get in touch with a source for a story. When you conduct an interview online or use social media to set up a telephone or face-to-face meeting with a potential source, follow these tips:

1. Identify yourself as a reporter working on a story. Many people unfamiliar with the news media don't understand that journalists assume all communication between a reporter and a source is on the record unless the reporter and source agree otherwise beforehand.

2. You can consider anything you find on a social media site to be on the record. Don't be afraid to hold powerful people accountable for their online behavior. There is usually no reason to let someone retract or change a newsworthy quote that you receive over social media, but be reasonable and give your source every opportunity to clarify the comment, or express regret for posting it. Give them the opportunity to say whether they still feel the way they did when they posted the comment.

3. When contacting sources via social media for the first time, be formal and polite. Potential sources should have no question that you are a professional and that you respect their time and circumstances. Separated by a computer screen and accustomed to sending short text notes to our friends, it can be easy to forget that the usual tone of our casual online conversations can send the message that we are sloppy, perhaps even rude. Either of these two perceptions will likely kill any hope of clinching an interview.

4. When you first contact a potential source, provide all of your contact information and the best times to reach you. Many people are concerned about giving their private information over the Internet. Allay their fears by letting them come to you.

5. Demonstrate that you've already done your basic homework by asking one very specific question that highlights your depth of knowledge about the subject. People love to teach journalists about themselves and their areas of expertise. But they resent being asked questions that could be answered by a simple Web search.

6. Provide links to your professional profile or to previous work you have done, especially if it is on a similar topic. These links should show that you are a well-trained professional reporter and that you are sincere and careful.

Finally, consider the serious risks of using any information from a social network that cannot be verified at least with a phone call to the source or, preferably, with a face-to-face conversation. In 2009, a former lobbyist for Wachovia caused confusion when a reporter writing a story used a profile of the lobbyist on the LinkedIn social network. The profile said that the lobbyist had once worked for the governor of North Carolina. He hadn't. But the information went into the journalist's story as fact. The lobbyist later denied that he was trying to inflate his resume, saying only that he didn't realize he even had a profile on

LinkedIn. Regardless of the reason the incorrect information was on the lobbyist's profile, once the reporter used the information in his story *he* became responsible for its inaccuracy.

SORT OUT THE FACTS

As we've seen time and again, the Internet is full of information—some of it accurate and some of it not. As a journalist, your credibility and influence depend on your ability to distinguish the good information from the bad. While Google and other search engines use some 500 million variables in their attempts to give you the most relevant and reputable sources of information, you can't leave the pursuit of truth up to an algorithm. In thinking about the challenge of finding valid information on the Web, start with skepticism. As with the content of a paper document or the statements of a phone interviewee, you need always to ask yourself not only *if* inaccuracies are being conveyed, but *why?* Why might inaccurate information get on the Web?

Who Created a Website?

You can tell a lot about a website from its name, specifically its **domain name.** A domain name is usually the URL of a site's homepage, such as cnn.com or nytimes.com. Each domain name is controlled by one, and only one, entity. Website publishers create domain names when they pay to register them with a company that specializes in this type of licensing. These domain-registering companies—indeed, all computers on the Web—share a common directory of domain names. As such, a user request for a document on a specific domain will transmit through the appropriate computer network.

A name can't always be trusted, however. In 1993, Adam Curry, a host of a video music show on MTV, paid to register and control the domain name mtv.com. When Curry left the company, MTV sued its former employee for the return of its name. Curry handed it over as part of a settlement, and he now appears online at curry.com.

In addition to searching for the registrant of a domain name, journalists can also simply look for a contact phone number or address on a website. People and organizations that prominently publish contact information on their websites typically allow journalists to verify information in person or over the phone.

 Tool: WhoIs ───

How do we know that Adam Curry runs the site at curry.com—and that he doesn't run the website at mtv.com? We can search the database that matches domain names with computers and their owners. The database is called WhoIs and can be accessed from several different websites. A good one to start with is http://www.internic.net/whois.html, operated by the Internet Company for Assigned Names and Numbers (ICANN).

A search for "curry.com" on Internic's WhoIs server yields this result:

```
Whois Server Version 2.0

Domain names in the .com and .net domains can now be registered
with many different competing registrars. Go to http://www.internic.net
for detailed information.

Domain Name: CURRY.COM
Registrar: NETWORK SOLUTIONS, LLC.
Whois Server: whois.networksolutions.com
Referral URL: http://www.networksolutions.com
Name Server: NS97.WORLDNIC.COM
Name Server: NS98.WORLDNIC.COM
Status: clientTransferProhibited
Updated Date: 26-feb-2010
Creation Date: 06-jun-1994
Expiration Date: 05-jun-2015

>>> Last update of whois database: Sun, 21 Mar 2010 01:44:29 UTC <<<
```

Internic's WhoIs server shows that the curry.com domain was registered on June 6, 1994, and that Network Solutions is the registrar.

```
Registrant:
Curryco, Ltd.
Keizersgracht 499
Amsterdam, NH 1017 DM
NL

Domain Name: CURRY.COM
```

Promote your business to millions
Learn how you can get an Enhanced Busir

```
Administrative Contact :
Curry, Adam
dnsadmin@mevio.com
463 Bryant Street
San Francisco, CA 94107
US
Phone: 415-519-6150
Fax: 973-857-9612

Technical Contact :
Network Solutions, LLC.
customerservice@networksolutions.com
13861 Sunrise Valley Drive
Herndon, VA 20171
US
Phone: 1-888-642-9675
Fax: 571-434-4620

Record expires on 07-Jun-2015
Record created on 06-Jun-1994
Database last updated on 26-Feb-2010
```

The WhoIs directory at Network Solutions provides some potentially useful contact information for the owner of the curry.com domain.

The search yields some information, but it doesn't tie Curry to the site. Instead, it points us to the **registrar**—the name of the company Curry paid to register his site. In this case, you can see that the registrar is at http://www.networksolutions.com/. The WhoIs database search for that registrar is at http://www.networksolutions.com/whois/index.jsp.

A search for "curry.com" on the **Network Solutions** site gives us a lot more information, including Curry's address and phone number, or at least those he gave when the site was registered. You'll see both a technical and administrative registrant for curry.com. In many cases these are different. The administrative registrant is the owner of the site.

Unfortunately, the WhoIs directory does not contain the names of all owners of all websites. The WhoIs database does not include listings of the people who control the subdomains at popular blogging services such as Wordpress or Blogger, nor does it list people who have private accounts that are listed as subdirectories on a Web server. A search of WhoIs, for example, could not verify whether the Los Angeles Times actually controls the account on the Flickr photo-sharing site at http://www.flickr.com/photos/latimes/.

Also, many website domain name registrars allow clients to hide their true identities by populating the WhoIs database with the generic contact information of the registration company itself rather than the person who is actually responsible for the content on the site.

(Q) Online Module 6

Screencast on navigating WhoIs

On Wikipedia—the top result for many search queries—the person who made an edit to a page can be hard to determine. If the person has not registered with Wikipedia, then the system records only the **IP address**—Internet Protocol address—of the computer from which the edit was made. While it can be difficult to trace an IP address back to a specific person, it can be done. Journalists and computer programmers have won awards for using IP addresses to uncover that some businesses and politicians were making inaccurate, anonymous edits to their own pages on Wikipedia.

When users do register with Wikipedia, they are not required to use their real names. But whatever pseudonym they choose does follow them across all of their activity on the site. Some Wikipedia users register with more than one pseudonym, even though Wikipedia tries to prevent this.

Wikipedia users can create profile pages for themselves on the site. You can find a person's profile by clicking on a user name in any article's history page. There is no standard template for a profile page, however. Nor is the information contained on profile pages ever vetted.

Why Was a Site Created?

People tend to act in their own self-interest, so it makes sense that websites reflect the interests of the person or organization that created them. For example, in the important area of health and medicine, manufacturers of drugs and dietary supplements publish websites in order to make their best arguments about the value of their products. Government agencies and independent researchers also use the Web to discuss their perspectives on the best treatments for various diseases and conditions. In a search result for a query on a specific drug or disease name, links to pharmaceutical companies will be commingled with links to government and academic sources. It is not unreasonable to assume that companies in the business of making money are going to highlight the information about their products that will help them make the most money. Sometimes this information is accurate, complete and a valuable resource for consumers. Sometimes it is incomplete, misleading and downright dangerous.

Websites offer disputants in a controversy a platform on which to air their claims. For example, in a 2004 book journalist Bob Woodward wrote about the Bush administration's activities leading up to the U.S.-led invasion of Iraq. The book included a portion of Woodward's interview with then Secretary of Defense Donald Rumsfeld. During the interview, Rumsfeld said that he had told the Saudi ambassador to Washington in January 2003 that he could "take that to the bank" that the invasion would happen.

Rumsfeld denied that he had ever said such a thing. The Defense Department posted on its website a transcript of Rumsfeld's conversation with Woodward as proof that the book was wrong. The only problem was that Woodward had made his own transcript, and it showed that the version posted online by the Defense Department had left out the relevant portion of the interview. Rumsfeld claimed that the portion in question had been omitted because he had wanted the comments there to remain off the record. In mid-2010, the official transcript on the Defense Department website still did not include the missing portion of the interview.

When Was a Site Created?

On April 17, 1973, President Richard Nixon's press secretary stood before a group of reporters who were grilling him amid the unfolding Watergate scandal. The administration was preparing to admit something that both Nixon and his press secretary had long denied—that people on the White House payroll were involved in the scandal. In an effort to avoid saying that he and the president had been misleading the press, Ron Zeigler explained, "The president refers to the fact that there is new material. Therefore this is the operative statement. The others are inoperative."

When you find a Web page, you may be looking at information that was true—or not—when it was printed. But if the page is too old, that is, to use Zeigler's creative sidestep, if there is "new material," then you may be looking at a page that is in fact "inoperative." Outdated information abounds on the Web. It is important for journalists to remember that one of the strengths of the Web—the availability of vast archives of news reports and source documents—can also be one of its weaknesses.

Look for date stamps on news articles you find online. The publication date of a story is often either at the very top or the very bottom of the page. If you can't find a timestamp in the article itself, try looking through the HTML code. Sometimes in the header section you can find metadata that indicates the date on which an article was originally published. Also, look for any indication that the version of the article you are seeing is the most recent. You may be seeing a new version that has removed the information you expected to find there. Or, you may be seeing an outdated version of a story that has been updated elsewhere on the site.

When dealing with newspaper or magazine articles, be aware that the date it was first published online may be different than the date it was published in the print version. Finally, beware of websites that use your computer's clock to timestamp their articles. This practice can make it appear as if an article was just published when in fact it was not.

Wikipedia articles all have a "history" page that chronicles each instance a change was entered. If you suspect that information on Wikipedia is wrong, you can compare the time and date that the suspect information was added to the article with the time and date on other sources that may offer conflicting information. Especially suspect are Wikipedia edits that are either very old or very new. Wikipedia has been known to break news before it reaches CNN—it's just that the "news" is not always true.

What Are the Site's Sources?

There is no requirement that people who publish information online attempt to verify the information they publish. In 2005, Bill Moyers, a journalist and former press secretary for

President Lyndon Johnson, gave a speech at Harvard University that contained information he culled from an article on the environmental news website Grist.org. The information was apparently incorrect, but that didn't stop newspapers and websites across the country from repeating the information in their coverage of Moyers' speech.

Trustworthy websites will make the sources of their information clear. The very best will even link their claims directly to the original source document. Links are a great way to determine whether a page is trustworthy.

Trustworthy websites also tend to be linked from other trustworthy sites. You can use the "link:" search operator in Google Web search to scan a list of the other sites that link to your potential source page. You can also use a site called **Backtweets.com** to see who on Twitter is linking to a page. If you see that a lot of other people you already trust are also linking to the page, then you can consider those links endorsements, though not proof, that the information on the page is accurate.

The authority of a page's author in other media is another good way to assess trustworthiness. Once you know who has created a page, it is worth looking to see where else the author has been published or asked to speak.

When using Wikipedia as a source, probably more important than knowing who edited a page is knowing the source that the person used to justify the edit. Wikipedia articles are annotated throughout with numbers set inside brackets. Each of these corresponds to a footnote at the bottom of the page. These footnotes often provide links to the primary source that was used to justify the change.

A word of caution. Documents that journalists would consider a primary source often differ from those a Wikipedia editor might consider a primary source. For example, an editor of Wikipedia might consider a newspaper article that includes references to a leaked memo or an interview quote a primary document. But the newspaper article itself is not the primary source. In fact, it is the leaked memo or the person who offered the quote that is the primary source. A thorough journalist will take the additional step of going all the way back to the true primary source. Attribution in a news story should rarely be to Wikipedia itself. You should attribute the information to the source to which Wikipedia links. (And, of course, you need to visit the source to verify that the Wikipedia editor paraphrased it accurately.)

Tool: Wikipedia

Articles that appear on Wikipedia differ from many other kinds of amateur content on the Web in an important way: they are not primary sources. Journalists should never use them as such. Assuming that the identity of a blogger or other online content creator can be verified, the thoughts and opinions expressed there can be directly attributed to the author. Wikipedia, on the other hand, like all encyclopedias, is meant as a general reference tool. It offers journalists and others a general overview of a topic while pointing them to the primary sources that were used to create the reference article.

Unlike a traditional reference book, however, Wikipedia does not exercise strict editorial control via a small group of authors and editors. Instead, its articles are accessible to any would-be editor, including you. This difference means that Wikipedia's strength is its breadth and comprehensiveness; its main weakness is its vulnerability to unprofessional writing, misinformation and outright lies.

Wikipedia has been known both to spread lies and to reveal information that has been suppressed by other news outlets. For 132 days in 2005, Wikipedia contained groundless allegations that journalist John Seigenthaler Sr. was involved in the assassinations of John and Robert Kennedy.

In 2009, Wikipedia's user-editors tried in vain to report the accurate information that New York Times reporter David Rohde had been kidnapped in Afghanistan. Reporters and editors at The New York Times worked with Wikipedia founder Jimmy Wales to keep the truth about Rohde's kidnapping a secret. According to a New York Times article, "Times executives believed that publicity would raise Mr. Rohde's value to his captors as a bargaining chip and reduce his chance of survival." This kind of decision is certainly understandable coming from news organizations trying to save the lives of staff members. But now Wikipedia's user-editors are having their say in these types of ethical dilemma. After seven months in captivity, Rohde and his translator escaped unharmed.

Wales has said he believes that neither Wikipedia nor any other encyclopedia should be used as a primary source of information. All encyclopedias, he noted, are intended to collect existing knowledge, not create new knowledge. The quality of information of any secondary source is only as good as the primary sources on which it relies. People who participate in the editing of Wikipedia often use the phrase "verifiability, not truth" to express the idea that it is up to Wikipedia's readers to check the accuracy of the content and make their own assessments. To give readers a better chance of doing this, Wikipedia depends on transparency and annotation. Readers must be able to see what changes have been made, at what time and by whom. They must also be able to easily see the primary source that the editor used to justify the change.

Screencast tour of Wikipedia article history page

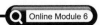

Tutorials on Wikipedia and judging information veracity

There's an old adage in journalism: "If your mother says she loves you, check it out." It's meant to help young reporters understand that no single source—no matter how reliable—is good enough to go unverified. At least one other independent source is required in all instances. The adage could perhaps be updated for the 21st century: "If Wikipedia says it loves you, check it out."

NEWS JUDGMENT

KILLED BY TWITTER, RESURRECTED ON WIKIPEDIA

Jared Fogle, the spokesman for Subway sandwiches, knows firsthand both the positive and negative effects of the democratic nature of online news and information. At JaredRemembered.com, Fogle is the subject of a cruel hoax. According to the site, he died "yesterday" from "abnormal abdominal adhesions resulting from his 1998 gastric bypass surgery." Only one problem—Jared Fogle is not dead.

How could the satire of a single website break through the noise of trillions of Web pages, all competing for attention? One answer is social media. Kevin Rose is one of the founders of Digg.com, a site on which visitors can submit and vote news stories up or down. On June 25, 2008, this guru of social media somehow found JaredRemembered.com and sent out the following message on Twitter: "RIP Jared—http://jaredremembered.com/." Rose is no journalist, but that didn't matter when it came to the size of the platform across which he was able to spread his rumor—the number of people who received this message exceeded the circulation numbers of most newspapers in America.

But people are curious and skeptical. They want to know more. They want to see for themselves. So what did they do? They turned to Google, as you can see:

Google Trends showed a spike in the number of people using the search term "jared fogel."

The popularity of "Jared Fogel" as a search term spiked in the hour after Rose sent out his Twitter message. This is not unusual. Millions of Americans turn to Google as the first stop in their efforts to find out more about a breaking news story. Consider the example of Google search trends on June 24 and June 25, 2009. On June 24, searches related to the news that South Carolina Gov. Mark Sanford had admitted to having an affair in Argentina when his office had said he was hiking the Appalachian Trail were most prevalent. But the next day, June 25, pop singer Michael Jackson and 1970s pinup girl Farrah Fawcett both died, and searches related to their deaths prevailed—along with searches related to rumors (false in this instance) of actor Jeff Goldblum's death.

But let's get back to Jared Fogle. Following are examples of what people might see when they turn to Google to verify the rumor of his death:

The top results for "jared fogel" on Google Web search.

The top result on this term, as on so many search terms, is Wikipedia. On its page for Jared Fogle, his death has been reported and removed several times. Let's check out the "History" page for Fogle's entries. Here's a summary of what happened to the page on June 25, 2008:

- 7:02 p.m.—Fogle is dead.

- 7:10 p.m.—Not quite dead yet.

- 8:42 p.m.—Dead again. At this point someone spends the next 11 minutes adding to the page fantastic details about his death. At one point, however, the anonymous editor seems to doubt his or her technical accuracy. (The possibility of factual inaccuracy never seems to have dawned on this editor.)

- 9:00 p.m.—Fogle is ba-aaack.

- 11:09 p.m., June 26—Another anonymous editor makes a gutsy defense of the 8:42 edits that falsely asserted that Fogle was dead.

- 11:30 p.m.—The truth hasn't been completely restored, but some progress has been made.

- 12:34 a.m., June 27—His death is called a hoax.

- 2:20 a.m., June 28—Someone still wants to duke it out, and edits the page to say that he's dead.

- 2:21 a.m., June 28—After one minute, the error is corrected. The page stays free of the error until July 11, when Fogle briefly dies again in the wiki world.

00:34, 27 June 2008	CJS102793 (talk I contribs)	(9,887 bytes)	*(his death was a hoax)*
00:32, 27 June 2008	CJS102793 (talk I contribs)	(9,956 bytes)	
00:08, 27 June 2008	76.109.81.255 (talk)	(9,955 bytes)	*(fixing spacing error)*
23:30, 26 June 2008	134.71.106.120 (talk)	(9,954 bytes)	
23:09, 26 June 2008	67.87.184.150 (talk)	(10,135 bytes)	*(revert - not vandalism)*
21:00, 25 June 2008	Jarbon (talk I contribs)	(9,890 bytes)	*(rv vandalism)*
20:53, 25 June 2008	97.82.199.28 (talk)	(10,217 bytes)	
20:53, 25 June 2008	97.82.199.28 (talk)	(10,212 bytes)	
20:50, 25 June 2008	97.82.199.28 (talk)	(10,142 bytes)	
20:47, 25 June 2008	97.82.199.28 (talk)	(9,963 bytes)	
20:45, 25 June 2008	97.82.199.28 (talk)	(9,952 bytes)	*(Editing to show his death.)*

The history tab on Jared Fogel's Wikipedia entry shows when and how it was changed.

From spoof website to social media, search engines and Wikipedia, the story of Jared Fogle's alleged demise provides a quick tour through the pitfalls of cultivating quality links and quality sources on a platform where anyone can enjoy the freedom of the press, even if they don't exercise the responsibility that comes with it.

NEWS JUDGMENT

Tool: RSS

In time, you will learn which sources you can turn to again and again for trusted information. The list of sites you track, however, may still be extensive. Journalists commonly read dozens of sites every day. One of the most popular tools they use to keep track of all of these sources is **Really Simple Syndication,** or **RSS.**

RSS was developed and became popular between 1999 and 2003, just at the same time that blogs were growing in popularity. Blogging content management systems and RSS helped speed the disaggregation and diversification of the news media.

RSS is a version of **XML,** or **eXtensible Markup Language.** Many sites automatically publish RSS files—also known as feeds—each time they add new information. When new information is added, a description of it and a link to it appear at the top of the RSS feed.

There are many ways to find RSS feeds. Directories of RSS feeds exist, and you can find them inside popular feed-reading applications. Another way to do it is to visit your favorite website and look for this icon:

Tutorials on subscribing to RSS feeds in Internet Explorer and Firefox and how to use Google Reader and Bloglines

ONLINE LEARNING MODULE 6

ACTIVATE THIS MODULE: journalism.cqpress.com

Throughout the chapter, we looked at how journalists and other professional researchers might approach some hypothetical situations. These examples show that the only way to become an efficient and discerning online information seeker is through experience and a lot of repetition.

On my blog, I frequently highlight examples of journalists who are effectively using social media to strengthen their reporting, and I also post links to new tools for finding and organizing online content related to your beat.

When you buy or activate this chapter's online learning module, you will have access to:

- A digital version of this chapter's text.
- Interactive flashcards for the terms used in this chapter.
- A printable tip sheet outlining how to use social media for reporting.
- A quiz to test your mastery of the material in this chapter.
- Screencast tutorials that provide step-by-step introductions to using advanced Google search techniques as well as instructions for Twitter, Wikipedia, WhoIs and RSS.
- Online exercises that give you hands-on experience using citizen media and social networks for reporting strong stories.

As you complete the module's online exercises, you will:

- Evaluate the accuracy of information in a real-world research question.
- Discover real-world uses of social media by leaders in your own community.
- Apply your knowledge of Twitter and Wikipedia to find reliable sources.
- Use RSS to keep up with news on a beat.

ONLINE LEARNING

CHAPTER 7 LINKING

In this chapter, you will learn how to:

- Select the most accurate, relevant and specific links for your story.
- Choose the right words to serve as a linked departure point from within the text of a story.
- Organize "sidebar" links and write effective departure text for links that appear next to a story.
- Read and manipulate the HTML code that creates links.
- Avoid ethical pitfalls, such as linking to offensive or potentially illegal material.

Brian Palmer is the guy you want to have on your team on trivia night. His friends tell him he has finally found a job that fits his habit of telling them odd little facts about what's happening in the world. Palmer, a one-time lawyer at a large Washington, D.C., firm, is now a freelance contributor to a daily column on Slate.com called The Explainer. Three times a week he spends his day frantically researching and writing 500 to 700 words just slightly off to the side of the big news of the moment.

"The purpose of The Explainer is to answer the unanswered question in the news," Palmer says. With only slight exaggeration he adds, "Questions that are beneath the dignity of a normal reporter to ask. Or questions that are too tangential to end up in a news story." Things like "Why don't figure skaters get dizzy?," which came up during the 2010 Winter Olympics, and "What, exactly, are natural causes?," which came up after actress Brittany Murphy died at age 32.

The columns are drawn from topics in the news, but Palmer's job is to think up and then answer questions that most news consumers didn't even know they had. That means starting work sometime before 7 a.m. First up, Web searches to get the basic facts; then, calls to experts to fill in the gaps and confirm that what he found online is accurate. But while Palmer eventually spends as much as two or three hours interviewing sources for some of his columns, you'll never see quotes from those interviews in The Explainer. Taking the place of the quote—which is a standard feature of most news stories, used in large part to show readers where a reporter got his information—is the **link.** The Explainer uses lots and lots of links.

Palmer and the other Explainer writers add links to their columns for three primary reasons: to explain jargon, to increase the trust of readers, and to better entertain and inform readers. Says Palmer, "The best links are the ones that I think, 'This is fascinating. I can't put this in the piece, but [if I were a reader] I'd love to read this.' Links are put in there for readers who are more curious than the average person."

Palmer begins collecting potential links for his column as soon as he chooses a topic. As he finds interesting or informative pages related to his topic, he saves them in his browser's bookmarks folders—one folder for each column he writes. But not all of the pages he bookmarks are linked to the final column. The links that do make it into the column must be accurate—he links to Wikipedia, for example, only when he is able to confirm the facts with another source—and immediately relevant to the column's topic. He is careful to avoid making people click more than once to find desired information; if he sends them too far away, he knows that they might not come back. Finally, the links have to be what Palmer calls "interesting." It is in the process of crafting interesting links that the hard work and artistry of writing the column come into play.

For a column on what whale meat tastes like, Palmer came across a World War I–era New York Times article that described a U.S. government effort to get Americans psyched about munching on the marine mammal. "I just found it in Google," he says. "But I tend to go much deeper into Google results than most people. I go into page eight, nine, ten."

Palmer didn't just have to work harder than the average Googler. He also had to have an eye for any link **destination** that would reward his readers if they took the time to click. What was it that caught his eye about the government's whale sale? A person in the article who opined that whale meat was "'as delicious a morsel' as the most aesthetic or sophisticated palate could possibly yearn for." These 15 words made it into Palmer's column. And so too did a link to the remaining 1,586 words of the original article.

Crafting good Explainer columns relies as much on choosing the right linking text as on choosing the right links. The linked text should be what Palmer's editor calls "active words." Often, the linked words are a verb and the object of the verb. In the sentence "Federal authorities held a luncheon (PDF) at the American Museum of Natural History in 1918, trying to push whale as a home-front substitute for the beef that our troops craved," Palmer linked the words "held a luncheon." The letters **PDF** tell readers that a **portable document format** will open up when they click on the link.

If The Explainer reports that "a study showed" something, those words get linked to the actual study that is paraphrased in the column. And when Palmer cites a little-known organization or person, those proper names usually get linked as well. "If it's the Justice Department, we wouldn't link to that. But if it were something like the North American Man/Boy Love Association, we would link to that."

But as nice as the links are, for Palmer the writing comes first. He never rewrites a sentence in order to make a link fit better. If there isn't a way to place a link in the text so that the link's destination and purpose are clear, Palmer leaves it out. "I don't like to do the parenthetical," he says. "The piece itself should be able to stand out on its own. It would be the equivalent of if I'm talking to you and every few words I broke my thought in half. . . . It would not be the best way of explaining something. The links are peripheral. And I don't want to add too much info in a confusing way."

At its core, journalism has always been about linking—linking one group of people to another, linking sources to readers. When White House science adviser Vannevar Bush in 1945 imagined and wrote about the ideas that would eventually coalesce as hyperlinks, he characterized the people who would use them as "a new profession of trail blazers, those who find delight in the task of establishing useful trails through the enormous mass of the common record." Part librarian, part investigative reporter—someone like Brian Palmer.

CHOOSING THE RIGHT LINK DESTINATION

Not all links are created equal. Good links make stories more transparent and add depth. Bad links are distracting, misleading and even unethical. In order to be a good journalist, you have to learn how to select and present the right links. But with more than a trillion Web pages of potential destination, how does the journalist choose the right ones?

In journalism, good links have a lot of the same qualities as good human sources. They are accurate, relevant and specific.

Accuracy

Journalistic links must demonstrate two standards of accuracy. The pages to which you link must contain accurate information, and the **HTML** code you use to insert the link must send visitors to the right address.

A link to a page is a recommendation. When you link to a page, you're not legally responsible for the information that readers encounter there, but the pages to which you link do reflect upon you and your news organization. Just as you wouldn't recommend a ratty restaurant to a friend, you should avoid directing your readers to an inaccurate or offensive Web page. To do so would erode the trust that people have in you. The links you put in a story are part of your reporting, and you should vet them with the same diligence you use when checking all of your other sources. You can learn some techniques for finding and verifying accurate link destinations by reading Chapter 6, on online news research.

Accuracy isn't important only when it comes to the content of the destination page; accuracy is also important in the creation of the actual HTML code directing the link. Making sure that all the links in a story go to the right page is a critical part of the copyediting process of every online news story.

The Gotham Gazette is certainly not the only news site to have published a broken link, but an example from a March 2010 story illustrates the damage that can be done by even a small error in HTML code. The story, about the impact of a plan to close prisons in upstate New York, was a wonderful example of using links: in 26 paragraphs the story offered 14 links. The only problem? Eleven of them were broken.

None of the links were badly broken. All had the same error. If they were interested enough, most readers could figure out how to find the destination page to which the Gotham Gazette article intended to send them. But it is sort of like publishing the first few paragraphs of your story on the front page of the paper and telling readers the rest of the story is on page 4 when really it is on page 5. Readers would figure it out, but many of them will wonder whether they can trust a news source to be careful with the facts if it isn't careful with the layout.

 Tool: Use HTML to Create Links

Here is the HTML code from three links in the Gotham Gazette's article. Two work and one doesn't. Can you tell which one is the broken one?

```
<a href="http://www.gothamgazette.com/campaigns/whosrunning.php?
searchterms=paterson&submit=search">Gov. David Patterson</a>
```

```
<a href="http://publications.budget.state.ny.us/eBudget1011/
ExecutiveBudget.html ">proposed</a>
```

```
<a href=http://www.huffingtonpost.com/2009/12/28/lake-champlain-
bridge-exp_n_404868.html">Lake Champlain Bridge was destroyed</a>
```

The broken link is the third one. It is missing a quotation mark between href= and http://. That missing quotation mark means that visitors' browsers don't understand where the a element's href attribute ends and where the value of the href attribute begins. If you don't understand how HTML elements, properties and values work, then you won't be able to copyedit or fix online news stories like this one.

Chapter 5, on editing news for searchers and scanners, introduces the **HTML tag,** which is also called an **element.** HTML's element for creating links is the <a>, or anchor, element. But the anchor element, like many HTML elements, has several attributes you can use to customize how the elements appear and behave on your site. That is, for each **attribute,** there is a corresponding **value.** Here is a breakdown of the third link listed above:

The element is <a>. This tells the Web browser to mark the location of the document as an "anchor." Like many HTML elements, it is used with a corresponding closing tag, which is </a>.

The attribute of the <a> element in this example is href. This attribute specifies the location of a page or file on the Web. It creates a link between the element and a destination anchor. Each <a> element can have only one href attribute. The href attribute creates a Hypertext REFerence for the visitor's browser.

The value of the href attribute in the broken link is http://www.huffingtonpost .com/2009/12/28/lake-champlain-bridge-exp_n_404868.html. Each anchor has only one href attribute, and each attribute has only one value. The value of the href attribute must be a valid Web address, which is also known as a **Uniform Resource Locator**, or **URL.** This value tells the visitor's Web browser a specific and unique location where it should locate and then open a particular file.

As you can see in our examples, the attribute and its associated value are connected by the = sign. Think back to your days learning algebra. In algebra, each variable, X, has a corresponding value that, once plugged in, allows you to solve an equation. In HTML code, you can liken the attribute to an algebraic variable; once it is assigned a value, it will take you to a specific destination. In our example, href="http://www.huffingtonpost .com/2009/12/28/lake-champlain-bridge-exp_n_404868.html" is logically similar to the algebraic construction X = 4.

The problem with the third link in our example is that it is not set off by an opening quotation mark. When browsers don't see that opening quotation mark, they don't know what to do. Instead of going to http://www.huffingtonpost.com/2009/12/28/lake-champlain-bridge-exp_n_404868.html, browsers try to go to http://www.huffing tonpost.com/2009/12/28/lake-champlain-bridge-exp_n_404868.html." It's the same URL, but with a stray quote. Humans can easily see what the producer intended, but computers interpret instructions literally. Browsers won't guess and don't give half-credit for half-right HTML code.

That said, the computer programmers who build Web browsers know that people who write HTML code sometimes make mistakes. So they program the browsers to interpret common errors. In fact, in one sense the problem with our broken link here is that it is not broken enough—if it had been missing both an opening and closing quote mark, most browsers would have understood the error and sent visitors to the right page. One challenge for Web programmers is that not all browsers anticipate the same errors, and not all Web browsers attempt to correct those errors in the same way.

Producers also have to be very careful with the way they write the actual URL itself. To understand how to write clean URLs, you first have to understand the different pieces of a URL.

http://www.huffingtonpost.com/2009/12/28/lake-champlain-bridge-exp_n_ 404868.html

This is called the **protocol.** It tells the browser which set of rules it should follow to communicate with the server where the destination file lives. In almost all cases of Web page links, you will use the **HyperText Transfer Protocol**, or **HTTP.**

http://**www.huffingtonpost.com**/2009/12/28/lake-champlain-bridge-exp_n_404868.html

This is the **domain name.** Although it is technically inaccurate to do so, you can start your understanding of domain names as the name of the computer—or collection of computers—that serves up a particular website or service. Typing the domain name by itself into a browser's address bar will usually take you to the site's **homepage,** also known as the **root directory**.

http://www.huffingtonpost.com**/2009/12/28/**lake-champlain-bridge-exp_n_404868.html

This is the **directory path**. It is read from right to left and follows a hierarchical logic. The directories on the left are at higher levels than the directories farther to the right on the path. The slash marks denote boundaries between the names of each **directory.**

In this example, the "2009" directory is inside the root directory, the "12" directory is inside the "2009" directory, and the "28" directory is inside the "12" directory. When you're talking about the relationships between directories, you say that the directories on the left are the ancestors to the directories on the right. You also say, in our example here, that the "12" directory is the **parent** of the "28" directory and the **child** of the "2009" directory. If we assume that there is a directory on The Huffington Post at "/2009/11/," that would mean that the "12" directory and the "11" directory are siblings. In some cases, the directory structure represents the physical location of actual files and folders on a computer server. In other cases, however, the directories and their hierarchies are purely conceptual and represent no actual physical location.

http://www.huffingtonpost.com/2009/12/28/**lake-champlain-bridge-exp_n_404868.html**

This is the **file name.** It represents an actual digital computer file.

In most cases, online news producers use the entire URL—starting with the protocol and ending with the file name—when creating a link between one page and another. This is called an **absolute link.** When you link between one domain and another, you must use absolute links.

If you are creating links between documents that reside inside the same domain, then you might want to use a **relative link.** This means that the location of the destination resource is relative to (you might even say "a relative of") the page from which site visitors depart. For example, you might create a link from http://www.huffingtonpost

.com/2009/12/28/lake-champlain-bridge-exp_n_404868.html to <a href= "page2.html">another page</a>. In this case, browsers would infer that both the departure and destination files are in the same parent directory—that is, they are siblings. You can also use two periods before a file name to tell browsers to go up one directory level before looking for the destination file. So, a link from http://www.huffingtonpost. com/2009/12/28/lake-champlain-bridge-exp_n_404868.html to <a href=". ./ page3.html"> yet another page</a> would send browsers to http://www.huffing-tonpost.com/2009/12 "page3.hmtl" inside the "28" directory.

There are advantages and disadvantages to creating relative links. Relative links make it easy to move groups of files from one domain to another, or from one directory to another, as long as the relationships between them remain the same. However, relative URLs can result in a broken link if either the departure or destination file has moved while the other file has stayed put.

Finally, you can in some cases create links that point to specific places within a destination document. This is called an **anchor link.** Anchor links allow you to create links that send a browser to the specific location of any other HTML element, as long as the destination element has been given a name. HTML elements are given names using the name="" attribute. This attribute works in almost every HTML element.

For example, perhaps you've published a biographical profile of your local state senator. The profile contains several sections: career resume, personal facts and votes on recent issues. You could create HTML elements that name each of the sections and that are placed at the tops of each section. They might be <a name="resume">, <a name="personal"> and <a name="votes">.

You could then create linked text at the top of the page that sends visitors directly to each section of the page without scrolling. It would look like this:

```
On this page: <a href="#resume">Resume</a> | <a
href="#personal">Personal</a> | <a href="#votes">Votes</a>.
```

The name and href attributes are the two most commonly used attributes with HTML links. You may also want to use the target attribute. The **target attribute** allows you to control whether the destination page opens in another browser window or within the same browser window as the departure page.

Screencast on linking text in Drupal and Wordpress

Relevance

Editing news isn't as much about deciding what information to include as it is about decid-ing what information to leave out. It's the same with links. The broader the focus of your story, the greater the number of links that might be relatable. It is your job to winnow these options and provide your readers with a manageable list of truly relevant links.

The best way to determine which links are relevant is to ask yourself, "What are the primary news elements of my story?" That is, is it the "Who?" "What?" "When?" "Where?" "Why?" or "How?"—or some combination thereof—that is most relevant to the story? The links you choose should relate to the news elements that are the most important to each particular story.

For example, in a feature profile about the mayor you might note that he was born in Kansas and that he really enjoys playing bebop on his tenor saxophone. A link to photos of the mayor with his family in Kansas might be relevant; a link to the weather in his birthplace probably is not. A link to audio of the mayor playing his saxophone might be relevant; a link to the Wikipedia entry on the tenor saxophone probably is not.

Providing links that are only tangential to the story can confuse your readers, who will click on them but then struggle to construct a connection between the main story and the link destination. Bad links not only undermine the value of the good links on your site, but they carry another danger: sending your audience off on a wild goose chase to another site from which it may well not return.

As is the case at many newspapers, reporters at The Wall Street Journal have the primary responsibility for suggesting to the Web producers links that should be added to their stories. When reporter Sarah McBride worked for the Journal, she developed a strategy for deciding which links would be the most relevant. For each link she considered suggesting, she'd ask herself, "Would that topic make a good graphic in print?" If the answer was yes, the link was probably a good idea.

Specificity

Links should take readers directly to the information referenced in the story. If your story includes a reference to a press release issued by Microsoft, it is better to link directly to that press release on the company's press page, http://www.microsoft.com/presspass/default.mspx, than simply to link to the Microsoft homepage, http://www.microsoft.com. If your story is about a new environmental regulation in California, it is better to link directly to the text of the new regulation, than simply to link to the homepage of the California Environmental Protection Agency.

Visitors should never have to click more than once to get from your site to the relevant material on a destination site. They should never be left thinking, "Where am I?"

Types of Link Destinations

Journalists employ links both to give their reporting greater depth and to offer transparency. Three basic types of link destinations help them to do this: source material links, full details links and backgrounder links.

Source Material

Just as transparency in government improves our ability to hold public officials accountable for their actions, transparency in journalism provides the audience with the opportunity to hold reporters accountable for the assertions they make in their stories. Journalists have long valued transparency, which is why they include direct quotes and detailed attribution in their stories whenever possible.

Hyperlinks allow journalists essentially to footnote every claim they make. They might do this by linking to databases or PDFs from which they drew selected facts, or to audio recordings of complete interviews with sources, or to videos offering eyewitness evidence. When considering which links to add to a story, ask yourself this question: "What links would show readers where this story came from and help them hold me accountable?"

Direct sourcing links point readers to the specific documents or interviews you used as part of the reporting process. Sometimes these are HTML documents or PDF files that exist on other sites. But sometimes—especially when the documents have been leaked to you from a source—you will have to create a digital version of the document and upload it to your own site so that you can share it with your audience. To create a PDF file from a paper document, you will need to scan the paper into a computer and then convert it to the portable document format.

Source material for your story isn't always text. It can also be a multimedia element, such as the audio of interviews you conducted for the article. Chapter 8, on multimedia reporting, introduces the technical skills needed to record, edit and post an audio or video file. Beyond these technical questions, you will also need to consider some journalistic questions when deciding whether to post a complete interview online:

- Is the audio or video quality sufficiently high that it won't be distracting or annoying to the audience?

- Is the content compelling enough—even for a subset of the story's total audience—to justify the effort of posting the complete interview?

- Did the source say anything that was off the record or not for direct attribution? If so, you will need to remove these portions of the interview and explain to your audience the reason why you removed them.

- Did the source have a reasonable expectation that everything she said might be published? For example, even if you told her that you might post the whole face-to-face interview you are conducting in her office, will this include the recording of a personal phone call the source had to take in the middle of the interview?

- Did the source or the interviewer say anything that she would not have said in a public forum?

- Are there competitive or reporting reasons to temporarily withhold some of the information gathered in the interview? For example, does the interview contain material you'd like to explore further for a later story?

A reporter's observations and experiences can also be source documents if they are captured in audio or visual media. If a reporter witnesses a newsworthy event, photos or videos of the event often help users put a story in context or judge the event for themselves. Professional and amateur news videos of riots and protests in restrictive nations like Iran or China have forced those governments to acknowledge events they might have otherwise denied.

Finally, don't forget to scour social media such as **Twitter** and **YouTube** for comments that either a public figure or the "**man on the street**" might have made about the topic you are covering. Links to accurate and authentic social media content can make for compelling quotes.

Full Details

In addition to helping make reports more transparent, links can also add depth to a story. Links to your own source materials provide depth, but journalists can also leverage external resources for the benefit of the visitor who needs more detail.

People's increasing ability to customize their news consumption notwithstanding, journalists for general interest news organizations must still craft their stories for a broad audience. Often they introduce or explain an element of politics, business or science with which at least some of the audience is completely unfamiliar. For most readers, a cursory overview will suffice. But others may want to know more about a topic. Links allow journalists to offer their audience the choice to read more.

When adding links to a story, ask yourself "What links will help readers who need or want to know more about this subject?" In stories about specialized topics—for example, on government, business, medicine or law—reporters are often able to access lengthy, in-depth documents concerning the subject of their story. When working against a deadline or inside space limitations, however, journalists often don't have the luxury of sifting through every page of every report in order to integrate large amounts of detail into their article. And for most readers, this is just fine. But for others, detail might be essential. Links offer the journalist a ready solution: they are a way to provide detail without adding needless verbiage to a story.

Backgrounder

Just as some of your visitors may be looking for added depth about the information in your story, others may be reading about your topic for the first time and would appreciate links that put your specific story in a broader context. Some examples of backgrounder links are the archives of your own news organization, company profiles, encyclopedia articles, timelines, **FAQs** and biographies.

Backgrounders: Pages on NYTimes.com that provide more in-depth information.

Source Material: Link to organizations' websites.

More Details: Link to text of full medical study.

NEWS JUDGMENT

LINKING TO OFFENSIVE OR ILLEGAL MATERIAL

Journalists today face all manner of compelling ethical dilemmas about linking to offensive or potentially illegal material.

In December 2008, reporter Brian X. Chen wrote a blog post for Wired.com that included a link to a site where visitors could download a hacked copy of Apple's OS X **operating system,** which could be used on non-Apple computers. The pirated software was hardly a secret; other blogs and user forums had been linking to it. But when Apple saw the link on Wired's site, it complained. Wired's editors removed the link and had Chen rewrite the post so that it described another, legal method of installing OS X on a PC.

Of course, linking to someone doing something illegal is different from actually doing something illegal. After Republican vice presidential candidate Sarah Palin's Yahoo mail account was broken into in 2008, University of Tennessee student David C. Kernell was arrested and charged with several crimes related to the break-in. The crime became public after someone anonymously posted pictures of Palin's inbox and several of her e-mails to a site called Wikileaks.org. And it became even more public after reporter Michael Falcone linked to the images on a New York Times blog. While Kernell faced prison time in 2010 after being convicted of two federal crimes, nobody from Wikileaks or The New York Times faced charges in the matter.

Not all judgments about links involve questions of legal liability. Some fall into the realm of taste. Newspaper editors have long thought carefully before publishing graphic photos, especially on their front pages where people have no choice about seeing them. But on the Web, editors and producers have embraced the practice of

CHOOSING THE RIGHT DEPARTURE POINT

Once you've figured out where you want to send your readers, you need to decide how you're going to get them there. When journalists create links from words inside the **body** of an article, the hypertext is called an **inline link**—the linked text is inside the story itself. When links related to an article are placed outside the story, the hypertext is called a **sidebar link**—the linked text is placed to the side of the story.

Journalists must be careful when choosing which words inside a story will link to other pages. Poorly placed links can be annoying, or even misleading.

Inline Links

An inline link works best when the destination to which it links is described directly, completely and clearly in the body of the article text. Inline links should be so closely related to the story that they are nearly indivisible components of it.

publishing or linking to images that are more graphic than those they might run in print. This is because in these instances the audience has a choice. A user must actively click on a link in order to see the potentially offensive material.

In 2002, the Boston Phoenix newspaper was widely criticized when it linked to a video of the beheading of Wall Street Journal reporter Daniel Pearl, who was kidnapped while reporting in Pakistan. Dan Kennedy, a former writer for the paper, had heard about the video, found it within five minutes of searching the Web and e-mailed the link to his editor, who decided to post it.

Kennedy felt that his paper's unusual decision was the right one. "[T]he video was already available, on a website that publishes gross-out photos of accidents, autopsies and the like for the viewing pleasure of its perverse audience. The Phoenix did not so much make the video available as it put it in its proper context," Kennedy wrote in a 2009 piece for Nieman Reports.

But the slain journalist's father wrote in The New York Times that the Phoenix's decision was not only devastating to his family but that by making it easier for its visitors to see the beheading video, the Boston weekly was "inviting more abductions and more murders" and "helping the enemy destroy our role models."

Bob Steele, then director of the ethics programs at The Poynter Institute, looked at the newspaper's choice through the prism of the Society of Professional Journalists ethics code, which asks journalists to balance their obligation to report the truth with their responsibility to minimize harm. "I just don't believe there is any journalistic imperative to show these terrible images of Daniel Pearl's death to the general public," Steele wrote on the Poynter site. "I don't believe we learn anything substantive or new."

The best type of word to use as a link is a noun that describes the destination page you are recommending to your readers. For example, if you are writing a story about a robbery, you might include the following sentence: "The three men were wearing ski masks, according to a police report." You could use the words "police report" to link to a PDF file of the police report. The words "police report" describe the destination directly, completely and clearly. If you decided to use the words "three men" to create a link, then the reader might expect information that is directly related to that subject—perhaps surveillance camera photos, or text descriptions or the names and addresses of the men.

Keep in mind that the words you use to form a link will create expectations in your audience. Journalists who create one expectation but deliver something else will erode their readers' trust. Following are some suggestions to help guide you in choosing the appropriate words to use as links. These words are quite often derived from a consideration of the most important news elements in your story:

- Who—Link people's names to biographies.

- What—Link the names of companies and organizations to their homepages, or to encyclopedic profiles of them on your own site. You can also link to photos or definitions of unusual objects in your stories.

- When—Dates are rarely linked in news stories. One prominent exception is Wikipedia, which links dates to pages that contain milestones that took place on that specific date.

- Where—Location nouns are often a great departure point to a map. Location names can be linked to encyclopedic profiles or demographic data about the location.

- Why and How—The "Why?" and "How?" news elements are rarely encapsulated in a single noun or even in a single short phrase that you can use as a link. When journalists create links related to these news elements, they often use a verb as the departure point. We'll discuss the use of verbs as linked text later in this chapter.

Although news stories often repeat the same key nouns over and over, readers might get confused if they see several instances of the same word all linked in a single news story. Readers may wonder whether several hyperlinked instances of "Obama" in a story all go to the same place, or to different places. To avoid confusion, it is best to link only the first instance of a word in the story. There is a single exception. Because readers are slowed by the appearance of linked text within the body of a story, it is best not to link any words that appear in the lead of an article. If the first instance of the word is in the lead, then wait to link it in the second or third (or whichever paragraph it next occurs).

While links can provide value to the audience, too many links on a page can become distracting. In his 1997 book "Hot Wired Style," Jeffrey Veen warns against too many "little blue scars" all over the page. You will also want to avoid linking more than three to five consecutive words. Linking more than five words is both visually distracting and imprecise. With so many linked words, how is the reader supposed to know what destination awaits him when he clicks? A journalist's job is to help focus the audience's attention on the information that matters most. Even the simplest of sentences—"The boy read the book."— has at least two nouns that could send readers to different destinations. Readers might wonder whether they will get a biography of the boy, a summary of the book or a photo of the boy reading the book. As such, it is best to link as few consecutive words as possible.

In some cases you will want to link the verb of a sentence rather than the noun. Nouns link to things. Verbs link to actions. Linked verbs indicate to readers that they will see one of two things at the destination: a visual representation of the action or a contemporaneous account of the action.

Look at the placement of the linked words in these two similar sentences:

- The mayor <u>spoke</u> last month at the opening of the new cultural center in downtown Ottumwa.

- The mayor gave <u>a speech</u> last month at the opening of the new cultural center in downtown Ottumwa.

In the first sentence, the verb "spoke" is used as the link. Readers are likely to expect this link to take them to a video of the speech, or perhaps the archived news story that was written to cover the speech when it was first given. In the second sentence, the noun "a speech" is linked. This link is more likely to take the reader to the transcript of the speech.

Sometimes it can be hard to find just the right word to link inline. While you might be tempted to insert a sentence into the narrative that commands a reader to "click here"—don't. Sentences like this interrupt the narrative, which is the primary reason that your audience is on the page. Always use existing words that best describe the destination to create your links.

Sidebar Links

Sometimes it is more practical to put links next to the main content on a page rather than directly inside the story. On some news sites, these links are placed to the right of the main content. On other sites sidebar links appear at the bottom of the page, and at still others sidebar links are placed inside a boxed area between the paragraphs of the main story.

Putting links outside the body of the article has some advantages, but also one big disadvantage. On the plus side, links outside the article are less likely to distract readers from the main content. Also, the wording of sidebar links can be tailored to the destination. On the minus side, sidebar links may be overlooked—and as a result go unused.

Links outside the article tend to be related to the overall concept of the story rather than to a specific noun or verb within the story. Following are three scenarios in which a sidebar link would work better than an inline link:

- Pointing the audience to previous coverage of the story. Examples include episodic stories, such as stories about a sports season, a criminal trial or an ongoing civic debate about panhandling ordinances, or a story that is part of a longer series.

- Pointing the audience to different angles of coverage on the same story. Examples include stories that are told in different multimedia formats such as a photo gallery or a video. A straight news story might also include links to related opinion, analysis or feature pieces.

- Pointing the audience to long lists of documents or related tools, such as a database or calculator. An example of a long list of documents might be witness affidavits in a trial, or campaign finance report documents from several candidates in an election.

With so much of the online audience entering news sites from a specific article page rather than the homepage, sidebar links can also be used to ensure that "every page is a homepage." You can read more about the way that the online news audience uses article pages as homepages in Chapter 3, on the online news audience.

fee to play on athletic teams.

A bit of bright light seemed to appear Tuesday evening, when Gorman asked the school board to approve a budget that will increase county dollars to CMS and avoid the layoffs, which would affect 600 teachers and 164 teacher assistants.

But the superintendent made it clear Wednesday that this budget proposal might be "closer to a dream."

Gorman said he is seeking the increase from the county in the middle of a recession because "a former school board member (George Dunlap) who is now a county commissioner told me to ask for what I really need."

What he really expects, he said, is for the state to reduce CMS's appropriation by 4 percent from the current year, and the county to cut its contribution by 6.5 percent. That would leave the school system with $78.2 million less than what its leaders say is needed.

Farther down the road is more potential trouble.

Federal stimulus money that is paying some teachers' salaries in this and the upcoming school years will disappear in July 2011.

MORE INFORMATION

- City's budget plan has raises
- Longer breaks mark CMS 2011-12 calendar
- **Siers Cartoon:** New CMS sandwich
- A different CMS

| EVENTS | DINING | MOVIES |

Goodnight Moon
Friday, April 16, 7:30PM
Children's Theatre of Charlotte

Carolina Chocolate Drops w/special Guests Pat 'Mother Blues' Cohen & Ian Thomas
Friday, April 16, 8:00PM
Neighborhood Theatre

More Events   More Venues

RECENT BLOGS

THIS OLD STATE
Obama v. Bush: Close call

CAMPAIGN TRACKER
Poll shows 8th District Republicans split

CAMPAIGN TRACKER
Playing nice in the sandbox

PAPER TRAIL
Park and rec, building fee changes loom

THIS OLD STATE
Basnight: Navy's "awful idea" for OLF is "WRONG"

The Charlotte Observer puts related links on the side of its story text.

USA TODAY | ■ Home ■ News ■ Travel ■ Money ■ Sports ■ Life ■ Tech ■ Wea

News » World ■ War casualties

State Department: Russian adoptions not suspended

Updated 1h 27m ago | Comments 🖃 234 | Recommend ⬦ 13   E-mail | Save | Print | RSS

In this image taken from Rossia 1 television channel TV, 7-year-old adopted Russian boy Artyom Savelyev gets into a minivan outside a police department office in Moscow on April 8, 2010.

⊕ Enlarge   AP

USA Today puts related links between two paragraphs of its stories.

MOSCOW (AP) — The Russian Foreign Ministry said Thursday that all adoptions to U.S. families had been suspended, a week after an American woman sent her 7-year-old adopted son back to Russia on a plane by himself — but the issue remained confused, with the U.S. State Department saying there was no freeze on such adoptions.

There appeared to be uncertainty inside Russia, as well. The Education and Science Ministry, which oversees international adoptions, said it had no knowledge of an official freeze. And a spokeswoman for the Kremlin's children's rights ombudsman said that organization also knew nothing of a suspension.

In Washington, the U.S. State Department said Thursday that it had been assured that the adoptions had not been stopped.

CONTROVERSY: U.S. seeks to defuse adoption flap

Share
b Yahoo! Buzz
m Add to Mixx
f Facebook
t Twitter
More
Subscribe
myYahoo
iGoogle
More

"Our embassy in Moscow and officials in the department have been in contact with Russian officials to clarify this issue," State Department spokesman P.J. Crowley said Thursday. "We've been told there's been no suspension of adoptions."

"We will focus initially on those [mines] that we regard as somewhat troublesome," says Ron Wooten, the director of West Virginia's Office of Miners' Health Safety and Training.

State investigators are expected to begin their work Friday. Manchin says he wants the higher-risk mines inspected in the next two weeks.

Just three weeks ago, federal mine safety officials and representatives of mining companies and unions gathered at the Labor Department in Washington to mark 2009 as the industry's safest year on record.

NPR's Robert Benincasa contributed to this report, which also includes material from The Associated Press

> NPR puts related links below the text of its stories.

Related NPR Stories

- Despite Disaster, Mine Owner Gets Mixed Reviews April 14, 2010
- Documents Reveal Extensive Violations At Mine April 9, 2010

✉ E-mail   ◁ Share   💬 Comments (10)   ✓ Recommend (12)   🖶 Print

Around the Nation >	**Podcast + RSS Feeds**	**Talk of the Nation Newsletter**
· Tea Party Express Comes To A Head On Tax Day	Podcast RSS	Hear the show and get previews of

One exception to the established rules about linking in news stories involves sidebar links. Links that are next to a story rather than inside a story don't necessarily have to be directly related to the story. In some cases, providing readers with sidebar links to *un*related material can help alert them to news they might not be actively seeking but in which they would be interested anyway. The goal with unrelated sidebar links is to mimic some of the serendipity that newspaper and magazine readers say they enjoy most about those formats.

There are two types of unrelated sidebar links that can appropriately be placed on a story:

- Latest headlines for stories about the same general topic, such as sports, business or politics, or latest headlines across all subjects.
- Popular content, such as most e-mailed or most commented-on stories on the site. Many news sites automatically publish links to their most popular content or latest news headlines to the sidebar link area of every story.

Once you've selected your sidebar link destinations, the next step is to craft the text on which readers will click. Sidebar link text should be a label for the destination page. It provides relevant information about the format and content of the destination. It is short— just three to five words—and it emphasizes nouns; often there is no verb at all. Here is one example of how a story headline can be converted into a label for a sidebar link:

Sotomayor Overcame Obstacles to Sit on Nation's Highest Court

becomes . . .

Biography of Sonia Sotomayor

Following are additional examples of label links that do not include verbs:

Map of Park Locations

Police Report of Incident

Palin's Resignation Letter

In some instances, it is best to use a full headline as the sidebar link text. Labels work well when the destination of the link is something other than a traditional news story. But when you want to link to other articles on your site that are related, using the full headline text is best. When you do this, the link text should match almost exactly the headline on the destination article so that readers don't become disoriented and think they clicked on the wrong link.

For example, you would not want the words "California Budget Crisis Resolved" to link to an article with the headline "Schwarzenegger, Legislators Reach Agreement." With no words in common, readers not familiar with the story might not draw the connection between "Schwarzenegger" and "California," and they might have to scan the story to be sure that the "Agreement" was the thing that resolved the "Budget Crisis." It's not that readers couldn't figure this out, but if you make them do any extra work, they might just leave.

When linking to articles it is useful to include the date that the original story was published, if space permits. Many news publications put this in unlinked type next to the headline:

Budget Cuts Threaten Paramedics' Response Time (July 2009)

Providing the date along with a headline helps readers quickly place the headline in context. In this example, readers could easily understand that the budget crisis in the destination article was a different year's budget.

Sidebar links serve as labels for their destination; but sidebar links themselves should be labeled. Most article sidebars contain numerous links, both editorial and promotional. Promotional links connect to advertisers' sites. The separation between editorial content— that is, content created by journalists—and advertising content is crucial. News organizations must ensure that the audience understands that money, in the form of advertising dollars, is not influencing news judgment. To maintain audience trust, advertising links should be clearly labeled. At the same time, editorial links also need to be well organized and well labeled so that readers can readily find what they are looking for.

In many cases, the labels for groups of sidebar links are generic and automatically generated by the content management system. Ideally, they should be edited so that they are as specific as possible. Take a look at the following four examples, from worst to best, of labels for a **linkset**—a collection of links that goes, in this instance, to previous news stories all covering the same topic:

More Information

OK. It's "information." But what *kind* of information?

Related Links

At least we know now that the links are related to the story in some way. But *how?*

From the Archives

Now we know it's related because it's old. But what *is* it?

Past News Articles

Aha! Now we know exactly what we'll find if we click the links. This is a specific and clear label. And it is short. Linkset labels should be kept to three to five words.

The labels on sidebar links not only need to be specific, they also need to be descriptive. And when a group of links is involved, that description needs to apply to each link in the set. In most cases "Video" is a better label than "Multimedia" because it is more specific. But that only works if all the links underneath the label do in fact go to video stories. If one of the stories is a photo gallery, "Multimedia" is the only accurate choice.

When you do have multiple types of media underneath a single label, each link will need its own label. If the link label is "Past Coverage" and some of the coverage was done with video while other coverage was done with text, then you can help your audience by identifying the media type in front of the link label:

Past Coverage

> Video: Highlights of the Game
> Audio: Interview With the Coach
> Text: Player Statistics

If most of the items in the list are of a single media type, then you need to label only the links that go to different media:

Related Coverage

> Tiger Pitching Gets It Done Again
> From Shelter to Shutout, Childers Finds a Home on the Field
> Video: How to Throw a Knuckleball

Presumably, the first two links do not go to video content. If most of the stories on the site are text articles, then text is the presumed format of the first two links.

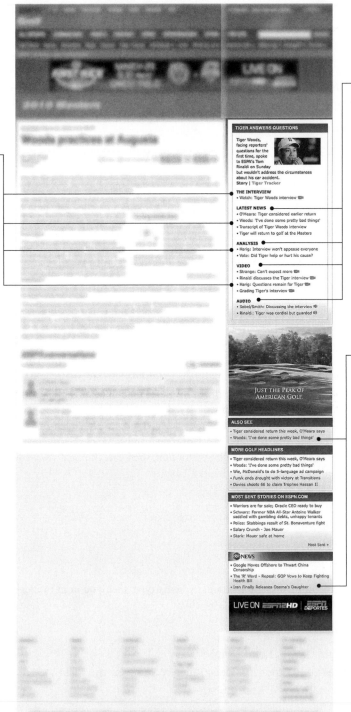

These links (Watch: Tiger Woods interview, Transcript of Tiger Woods Interview, Vote: Did Tiger help or hurt his case, Grading Tiger's interview) are written as labels.

These labels (Latest News, Analysis, Video, Audio) are hierarchical. Each one describes all the links below it. All of these four labels are described by "Tiger Answers Questions."

The links in these three boxes are not directly related to the story. But note that the collection of links that is the most similar—More Golf Headlines—appears on top and the least similar—ABC News—is placed on the bottom of the stack.

Index Page Links

Index pages on news websites serve as a navigation tool. The index page allows readers to access the individual stories and tools on a website. A Business News section front page is an index page; so too is an automated list of Associated Press news headlines. The homepage is the most popular and important index page on a site. Here editors and producers set the agenda and tone for the entire site. One way they do this is by grouping links together to create packages of information. Packages often include the headline and summary of a main story along with a collection of between one and three lines of links that go to items related to the main headline in the package.

The guidelines for choosing which links to include in these lists, as well as the guidelines for how to write the text of the links, are identical to the guidelines for choosing and writing sidebar links in an article. Related links in a **homepage package** often point to stories that are about the same topic and that were published on the same day as the main story. The text of the link should be styled as a headline. If a related link points to an online feature or tool, then that link should be written as a label without a verb.

Here is an example of a package from the Fox News homepage:

Your Tax Dollars to Sell Obama's Health Care Plan

EXCLUSIVE: White House confirms it used taxpayer dollars to hire private company to distribute e-mails, including unsolicited spamming to push health plan

• YOU DECIDE: Should Tax $$ Be Used to Lobby Reform?

• Kennedy Visit May Rally Dems | Obama Rips Critics

• Divides Emerge in Reform Talks | FULL COVERAGE

Fox News homepage.

Notice that the related links feature headline-style links as well as one label—"FULL COVERAGE."

In the Fox News example a vertical line separates the related links. This is called a **pipe**. Like long headlines and summaries, long lists of related links can be difficult to scan. One way to improve the scannability of long lists of links is to place two or more items on the same line and separate them with a pipe. This technique also saves vertical space in a page's layout.

The first line that uses a pipe in the Fox News example is done well; both items on the line are news stories, and the two stories are connected by the common theme of actions taken by Democratic politicians. The second use of the pipe, however, leaves readers unsure. Will clicking on "FULL COVERAGE" send readers to an article detailing the emerging divide in the reform talks, or will it send readers to a page containing full coverage of the White House's health care lobbying? In fact, the actual destination of this link proved to be a page in the "Politics" section of the site that had the "latest stories and videos about Health Care from FOXNews.com"—which still left questions. The Fox News site also has a section called "Health." In this instance, readers will be confused—are they heading to a story that discusses "health care reform," or to a story on a "health care" topic?

Here is another example of a way that labels and pipes could be used to present five links on just three lines of text:

Related Coverage

> Obama's Speech: <u>Video</u> | <u>Text</u>
> Reaction: <u>Dionne</u> | <u>Brooks</u>
> <u>State of the Union Address History</u>

On the first line, one link goes to "video" of the speech while the other goes to a "text" transcript. The common subject—"Obama's speech"—is unlinked to make it clear that it is a label and not a link. On the second line, one link goes to a piece by "Dionne" and the other goes to a piece by "Brooks." Both pieces are in "reaction" to the speech. Finally, on the third line, a traditional link appears to a page that contains a historical account of previous State of the Union speeches.

In these examples, the pipe is used to visually separate one link from another. Without the pipe, it might appear as if "Video Text" is a single link to a single destination.

ONLINE LEARNING MODULE 7

ACTIVATE THIS MODULE: journalism.cqpress.com

Journalism has always provided connections for the communities it serves, and with the Web's hypermedia these links have become much more literal. To retain and build trust, however, you must make clear and conscious decisions about how, when, where and why to connect one piece of information to another—or one member of the audience to another.

I use links on my blog to connect students using this text to each other and to highlight examples of how news organizations are using links to increase the transparency and relevance of their reporting.

When you buy or activate this chapter's online learning module, you will have access to:

- A digital version of this chapter's text.
- Interactive flashcards for the terms used in this chapter.
- A printable one-page tip sheet for choosing appropriate link departure points and destinations.
- A quiz to test your mastery of the material in this chapter.
- A video screencast that shows you how to code HTML links.
- Exercises that give you hands-on experience building links for news stories.

As you complete this module's online exercises, you will work with real news stories to:

- Select the most accurate, relevant and specific links for your story.
- Choose the right words to serve as a link's departure point from within the text of a story.
- Organize "sidebar" links and write effective departure text for links that appear next to a story.
- Read and manipulate the HTML code that creates links.
- Write an "FAQ" using links.

ONLINE LEARNING

CHAPTER 8 MULTIMEDIA REPORTING

This chapter will teach you how to:

- Shoot, edit and distribute digital photographs.
- Record, edit and distribute digital audio interviews.
- Create a podcast.
- Record, edit and distribute digital video interviews.
- Record, edit and distribute environmental videos.

On Jan. 20, 2009, dozens of Washington Post photographers and videographers hit the freezing streets of the nation's capital to bring back live images of history in the making. The inauguration of Barack Obama was a huge story for the world and for the Post, where it represented the convergence of two franchise beats: national politics and local news. Descending on the city for this historic moment were well over a million Americans who would bear witness to parades, speeches, concerts and black-tie galas—millions of eyeballs all seeing pieces of a single historic event. Tom Kennedy, the Post's multimedia editor, and his staff faced an enormous logistical task: how to use photos, audio and video to capture all of those pieces and create a single comprehensive narrative.

For Kennedy, Inauguration Day meant more than 24 straight hours of work. He'd done months of planning with programmers, writers, producers, editors, marketers and designers to prepare for this momentous day when thousands of digital images would be pouring into the newsroom. As events unfolded, editors and online producers continuously scoured the images, selected the best and posted them to the Post's website as quickly as possible. Meanwhile, the site was streaming live video of the inaugural speech and interviews and commentary from journalists and guests in the newsroom. And on the photo-sharing website **Flickr,** 57 registered users uploaded 455 items to a special group pool created by the Post to gather even more photos from its audience—just in case its staff missed anything.

Kennedy had been thinking about a day like this for more than 20 years. In May 1985, he was the deputy photo editor of The Philadelphia Inquirer when police set fire to a row house in the city occupied by a commune called MOVE. The fire spread quickly from the house to the surrounding neighborhood. Everyone—including photographers—was forced out of the path of the deadly blaze. As Kennedy sat with other editors to choose the images they would use in each edition of that day's papers, they watched live video from a camera that had been strapped to the top of a pole above a television news van and abandoned inside the perimeter. A colleague of Kennedy's grumbled. The photos available to them for use in the newspaper were literally hours behind the story they were seeing unfold on live TV.

"I realized that from that day forward if papers were ever going to compete with television for visual journalism, they would need to find a way to move and publish photos digitally and in real time," says Kennedy. But if newspaper reporters were ever going to compete with television in visual journalism, they would need to learn how to shoot, edit and produce a variety of multimedia in formats that even television had yet to imagine.

Oh, and Kennedy eventually got even with television. During his decade at the Post, his staff earned several Emmy, Peabody and Murrow awards—awards traditionally given to television journalists, not newspapers.

In this age of digital journalism, the traditional strengths and weaknesses of television and newspapers have evaporated. Newspapers are able to use live video when a story calls for it. Television journalists can write and post online detailed reports for which they don't have pictures. When it comes to digital journalism, all forms of media are created equal. Text, audio, video and photographs are each just collections of data. This means that journalists can use any or even all of these forms of media to tell a story online. But this wide range of choices creates two challenges for multimedia reporters—they must choose the best combination of technologies to tell each story, and they must learn to use those technologies well.

Multimedia reporting is about the convergence of different storytelling tools all in service of a single story. The best multimedia stories allow text to tell that part of the story that text can tell best—analysis, trends and unseen motivations—and audio or visual media tell the parts of the story that those media can tell best—human emotion, conflict and the physical setting in which the story unfolds.

When writer Scott Baldauf and photographer Melanie Stetson Freeman set out to tell the story of AIDS in South Africa in 2007, they produced a multimedia package of stories for their newspaper and its website. Baldauf's text tells site visitors about the unobservable context of a story—that "71 percent of deaths among adults ages 15 to 49 are caused by AIDS" in South Africa and that "housekeeper Olga Thimbela earned about 700 rand a month ($100)." These are important pieces of information that are difficult to illustrate visually. How do you take a picture of 71 percent of all the deaths in a country? How do you take video of the receipt of payment for housekeeping work?

Baldauf's writing, though, as strong and effective as it is, can't transport us to the scene or put raw human emotion squarely before us as effectively as Freeman's photographs. Her photos show us how the story of the AIDS epidemic is being played out in a nearly monochromatic room colored only by worn and ragged stuffed animals. The photos force us to stare into the eyes of a poverty-stricken woman who has opened her home to her six nieces and nephews orphaned by the disease.

And while we're looking into her eyes, we hear Thimbela's voice.

South African couple takes in AIDS orphans

Olga and Pontsho Monamodi added six children to their family after Olga's sister and aunt both died.

Melanie Stetson Freeman's photographs and audio gave this Christian Science Monitor story about AIDS in South Africa an emotional appeal that words would have difficulty capturing.

It's broken by sniffs and sighs as she describes the death of her sister and aunt. This combination—Thimbela's voice laid on top of those photos and presented alongside Baldauf's words—demonstrates the power of multimedia reporting.

Multimedia reporting is much more than just delivering a story through multiple channels of distribution. An example of the latter, known as **multichannel distribution,** would be a National Public Radio show that is broadcast over the FM frequency, XM satellite radio and via a podcast on iTunes. Or it is the same Associated Press story that shows up both in a newspaper and on a website. Multimedia reporting is also much more than simply reporting a story twice in different media formats—a complete text version of the story distinct and separate from a complete video version of the story, for example. This is called **parallel reporting**.

In larger newsrooms, the tasks of multimedia reporting are spread across a variety of specialists ranging from videographer to computer programmer to investigative reporter. In smaller newsrooms, each journalist is required to be familiar with all forms of multimedia reporting. This jack-of-all-trades has been dubbed the **backpack journalist** because he or she carries a variety of small audio and video reporting tools at all times, typically in a backpack.

Because of the differences in the way that multimedia reporting is done at large and small newsrooms, it encompasses a wide variety of formats and an equally wide range of quality. It includes the poorly composed and low-resolution cell phone camera photos taken in London's subway system as passengers escaped from a bombing there in 2005. It includes

A passenger with a mobile phone camera was able to capture this low-quality but one-of-a-kind photo of the scene inside the London Tube after the bombing in 2005.

SOURCE: Adam Stacey/Creative Commons. Permission from Creative Commons: http://moblg.net/view/77571/london-underground-bombing-trapped and http://creativecommons.org/licenses/by/2.5/.

videos and animated graphics on newspaper websites that have won awards normally reserved for television news organizations. And it includes CNN's presidential debates in which citizens and candidates used YouTube videos to ask and answer questions.

No matter the size of the newsroom, journalists must be familiar with all of the techniques and tools available to tell a story as clearly and accurately as possible in any medium. In this chapter, you will learn about these techniques and try out the immediate tools you will need to get started on your career in multimedia reporting, whether as a backpack journalist or an online video producer.

WORKING WITH DIGITAL PHOTOGRAPHY

A few years ago, The Washington Post created a marketing campaign around the slogan, "If you don't get it, you don't get it." In other words, if you did not acquire a copy of the newspaper, then you would lack comprehension about the world around you. The same tag line could be used for multimedia reporters. But in this case, "If you don't get it, you don't get it" means that if you don't capture the event with your camera or audio recorder, then it might as well not have happened.

When Pulitzer Prize–winning reporter Bill Dedman was putting together a story in 2009 and 2010 about one of America's richest women, 103-year-old Huguette Clark, who had no heirs and lived in none of her multimillion-dollar homes, one of his colleagues at msnbc.com suggested he tell it with photos. At that moment, Dedman's challenge doubled. Not only did he need to find the facts, he had to find the photos. msnbc.com turned to a variety of sources—from a Connecticut Realtor to an aerial photographer in California—to get pictures of Clark's homes. Dedman himself photographed her Fifth Avenue apartment building. Why? Because without the photos he could have written a story, but he couldn't have built his photo gallery.

Dedman certainly knew how to write up a good story, but he also had to be able to shoot good photos. That meant he had to know his tools. If his photos had been out of focus or obstructed by a pedestrian's head, the shots would have been unusable. Luckily for Dedman, apartment buildings don't just disappear; if his first go at photographing her building had turned up poor pictures, he could have tried again another day. But remember that series about AIDS in South Africa? What would have happened to that story if the writer and photographer had returned to their Boston newsroom only to find they had no usable photos of Thimbela's adopted children, or that the audio recording of her tear-filled narrative had been inaudible over the din of dinner being cooked in her kitchen? Their subject's story may never have been told. Epic multimedia failure!

The first rule of digital photography is to always carry your camera with you. The second rule is to take a lot of pictures. You don't have to use all of them—and you definitely shouldn't. But if you don't take the picture, then you'll never be able to use it.

Tool: Digital Cameras

As with all digital reporting tools, digital cameras come with a variety of features, and choosing the right camera is a matter of balancing price with quality. Because prices tend to drop over time even as quality and the range of features increase, it is tough to offer advice based on price range or specifications that won't be quickly out of date. Instead, here are some things to consider when choosing and using a camera for news reporting.

Recording Sensors

Digital photographs are made by thousands of tiny samples of light that are recorded by the camera. These sensors are arranged in columns and rows, and are commonly called **pixels**. One **megapixel** is equivalent to 1 million pixels.

So, if you are using a camera that has 6 megapixels, then it will have 2,816 columns of sensors and 2,112 rows of sensors (2,816 pixels × 2,112 pixels = 5,947,392 pixels, or rounded up 6,000,000 pixels; 6,000,000 ÷ 1,000,000 = 6 megapixels). Quite simply, the more megapixels you have in your camera, the more detailed your image. Photos that are made with more pixels allow editors to zoom to a greater level of detail before losing noticeable quality. Photos recorded with more pixels can also be printed at larger sizes without losing quality, but that is not relevant for online photo display.

Zoom

Many digital cameras are marketed as having both optical and digital zoom. **Optical zoom** is more important, because it allows you to make the subject larger in your frame without the image distortion that comes with **digital zoom**. The effect of digital zoom can be achieved when you edit your photos. For example, you can enlarge a portion of your photograph; however, keep in mind that when you do this your resolution is reduced, which results in a poorer-quality image.

In addition to built-in optical zoom capabilities, digital cameras can also accommodate different lenses that can be purchased separately. This is true even of some high-end point-and-shoot cameras.

Storage Media

Storage media refers to the device that is used to store the digital photographs that you have taken. The best cameras offer a removable storage media option. If you don't have to rely exclusively on your camera's built-in memory, you will be able to take and then store many more pictures. You should buy as much storage space as you can afford.

Some cameras, like those that come on many mobile phones, simply store the photos to the device itself, which means there is no way to remove the photographs while you are using it to take pictures. And often there is no way to add additional storage memory. Cameras that store photos to removable media can allow you to replace media if you fill it up while still in the field reporting the story. They also allow you to give the media to another person to edit the photos while you are shooting.

The **CompactFlash card** (also known as CF) and **Secure Digital card** (also known as SD or SDHC) are the most widely used removable media formats in digital cameras. Compact-Flash cards are more common in higher-end cameras because they have a higher maximum storage space than SD cards and are faster at recording and transferring digital files. SD cards, however, usually have sufficient capacity for most reporting uses. SD cards tend to be smaller and less expensive.

The size of removable storage media is measured in megabytes (MB) and gigabytes (GB). One **gigabyte** is the equivalent of 1,000 megabytes. The number of photographs that you can store on one memory card depends on (1) the amount of memory on the card, measured in megabytes or gigabytes; (2) the number of megapixels (sensors) you use to take the photograph; and (3) the compression rate at which you store the photo on the memory card.

A digital photo is compressed by the camera in order to reduce the photo's file size. The most common **compression** format for digital photos is the **JPG format,** denoted in file names by the ".jpg" suffix. Put very simply, the camera looks for pixels near each other that all have the same colors. It then records the information from one pixel and uses it to represent all the other pixels. This process is called **sampling,** and it is used as well to compress digital audio and video files. A good analogy to describe sampling would be to think of a big pot of soup. You can taste—or sample—just a single spoonful and still get a good idea of what the soup tastes like. You don't have to eat the whole pot.

Every camera will come with slightly different instructions on how to adjust the number of recording pixels and compression rate, so be sure to familiarize yourself with the camera's operating manual before you get started. While lowering the number of recording pixels increases the number of photos that you can save on a memory card, and increasing compression allows you to save more photos on a memory card, remember that both techniques will reduce the quality of your photos. Experiment with your camera's various settings to find the combinations that provide you with the best results for the amount of memory you can afford. But be sure and do this *before* you get started on your reporting. Once a photo has been taken, you will not be able to increase the number of recording pixels or reduce the compression to improve your image.

To determine which combination of resolution, compression and storage works best for you, you need to know just how many photos your memory device will hold. A 10-megapixel photograph (one that is recorded with 10 million sensors) is usually anywhere between 2.5 MB and 5.5 MB, depending on the amount of compression you use. This means that a 2 GB memory card could store anywhere between 360 and 800 still images. The same memory card could store anywhere between 650 and 1,000 images taken with 6 megapixels (6 million sensors). While these are rough estimates, they give you an idea of how resolution, compression and memory size all relate to one another.

Video

Many digital cameras can also capture video. This is a nice feature to have on a camera because it means that you'll have an extra tool for reporting in case of emergency. If your aim is to do serious video reporting, however, it is better to purchase a separate video camera that is made specifically for that task. This chapter's section on digital video cameras offers additional information on the digital video specifications important to journalists.

Batteries

Having a great camera doesn't do you any good if you can't use it. Always be sure to bring an extra set of fresh batteries wherever you go. Even if you've just put new batteries in your camera, keep a set in reserve. Some cameras come with custom rechargeable batteries. This means that you must be sure that they are fully charged before going out into the field. You should also consider in advance how you will recharge them if the need arises. Most cameras on a fresh set of batteries will shoot anywhere between 100 and 400 photos before dying, depending on the battery technology, the air temperature (very cold air drains batteries) and the other features you are using on the camera while shooting.

A word of warning: digital audio and video equipment can get very expensive very quickly. The reporting kit used by multimedia company MediaStorm runs into the mid four digits. You can see the complete list of equipment used by MediaStorm's documentary journalists at http://mediastorm.org/submissions/gear.htm. Keep in mind that the quality of inexpensive tools is always improving. Journalism professor Mindy McAdams put together in 2007 a list of inexpensive equipment for the fledgling multimedia reporter. Have a look at http://mindymcadams.com/tojou/2007/basic-kit-gear-for-the-multimedia-reporter/.

Basics of Photo Reporting

At first blush, taking a photo for a news site can appear to be as simple as "point and click." Digital photography is a hobby for about 85 percent of Americans between the ages of 18 and 64 who own their own digital camera—a tool that a little more than 10 years ago was a luxury reserved for professionals. And it's not just Americans who have taken up digital photography with gusto. You can travel to almost any tourist destination in the world and hear the English words "Say Cheese!" Digital photography is truly a worldwide phenomenon.

TEN TIPS FOR TAKING NEWS PHOTOS

Photography is an art and a science worthy of a book all its own—and, in fact, there are many available that you might want to invest in. To make a start, however, follow these 10 simple rules on how to use images to report the news.

Rule 1: Have a working camera with you at all times.

Rule 2: Have one—and only one—clear subject in your photo. The subject should be in focus and stand out from everything else in the photo. A street is not a subject. Seven people walking down the sidewalk is not a subject. One person walking down the sidewalk is a subject.

Rule 3: Take a lot of photos. For every subject, take 10 photos.

Rule 4: Act natural. Journalists are in the business of recording the world as it is. You want to capture the way your subject would look if you weren't there. Make yourself and your camera as invisible as possible. Capture the subject "in action"—not posed in front of the camera.

Rule 5: Move around. Take pictures from far away, a "normal" distance and up close. Don't use zoom as a substitute for getting up close to a subject. Move as much as you can without violating Rule 4.

Rule 6: Don't center your subject. Photos with their subject right in the center are boring. Think of your photograph as a 3-x-3 grid, and then place your subject at the intersection of those imaginary grid lines. This is known as the **rule of thirds**.

But, news photography is just the opposite of "Say Cheese!" photography. News photography is about capturing unscripted moments that show us the world as it is, not as we wish it to be. Good photo reporters know that theirs is a physically demanding job that requires them to move quickly. Good photo reporters are bold enough to get inches from a subject's face and subtle enough to do it without being noticed. The very best news photography captures a single moment that tells a story of emotion or conflict in a dynamic world that does anything but stand still.

Editing Digital Photographs

Journalists work on deadline. They want to get their photos off their cameras and onto their computers as quickly as possible. And because journalists shoot so many photos, they end up transferring many more photos than they actually need. This is where editing comes in.

Rule 7: Place subjects so that they are moving or looking into the photo, rather than out of it. If a person is pointing to the right, be sure she is at the left of your photo. If the subject is a helicopter approaching the landing pad, put the helicopter at the top of your photo.

Rule 8: Keep the light behind you. Make sure the subject's face is fully lit. Never shoot into the sun. Better yet, avoid sunny days altogether if you can. Shooting in light cloud cover prevents a lot of shadows. And it reduces the chance that your own shadow ends up in the photo—that's rule 8a.

Rule 9: If it can be avoided, don't use flash. Instead, take your camera off automatic mode and learn how to use your camera's **shutter speed** and **aperture** settings to get the right lighting and depth of field. The **shutter speed** is the amount of time—usually measured in fractions of a second—that the camera's sensors "see." The **aperture** is the size of the opening through which the camera lets light into the sensors.

Rule 10: Be aware of the background. You don't want a tree that is right behind your subject to look as if it is growing out of her head. Also, you don't want to take a mug shot—make sure your subject isn't backed up against a blank wall. Finally, think about which colors are in the mix; for example, avoid taking a picture of a red flag in front of a red building.

Many of these rules also apply to video reporting.

A tool called a **card reader** is the fastest way to transfer photos. With a card reader, you can remove the memory card from your camera, insert it into the card reader and then attach the card reader to your computer. Of course, if you don't have a card reader you can still transfer your photos. Most cameras will allow you to connect them—and the photos they contain—directly to your computer through a **USB** cord.

Most consumer cameras come with built-in software that allows you to transfer and manage your collection of photos. While this software provides the basic tools to organize and edit photographs, it often forces you to transfer and organize files in ways that might not be optimal. Professional journalists turn to software designed specifically to meet their needs.

When moving files from a camera to a personal computer or common server, it is important for journalists to use a standardized naming and organizational convention for all of their digital media. This makes it easier for you to find the photo you need on deadline and easier to share those photos with other people in your newsroom. Which standard you choose is less important than coming up with one that works well for you and that you will be able to utilize consistently.

You will probably want to store all of your photos in one place, separate from other media—perhaps in a separate folder or directory, or on a separate server or hard drive. Once you have all of your photos in one place, you might want to organize them in a date hierarchy. For example, if all of your photos are in a directory called "Photos," then you may want to create subdirectories based on the year the photo was taken: 2009, 2010, 2011 and so forth. Inside each of these year directories you could create 12 subdirectories for each of the 12 months of the year. Within these month directories you could even create a directory for each day in the month.

Other organization schemes might be to arrange photos by the photographer's name or by the subject matter. The important thing to consider is your needs. When developing a scheme first ask yourself, "How would I like to search these photo archives in the future?"

Each digital file should be named. As such, you will need to develop a **naming convention**. To start with, ask yourself, "How can I differentiate between two photos taken of the same subject on the same day? Or two photos of the same subject taken on different days?" Of course, you might be able to open each photo and tell just by looking at it, but taking the time to do this will slow you down considerably—and of course, you are working on deadline. Developing a naming convention and then applying it to your files will increase your efficiency and allow you to cull the exact photo you are looking for without searching through multiple files or multiple photos.

Digital photos can be used over and over again. Keep in mind that you may want to edit a photo differently for different uses. This is why it is important for you to never—never!—edit the original version of a photograph. When you get ready to edit a photo, follow these steps:

1. Make a copy of it.

2. Give the copy a name that indicates it is a different version but still related to the original photo. For example, if you took a picture of an ostrich and wanted to edit it into an 80-pixel by 80-pixel **thumbnail** image for the homepage of your site, you might call it "ostrich-edited.jpg" or "ostrichv1.jpg" or "ostrich80.jpg" or "ostrich-thumbnail.jpg" or "ostrich-homepage.jpg." Just as you have standard naming conventions for the original photos, it is also important to develop a standard naming convention for each of the versions you create.

3. Save the copy to a different directory. This further avoids confusion between the copy and the original.

Tool: Photoshop

You will want to edit almost every photo you take. You can perform basic photo editing functions using the software that comes pre-installed on your computer. On the Windows operating system, versions of Microsoft's **Photo Gallery** come pre-installed. On the Macintosh operating systems, a version of the **iPhoto** application comes preloaded on new computers.

There are other, free photo-editing applications available online that perform basic editing functions. **Picasa** is free photo editing software from Google. **GIMP** is another free, open-sourced application with multiple menu bars and popular features. You can read more about GIMPshop and download it at http://www.gimpshop.com/index.shtml.

These free versions are all great for students and journalists on a budget. None of them, however, has the advanced features—or the price tag—of **Photoshop**, the most widely used professional photo editing software today. Photoshop, which is made by **Adobe**, offers an incredibly broad and powerful set of editing tools. This breadth can sometimes mean that people using the program for the first time are overwhelmed by options. Online news producers must be familiar with at least the basic functions of Photoshop, for example, tools for cropping, resizing and saving a photo for use on the Web.

Screencast on how to crop, resize and save photos

Cropping a Photo

Cropping a photo is the process of cutting off one or more of its edges. This might be done to ensure that the photo has one and only one clear subject. Cropping can also ensure that a photo maintains the correct aspect ratio when it is resized for the Web.

Here is a photo that has no clear subject:

These photos of Jockey's Ridge were taken just a few miles from Kitty Hawk. In the first, there is no clear subject.

SOURCE: Ryan M. Thornburg

And here is the same photo that has been cropped so that it has one and only one clear subject:

This second shot zooms in and crops the photo to capture an image reminiscent of the Wright Brothers' historic flight.

SOURCE: Ryan M. Thornburg

Sometimes you will have to fit a photo that is wider than it is tall into a space that is taller than it is wide. Or perhaps you'll need to place the photo into a space that is perfectly square. In either of these cases, you will probably need to crop your photo so that it will fit the **aspect ratio** of the spot it needs to fill. For example, the photo to the right has a 3:2 aspect ratio—that is, for every 3 pixels of width it has 2 pixels of height. Below it, you see the same photo cropped to fit a square space. The aspect ratio of this photo is 1:1—for every 1 pixel of width there is 1 pixel of height.

This photo of a Belted Galloway cow has a 3:2 ratio.

How do you know what size your photo is? And how do you know what size it is supposed to be? If you are editing a photo to fit into an existing hole on a Web page—for example, to replace a photo already on your site—there are three easy ways to find the correct dimensions of a photo on a website:

A square area was selected and cropped from the larger photo.

1. Open the Web page of your intended destination. Right-click (command-click on a Macintosh) on the photo that already appears on the page and select "View Image" (in Firefox). The width and height will appear in the browser's title bar. Width is always listed first, so a photo that is "426 x 200" is 426 pixels wide and 200 pixels tall.

2. If you are using the Firefox browser, you can use the **Web Developer Toolbar** Add-on to find the size of a photo. Download and install the Add-on, then choose "Miscellaneous" and "Display Ruler." Use the ruler to measure width and height of any space on a Web page.

3. Finally, you can view the source of a Web page and look for the HTML code that shows you the dimensions of the photo.

Online Module 8

Photo editing screencast for aspect-ratio demonstration

Once you know your dimensions, you will need to determine the dimensions of the original photo. In Photoshop, just above the form fields you use to resize the picture, you will see a label called "Pixel Dimensions" followed by a number. This number tells you how large the resulting image file will be. As you reduce the dimensions of your photo, you can see the effect on file size. It is best to crop a photo to the correct ratio before resizing it.

Resizing a Photo

Web-published image files should not have dimensions that are greater than the dimensions at which they will appear on the visitor's screen. If the space on the website where you will display the photo allows only for an image that is 200 pixels wide, then you don't want to upload a file that is 600 pixels wide. You can use your photo editing software for **resizing** the photo before you upload it.

Be careful to maintain the correct ratio of width to height. If the original photo is 600 pixels wide and 400 pixels tall, then you would not want to resize only the width down to 200 pixels, leaving the height at 400 pixels. This would cause a horizontal photo to become a distorted vertical one, making your subjects all look very skinny.

The easiest way to maintain the correct proportions of a photo is to use Photoshop's "constrain proportions" option, which will automatically resize one dimension proportional to the size you enter for the other dimension. In our example of the 600-pixel-wide photo being squeezed down to 200 pixels, Photoshop would automatically calculate for you that the height should be 133 pixels. Other photo editing programs offer similar options.

Photo at original height and width.
SOURCE: Ryan M. Thornburg

Here the width and height of the original photo were reduced in equal proportion.

If you reduce the width of a photo, but forget to make a proportional change to its height, you can end up with some truly lean beef.

While it is possible to change the dimensions of a photo using the height and width attributes of an HTML image element, this is not a good idea because it requires you to download the full-sized original document to the visitor's Web browser before the browser can use the HTML code to resize it.

A final word on resizing photos. Never attempt to make your photo larger than the original. Once a photo has been created—or sampled—at a certain pixel rate, you can't add more pixels to it. This means that if you attempt to enlarge a photo it will be forced to stretch its pixels over a wider area. This creates an undesirable effect called **pixelation.** A pixelated photo looks like a mosaic of tiles.

Choosing the Right Resolution

Publishing photos online means finding a balance between two things: the quality of the image and the time it takes to download. On the one hand, the larger the file size, the longer it will take to download and display on a visitor's browser. On the other, the larger the file size, the greater the **resolution** and hence the better the quality of the photo that is ultimately displayed. The resolution of a photo is measured in the number of "pixels" per linear inch of screen. The word "pixel" in this sense refers not to an

Online Module 8

Photo editing screencast for resizing demonstration

Here, the cropped, square image (from page 205) has been enlarged, making the grass and the cow's hair appear "fuzzy."

image sensor as it did when we were discussing digital cameras earlier. Here, a "pixel" is the smallest unit of light that is displayed on a screen.

While printed photos may reproduce at a resolution of several hundred dots per inch, Web photos do not need to be more than 72 pixels per inch. If you're using Photoshop, the "Save for Web & Devices" tool under Photoshop's "File" menu usually does a sufficient job balancing the size of your photo with the quality. Other photo editing programs have similar preset specifications.

Almost all photos on news websites are saved as JPG files. A JPG file is a compressed version of the original file. You will almost always want to save any photo you publish to the Web as a JPG file type.

Publishing a Photo

Once you are satisfied that your photo is the correct size, and you have saved it as a 72-**ppi** (pixels per inch) JPG file, you're ready to upload it to the Web either using **File Transfer Protocol,** or **FTP,** or a Web-based image upload tool that comes with the blogging platform or content management system you are using. You cannot put a photo on a Web page until the photo file is uploaded to the Web somewhere.

Tutorials on using photos on Wordpress

Uploading a photo to a blog or CMS is very similar to uploading a photo to Facebook or any other social networking site you may have used. If you are interested in gaining a broader audience for your photos, you may also want to upload them to a photo-sharing site such as Flickr.

Photoshop Resources

There are many free online tutorials to teach you the basic functions of photo editing applications. However, there are multiple versions of Photoshop, so be sure that the tutorial you are viewing matches the version you are using. Many of the basic functions remain the same across versions, but each version contains both significant and minor differences to the workflow or menus. In the last decade or so, Adobe has released major updates to Photoshop about every two years. Photoshop CS5 was released in April 2010. In addition to the frequent version updates of Photoshop, at any one time there can be several editions out on the market, from the low-end Photoshop Elements to the ultra-high-end Photoshop Extended. Keep in mind too that the Macintosh versions of Photoshop differ slightly from the Windows versions.

Online Module 8

Photoshop tutorials and resources

NEWS JUDGMENT

ETHICAL PHOTO EDITING

Manipulating digital photographs for both entertainment and malice has become so routine that the name of one of the most common digital photo editing applications, Photoshop, has become a verb. But "photoshopping" an image in a way that changes the story it tells is a violation of journalistic ethics. While it is easy to remove a distracting tree or change the direction in which someone is running to improve the visual quality of the photo, such changes distort the reality the photographer recorded. Manipulation of your photo record is never appropriate in the journalistic setting.

Following are three additional ethical considerations to be taken into account when dealing with digital images:

1. Using photos taken by other people. In general, you should not use photos that you have found elsewhere on the Web. In most cases, photographs are copyrighted, which means you cannot use them without asking permission of the owner of the copyright. Typically this is either a photographer or the site on which it was published. If you do wish to use a photo under copyright, be aware that copyright holders will oftentimes require you to pay a fee for a license to use the photo. Licensed use may be limited to a certain number of uses, or a specific duration, or a named geographic area, or certain media. Licenses can also be unlimited.

Even if you don't download a photograph from another Web page and then re-upload it to yours, you may be violating copyright if you use HTML code to display a photo that appears on another site within the context of your own site.

NEWS JUDGMENT

Some digital images are published with the hope that they will be re-used. While promotional images from a company or political group typically have low journalistic value, they are often free for journalists to use. Photographs created by the U.S. federal government frequently fall within the public domain, which means they are free to use as well. A Web search for "public domain photographs" will yield several resources.

Some photographers publish their work under a **Creative Commons license**. This means that they allow their images to be reproduced under certain conditions. You can search for images with Creative Commons licenses by conducting a search at http://search.creativecommons.org/.

A good guide to this issue is the Intellectual Property section of the **Electronic Frontier Foundation's** Legal Guide for Bloggers at http://www.eff.org/issues/bloggers/legal/liability/IP.

2. Removing things. Don't crop people or things out of the middle of the photo. You can make a shot tighter by cropping items out of the edge of the photo, but if you took a picture with a light post growing out of the top of your subject's head, then you're either going to run a photo with a light post growing out of the top of your subject's head, or you won't run the photo.

3. Adding things. Don't add things to a photograph. If you take a photo of the match-winning shot in a soccer game and find that the ball is actually out of the frame, you can't copy a soccer ball from another photograph and paste it into yours. Even if the ball was there just one second earlier, you're still manipulating reality by that one second.

Visit the **National Press Photographers Association** code of ethics, posted at http://www.nppa.org/professional_development/business_practices/ethics.html, for more information on ethical photo editing.

DIGITAL AUDIO

On the 40th anniversary of the first human footstep on the moon, America Online built a photo gallery of 10 historic photographs that told the story of the Apollo 11 mission. The images are iconic—a rocket being thrust into space atop a column of fire, the brilliant reflections of the lunar module's metal sides contrasted against the dull surface of the moon and, of course, the imprint of a shoe that was the first not made on the Earth's surface. And yet, it is the audio behind several of these images that really puts you in the moment—the thundering power of the engines at take-off, the relief in the voice of a technician from mission control and the words that many Americans can't read without connecting them in their minds to the crackle of a microphone as it sent Neil Armstrong's voice across 200 thousand miles of airless, black space: "That's one small step for man; one giant leap for mankind."

To relive the thrill, go to http://kids.aol.com/KOL/2/HomeworkHelp/article/moon-landing-pictures. You will no doubt agree, whether it is on radio, on television or on the Web, audio is a powerful storytelling tool that puts images in context and allows the audience to hear the emotion in a subject's voice.

Digital photos capture a single moment in time. But digital audio—and digital video—captures a sequence of consecutive moments. This means that the technical elements of audio and video recording are somewhat more complicated than those of digital photos, and it also means that the key storytelling element has shifted from space alone—that is, from width and height—to time.

 ## Tool: Digital Audio Recorders

Recording audio for a news report requires the right equipment. As with digital cameras, digital audio recorders come in a broad range of quality and prices, from as little as $50 to $70 for a voice recorder to upwards of $500 to $700 for top-of-the-line audio recorders. Here are some things that are important to know about digital audio recorders.

Recording Format

While almost all digital cameras store photos in the JPG format, audio recorders save their files in a wide variety of formats. In general, you have two basic considerations: you can work with an **uncompressed audio format** or a **compressed audio format.** Your choice of format will depend to some extent on which type of operating system you use. Some audio formats work more easily on Macintosh operating systems while others work better on Windows. Uncompressed audio files are as much as 10 times larger than files in a compressed format, but the sound they contain is also higher in quality.

If possible, you should record and store your original audio files in a high-quality, uncompressed format. However, because many recorders don't have removable storage media, files are often saved in a compressed format in order to save space. Following are some common audio file formats:

- **WAV**—The Waveform audio format is an uncompressed file format for use on Windows and Macintosh operating systems.

- **MP3**—A very widely used compressed file format, formally know as the MPEG-1 Audio Layer 3 format.

- **WMA**—Windows Media Audio is a file format, typically compressed, that was made for use on Windows operating systems.

- **AIFF**—The Audio Interchange File Format is an uncompressed file format for use on Apple operating systems.

- **AAC**—The Advanced Audio Recording format is a compressed file format similar to an MP3. It is used by Sony gaming consoles and Apple devices.

Storage Media

The recording media for digital audio recorders are primarily the same as for digital cameras—CF, SD and SDHC cards. These media are all removable. Some recorders not do have removable media, which means that your recording time will be limited to the amount of storage on the device itself.

Sample Rate

The **sample rate** of a digital audio record is the number of times in one second that it samples sound. To go back to our soup analogy, if sound were a pot of soup, the sample rate would be the number of times per second that you dip your spoon into the pot. Sample rate is measured in kilohertz (**kHz**). If an audio recorder were to sample sound once per second, then the sample rate would be 1 kHz. A sample rate of 44.1 kHz is considered "CD-quality."

Bit Depth

Bit depth is how much information the recorder collects with each sample. To extend our analogy a bit further, it is the size of the utensil you dip into your bowl of soup. For example, are you using a teaspoon or a ladle? You can dip a teaspoon and ladle into a pot of soup at the same "sample rate," but the ladle is always going to grab a lot more soup than the teaspoon. A bit depth of 16 is considered "CD-quality."

Sometimes bit depth is confused with "bit rate." The **bit rate** of a compressed audio file determines its quality. Bit rates measure the amount of data stored per unit of time. It is measured in kilobits per second (**kbps**). MP3s are often produced at 128 kbps. We will examine bit rate in more depth later in this chapter.

File size is a function of the bit depth and sample rate. Higher sample rates and bit depths mean higher-quality audio; however, they also mean larger files and therefore less recording time. Professional journalists typically record in the WAV file format at 44.1 kHz and 16 bits for Internet-based audio. If the audio will be used in online video presentations, the sample rate will often go up to 48 kHz. When creating audio for the Internet, there is usually no reason to record at more than 48 kHz and 24 bits. In all likelihood, your files will end up as 64 kbps compressed MP3 files, but it is good practice to start off with as high a quality as you can afford.

Microphones

A **microphone** feeds sound into the audio recording device. Internal microphones will almost always record a lower-quality sound than external microphones. The highest-quality microphones connect to the audio recorder with a three-pronged plug format known as **XLR**.

Some lower-end audio recorders allow only connections for a 1/8-inch **mini-plug**, the kind of plug you find on most portable digital audio players. For these recorders, you will either need to limit your microphone use to those with mini-plug jacks or you will need to buy a separate adapter that allows XLR microphones to plug into a mini-pin receptacle.

XLR cables can be identified by their three prongs arranged as a triangle.

There are many different types of microphones. For field reporting, the biggest consideration in determining which kind of microphone to use is how much environmental, or background, noise you want to collect. Depending on how a microphone is made, it can either pick up sound in all directions, only one direction or some combination.

A microphone that picks up sound in all directions at once is called an **omni-directional**

The 1/8-inch audio jack is standard across many consumer devices.

microphone. The advantage of omni-directional microphones is that the reporter doesn't have to point the microphone right at the primary subject. The disadvantage is that they collect a lot of the surrounding noise. A microphone that picks up sound primarily in one direction is called a **cardioid microphone** because its sound pick-up pattern looks like a heart. The advantage to cardioid microphones is that they don't pick up a lot of background noise. The disadvantage is that the reporter has to make sure the microphone is pointed directly at the subject at all times. Finally, the **hypercardioid microphone** is the most directional of all of the microphones; its long cylinder means that it is sometimes called a **shotgun mic**.

Good microphones are not cheap. Prices can easily run into the three-figure territory.

Table 8.1 Microphones

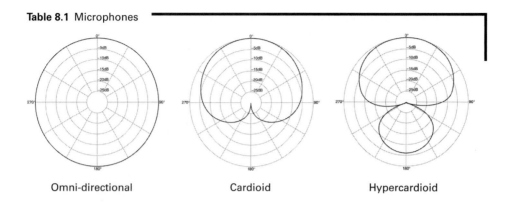

| Omni-directional | Cardioid | Hypercardioid |

Headphones

A professional audio recorder has a headphone jack. This is because professional audio technicians always wear headphones, even if it looks goofy. Wearing headphones while recording is the only way a reporter will know exactly what a microphone is picking up—and, as important, what it is not picking up. It does not matter what your ears hear. It only matters what the microphone hears.

Batteries

You can count on getting somewhere between four and six hours of recording time out of a digital audio recorder. If the recorder uses standard, interchangeable battery sizes such as AA, you can extend that time quickly by replacing the batteries. If your recorder has a proprietary rechargeable battery format and you want to record more than four to six hours of sound, then you will need to be near an electrical outlet for recharging.

Basics of Audio Reporting

Conducting an audio interview for a multimedia news report is completely different from interviewing someone for a text-only story. The mechanics of the interview—for example, your posture, your proximity to the subject—all change. The questions have to change a bit, too, so that they elicit not just the information you want but the style of answer that will make sense after editing. Finally, the relationship between you and your subject will feel different. What in a conventional interview setting is an intimate conversation in a recording setting is a conversation that has to contend with a not-so-intimate third wheel—the microphone.

When scheduling interviews, explain to your subject that you will be using a small, hand-held recorder so you can publish the interview on the Web. Be up front about your intention to record. At the same time, reassure your subject about the recording process itself, letting him know that it will be painless (even if your questions aren't). Talking into a microphone makes most people self-conscious. But giving your subject any sense that you are attempting to hide the fact that you're recording the interview will lower his trust in you.

When you begin the interview, start with some small talk about yourself, the weather or some noncontroversial topic about which you know the subject is interested. If you can, take a few minutes to chat before taking out your recorder—and keep talking while you're getting set up. By the time you go to your first interview, you should have done enough test runs with your tools so that you can set them up without thinking about it.

Five Tips for Recording News Audio

Following are five useful tips to follow when recording news audio:

1. **Run a sound check before you begin.** As you start to record, make sure everything sounds good before you start asking your questions. Run a sound check and watch your recorder's level monitors. Make sure that they are moving, but not hitting the extreme right or top of the bars, even when the test voice is at its loudest. If the levels are regularly hitting the far right side of the meters—typically 0 decibels—your recording will sound too "hot." This means that the loudest sounds will exceed the dynamic range of your recording settings and may be clipped off, which can result in an audible clicking noise in your recording. To eliminate this problem, reduce the **gain** slightly.

Online Module 8

Screencast on how to tell the difference between audio that's too hot or just right

2. **Reduce background noise.** Listen before you record. Are there any buzzing vending machines, air conditioners or light bulbs in the background? Is the noise of outside car traffic distracting? You might need to make a few adjustments to minimize external noise. When you do start recording, is the subject sufficiently loud in your headphones?

3. **Hold the microphone carefully.** When you conduct the interview, you should hold the microphone about five or six inches away from your subject's mouth, slightly off-center. The grip shouldn't be too tight, and you should move the microphone as little as possible. The movement of your fingers on the microphone will be picked up in the recording. If you set the microphone on a table, everything that comes in contact with the table will leave a blemish noise on your recording. Never—never!—let your subject or anyone else hold the microphone during an interview.

4. **Don't interrupt.** Once you have the proper set-up, try to forget about it and focus on listening to your subject in the interview. Do your best to keep your mouth closed while the subject is speaking. Every time you say "uh-huh" or interrupt to redirect or clarify an answer, you render the subject's response unusable.

The first few times you conduct an audio interview, you'll probably be amazed at how often you use that simple "uh-huh" to reassure the subject and let the person know that you're interested in what she has to say. Once you've retrained yourself to listen without talking, you can practice listening while looking. In audio interviews, as in video interviews, reporters need to maintain a comfortable but consistent eye contact with their subject. This does two things: it prevents the subject from staring at that forbidding microphone you've just stuck in her face, and it conveys to the subject that you're paying attention and are interested.

5. **Take notes and record timestamps.** Finally, it is important to realize that recording audio of an interview doesn't give you permission to stop taking notes. When you edit the recording, you will find that the notes you took during the interview are an invaluable resource. Your notes don't need to be a verbatim rendering of the audio, but they do need to capture the key ideas in the order that the subject presented them. And, most important, they need to record the timestamp at which the person said each quote. By peeking down at the recorder's time code as it is rolling along, you'll know exactly where in that 30-minute recording are the 30 seconds you need for your story.

After just a few sessions of editing audio, you will recognize an important difference between gathering digital photos and gathering digital audio: unlike sorting through digital photos, it is very difficult to sort through digital audio to find the just-right clip. It is much easier to scan photos than to scan audio. Your notes will help. But while you may want to shoot 10 times as many photos as you think you'll use, you can also expect that the time it will take you to edit audio will be about three to five times as long as the amount of time it took you to record.

Turning Your Computer Into an Interview Studio

Not all audio recording is done in the field. Sometimes you may be recording your own voice—perhaps for distribution as a podcast. In professional environments, this is called studio recording. With a personal computer and a few basic tools, you can turn just about any environment into a makeshift audio studio.

When recording directly to your computer, you will need some sort of audio editing software such as **ProTools, Sound Forge, GarageBand** or **Audacity.** This is the only mandatory requirement. Use the "record" button in the audio editing application to record your voice into the computer.

You can use your computer's speakers and internal microphone to record your voice, but the sound quality will be poor. It is better to use external headphones so that you can listen to your voice as it is recording and an external microphone that is plugged into your computer. You will need to "tell" both your computer's operating system and your audio editing application that you want to do so. This can be done via your computer's preferences menu by selecting audio input and output and by setting the correct input and output devices inside your audio editing application.

Online Module 8

Screencast on how to select the correct audio input and outputs

Avoid recording interviews over the telephone if at all possible. Achieving high-quality sound over the phone is very difficult. It requires a lot of editing work to adjust the sound, an expensive piece of hardware called a mixer, or both. If you must use the telephone, be sure to tell the person on the other end that you are recording the call.

A final—and least desirable—option is to use some sort of **Voice-Over-IP,** or **VoIP**, chat software to conduct an interview. **Skype** or **iChat** are two examples of VoIP applications. To record the conversations, you will need yet another application, such as **Audio Hijack** for the Macintosh or **Total Recorder** for Windows.

Editing Digital Audio

Once you've captured your interview on your audio recorder, you will need to upload it to your computer for editing. Each model of digital recorder is different, but you will probably either connect the recorder directly to the computer using a USB port or remove some type of memory disk from the recorder and insert it into a slot on your computer. You will then copy the files off your recorder and onto the computer, just as you would transfer any other files from an external device. Some recorders attempt to force you to transfer and edit the audio using the proprietary software that comes with it; it is not necessary to use this, however. It is generally better to work directly through your computer's file system.

After you've transferred the files, you will need to make sure that they are in a format that is compatible with your editing software and operating system. For example, if you recorded your audio as a WMA file format, it will not play on Apple computers unless you download and install a program called **Flip4Mac**. There are several free applications—for example, **Switch**, which you can download from the Web—that can help you convert audio file formats.

As with your digital photo files, follow through with good management of your audio files: be sure that you don't edit the original files, give each file a unique and descriptive name and organize the files in a manner that makes sense to you.

 ## Tool: Audacity

Unlike photo editing software, audio editing software does not come pre-installed on most computers. You can import almost any audio file format into almost any editing application. The edits you make on a piece of audio typically will not affect the original file.

Popular professional editing applications such as ProTools, Sound Forge or Audition cost several hundred dollars, whereas Audacity is a free, open-source solution that is widely used by journalists and journalism students on a budget.

- Audacity can be downloaded for either a Windows or Mac computer at http://audacity.sourceforge.net/download/.

- To export your audio files in the MP3 format, you will also need to download and install a software component called LAME, which is available at http://audacity.sourceforge.net/help/faq?s=install&item=lame-mp3.

Screencast on how to use Audacity to edit and save audio

Tutorials for audio editing applications

Editing an Audio Interview

The most common use of audio in news reporting is to record an interview. Even for print journalists, audio recording of interviews provides important source material that can be referenced when writing up text articles.

In a few rare cases—for example, when the interview subject is particularly prominent or controversial—a reporter might want to post the audio from the entire interview. But in general posting unedited interviews should be saved for those instances when it is necessary to demonstrate a high level of transparency to a skeptical audience or when the conversation is so compelling that it warrants the audience's extra attention.

Most of the time, journalists will edit recorded interviews before posting them. For the uninitiated, editing an audio or video interview presents unique challenges. Journalists who are accustomed to pulling quotes out of an interview for a text story quickly realize that they are unable to wield one of their most reliable tools: the paraphrase. When editing audio or video, the only material available is the raw recording: the exact words the interview subject said in the exact order she said them.

In most cases when working with digital audio, you will be editing what radio journalists call an **actuality.** An actuality is what a layperson might call a sound bite—a direct quote from a source that stands alone. There are several ways you might use an actuality in an online news story, for example, as a link from a text article, as part of an audio narration to a photo slide show or as part of a complete audio story distributed as a podcast episode.

Actualities are typically very short—somewhere between 5 seconds and 15 seconds long. But you might prefer to post a lengthier audio. For example, you could create a link to a full interview or a complete speech from an article where the interview or speech has only been summarized. Or, you may wish to post both—two different versions for two different audiences.

To edit an actuality you will need to isolate it from the rest of the audio you recorded. You can do this by either removing all of the sound both before and after the quote or by highlighting the exact quote and then cutting it and pasting it into a new audio track. When pulling a quote out of an interview be sure and leave a silent space both before the quote begins and after it is complete. Words should not be clipped too closely.

Listen to two versions of the same clip—one with hesitations and stutters and one without

Pulling a quote is the most basic kind of editing you will do. But you don't have to stop there. If you need to you can clean up your audio. For example, you can edit the "ums" and other pauses or hesitations of your subject that prove distracting. To do this, you will need to zoom closely in on the waveform to ensure that you cut only pieces of clutter and not the quote.

Depending on how you set up the microphones during an interview, your own voice may be on the recording. In most cases you will want to remove your voice before posting the interview or clips from it. Be sure that your subject's comments make sense when removed from the context of your questions. The best way to do this is *during* the interview: listen for clips that contain valuable information but that might be misunderstood without a framing question. In such cases, don't hesitate to ask your subject to restate the comment in a way that supplies the required context. Getting an interview subject to both frame and answer a question is a skill all good journalists need to develop.

In some cases, for example, in a podcast show, you might want to include your voice as well as the voices of one or more interview subjects. The process of ordering various tracks of audio is called **mixing**. Mixing audio is both an art and a science—you have to know how to use a particular tool to create an audio aesthetic that sounds good to you and conveys your story accurately.

To create a **mixdown**, you will first need to import several audio files into a single project or workspace inside your digital audio editing application. Each clip or voice should be on its own track, with the most important track on the top and the least important track on the bottom. Each track should be identified by a unique name. Once you have ordered your tracks it is time to impose continuity. To do this you will need to master the art of **fading.** To maintain continuity across tracks a fade should be done smoothly with no distracting break—as you quickly fade out of one sound clip you will need to fade in as quickly to the next. In fact, the two fades should overlap a bit. But be sure that no overlap in content occurs. The content that you want the audience to hear should be at full volume on both tracks. When fading music or ambient noise in or out, fading can be done more slowly.

Finally, review the end mix before you post it. Here is a quick checklist of what to listen for in your audio file:

1. Are all voices clear? Are they too quiet? Muffled by background noise? Is the sound too "hot"?

2. Is the volume constant across the entire piece, regardless of who is speaking?

3. Is the final recording free of districting background noises?

Exporting and Compressing Audio

Once you are satisfied with your final mix—or run out of time before deadline!—you will need to export the audio project as a single file that can be downloaded or played from the Internet. Remember that sound quality and file size are inversely related. Higher-quality files will be larger and take longer to download. Lower-quality files will be smaller and take less time to download. You will need to find the correct balance between the two.

In almost all cases, you will be exporting your audio report as some sort of compressed audio file format, such as an MP3. Most of the podcasts produced by NPR and American Public Media are compressed as 64-kbps MP3 files at 44.1 kHz. A few music-related podcasts that require higher fidelity are compressed at 128 kbps and 44.1 kHz. As a rough guide, you can expect that an MP3 file compressed at 64 kbps and 44.1 kHz will be 1 MB for about every two minutes of sound. At 128 kbps, the files are a little less than 1 MB for every one minute of sound.

For the journalist working on deadline—take note: exporting and compressing a final audio project can take as long as the length of the audio file itself. So, if your audio report runs to three minutes, then expect the report to take about three minutes to export.

Distributing Digital Audio

Once you have your MP3 file, you will need to upload it to a server in order to use it on your website. Uploading an audio file is no different from uploading a digital photo. You will either transfer the file via FTP or use a Web-based file-uploading tool that comes with your blogging or CMS platform.

Once an audio file is uploaded to the Web, it becomes available at a specific URL. For example, a file called "test.mp3" uploaded to your Web server might be found at http://www.yourwebserver.com/audio/test.mp3. You can now link to the MP3 just as you would link to any other HTML or JPG or PDF file on the Web. If you conducted an interview with the mayor, you might insert a link at the bottom of your story that reads: "Listen to my interview with the mayor." The HTML would look like this: `<a href="http://www.yourwebserver.com/audio/test.mp3">Listen to my interview with the mayor.</a>`

A listener who clicked on these words would, in most browsers, see a basic audio controller in the browser window and hear the audio of the file. A browser will open an external program, called a **plug-in**, to play the sound file. The three most common plug-ins are **Flash, Windows Media Player** and **QuickTime**.

You can also embed an audio file directly within a Web page. In this case, the visitor would see the audio player embedded within the body of the page. This is just like embedding a photograph in a Web page. To embed the "test.mp3" audio file, you might use the following HTML code within the body of the page:

```
<OBJECT classid='clsid:02BF25D5-8C17-4B23-BC80-D3488ABDDC6B'
width="144" height="60" codebase='http://www.apple.com/qtactivex/
qtplugin.cab'>

<param name='src' value="http://www.yourwebserver.com/audio/test.
mp3"> <param name='autoplay' value="false">

<param name='controller' value="true">

<param name='loop' value="false">

<EMBED src="http://servername/path/to/media.file" width="320"
height="255" autoplay="false" controller="true" loop="false"
pluginspage='http://www.apple.com/quicktime/download/'> </EMBED>

</OBJECT>
```

In this example, the browser is being asked to play the audio file with the QuickTime plug-in. This method uses the HTML `<object>` **tag**, which is an official part of the HTML specification, as well as the `<embed>` tag, which is not part of the official HTML specification even though it is widely used by some browsers and is necessary if they are to play inline media files. In a new version of HTML, called **HTML5,** these methods will be standardized and likely change significantly. In early 2010, YouTube began experimenting with HTML5 video tags, and the most recent versions of all major browsers now support some—but not all—HTML5 elements.

Tool: Soundslides

It goes by many different names—slideshow, audio gallery, narrated photo gallery—but whatever you call it, the combination of still photographs and sound is an effective way to tell a story. And because it consumes less bandwidth than a video, it has become one of the most widely used multimedia techniques at news websites.

To fill the demand for this style of multimedia story, an enterprising journalist in North Carolina created an inexpensive and easy-to-use application called Soundslides. Using a simple workflow and user-interface, Soundslides allows you to import photos, write captions for them, put them in a specific order and then add a sound file that plays underneath them. After the photos and audio are arranged, the story is exported as a complete package of files, including the HTML and Flash files that you need to publish the audio slide show to the Web. Publishing it is as easy as uploading a single folder to your website.

The know-how necessary for creating a Soundslides show is not difficult for students who already know how to use Photoshop and Audacity, who know how to upload files via FTP and have just enough knowledge of HTML and CSS to ensure that the slide show appears properly on a Web page after production is complete. The editorial choices, however, require some planning.

Slideshows created with Soundslides are linear—that is, the audience will start at the first photo and move sequentially through each photo until it arrives at the last photo in the series. This means that you will want to use your photos to create a narrative arc. Consider each of the storytelling components: When do you introduce a character? How and when do you show conflict? What is the climax of your story? And what will be your visual resolution?

Many slideshow producers begin by creating and editing the audio story first, then adding the photos afterward. Some examples of audio content include a "behind-the-scenes" account of an event or the voice or voices of the people featured in the story. Once the audio portion is in place, the photographs can be selected and synchronized to the sound. It is essential, of course, that the spoken words are correctly matched to the relevant images.

The secret to a good slideshow is a good story—and a good rhythm.

Tutorials on how to produce a slideshow with Soundslides

Podcasting

The term "podcast" refers to one of three things: a series of audio files, a particular episode within the series or the digital text file that is used by a listener to subscribe to the series. The only difference between publishing an MP3 file on the Web and publishing it as a podcast is that people can subscribe to MP3s that are published as podcasts. Hence, if your MP3—however interesting and newsworthy—is not part of a series, then there is no reason to publish it as a podcast.

The guidelines for creating a successful podcast are in many ways the same as those for blogging. Chapter 10, on blogging, details the importance of picking a niche target, providing short and frequent updates and engaging with your audience. The creators of a podcast must not only ensure that it is well written, but that it is technically well produced too.

The length of a professionally produced podcast can range anywhere from just a few minutes to an hour. As a general rule, the less frequently you update your podcast, the broader the topic and the more voices featured on each show, the longer your podcast should be. A frequently updated podcast on a narrow topic narrated only by you should be very short. Three minutes is probably a good maximum length for any single topic in a podcast. And five, three-minute segments is probably the maximum length for any podcast that is just getting started. The advantage of podcasts versus broadcast radio shows is that there is no requirement to adhere to a strict time maximum or minimum. You can let content drive your decisions about length.

In many ways the structure of a podcast, regardless of its length, is similar to that of a good audio or video news program in broadcast. A podcast episode should follow the same basic structure. Here are the five steps:

1. **Make an introduction.** Tell your audience which episode they are about to hear, including the date it was originally posted. Introduce yourself and the topics the podcast will be covering. Remember, this may be the first time that a listener is tuning in—or the millionth.

2. **Present the "lead" of the first segment.** In broadcast, leads need to both summarize the upcoming story and grab the listener's attention. Remember that your audience will be seeing something else while it is listening to your show. This means that your sound will be competing with a "view" for your listener's attention—as often as not, the "view" will be one of dozens of cars racing along the interstate.

3. **Tell the story.** As you present the details, use very short sentences. Don't hesitate to reiterate key points. A word or phrase that may be perfectly clear in writing may need to be simplified and clarified in audio. Be sure to listen to the final version of any story to make sure it is clear before you post it.

4. **Recap.** After you've told listeners what you're going to tell them, then told it to them, you need to finish up by telling them what it was you told them. Repeating the key points of your story gives the audience a sense of closure.

5. Tease the next segment or episode. Let people know what they can expect to hear next and when they will be hearing it. This is also a good time to point people back to your Web page or other resources. You may choose to include music between segments to provide an aural break.

Before you set out to produce your own podcast, it is a good idea to spend some time listening to what's already out there. The shows sponsored by public radio organizations such as NPR, American Public Media and Public Radio International are almost all high quality both in terms of content and production value. ESPN also offers several high-quality podcasts. In iTunes and other podcast directories, you will find literally thousands of shows as well as lists of which shows are popular at any given time. Listen to as many as you can and note your likes and dislikes. Chances are you'll find some styles and techniques that you can model as you get started on a podcast of a subject that interests you.

DIGITAL VIDEO

The next time you visit a news website, take a look at some of the video stories posted there. But do it with a critical eye. First, watch a few videos without the sound. Even if you don't understand the details of the story, could you tell who the primary subjects were? Did the content of the shots and their order and the pacing at which they were displayed convey some sort of narrative arc, with an introduction, a climax and a conclusion? The best news videos will. Now, take a look at some other videos on the site. This time, close your eyes and just listen to the sound. Are there sounds that allow you to imagine what the scene looks like? Can you tell whether the voices are far away or close? Is the mood of each speaker apparent?

While video stories are comprised both of video and audio, they should be more than just a visual sequence set on top of an audio timeline. While the technical elements of video reporting must be accomplished with precision, it is the storytelling that captures the attention of the audience. And good storytelling is the product of good editing. After all, it is the editing process that weaves together the sights and sounds to create a whole that is greater than any of its parts.

As a journalist you already know how to tell a good story. The key to great video reporting is to become equally adept with the technologies involved in its creation. When the technical aspects of recording and editing become second nature to you, nothing will get in the way of your ability to transport your audience to a time and place that is both relevant and memorable. In fact, mastering this new set of skills might just take your reporting to a whole new level.

 Tool: Digital Video Cameras ⎯⎯⎯⎯⎯⎯⎯⎯⎯⎯⎯⎯⎯⎯⎯⎯

Digital video cameras can cost anywhere from $150 to $15,000. Obviously, with such a range of prices, there exists an equally vast range in quality and available features—more so than with either digital still cameras or digital audio recorders. Picking the right camera depends on which features will best complement your news organization's workflow as well as the manner in which the video will ultimately be delivered. The focus here will be on cameras that can be used for quick turnaround of video distributed to desktop or laptop computers connected to the Internet.

The developing trend for video journalists is the move away from standard definition (SD) to **high definition (HD)** video. Along with a push toward a higher-quality video image is a related push toward higher bandwidth for video delivered over the Internet—both via traditional land lines and via wireless mobile devices, whose market has grown phenomenally in recent years. The higher the quality of video, the longer it takes to deliver over the Internet. A single HD video frame can require up to six times more data than an SD frame. The trends toward high definition and high bandwidth tend to drive each other.

Most of the best professional multimedia journalists have already made the switch to high definition. The primary reason for this is business driven: even if the final product ends up as a standard definition video delivered over the Internet to computers or mobile phones, video journalism that is shot in high definition can later be relicensed for broadcast or for Blu-ray disc distribution. It makes good business sense for a video journalist to enter the market with the best product possible. If profitability depends on wider distribution to a larger audience interested in the highest-quality product, then purchase of the kind of equipment that best captures hard-to-get stories and images is a smart investment.

Storage Media

The balance between image quality and size of file (and therefore download time of your completed video story) is not the only factor to be considered when choosing between standard or high definition video. Shooting in high definition also consumes more storage media on a camera than shooting in standard definition. This means that when you are shooting out in the field you will need to carry with you more storage media.

Like digital still cameras and digital audio recorders, many digital cameras record to SDHC (Secure Digital High Capacity) cards. These come in a variety of "classes." Video should be shot on SDHC class 4 or above. SDHC cards come in a variety of sizes. If you are shooting in standard definition, you will get about 19 minutes per 1 GB of card memory. In high definition, you will get about 7.5 minutes of video per 1 GB of card memory if the video files are compressed; if the HD video files are not compressed, you will get only about one minute of video per gigabyte.

Some cameras use SDHC cards in conjunction with an internal memory that cannot be removed from the camera. This is known as **flash memory,** or sometimes **solid state memory** because it has no moving parts. The advantage of flash memory is that you will never be without some type of recording media. The downside is that you have to stop shooting in order to upload video files from the camera to a computer. With SDHC cards, you can hand the card over to an editor and then keep shooting. Some low-end video cameras offer flash memory only, without the option of adding an SDHC card.

In one respect, video cameras are a bit of an oddity among digital recording devices. Unlike still cameras or digital audio recorders, many digital video cameras still record to tape. A tape will typically store either an hour of SD or an hour of HD video. Standard definition–recording tape is known as **MiniDV tape**; high definition–recording tape is known as **MiniHD tape.** Either of these recording options is considerably cheaper than recording to an SDHC card—typically half the cost. However, it takes much longer to upload, or "capture," video stored on tape than it does to upload video stored on an SDHC card. Moving video from a tape to an editing computer happens in real time. This means that if you shoot an hour of video, you will have to wait an hour before you can even get started on editing it. Moving digital files from a card to a computer is as simple as dragging and dropping the files from the card to the hard drive. Something to keep in mind when working on deadline!

Resolution

As with digital still cameras, the resolution at which you shoot will affect both file size and image quality. In high definition, you might shoot at 1440×1080 pixels or 1280×720. In standard definition, you might shoot at 1080×1080 or 640×480. The larger the pixel numbers, the higher the resolution—and the higher the resolution, the better the image quality. But remember, higher resolution means a larger file—which means more time needed to download.

Frame Rate

The **frame rate** is the number of images per second that a video camera captures. Most video cameras shoot at 30 frames per second. Movies are filmed at 24 frames per second. The higher the frame rate, the smoother the motion of the objects in your video.

Some cameras also allow you to record video as either progressive scan or interlaced. These two terms describe the way that the final picture is "painted" on the screen after it is recorded. **Interlaced video,** the format used on broadcast television, first paints all the even-numbered horizontal lines of an image and then paints all the odd-numbered lines. **Progressive scan video** paints each horizontal line of an image in sequence—first Line 1, then Line 2, Line 3 and so forth. Progressive scan is used on most computer screens and results in a better image quality. However, it requires more bandwidth than interlace. Interlaced video displayed on a computer screen will look jagged.

Cameras that shoot to tape record interlaced video. The video they record needs to be **de-interlaced** during the editing and production process. The issue of interlaced and progressive scan video will be revisited later in the chapter in our discussion on exporting video for the Web.

File Format

If your camera records to an SDHC card, you'll want to be aware of the file format in which it stores the video. Video file types, container formats and compression codecs can be maddeningly confusing. For example, not all files with the **filename suffix** ".avi" use the same video **codec,** and they may behave differently on different editing platforms. Quick-Time files, which use the ".mov" suffix, are a **container format** that may use a codec for the audio portion of a file that is different from that used for the video portion of the file. Finally, the MPEG-4 file type can use the same codecs as QuickTime files, but use two different filename suffixes: "**.mp4**" and "**.m4v**."

CCDs

Video cameras use either one light **sensor chip** or three light sensor chips to record moving images. These sensor chips are called **Charge Coupled Devices**, or **CCDs**. Cameras that use three CCDs split light into the three primary colors—red, green and blue—and as a result are able to produce truer color.

Low Light Performance

Adequate lighting is critical when recording digital video, and some cameras are made to shoot better in lower light than others. The light ratings on cameras are measured in **lux.** Absolute darkness is 0 lux. Journalists should use cameras that have a light sensitivity rating of no more than 7 lux.

Zoom

Better cameras have higher degrees of optical zoom. Journalists will want to use video cameras that are able to zoom in on an object by a factor of anywhere from 10 to 40 times.

Microphones

While many video cameras record audio with an internal microphone, you will get higher-quality audio if you use an external microphone. Just as with digital audio recorders, XLR microphone inputs produce a higher-quality sound than microphones that connect through a 1/8-inch mini-plug. If you are filming an interview with just one camera, you may find it useful to use one that has two XLR microphone inputs, one for each person you are filming. As with digital audio recording, be sure to wear headphones so that you can hear exactly what is being recorded.

Output Connections

If you are shooting to tape, you will want to use a video camera with a **FireWire** output, also known as an i.Link or IEEE 1394 output. If you connect a camera to a computer with a FireWire connection, then you can use many high-end video editing programs such as Premiere or Final Cut to control the playback of videotapes in your camera.

Cameras that have USB output jacks can also connect to your computer, allow you to easily select video files on the SDHC card or flash memory on your camera and move them to the computer you will use to edit them. If you cannot connect your camera directly to a computer with a USB cord, then you will need to purchase a card reader that will allow your computer to read memory cards. The SDHC card is placed into the card reader, which is in turn plugged into a USB port on the computer.

You may also want to play the video on your camera directly into a monitor. In this case, your camera will need audio and video output jacks that can be connected directly to one of the audio and video input jacks on your monitor.

Accessories

Following are some of the more important accessories for shooting news video:

- Microphone—A wireless **lavaliere microphone** can be discretely clipped to an interview subject's tie or lapel. Shotgun microphones can be held above the camera and capture audio directly in front of the lens while excluding other ambient noise.

- Tripod—Hand-held shots will almost always have some jiggle to them. Tripods are the best way to avoid this. Use one whenever you are able to set up in advance.

- Light kit—Shooting video requires a properly lit subject. Shadows across faces can be distracting to viewers and even make interview subjects look menacing. This means that you need to be ready with additional lighting. Light kits are the solution.

- Batteries and battery charger—Many video cameras use large batteries that are not universally sized. This means that you will either need to limit your shooting time to the duration of one battery, bring spare batteries or be near an electrical outlet where you can recharge the batteries.

- Camera bag—Even the most basic set of video equipment can become unwieldy if not well contained and well organized—not to mention expensive to replace if not well protected. A sturdy, well-designed camera bag will alleviate any worries.

Basics of Video Reporting

Shooting video is like taking a photograph and recording audio all at the same time. When you shoot video, the techniques you use will depend on the type of story you are trying to tell. Your videos will be one of two types:

- **Interview video**—The purpose of an interview video is to record the exact words, voice tone and body language of an interview subject.

- **Environmental video**—The purpose of an environmental video is to capture and communicate the sights and sounds of a particular place at a particular time.

Of course, you may end up using both kinds of video in your final product. But when you are recording, you will be focused either on an environment or an interview subject.

Interview Videos

Setting up for a video interview takes more time than setting up for an interview that will not be recorded. It can take 15 to 30 minutes to set up the camera and lights that are needed to make a visually appealing video. Be respectful of the time your subject is giving you for the interview; do not make them wait while you fiddle with camera and lighting settings. When possible, choose a location where you will be able to set up your equipment in advance of your subject's arrival.

People behave differently when they are facing a camera. Oftentimes this is because they are nervous. It is natural for an interview subject to be concerned about they way they will look or sound on camera. Part of your job is to put them at ease so that you both can focus your energy on gathering information. To help relieve your subject's anxiety, it is always a good idea to make small talk with him before you start recording. Even consider talking with your subject about the equipment you will be using during the interview. Understanding the process will help make him more comfortable.

Shooting video interviews requires a substantial amount of practice. Here are some things to keep in mind as you get started:

1. **Use a tripod.** You want the camera to be as steady as possible, so if you don't have a tripod then you will want to lean on something that helps keep your arms steady. Take slow breaths, keep your arms close to your body, put your feet at shoulder-width and bend your knees slightly. The position of your entire body can affect the quality of your video.

2. **Do not pan the camera from side to side.**

3. **Do not zoom during a shot.**

4. **Always use lights—and then use more.** Check to be sure there are no shadows on the subject's face.

5. **Put the camera at the eye level of the subject.** Shooting up at the subject's face gives an illusion of added power while shooting down at the subject's face gives an illusion of insignificance.

6. **Shoot tight—and then tighter still.** You want your audience to be able to see the expression on your subject's face, even if it is watching the video on something as small as

the screen of a mobile device. It's OK to cut off a bit of the subject's forehead, even. But be careful not to frame the shot so that the subject's chin looks as if it is resting on the bottom of the frame.

7. **Have the subject look at you, not the camera.** If you place yourself slightly to the left or right of the camera, the subject will look more natural.

8. **Be quiet.** When the subject is responding, don't interrupt with "yeah . . . mmm, hmmm," and don't shuffle papers.

9. **Shoot some environmental shots** that can be used when you need cutaways. A **cutaway** can be edited in later to "cover" a long answer by the subject or to be used as transitions between two parts of an interview or two different speakers. If your schedule allows it, try to shoot the cutaways after the interview. This makes it easier to match them to the comments of your subject. Cutaways should match—or at least not contradict—the words that the audience will hear while the cutaway shot is on the screen.

10. **Don't shoot too much.** Unlike still photographs, it takes a long time both to capture and sift through video during the editing process. If you are shooting to tape rather than a memory card, you should be especially cautious about not shooting too much.

Environmental Videos

As with interview videos, environmental videos require forethought and planning. All the basic rules of interviewing apply: keep the camera steady, use as much light as you can and don't zoom or pan. Here are some additional considerations:

1. Look, shoot, interview, reshoot. Take the time to consider all angles before you start shooting. Once you have an idea of how the setting looks from different perspectives, and how the subjects move around within that setting, go ahead and shoot. If you will be interviewing people in their environment, you also may need to do some additional shooting after the interview so that you can capture the events, objects or processes the subject mentioned in the interview. Remember, when you are telling a story with video you need to capture all the relevant elements—if you don't it will be very difficult for your audience to grasp the meaning of the story.

2. Move around between shots. Shoot from one angle, stop the camera and shoot again from another angle. Don't just move right and left; if possible move up and down as well. Just don't move *while* shooting. Also, be sure to shoot from different distances. When you are showing a process in particular, it can be helpful to shoot the same process several times, each time from a different angle or distance. Then, when you are editing the piece, you can "move" the viewer from a broad view of the environment to close-ups of specific objects in the environment. This mimics the way a viewer would navigate an unknown environment if she were physically inside it.

3. Think about shooting sequences. To tell a story that unfolds over time, you will have to visually show the viewers what happens first, next and last.

4. Lead your target. If the subject of your video is moving, be sure to keep some space in front of the subject at all times. Never let a subject jump or fall out of the frame.

5. If zooming in is truly the only way to produce a desired effect, then you will want to first zoom all the way into your final shot and frame it. Then zoom the camera back out and begin shooting. When you zoom, do it. Very. Slowly.

Editing Video

Now that you have recorded your video, it is time to edit it. Or, you may find yourself editing video shot by someone else. Although there are many different brands of digital video editing software, most provide the same basic functions.

Regardless of which video editing software you use, the process of editing video will follow three basic steps: (1) move the video out of the camera and into the editing application by capturing, importing and logging clips; (2) organize the video clips with cuts and transitions; and (3) compress and export the video for distribution on the Web.

Tool: Premiere

Of the myriad choices a video editor is faced with, the first is selecting the right editing software. **Premiere,** made by Adobe, is a popular choice among professionals and is available for both Macintosh and Windows operating systems. Another popular editing application is **Final Cut,** which is only available for the Macintosh. Many amateur bloggers and low-budget newsrooms use **iMovie,** for the Macintosh, and **Windows Movie Maker,** for the Windows operating system.

Screencast on capturing, editing and exporting video files

Online Module 8

Tutorials for working with Premiere resources

Premiere and Final Cut are vastly more powerful and complicated than iMovie or Windows Movie Maker. The instruction manual for Final Cut Pro is more than 2,000 pages long! The good news is that once you've learned your way around the most common functions of any of these video editors, you will be able to get right to work.

Importing, Capturing and Logging

Importing, capturing and logging video can be the most time-consuming process in the entire video reporting and editing workflow. More than one news story has been dropped from a website's news budget because the journalists working on it failed to take into account the time needed for this technical process. Good video reporters working on tight deadlines become more selective about their shots as they become more familiar with the demands of the editing process.

When video comes in from the field, the first thing you must do is import your video into the editing software. This doesn't mean just opening a file, as you would when working with digital photo files in Photoshop. **Importing** video into an editing application means that you are not working with the original video file. The upside of this is that your original footage is preserved for re-use in another story; the downside is that more time is needed for the extra step of importing.

If you have shot your video to a flash memory drive or a removable SDHC memory card, importing video will be simple. First you drag the file from the external memory and drop it onto the hard drive of your editing computer. After you open your editing application, find the submenu item labeled "Import." Once you select it you will be asked which video file you wish to import. Select the file and wait—as noted above, importing a video file takes time.

If you have shot video to a tape, then you will have to connect your camera to the computer using a FireWire connection. You will use your editing software to "play" the tape on the camera and "**capture**" the video into the editing application. The amount of time it takes to capture video shot to tape is equal to the amount of video you shot. So, if you recorded an hour of video in the field, then you will need to wait an hour while the software captures the video from the tape. Capturing video requires a lot of computing power, so be sure to close all other applications while the computer is at work.

Logging footage is the practice of choosing and naming short segments of video that you've shot on your tape before capturing them into the editing application. With small amounts of single-subject footage, logging is not necessary. But when you have hours of tape of various subjects and various shots, logging is critical in order to reduce the time it takes to capture and edit the final cut of the story.

When logging a tape, you will use an editing application to play and watch the video. When you see video you want to use, you will set an "**in point**," usually by pressing a specific button on the keyboard. At the end of the video segment, you will set an "**out point**," again by pressing a specific keyboard button. Don't import more video than you need. Doing so only wastes time on deadline.

Before importing all of your clips, import a test clip so you can check to be sure you hear sound and see video. If you can't hear the audio—and the audio level meters aren't moving—or if you cannot see the video, check to make sure you are working with a file type and container format suitable for your operating system and editing software.

Cuts and Transitions

Once you've finished importing your video, you will see a timeline in your video editing application that looks like the timeline in audio editing software. If you're editing a simple single-subject interview, then editing the video will be very much like editing audio. If you collected **B-roll**—that is, a secondary roll of film from which to make cutaways—you may use it to cover cuts in the video. These cutaways are used to visually cut away from the subject of the interview. If you do use B-roll, be sure to match the image to the spoken words. For example, if your subject is talking about the influence of her mother, cut to a shot that shows an old photo of the subject and her mother on her desk.

If your video is more complicated and involves multiple shots, avoid jumpcuts. A **jumpcut** is a transition that shows the same person in adjacent shots, but in a different position. This makes it look as if the person—or some part of the person's body—has "jumped" from one spot to another.

Whatever you do, resist your inner Picasso: *don't* use "artistic" transitions or other effects. Employing anything other than basic transitions can make your video look amateurish and may even convey to the audience an unintended opinion about the subject of the video.

Try to use matched action, especially when your video story involves the "How" news element. **Matched action** is the technique of showing the same action from different distances or slightly different angles. To do this in the editing stage, you will have had to think about it during the shooting process. If you don't shoot the scene from different lengths and angles, then you won't have the material necessary to achieve matched action during editing.

Order your shots. If you have multiple shots, first use a wide shot that allows the audience to establish the location of the story. This is known as an **establishing shot.** After you have established the setting of the story, then use close-ups to convey the details. This technique mimics the way that people visually scan unknown environments.

Finally, add titles. A **title** is the word or words you put on the screen to supply context. Titles can be placed in frames of their own, or they can be placed over the top of the image. Title frames that appear at the beginning of the video can introduce the time, place or topic of the story; they can also be used in the middle of a story to introduce "chapters." Title frames almost always center the text vertically and horizontally in the middle of the frame. When titles are printed on top of the image, they are often used to introduce the name and significance of each new speaker. They can also be used to set the time or location of the story. When titles are placed over images, be sure to put them on the lower third of the screen, flush left or right. This is the reason that titles over video images are known as "**lower thirds**." Whether you use text or audio, be sure to establish the time and setting of your story as well as the names of all of the speakers. When video is posted on the Web, you can't always control the time or place your audience sees it. This makes it all the more important that the audience be provided with the age of the information in the story as well as its setting and source.

After you've finished editing, have a colleague look at your video. A second set of eyes is one way to safeguard against problems in the storytelling that you did not catch. She may also catch misspellings in titles. Errors in a video are extremely difficult to fix once published to the Web.

NEWS JUDGMENT

TAKING QUOTES OUT OF CONTEXT

Newsmakers who believe they have been misrepresented in print or on TV often complain about being quoted out of context. Literally, of course, they're right. Unless your news report consists of every word uttered in the universe at the time of the interview, you are presenting facts and quotes without the complete context that accompanied them. Making choices is a journalist's job—and making *ethical* choices means including enough context so that each quote accurately represents a speaker's meaning.

Editing quotes, whether for print or broadcast, can pose tough questions. Should you remove stumbles or stutters or places where the speaker meandered off before returning to the point? The inexperienced reporter might answer yes; after all, stumbles distract from a speaker's meaning. Sometimes, however, spaces and hesitations clearly convey a tone or nuance that is essential to the story. Subtleties such as these cannot be conveyed through words alone. And removing them from an audio or video interview can in fact compromise the accuracy of your report.

Manipulating the audio or video of an interview in any way that misrepresents the content or context of a quote is clearly unethical. It would be simple to think, "It happened; I saw it; it's true." But we all know that editing can change the way people perceive the truth. It may be the truth, but not the *whole* truth.

To illustrate, consider an interview that then-candidate Barack Obama gave to George Stephanopoulos of ABC News in 2008. In a 12-second clip posted on YouTube, Obama is heard saying: "You're absolutely right that John McCain has not, uh, talked about my Muslim faith." This clip was widely circulated on the Internet and cited by Obama opponents as evidence that he was secretly Muslim and not Christian as he claimed.

Was this proof that Obama was hiding his true religion? Obama did say those words. But when you are exposed to the context—to the two minutes that surrounded that 12-second quote—your understanding of Obama's statement is completely altered. In the longer clip, you watch as Obama stumbles over the wording of his answer, and when Stephanopoulos questions him, he clarifies: "What I'm saying is, [McCain] hasn't suggested that I'm a Muslim." Click on the two links below and see for yourself.

- The 12-second clip: http://www.youtube.com/watch?v=XKGdkqfBICw
- The two-minute clip: http://www.youtube.com/watch?v=iQqIpdBOg6I

Most professional journalists wouldn't deliberately mislead their audience. But, in fact, it is all to easy to change meaning purely by accident. The skilled journalist is ever-vigilant and knows the danger zones. For example, don't re-order the sequence of a person's statements in a way that makes those separate quotes sound like one continuous quote. If you do need to play quotes out of order, be sure that you clearly convey to the audience that the two clips were not consecutive.

To many news consumers, seeing *is* believing. Photos and video *are* more trusted than text descriptions. Your job as a journalist is to ensure that they can believe what they see. Following are links to sites offering further insights into the professional ethics of editing audio and video:

- http://mindymcadams.com/tojou/2007/truth-in-audio-have-you-crossed-an-ethical-line/
- http://www.cpb.org/stations/radioethicsguide/
- http://www.j-source.ca/english_new/detail.php?id=1638

Compressing and Exporting Video

After you've edited your video, you are ready to set the compression and export settings. These settings determine the quality and file size of your final video. There is no magic compression formula that is universally ideal, and there are literally millions of possible combinations of export settings in iMovie alone. As you get started with video editing you may find that you need to tweak the compression settings and export the video several times until you get the balance just right. Differences in a video's length or its audio or video content may require a bit of fine tuning.

Here, however, is a good place to start:

Video

- File format: MPEG-4 (.mp4)
- Compression codec: **H.264**
- Keyframes: automatic (should be about 1 keyframe every 10–50 frames)
- Framerate: 30 fps
- Resolution: 640 x 480 (SD) or 1280 x 720 (HD)

Audio

- File format: AAC
- Sample rate: 44.1 kHz stereo, or 22.05 kHz mono
- Bit rate: 64 kbps

Other popular options you may want to try include the following:

- Exporting the video as a QuickTime (**.mov**) file, using the H.264 compression codec
- Using the MP3 format instead of AAC
- Exporting as a Flash video (.flv) file
- Reducing the resolution to 320 x 240
- Reducing the framerate to 15 fps

Finally, if you are working with Windows Movie Maker, the free video editing application from Microsoft, you will only be able to export as either a Windows Media Video (.wmv) file or as an AVI file (.avi). If you save it as an AVI, it will be very large but you can still upload it directly to a video-sharing site such as YouTube or Vimeo. In fact, if you upload an AVI to YouTube you can then download it as a much smaller MPEG-4 video that uses the H.264 codec for video and AAC for audio. You can also use a free application such as **Handbrake** to change the format of the video from AVI to something more suitable for distribution over the Web.

Regardless of the specific settings you use for each video file, you will want to review the final copy to be sure the balance between quality and file size is appropriate for your audience. A good rule of thumb is to keep your videos at 1MB per minute for a low-bandwidth audience and at 3–4MB per minute for a high-bandwidth audience.

Distributing Video

Just as with digital photos and audio files, you will need to upload your news video to a Web server in order to share it with an audience. Many news organizations use designated servers to host audio and video content. These servers are owned and managed either by the news organization itself or by a company that specializes in hosting Web content. Many news organizations use video-sharing sites such as YouTube or Vimeo to attract a broader audience and reduce hosting costs.

To upload video to a sharing site such as YouTube or Vimeo, you will need to create accounts with them. The content you upload must conform to the sites' technical, content and use restrictions. In addition to these general consumer sites, other video hosting solutions are available from companies such as the Associated Press and **Brightcove**.

Online Module 8

Tutorial on how to upload video

Regardless of where you host your video, after you have uploaded it and added all the appropriate metadata such as date and title, you will use HTML to embed the video into your site. Your CMS may have a simple workflow that allows you to add video to your pages without HTML. If not, you will need to be familiar with HTML's <object> and <embed> tags, which were briefly introduced in the audio section of this chapter. The <object> and <embed> tags tell a Web browser how to display and play specific pieces of content, especially audio and video content.

Both YouTube and Vimeo distribute videos as Flash files. Once a video is uploaded to either of these sites, both services will provide you with the embed code you will need to use on your website.

Following are examples of the HTML code used for each of these services:

From YouTube

```
<object width="560" height="340">

<param name="movie" value="http://www.youtube.com/[videoname]">
</param>

<param name="allowFullScreen" value="true"></param>

<param name="allowscriptaccess" value="always"></param>

<embed src="http://www.youtube.com/[videoname]"
type="application/x-shockwave-flash" allowscriptaccess="always"
allowfullscreen="true" width="560" height="340">

</embed>

</object>
```

From Vimeo

```
<object width="400" height="300">

<param name="allowfullscreen" value="true" />

<param name="allowscriptaccess" value="always" />

<param name="movie" value="http://vimeo.com/moogaloop.swf?clip_
id=&amp;server=vimeo.com&amp;show_title=1&amp;show_
byline=1&amp;show_portrait=0&amp;color=&amp;fullscreen=1" />

<embed src="http://vimeo.com/moogaloop.swf?clip_id=&amp;server=vimeo.
com&amp;show_title=1&amp;show_byline=1&amp;show_portrait=0&amp;co
lor=&amp;fullscreen=1" type="application/x-shockwave-flash"
allowfullscreen="true" allowscriptaccess="always" width="400"
height="300">

</embed>

</object>
```

While differences are apparent in the coding, it is more useful to look at the important similarities. Let's start by looking at the <object> tag. In both cases the <object> tag has a "width" and a "height" attribute. The values for these attributes help determine the height and width of the video on your page. The values of the height and width attributes in the <object> tag must match the height and width values in the <embed> tag.

The <object> tag has several child tags that are variations of the <param> (parameter) tag. The way that the <param> tags are closed differs between the two services. Each parameter has a unique name. Two important parameter names are "AllowFullScreen" and "movie." For "AllowFullScreen" the default is "false," which means that your audience cannot enlarge the video to the full size of their screens. To change this default, you must indicate that the parameter should have a value of "true." The value of the "movie" parameter tells the browser where to get the actual video file; in these two instances the files are stored as an ".swf" Flash file.

A quick word about Flash file extensions. **FLV** or **F4V** are Flash "video" files. These files are imported into Flash project files, which have an ".fla" file extension. **FLA** files are then compressed and exported as **SWF** files, which are then published to the Web.

While embedding video with the QuickTime player is similar to embedding Flash video, there are nevertheless some important differences. Following is sample HTML code that tells a Web browser to display an HTML video:

```
<OBJECT classid='clsid:02BF25D5-8C17-4B23-BC80-D3488ABDDC6B'
width="320" height="255" codebase='http://www.apple.com/qtactivex/
qtplugin.cab'>

<param name='src' value="http://servername/videofile.mov"> <param
name='autoplay' value="false">

<param name='controller' value="true">

<param name='loop' value="false">

<EMBED src="http://servername/videofile.mov" width="320" height="255"
autoplay="false" controller="true" loop="false" pluginspage='http://www
.apple.com/quicktime/download/'> </EMBED>

</OBJECT>
```

You can see that both the <object> and <embed> tags have height and width attributes. These attributes function as they do in the Flash embed code. But the "movie" parameter found in the Flash embed code is replaced with an "src" parameter in the Quick-Time embed code. Both tell the browser the location where it will find the actual video file.

Finally, you will see that the QuickTime embed code features additional parameters. These control whether visitors see the controller bar, whether the video plays as soon as it loads and whether it loops back to the beginning after it ends.

 ## Tool: Flash

One of the most common tools for creating multimedia and interactivity is Adobe's Flash application. Along with Photoshop and Illustrator, it has become a fundamental tool for Web designers. Designers and programmers can use Flash to create multimedia, interactive applications (.fla files) that are compressed and delivered over the Web as ".swf" files. These files are then read by the freely available Flash Player application that is on nearly every computer connected to the Web.

Flash has several important uses:

- It enforces standardized control over the visual layout in a manner superior to either HTML or CSS.

- It allows for various media to be delivered in a single file and permits interaction between these media.

- It allows illustrators to animate charts, graphs and other information graphics or even drawings.

- It provides opportunities for users to create customized experiences by interacting with raw data, such as sports scores, weather reports, stock prices or election returns.

When working with Flash, reporters and editors create content using applications such as Microsoft Word, Photoshop, Illustrator and Premiere. This content is then laid out in Flash. The animation and interactivity is programmed in Flash, which uses a proprietary scripting language called ActionScript.

For a variety of reasons, multimedia delivery and especially interactivity are trending toward nonproprietary programming solutions such as **AJAX**, an acronym that stands for "asynchronous JavaScript + XML." Heated debate is ongoing among online designers and programmers about whether the forthcoming HTML 5 will end up by replacing many of the more pedestrian uses of Flash, such as the display of audio and video on a Web page.

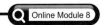

Tutorials on using Flash resources

On my blog, I write about and link to examples of how audio-visual reporting is being used in online journalism. Your questions and comments will help drive this discussion.

When you buy or activate this chapter's online learning module, you will have access to:

- A digital version of this chapter's text.

- Interactive flashcards for the terms used in this chapter.

- A printable tip sheet for shooting photos and recording audio and video for online journalism.

- A quiz to test your mastery of the material in this chapter.

- Links to free tutorials from across the Web that will help you learn more about the wide array of multimedia production tools available.

- Screencast tutorials that walk you through the editing processes discussed in this chapter. These screencasts show you exactly which buttons to click on current versions of digital multimedia editing applications.

- Hands-on exercises in which you download, edit and submit for review audio, video and image files chosen specifically to give you experience with the concepts and techniques introduced in this chapter.

As you complete the module's online exercises, you will:

- Crop, resize and save photos for the Web.

- Edit audio interviews and upload them to a website.

- Edit, compress and upload digital video interviews.

Note: Many of the exercises for module 8 require the use of third-party image and audio and video editing software such as Photoshop, Audacity or Premiere.

ONLINE LEARNING

9 COLLECTING AND USING DATA

This chapter will help you think of interesting questions that require data to answer. It will also teach you the basic skills you need to master to collect and assess data, including:

- Gathering data through first-hand observation and from public documents and site users.
- Organizing information in a spreadsheet to illuminate trends, identify outliers and answer journalistic questions.
- Publishing data online so that news site users can get the information they want on demand.

F acebook. Amazon. iTunes. Craigslist. Each, a world-renowned online application. And each, not much more than a big database.

An incredibly complex and dynamic database, to be sure, but a database nonetheless. A **database** works by reducing information into small, atomic pieces and then allowing users to relate those pieces back to each other in a dynamic and flexible way. These four sites have achieved success in large part because of their ability to present customized experiences to each person who uses them—or, to put it simply, they are successful because they have mastered the art and the science of collecting and using data.

Each of these applications is driven by a primary **entity**. For Facebook, the entity is a person. For Amazon, it was initially books. For iTunes, songs. For Craigslist, items for sale. And each of these entities has **attributes**. People have names, genders, ages and hometowns. Books have authors, prices, page counts, subjects and titles. Songs have artists, genres and release years. Items for sale have sellers, locations, categories and descriptions. The attributes of these entities relate to each other in some way. Books on Amazon may share an author. Songs on iTunes may come from the same album. Items for sale on Craigslist may share a category. A database stores all of these entities and their attributes in a way that allows a user to see and exploit the relationships among them.

When you put a database on a server connected to the Internet, and then build a **user interface**—buttons, search forms, hyperlinks—on top of the database, users can manipulate information to effect a desired outcome. They can even add new pieces of information or interact with other people who are using the same database. Essentially, the users of a database can get (and give) the information they want, when they want it. That's on-demand delivery!

Journalists use databases, too. In fact, you learned in Chapter 4, on content management systems, that the articles, videos and other content on most news websites are stored in a database and organized by online producers who are able to manipulate that database through an administrative interface. CMS databases also have entities—a story, for example. And stories have attributes, for example, authors or topics.

Databases in newsrooms don't just help manage stories, they help tell stories. Journalist Adrian Holovaty has developed online data-driven applications for The Washington Post and sold another news data project he developed, **EveryBlock**, to msnbc.com. In a famous blog post he wrote in 2006, Holovaty argued that journalists have always been collecting data, but that in print they were forced to turn that data into narrative stories. Online, data can be kept in its native format and made much more useful and accessible to readers who want customized information. Consider the following:

- "An obituary is about a person, involves dates and funeral homes.

- "A wedding announcement is about a couple, with a wedding date, engagement date, bride hometown, groom hometown and various other happy, flowery pieces of information.

- "A birth has parents, a child (or children) and a date.

- "A college graduate has a home state, a home town, a degree, a major and graduation year.

- "An Onion-style 'On the Street' feature has respondents, answers and a publication date.

- "A drink special has a day of the week and is offered at a bar.

- "The schedule of the U.S. Congress has a day and multiple agenda items.

- "A political advertisement has a candidate, a state, a political party, multiple issues, characters, cues, music and more.

- "Every Senate, House and Governor race in the U.S. has location, analysis, demographic information, previous election results, campaign-finance information and more.

- "Every known detainee at Guantanamo Bay has an approximate age, birthplace, formal charges and more."

You can read Holovaty's complete blog post at http://www.holovaty.com/writing/fundamental-change/.

Investigative reporters have used databases for decades. Their stories summarized their findings for print or broadcast outlets, and for a long time that is all reporters could do. Summarizing is still important, as few audience members have the time or patience to sort through a complex database. But in this Internet age, if people do have the inclination, they can certainly try. Posting databases online makes them available to anyone who wants to explore them. Anyone who is interested can look for and perhaps find information that is relevant to them. And anyone, if they're sufficiently dedicated, can hold a few powerful people accountable.

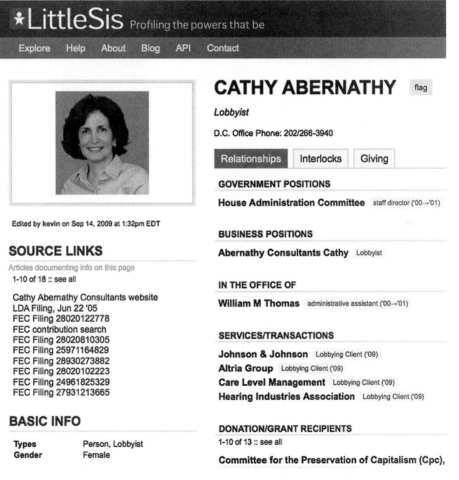

LittleSis.org is a nonprofit site that is working to create and publish profiles of "people and groups with significant access, influence, and wealth."

Data can certainly be found that will shine light in dark places . . .

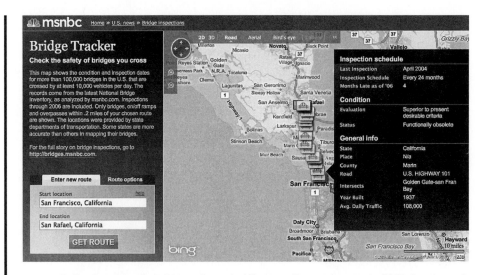

Following a deadly bridge collapse in Minneapolis, msnbc.com in 2008 dug through federal government records to bring to light a broad trend of delinquent bridge inspections as well as specific information about each bridge on any user's customized route.

And it can often help explain an increasingly complex world . . .

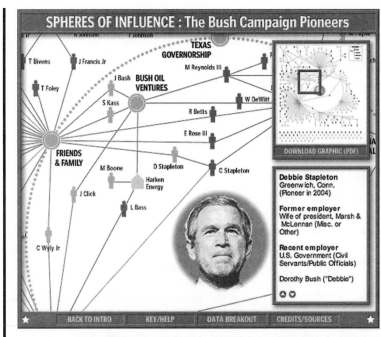

In 2004, the Washington Post used a database to show the web of relationships among President George W. Bush's top donors. Each person's symbol linked to a profile of information about that donor.

Data-driven journalism requires reporters and editors to follow a fairly rigid workflow. A journalist's job is to ferret out hidden information and then provide the context that helps the audience understand the information's significance. Without a smart plan, data-driven journalism projects will end up a scattered mess of information that offers nothing of use to the audience.

Before getting started, journalists must have a clear idea of what questions they want to help answer. What are the news elements of the story? What are the news values that make it interesting and important to the audience? This chapter will help you think of interesting questions that require data to answer.

The ability to understand and work with fielded data is fundamental to creating customized news experiences and distributing news and information to multiple platforms. It is no wonder that data-driven reporting and database programming skills are in such high demand in today's newsrooms. These skills are the foundations on which you will build your career; they supply the tools you will need to present your unique story ideas to a questioning audience. In the end, it is your imagination—and your perspiration—that will get the questions answered and the important stories written.

COLLECTING DATA

All good stories begin with a hunch. Ask a good question, and then find the answer that is relevant to your audience. But questions cannot be answered without information. Journalists have to know where to get the information, and how to identify sources that are reliable and complete, to answer a question.

Journalists acquire data in the following four primary ways: (1) through observation; (2) by importing from digital files stored on the Web, on a CD-ROM or on other digital media; (3) via submissions from site visitors who fill out a Web form; or (4) by "scraping" the unstructured text of a Web page or other digital document.

Reporter Observation

Perhaps the simplest way to acquire data for use in a news application is to observe it yourself. While there is plenty of data online, and plenty more hidden away in government databases and paper files, there is also a lot of information that nobody but a professional reporter will gather. For example, sometimes the information you want exists only for a very short moment in a very specific location. This means if you want the data, you'll have to get up from your computer and go see it for yourself.

Here are some examples of information that might be gathered through observation:

- The number and gender of people walking into a new museum

- The number of cars observed running red lights at a busy intersection during rush hour

- The height, width and number of political campaign yard signs in a neighborhood

- The number of lumens—a measurement of light—put out by street lamps in a high-crime section of town

- The responses you receive to a telephone poll question

Digital Files

Local, state and federal governments produce a lot of raw data that has already been formatted into discrete fields. Examples include data on campaign finance reports, business filings and tax returns, government budgets and school test scores. The **National Institute for Computer-Assisted Reporting** has a library of more than 40 datasets produced by government. Topics include airplane service difficulty reports, storm events, FBI crime data, fatal highway accidents, problems with medical devices and federal contracts awarded to private companies. You can learn more about the NICAR database library at http://data.nicar.org/node/7.

Q Online Module 9

Screencast with instructions on how to find and download campaign finance data collected by federal and state governments

Tool: XML: eXtensible Markup Language

By now you are familiar with the basic concepts of HTML, or hypertext markup language. HTML uses markup tags to separate the content of a page from its structure. **XML,** or **eXtensible Markup Language,** is another markup language. Its purpose is to transport and store data in a way that makes it easy to re-use and display in a variety of ways. Like HTML, XML is written in plain text that is easy for computer applications either on a server or a client to read. XML is a robust and useful way for organizations to publish data on the Web because it makes the data easy to gather and store in a database.

XML tags describe only the content inside them. Unlike HTML, they don't provide any information about the content's structure or how it should be displayed. Another important difference between HTML and XML is that HTML works only if the person writing it uses legal tags, that is, tags that have been predefined and agreed upon as having a valid use in HTML documents. In XML, there are no predefined tags. As such, it is extensible, or capable of being extended. And how you extend it is entirely up to you.

Many industries, including the news industry, use specialized versions of XML. For example, the International Press Telecommunications Council has created several "flavors" of XML that are specific to the news environment—NewsML, SportsML and EventsML. For the exchange of financial data, there is XBRL (eXtensible Business Reporting Language). Several U.S. states and European nations are using EML (Election Markup Language) to run electronic voting applications.

Of course, these special versions work only if people agree on specific standards. They were each created by committees whose members are conversant in the relevant subject and who could agree on useful standards. Newswire services are able to send information to their clients in NewsML only because the editors and technicians at all of the companies receiving the information agree on it as a common standard.

One of the most popular versions of XML is **RSS**, or Really Simple Syndication. News organizations use RSS to distribute their headlines directly to users of certain computer applications, such as Microsoft Outlook. Perhaps the most popular use of these RSS news feeds is via customized homepages such as My Yahoo or iGoogle.

Basic and advanced tutorials on XML

User Submissions

News organizations are beginning to benefit more and more from raw data supplied by the audience. The types of information that news sites are collecting range from the pedestrian, such as the prices readers are paying for organic foods at various local grocery stores, to the life-saving, such as the location of closed roads and public shelters during natural disasters.

User-submitted data is a good option in any of the following instances:

- When a large amount of information is needed

- When gathering each piece of data is very simple

- When the data changes rapidly

- When a site has a lot of visitors

- When the desired information is the type about which people are unlikely to lie

An example of a website that collects user-submitted data is GasBuddy.com. This site asks visitors to submit the locations of, and prices advertised at, filling stations in various cities around the country. The information gathered allows it to publish station-by-station prices. Consumers who access the site can then make informed purchasing decisions. No news organization would ask a single journalist to collect all the prices of all the fuel grades at all the gas stations in a city every day. But a wide group of users can divide the task so that no single person has an onerous burden. The only incentive to lie about the information requested is to trick motorists into visiting your gas station. But with a large group of users, such tricks would be quickly unmasked and corrected.

The Southern California affiliate of GasBuddy uses a simple form that allows users to submit data to the site.

Tool: Google Docs

In order to collect user data, you have to create a way for users to input information into a database. Most often this is done via a form on a news organization's website. Customized Web forms require knowledge of HTML as well as of programming and database languages. If you would like to learn how to create forms in HTML, you will find more information at http://www.w3schools.com/html/html_forms.asp.

But there are also some simpler solutions that can be used to test out the concept of asking visitors for data. For example, journalists can use **Google Docs** for free to create a Web page that will automatically accept visitor responses and insert them into a Google spreadsheet.

Screencast on how to set up a web form in Google Docs and publish it to your website

Tutorials on using Google Docs

Page Scrapes

Page scraping, or data scraping, is the practice of using a specialized computer program to convert human-readable paragraphs into data fields that can be stored, analyzed and presented from a database. Screen-scraping programs use a technique called **pattern matching** to figure out which information in certain paragraphs belongs in which fields of a database.

VIEW SOURCE

DATABASING MILITARY PRESS RELEASES

To get an idea of how pattern matching and screen scraping work, let's take a look at the text of two U.S. Department of Defense press releases about military fatalities. Here is the first:

"The Department of Defense announced today the death of a soldier who was supporting Operation Iraqi Freedom.

"Spc. Jonathon M. Sylvestre, 21, of Colorado Springs, Colo., died Nov. 2 in Kut, Iraq, of injuries sustained from a non-combat related incident. He was assigned to the 1st Battalion, 10th Field Artillery Regiment, 3rd Heavy Brigade Combat Team, 3rd Infantry Division, Fort Benning, Ga.

"The circumstances surrounding the incident are under investigation."

And here is the second:

"The Department of Defense announced today the death of a Marine who was supporting Operation Enduring Freedom.

"Sgt. Cesar B. Ruiz, 26, of San Antonio, Texas, died Oct. 31 while supporting combat operations in Helmand province, Afghanistan. He was assigned to Marine Forces Reserve, New Orleans.

"The circumstances surrounding the incident are under investigation."

Let's see if we can find a pattern of text that allows us to break these human-readable paragraphs into fields of data. Both start with the same pattern of letters: "The Department of Defense announced today the death of a." The next word indicates whether the service member was a "soldier" in the Army or a "Marine." This information could be submitted to a field in a database, perhaps a field called "service_branch." Then there is a pattern of matching text: "who was supporting." This is followed by a variable, either "Operation Iraqi Freedom" or "Operation Enduring Freedom." This variable could be submitted to a database field called "operation_name." In other words, the first paragraph of each of these news releases could be parsed into two data fields: "service_branch" and "operation_name." The two fields are always separated by the pattern of text "who was supporting."

Now take a look at the second paragraph. How might you use pattern matching to extract the rank, name, age, hometown, home state, date of death, location of death and military unit?

Computer programmers use a variety of languages to automate the pattern-matching process. Computer programs are very good at efficiently repeating the same pattern of task over and over again. The coding of Web pages can often make this task easier because of the use of tags to denote various pieces of information. This process is called **semantic tagging**. For example, look at the following HTML code of an article on The New York Times' website; you will find HTML and CSS tags that clearly identify discrete parts of the page that can be parsed into a database:

```
<NYT_BYLINE version="1.0" type=" ">

<div class="byline">By <a href="http://topics.nytimes.com/top/
reference/timestopics/people/h/javier_c_hernandez/index.
html?inline=nyt-per" title="More Articles by Javier C.
Hernandez">JAVIER C. HERNANDEZ</a>

</div>

</NYT_BYLINE>

<div class="timestamp">Published: November 6, 2009

</div>

<div id="articleBody">

<NYT_TEXT >

<p>For Americans who wake up each morning thinking about their job
hunt, Friday&#8217;s unemployment report offered little reassurance
```

```
that their search would soon pay off, even as the broader economy
showed signs of strengthening.</p>

. . .

</NYT_TEXT>
```

Screen-scraping programs could use the HTML/CSS <div> tags to identify the byline, the timestamp and the article body.

A word of caution. In many cases it is a violation of copyright law to retrieve and store original expressions published on a Web page or anywhere else. Screen-scraping techniques should be used only on data that is in the public domain. Information is considered in the public domain either because the government publishes it or because the information is commonly known raw factual data. Facts cannot be copyrighted. It may also be considered an unfair business practice or a violation of trespassing laws to use a computer program to access a website in a way that interferes with its operation. These types of legal issues differ from country to country and in fact continue to evolve on a case-by-case basis. Best advice? Tread carefully.

Tool: Screen-Scraper.com

It takes experience with advanced programming techniques to write code that will automatically grab data from live websites and get it to appear neatly in a database. But there are a few tools that journalists with only a basic understanding of data and online publishing principals will be able to use. One of the more popular tools is **Screen-Scraper.com.**

You can access a free demonstration of Screen-Scraper.com at work by visiting http://www.screen-scraper.com/media/video/video_tour.php.

Online Module 9

Screencast on using Screen-Scraper to grab information

ORGANIZING DATA

Gathering data is only the first step of the data-driven reporting process. Once you have your data in hand, it is time to continue reporting by looking for trends, patterns or anything unusual. Trends and patterns help journalists tell stories about the magnitude, proximity or timeliness of the information in a **dataset.** Outlying pieces of data help journalists tell stories about novelty and impact.

The way that you organize your data will depend in large part on the questions you are trying to answer: What exactly are you trying to measure? Do you have the data you need to measure it? And is the data structured in such a way that you can easily see the news value?

What Questions Are You Trying to Answer?

Before you start collecting data, you have to be able to imagine how your audience might want to use it. The best way to do this is to make yourself a list of questions you think a user might want to have answered. When we talk about organizing data, what we're really talking about is breaking down the information you've collected so that it can be used to answer questions you and your audience might have.

Data is great for answering the "Who?" "What?" "When?" "Where?" and "How much?" questions. It is not as useful in answering the "How?" or "Why?" questions. Following are some examples of simple questions that data would help to answer:

- How many/how much _____?

- Where are _____?

- Who are _____?

- When did _____?

- What is the biggest/smallest or the most/least _____?

- What is the average _____?

- What is the most/least common _____?

- What is the ranking of _____?

- In what order _____?

 Tool: Excel

In order to properly analyze it, journalists must create some kind of structural framework across which to lay their data. A particularly useful framework for working with basic datasets is the **spreadsheet,** and Microsoft's **Excel** is by far the most commonly used among journalists.

At first glance, you can tell that a spreadsheet has a lot more structure than a word-processing document. A word-processing document is just a big blank screen. The text you add is just one long string of letters, numbers and punctuation. Spreadsheet documents, on the other hand, are divided up by a matrix of horizontal and vertical lines.

Data must be formulated quantitatively if it is going to fit into the fields of a spreadsheet. For example, to say that "The day was warm" is a qualitative description of the day's weather. Adding specificity gives us a quantitative description: "The day was 78 degrees Fahrenheit." In the latter case, we are given the *quantity* of degrees that precisely define the day's *quality* of "warm."

If you don't have the specific degrees of a day's temperature, you can still convert the quality of "warm" into a quantitative measure by giving it a numerical value that differs from any other potential qualities. For example, you can create the following coded scale: "Hot" = 4, "Warm" = 3, "Chilly" = 2, "Cold" = 1. Here, qualitative measures of the weather have been converted into numerical, or quantitative, data that can be readily entered into a spreadsheet. A conversion even this basic allows reporters to perform simple statistical analysis later in the reporting process.

Screencast on using Excel to store and organize data

Tutorials and tip sheets on basic and advanced Excel functions

Once you have collected your data, inserted it into a spreadsheet and figured out what questions might be interesting and relevant to your audience, it is time to take a look at how each of the pieces of data connect to others. All data-driven journalism requires you to think about how the data you have gathered is related. It is these relationships, after all, that ultimately allow you to answer the relevant question or questions around which you are building your story. You can start by considering the elemental components of your data.

Do You Have the Right Data Elements?

A **data element** is the most basic piece—our so-called atomic particle—of information that you will have gathered. To start thinking about data elements, picture a spreadsheet on which you have entered a list of the students in your class. Each line on your spreadsheet stores information about one student—the data entity. And each **cell** of information on that line contains a data element for the entity—first name, last name, ID number, class and hometown, perhaps.

A data element must be narrowly and precisely defined. For example, a person's age is a data element. But a biography of the person is not. A biography is the connection of many different data elements into a narrative structure. Someone's age can be very precisely defined. When assigning a definition to a data element, you must be sure to clearly differentiate one piece of data from another.

The definition of each data element should also include the units in which the data is being measured and the possible valid values. Someone's age can be a data element. But you can express someone's age in terms of years, months or even days. There is a chance that "age" could be confused with "birthday," too. So it is important to use a clear data definition of age so that computer programmers and journalists—and eventually the audience—will know exactly what you are talking about.

The "age" data element might be defined as "the period of time that has passed since the day the person was born." If the age of a person is measured in years, the possible valid values are all whole numbers greater than 0. (This assumes that people who have not yet reached their first birthday would be given an age of 0 years. And it also assumes that someone could live to be an infinite number of years, which is obviously not a reasonable assumption.)

What about a data element for a person called "home"? Is "home" a good data element? Probably not. It is neither clearly defined nor precise. It typically means the location where someone lives, but does the data element contain the name of the city or the ZIP code or the street address or all three? Is it supposed to be a description of the person's residence, such as an apartment, condominium or house? In this instance, our data element has not been sufficiently "atomized." In fact, to store data about a person's "home," we can create several different data elements. These may include the following:

- Country
- State
- ZIP code
- Street name
- Address number

Each of these elements is precise and contains only a limited set of valid values.

You are now well on your way to building your story. You know what questions you are trying to answer, and you know which data elements you need to collect to answer those questions. But you still have one further question: "How do the data elements relate to each other?"—that is, what is the data structure?

Data structure describes the relationship between data elements. It is these relationships that allow you to answer your audience's questions. Let's consider a common news story that is driven by data—end-of-grade test scores at local schools. What questions would your audience ask about this subject? Consider the following basic questions:

- What were the scores for students at the school my children attend?
- What schools in the area had the highest scores?
- What schools in the area had the lowest scores?
- What schools improved their performance the most this year?

But your audience may also have some more complex questions. For example, consider the following, more analytical questions:

- Did schools with a high percentage of nonwhite students perform better or worse than schools with a low percentage?
- Across the entire district, how did the scores of boys and girls compare?
- Who are the principals at the highest-scoring schools?

Suppose that you have requested and received a CSV (comma-separated values) file from your local school district. A CSV file is a simple text format for a spreadsheet or a database table. The file has a row for each of the schools in the district as well as the following columns:

- School_Name
- Test_Year
- Total_Tested
- Test_Score
- Percent_NonWhite
- Percent_Female

(Note: the title of each column is a single word, without a space. In computer programming, it is very difficult for a computer brain to deal with spaces. A space in a column heading can be eliminated either by pushing the words in the head together to create a single "word" or by substituting the underscore symbol ["_"] where the space or spaces would normally appear.)

Can you now answer all of your audience's questions? Have you acquired the data you need—that is, are all of the necessary data elements present? And is the data stored in a way that is usable—that is, is the data structured such that you can tease out the relationships relevant to your audience's questions?

In fact, you can answer all of your audience's basic questions, though you will need to have test results from multiple years in order to determine whether a school's scores have gone up or down. The more analytical questions, however, are a different matter. How will you define schools with a "high" percentage of nonwhite students? Should you search for schools with nonwhite populations in a certain range, or should you add another column of data that puts each school into categories of "high," "medium" or "low" when it comes to their nonwhite student population?

With the data here, you wouldn't be able to search for district-wide demographic comparisons because you don't have the information you need to pull out the scores of individual demographic groups. Neither do you have the information you need to provide district-wide averages by gender—for that, you'd need to know the number of female students at each school, rather than just their percentage.

Nor does the dataset supply you with the names of the principals at the various schools. The CSV file supplied by the district does not contain this information. You could readily add it, however, through further reporting, and thereby bring additional value to the raw data distributed by the district.

Clearly, the only way to know whether you've gathered all the **datapoints** you need is to analyze the structure of your data through the lens of the questions you are trying to answer.

Is Your Data Accurate?

The type of data you acquire and the precision with which you organize it will determine your ability to analyze the data and present it in a context that is useful to the audience. As a journalist, the first analysis you will want to perform on any dataset you collect is one that determines whether or not it is accurate.

The first step in ensuring data accuracy is to acquire it from a reliable source. Is the information current? Did it come from the source that first created it, or has your data been passed from government department to government department? What are the ways that the people entering the data might have made typing errors?

If you are confident with the source of your data, then it is time to check whether or not the data makes sense. Remember, you collect data because you have a hunch about it. You have expectations about what it should show you. Understand that it is the *unexpected* that you are looking for. Remember, when the world doesn't behave as you expect—that's news.

For example, if a state law specifies that bridges are to be inspected every two years, and you have data showing inspection dates that are more than two years old, then you might have a story. If you know that the average voter turnout for your state is 60 percent, and you have precinct data that shows a turnout of 98 percent, then you might have a story. As a journalist, you're looking for anything unexpected or out of the ordinary. When you do find something unusual, you either have a story—or you have bad data.

By ordering your data in a uniform way—for example, from biggest to smallest, most to least or earliest to latest—you can look for outliers. For example, which company paid the most taxes? Order the data. See anything unexpected? Or, which neighborhoods had the most home break-ins last year? Order the data. See anything unexpected?

In many cases, you'll be faced with datasets that are hundreds or even thousands of records. For your particular story, you might be interested in looking for the outliers in only a specific subset of records. Perhaps, for example, a reporter wants to see which Democrats received the most votes in last year's congressional elections. In order to do this, a reporter would need to filter the data in a spreadsheet so that it showed only Democrats.

Information at the top or the bottom of the list doesn't always tell the whole story. You might need to dig deeper. You might need to look for patterns or trends. To do this you will need to be familiar with some very basic math formulas, for example, one that determines the difference between the values of two specific data elements. Spreadsheets allow journalists to easily perform math equations using data from two or more cells.

If a journalist reports the name of the person who had the most votes in an election, they should also report the margin of victory. To do this, you would need to subtract the number of votes received by the second-place candidate from the number of votes received by the winning candidate.

A journalist's audience is interested in the *latest* information. One of the nice things about databases is that math equations can be written in such a way that the equation will automatically update as the values in the cells change. For example, consider a close local election. Election returns are not static: as votes are counted the relative standing of the candidates can change. It is the job of the journalist to provide updates. A spreadsheet math formula will automatically update the relative standings of candidates as the returns come in, allowing the journalist to report on the latest election results.

Excel and other spreadsheet applications come with sets of predefined math formulas. These are called **functions.** For example, if you have three pieces of data and want to find the average, you could write the following formula:

$$(DATA1 + DATA2 + DATA3)/3 = AVERAGE$$

Or, you could simply apply one of Excel's premade functions, called AVERAGE(). It would look like this:

$$AVERAGE(DATA1:DATA3) = AVERAGE$$

Sometimes journalists want to display only information that meets certain conditions. Conditional formatting in a spreadsheet means that any statement can be put into the format *If A, then do B*. The values of A and B do not matter. An example of conditional formatting might be, "If the value of a record's 'Party' cell is 'Republican' then color the text of that record purple."

Conditional statements are one of the foundational concepts of computer programming and customized news presentation. Of course, the conditional statements used by robust Web applications such as Facebook or Amazon are much more complicated than the ones used in a spreadsheet, but the concept is the same.

Is Your Data "Normal"?

So far in this chapter we've been dealing with spreadsheets or simple online databases that contain only a single table. But what happens when you need more than one table? How can you draw conclusions across two or multiple datasets? Complex data-driven journalism requires analyses provided by a more powerful data application known as a **relational database.** You can think of a relational database as a group of spreadsheets linked together by specific relationships between a cell on one spreadsheet and a cell on another.

Before going further, let's examine the terms that are used to talk about data when it is stored in a relational database rather than a spreadsheet. A **row** in a spreadsheet is called a **record** in a relational database. Each record is one "thing," whatever that may be in your database. A **column** in a spreadsheet is called a **field** in a relational database. The fields are the different attributes of each record. Finally, each field for each record has a **value**—what is called a cell in a spreadsheet. In relational databases, a collection of records is called a **table.** A database needs to have at least two tables in order to be relational.

Database normalization is the process of re-organizing data so that there is no redundancy. Redundant information in a database slows its operation and makes it difficult to seek, retrieve and display data on a website. The database normalization process involves five steps, each of which is called a **normal form.** The first three normal forms are the most important and will be the ones we cover here.

Let's start with this example of a record from a database of donations to a political candidate:

Table 9.1 Campaign Contributions

DONOR	ADDRESS	PHONE	CANDIDATE	DONATIONS
Maria Garcia	1872 Pine St., Springfield, CA 95370	873-1234	Harry Anderson	$150 on April 17 and $50 on July 1
Carlos Garcia	1872 Pine St., Springfield, CA 95370	873-4321	Harry Anderson	$50 on July 1
Carlos Garcia	1872 Pine St., Springfield, CA 95370	873-4321	Rose McClintock	$150 on April 17
Harry Anderson	99 W. Mariposa Ave., Shaws, CA 95371	873-3333	Harry Anderson	$2000 on January 1

Perhaps the most important rule of database design is that each record must be absolutely unique. One way to ensure that this is the case is to give each record a unique identification number, or **UID.** Using UIDs ensures that, no matter how often the values of the record change, and no matter how similar two records are to each other, there will be no mistake that record 167 is always record 167 and always different from record 184.

Table 9.2 Campaign Contributions (With UID Added)

UID	DONOR	ADDRESS	PHONE	CANDIDATE	DONATIONS
1	Maria Garcia	1872 Pine St., Springfield, CA 95370	873-1234	Harry Anderson	$150 on April 17 and $50 on July 1
2	Carlos Garcia	1872 Pine St., Springfield, CA 95370	873-4321	Harry Anderson	$50 on July 1
3	Carlos Garcia	1872 Pine St., Springfield, CA 95370	873-4321	Rose McClintock	$150 on April 17
4	Harry Anderson	99 W. Mariposa Ave., Shaws, CA 95371	873-3333	Harry Anderson	$2000 on January 1

After you have created unique IDs for each database record, it is time to break each field down into its smallest possible pieces and make sure you have one, and only one, value in each table cell. This is called the first normal form. In our example, the address and name fields contain a variety of types of information. The donor and candidate fields contain both first and last names. The address field contains the house number, the street name, the city name, the state name and the ZIP code. The donations field contains the donation amount and date. Our goal in applying the first normal form is to break down each field into its smallest meaningful component pieces.

Table 9.3 Campaign Contributions (With Granular Fields)

UID	DONOR_ FIRST-NAME	DONOR_ LAST-NAME	ADDRESS	CITY	STATE	ZIP	PHONE	CANDIDATE_ FIRSTNAME	CANDIDATE_ LASTNAME	DONATION_ AMOUNT	DONATION_ DATE
1	Maria	Garcia	1872 Pine St.	Spring-field	CA	95370	873-1234	Harry	Anderson	$150 and $50	April 17 and July 1
2	Carlos	Garcia	1872 Pine St.	Spring-field	CA	95370	873-4321	Harry	Anderson	$50	July 1
3	Carlos	Garcia	1872 Pine St.	Spring-field	CA	95370	873-4321	Rose	McClintock	$150	April 17
4	Harry	Anderson	99 W. Mariposa Ave.	Shaws	CA	95371	873-3333	Harry	Anderson	$2000	January 1

Why do we do this? Think about how you would ask a database to answer the question, "How much money came from the city of Springfield?" The database can't answer this question unless there is a field called "city" and a value called "Springfield."

Notice that you could theoretically break down the address even more. You could separate the house numbers from the street names. But while doing so would break down the field into smaller pieces, it wouldn't result in a smaller *meaningful* piece. There is no significant journalistic reason to ask the question, "How much money did the candidate get from everyone who lives in a house numbered '1453' on any street?" While there can be no argument that technology is integral to effective database creation, there can be no doubt either that an effective database requires the nuance that can only be supplied by journalistic sensibility.

To complete the transition to the first normal form, we need to make sure that there is one and only one value in each table cell. In our example, Maria Garcia has made two contributions to Harry Anderson. The DONATION_AMOUNT field and the DONATION_DATE field for her donations contain more than one value. We need to split these apart by creating a new table with donation amounts and donation dates. Notice that when we split them apart, we end up creating a new record with a new UID. The existing UIDs do not change.

Table 9.4 Campaign Contributions (With One Value Per Field)

UID	DONOR_ FIRST-NAME	DONOR_ LAST-NAME	ADDRESS	CITY	STATE	ZIP	PHONE	CANDI-DATE_ FIRST-NAME	CANDI-DATE_ LAST-NAME	DONATION_ AMOUNT	DONATION_ DATE
1	Maria	Garcia	1872 Pine St.	Springfield	CA	95370	873-1234	Harry	Anderson	$150	April 17
5	Maria	Garcia	1872 Pine St.	Springfield	CA	95370	873-1234	Harry	Anderson	$50	July 1
2	Carlos	Garcia	1872 Pine St.	Springfield	CA	95370	873-4321	Harry	Anderson	$50	July 1
3	Carlos	Garcia	1872 Pine St.	Springfield	CA	95370	873-4321	Rose	McClintock	$150	April 17
4	Harry	Anderson	99 W. Mariposa Ave.	Shaws	CA	95371	873-3333	Harry	Anderson	$2000	January 1

Table 9.5 Candidates

CANDIDATE_ID	FIRST_NAME	LAST_NAME
1	Harry	Anderson
2	Rose	McClintock

After breaking each field down into the smallest possible pieces and making sure that there is one and only one value in each table field, we are ready to move on to the second normal form. In the second normal form, the goal is to remove any repeating entities in the original table. For example, we see that the candidate entity "Harry Anderson" is repeated. This is inefficient; we need to clean it up. We do this by creating a new table for any repeating values.

With the creation of this new table, our original table would change to look like this:

Table 9.6 Campaign Contributions (With Repeating Candidates Removed)

UID	DONOR_ FIRST-NAME	DONOR_ LAST-NAME	ADDRESS	CITY	STATE	ZIP	PHONE	CANDI-DATE	DONATION_ AMOUNT	DONATION_ DATE
1	Maria	Garcia	1872 Pine St.	Springfield	CA	95370	873-1234	1	$150	April 17
5	Maria	Garcia	1872 Pine St.	Springfield	CA	95370	873-1234	1	$50	July 1
2	Carlos	Garcia	1872 Pine St.	Springfield	CA	95370	873-4321	1	$50	July 1
3	Carlos	Garcia	1872 Pine St.	Springfield	CA	95370	873-4321	2	$150	April 17
4	Harry	Anderson	99 W. Mariposa Ave.	Shaws	CA	95371	873-3333	1	$2000	January 1

The candidate names in the original table now appear as numbers. These numbers correspond to the numbers in the UID **primary key** field in the new candidate table. In using the values from the primary key field from the candidate table and plugging them into the original table we have created what is called a **foreign key.** Foreign keys create relationships between two tables by matching the values of the foreign key to the values of the primary keys.

To achieve the third normal form, we need to ensure that information about different types of "things" is stored in different tables. Each type of "thing"—or entity—has its own table with its own primary key field. What are the entities in our database? Take a look:

- A *donor* . . .
- who makes a *donation* . . .
- to a *candidate.*

So, we have three entitites: a donor, a donation amount and a candidate. And that means we need to have three tables, one for each entity.

The point of creating successive normal forms is to remove from the original table any information that does not relate to the primary key. Remember that the primary key counts unique entities. And the only entity that in the original table was absolutely unique was the donation amount. A donation, which involves a specific donor, candidate, amount and date, can only happen once. However, candidates can receive multiple donations from multiple donors. And donors can make multiple donations to multiple candidates.

We've already started to move to the third normal form by removing the information about the recipient of the donation. But we also need to remove information about the donors:

Table 9.7 Donors

UID	DONOR_ FIRSTNAME	DONOR_ LASTNAME	ADDRESS	CITY	STATE	ZIP	PHONE
1	Maria	Garcia	1872 Pine St.	Springfield	CA	95370	873-1234
2	Maria	Garcia	1872 Pine St.	Springfield	CA	95370	873-1234
3	Carlos	Garcia	1872 Pine St.	Springfield	CA	95370	873-4321
4	Carlos	Garcia	1872 Pine St.	Springfield	CA	95370	873-4321
5	Harry	Anderson	99 W. Mariposa Ave.	Shaws	CA	95371	873-3333

You can see that this table isn't in the second normal form. We need to get rid of the repeating entities:

Table 9.8 Donors (With Repeating Donors Removed)

UID	DONOR_FIRSTNAME	DONOR_LASTNAME	ADDRESS	CITY	STATE	ZIP	PHONE
1	Maria	Garcia	1872 Pine St.	Springfield	CA	95370	873-1234
3	Carlos	Garcia	1872 Pine St.	Springfield	CA	95370	873-4321
5	Harry	Anderson	99 W. Mariposa Ave.	Shaws	CA	95371	873-3333

Finally, we arrive at the third normal form of our original table. It has one primary key (UID) and two foreign keys (DONOR_ID and CANDIDATE_ID). Two fields remain from the original table; these show the only information that is specific to our primary key (AMOUNT and DATE).

Table 9.9 Campaign Contributions (Normalized)

UID	AMOUNT	DATE	DONOR_ID	CANDIDATE_ID
1	$150	April 17	1	1
5	$50	July 1	1	1
2	$50	July 1	3	1
3	$150	April 17	3	2
4	$2000	January 1	5	1

With the database normalized, it is time to assess relationships between the three tables. There is now a **one-to-many relationship** between the donor table and the campaign contribution table. In other words, each *one* value in the donor table appears *many* times in the transaction table. There is also a one-to-many relationship between the transaction table and the candidate table. The donor and candidate tables are related only through the campaign contribution table. There is no direct relationship between the donor and candidate.

There are additional forms to data normalization, but you will only encounter them if you get into situations that require advanced data theory. Those situations, thankfully, are rare in newsrooms.

Figure 9.1 Relationships Between Tables

Table Name: Candidates

CANDIDATE_ID	FIRST_NAME	LAST_NAME
1	Harry	Anderson
2	Rose	McClintock

Table Name: Campaign Contributions

UID	AMOUNT	DATE	DONOR_ID	CANDIDATE_ID
1	$150	April 17	1	1
5	$50	July 1	1	1
2	$50	July 1	3	1
3	$150	April 17	3	2
4	$2000	January 1	5	1

Table Name: Donors

UID	DONOR_FIRST-NAME	DONOR_LASTNAME	ADDRESS	City	State	ZIP	PHONE
1	Maria	Garcia	1872 Pine St.	Springfield	CA	95370	873–1234
3	Carlos	Garcia	1872 Pine St.	Springfield	CA	95370	873–4321
5	Harry	Anderson	99 W. Mariposa Ave.	Shaws	CA	95371	873–3333

Tool: Access

Databases can be manipulated using a **relational database management system (RDBMS)**. Microsoft's **Access** is one of the most widely used desktop RDBMS applications, but there are others. **SQL Server** and **Oracle** are popular enterprise caliber databases, and **MySQL** is a popular free and open-source RDBMS that is often used for Web applications.

All relational database management systems perform four primary functions on data:

- Create records
- Read records
- Update records
- Delete records

These four functions are known by the acronym CRUD.

For people who are just getting started with databases, Access is a good jumping off point. It offers a menu that will be familiar to anyone accustomed to using Microsoft products, and its graphical interface will feel comfortable to anyone who has used a spreadsheet. Access also allows its users to take a peek under the hood, so to speak, and actually see the programming commands that make the database work.

Screencast on moving data from a spreadsheet to work within Access

Tutorials on Access, SQL and other Web database programs

Structured Query Language, or SQL (pronounced either S-Q-L or "sequel") is the language that developers use when they are working with databases. An **SQL statement** is a command that directs a database to perform a specific function. While SQL comes in several varieties, all employ the same basic commands in directing the action of an RDBMS:

- "Insert Into" to create records
- "Select" to read records
- "Update" to update records
- "Delete" to delete records

PUBLISHING DATA ONLINE

Databases have long been powerful reporting tools, but they weren't powerful *storytelling* tools until they began being published to the Web. On the Web, journalists use data to create animated graphics, such as a colored map of the United States on election night or a live, updated shot chart during a basketball game. They also create search forms that allow users to find exact information, for example, four-star hotels within two miles of the airport for less than $150 a night.

Data on the Web is not powerful just because the Web makes it accessible or because there is so much of it out there. Data published to the Web is powerful because it can be used both to make news more interactive and to provide answers on demand.

Journalists must take care, however. Publishing a "data dump" online has limited value to the reader. With the exception of increasing transparency—for example, data that has never before been made widely available may serve to illuminate a hidden aspect of government or business—most data dumps are just what the name implies: an apparently bottomless pit of discarded, unusable information. Journalists are in the business of making information accessible and *usable*. Their challenge, then, is to wield data in a manner that is useful to their audience.

The first step to creating a usable database is to put the database on a Web server and connect it to a Web page to make the information readily accessible. There are a couple of different methods for connecting Web databases with HTML Web pages. One common method is called **three-tiered architecture**. The three tiers include a presentation tier, a logic tier and a data tier.

The **presentation tier** is the HTML and CSS with which the audience interacts. The **logic tier** is the computer programming language that provides the logic, or rules, about how different pieces of data should be pulled from the database and sent to the HTML pages. **PHP** is a popular programming language for use at the logic layer. PHP and other programming languages must be installed on a Web server before you can use them to interact with a database. The W3Schools provides a free introductory tutorial to PHP programming at http://www.w3schools.com/PHP/.

Finally, the **data tier** is the set of data that is on a server in an RDBMS such as MySQL. The logic tier creates, reads, updates and deletes records from the data tier by receiving user input from the presentation tier and using it to run SQL statements on the data tier.

Many journalists work with database developers or Web programmers who know HTML, CSS, PHP and MySQL. Some other popular ways of publishing data to the Web include writing computer code with **frameworks** such as Ruby on Rails or Django. While discussion of these frameworks is beyond the scope of this book, as a budding journalist you should consider investing time in learning one or more of these languages. They can be valuable tools.

The easiest way to publish data online is simply to upload a CSV file to a Web server and link to it from your story. If nothing else, this gives visitors the chance to download it, import it into a spreadsheet application and do their own analysis. But this solution places a large burden on the audience—in most cases too large a burden, which would only propel frustrated visitors away from your site. If your story requires you to publish data this way, however, be sure to publish it as a CSV so the file can be opened and used by as many spreadsheet applications as possible.

If you have a limited amount of information, you may want to drop a simple HTML table onto your site. Rather than code an HTML table by hand, you can use a conversion tool such as Tableizer, which is available at http://tableizer.journalistopia.com/. Tableizer is a free tool created by online news producer Danny Sanchez.

VIEW SOURCE

A PULITZER PRIZE FOR POLITIFACT

In 2009, the Pulitzer Prize for National Reporting was awarded to the St. Petersburg Times for reporting that was presented primarily as a database. It was the first Pulitzer to be awarded to a project that originated on the Web.

Matt Waite, a 10-year veteran of newspaper reporting with no programming experience, launched PolitiFact in August 2007 to fact-check claims made by candidates running in the 2008 national elections. At the time Waite was just beginning to learn how to create dynamic, data-driven Web pages with a framework called Django, and PolitiFact was his very first project.

Waite said he was inspired by Adrian Holovaty's blog post, which had appeared the previous year, in which Holovaty described his vision of how newspaper websites needed to implement fundamental change. Waite's own blog post announcing the arrival of PolitiFact even sounded a bit like Holovaty's:

> If you think about it, a statement from a politician has consistent pieces. It has a speaker, that speaker has a political party, the statement has a subject and a forum in which they said it. After we fact-check that statement, we assign a ruling to it, summing up the veracity of what they say on a scale from true to false to pants on fire (a personal favorite). All of those things become fields in a database. Statements are all in their own database, and we also are writing more traditional stories on the statements. And those articles have some common pieces, like a byline.

You can read Waite's full post at http://www.mattwaite.com/posts/2007/aug/22/announcing-politifact/.

PolitiFact wasn't just a computer program. An immense amount of reporting from the staffs at the St. Petersburg Times and Congressional Quarterly—at the time, both companies were owned by the same parent—was needed to populate the database. By the end of 2009, more than 65 journalists had written, edited or researched the information that went into PolitiFact. The Pulitzer board cited PolitiFact's use of "probing reporters and the power of the World Wide Web to examine more than 750 political claims, separating rhetoric from truth to enlighten voters."

It takes a reporter's eye to see stories in the data and think about how the audience would want to use it, but reporters who want to build data-driven news applications like PolitiFact also have to be able to speak the language of computer programming. This chapter only touches on these aspects of data-driven online journalism, but to actually build an application you will need to learn how Web servers work and how to program them. Is it hard to do? Just ask Matt Waite. Or Adrian Holovaty. They taught it to themselves.

If you're interested in learning programming, here is a simple recipe to help you pull together and build the next Pulitzer Prize–winning database application:

1. Find some real-life data to play with. You might work with campaign contributions to your local state legislator, or crime reports covering the previous month in your city, or salaries of faculty at the nearest public university.

2. Learn **HTML** and **CSS.**

3. Learn **PHP** and **MySQL.**

4. Learn **Ruby on Rails, Python** or **Django.**

5. Learn **JavaScript** and **XML.**

What's in it for you? A job in a newsroom. Or maybe a $1 million grant like the one Holovaty received for his work. Or maybe a Pulitzer Prize, like the one Waite got for his extracurricular efforts. But why stop there? Shoot, maybe even a chance to change the world.

Search Forms

After you have determined the questions you can answer with your data elements and data structure, your next task is to develop a way for site users to search and sort through the data. In other words, what buttons will they need to press to get the answers to their questions? The questions you think your audience will want to answer will determine how you create your search forms.

A Web **search form** is created with HTML code. (You can learn more about coding HTML forms at http://www.w3schools.com/html/html_forms.asp.) There are four basic interface components for Web forms: (1) the textbox, (2) the pull-down menu, (3) the checkbox and (4) the radio button. Each of these interface components is an **input type.**

A **textbox** is useful when you have a lot of possible values for a particular column. But textboxes have two disadvantages: people often misspell the words they are trying to find, which results in a failed search, and the names with which people are familiar may not be the way the names are stored in your dataset.

To illustrate, consider a Web page about local education data. A textbox could be created so users could type in the name of a particular school. But if a parent searches for the

"MacDugal" school and the school's name is really spelled "McDougal," the search would return a false negative result; it would appear as if your database didn't contain any data for the school when it actually did. A user might also search for "McDougal," which may or may not return a result for the "James B. McDougal Middle School," depending on the way your search form interacts with the database (a consideration beyond the scope of this book).

One way to solve the problem of misspelling and uncommon data is to give users a limited set of choices. For example, if there are 12 schools in the district for which you have data, then a **pull-down menu** might be the best input type. This allows users to select the school for which they want information. Pull-down menus are prepopulated with a limited list of valid choices from which the user can select. In the case of our imaginary McDougal school, a user would likely be able to match her intent with one of the available choices even if it didn't match exactly.

With pull-down menus, though, users can select only one choice. Perhaps you think your users would like to see the results of more than one school at a time in order to compare them. In this case, you might consider using the checkbox input type. You could present a list of all 12 schools, with a checkbox next to each one. Users could then select as many schools as they wished and view all the results at the same time.

Finally, a **radio button** is an input type that shares characteristics both of pull-down menus and checkboxes. Like pull-down menus, radio buttons force users to select only one choice. But, as with checkboxes, the user can see all choices at once. Radio buttons might be a better choice than pull-down menus when the list of choices is relatively small, perhaps fewer than five.

Once you've decided how you want your users to tell you (or rather the database) which information they want, you'll need to decide whether a search for information in two or more categories is done as an AND search or an OR search. In other words, will the search return only schools that match the criteria the user has chosen for all the fields, or will the search return any results that match any of the fields?

 Tool: Caspio

Earlier in this chapter, you saw how you could use Google Docs to create a Web form to gather user-generated data. But you can't use this elementary method to create forms that will let your audience search a robust database.

Many newspapers are using a subscription service called **Caspio** to host their data and automatically create Web search forms to add to their sites. It is not a cheap solution. As of 2010, hosting even the smallest project cost several hundred dollars a year. But it is certainly easier than learning a programming language and less costly than hiring someone who knows a programming language.

An example of an online application that uses Caspio is "The Beamer File," which appears on the website of The Roanoke Times. The application allows readers to search and sort statistics from the career of Virginia Tech football coach Frank Beamer. It is accessible online at http://www.roanoke.com/data/viewdata.aspx?wdid=11&cid=6.

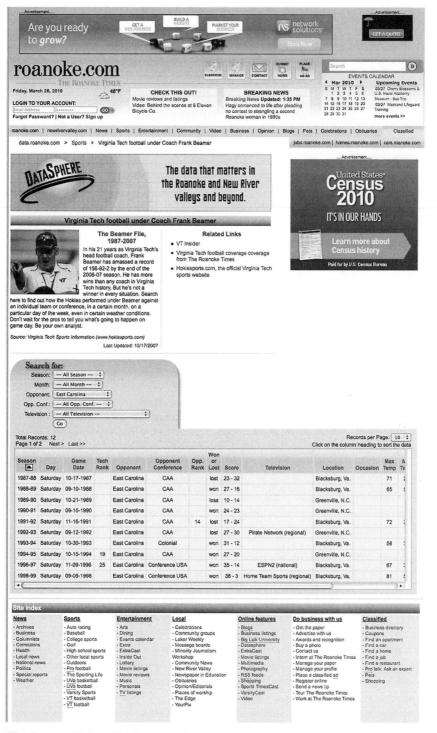

"The Beamer File" on The Roanoke Times' website is powered by a database.

Screencasts on uploading data into Caspio to search and sort data

Tutorials on Caspio and news sites that use the tool

Caspio automatically creates the Web database, the HTML page interface and the code needed to connect the two. Without Caspio, pulling together these technical steps would be your responsibility.

Creating Dynamic Charts and Graphs

Data visualization is the process of turning raw data—text, numbers and other information stored in fielded rows and columns—into a graphical representation. At its most basic, data visualization might be the process of taking the 2008 presidential returns and creating a pie chart that shows what percentage of voters cast their ballots for Barack Obama, John McCain or any other candidate.

But data visualization can also produce multimedia, interactive and downright artistic images. The online magazine Smashing maintains a collection of some of the most interesting data visualizations in both print and online media at http://www.smashingmagazine.com/2009/09/11/25-useful-data-visualization-and-infographics-resources/.

Data visualization is a professional field of art and science all its own, and as such not a topic for this book. However, there are several free online tools that can aid journalists who do not have sufficient background in informational graphic design to turn their raw data into something that a website visitor can quickly understand and even engage. Even if you have no intention of creating your own graphics, remember, as a journalist it is your job to initiate the process by noting when data you have collected would benefit from a visual presentation. Then, let your imagination run wild—and visualize.

 Tool: Many Eyes

Many Eyes is a Web-based data visualization tool that was created by IBM's Collaborative User Experience research group and made available for public use. To use the site (http://manyeyes.alphaworks.ibm.com), you must first possess data that you want to see visually. Once you've found it, you will need to "massage" it—that is, put it into a standardized format that the Many Eyes tool can understand. Once you've done this, uploading the data that you've stored in a spreadsheet is as easy as cutting and pasting the contents of the spreadsheet. With the data uploaded, the site provides you with many different visualization options. It's a fun tool to play with. Try it.

After you have created a visual presentation for your data, you can embed it on your website by cutting and pasting into your own Web page a small snippet of HTML code that is provided by Many Eyes. This code allows the interactive application to appear on your site, even though it actually resides on the Many Eyes website.

The New York Times is one of numerous news organizations that have used ManyEyes for data visualization. In late 2008, IBM and The New York Times partnered to launch the newspaper's own Visualization Lab, where users can upload datasets or explore datasets already uploaded by the newspaper staff. The New York Times Visualization Lab is accessible at http://vizlab .nytimes.com/.

Screencast on how to embed data visualization created with Many Eyes

Tutorials on news data visualization with links to examples

Mapping Data

Proximity is one of the most widely prized news values in any medium. In Los Angeles, a small earthquake in Pasadena is going to be much bigger news than a big earthquake in Cairo.

Maps have long been used in both print and television to show the audience the precise location of an event. But when a map is online, it can offer users layers of detailed information; it can even be controlled and customized by each person who visits the site. And with the rapid growth of location-aware applications on mobile phones, maps are becoming increasingly dynamic, able to change automatically as information is updated and users themselves move around.

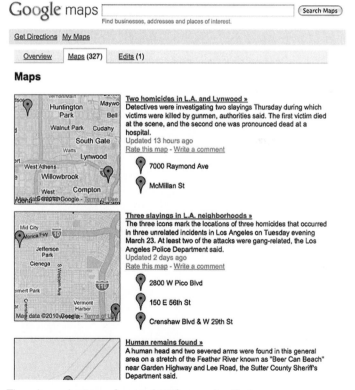

There is no shortage of examples of news sites that use maps to illustrate data. The Los Angeles Times has created more than 300 maps on Google. You can see all of them at http://maps.google.com/maps/user?uid=109103557032275200740.

Tool: Google Maps

There are two different methods for building **Google Maps.** The most useful—and complex—is to build a map application using the Google Maps API. **API** stands for "application programming interface." Using the API requires knowledge of JavaScript and **object-oriented** programming concepts, both of which are beyond the scope of this book. If you have these skills, however, there are all sorts of neat things you can do when creating a map or maps for your site. To see for yourself, access Google's list of case studies, which include examples from The New York Times and San Diego public television station KBPS. It can be accessed at http://maps.google.com/help/maps/casestudies/.

If you don't know JavaScript, you can still use Google's "starter spreadsheet" to quickly create a map for your data.

Screencast on mapping data and embedding maps on your website

Tutorials and links to dynamic online mapping tools

ONLINE LEARNING MODULE 9

ACTIVATE THIS MODULE: journalism.cqpress.com

The ability to deconstruct narrative news into points of data as well as the ability to use individual datapoints as the building blocks for a journalistic narrative requires experience and practice with the technology and tools of fielded information. Breaking news into small pieces can help you get the right information to the right people at the right time, without loading the news down with a lot of unnecessary words.

On my blog, you will find examples of the latest techniques and tools for presenting databased journalism online, along with discussion and commentary in which I encourage you to engage.

When you buy or activate this chapter's online learning module, you will have access to:

- A digital version of this chapter's text.
- Interactive flashcards for the terms used in this chapter.
- A printable tip sheet stepping out how to acquire, organize and present data on a news website.

- A quiz to test your mastery of the material in this chapter.
- Video screencasts that introduce the tools of data-driven journalism, such as Excel, Google Docs and Microsoft Access.
- Links to tutorials from across the Web that guide you from the most basic to the more advanced uses of XML, SQL, Excel and Access.
- Hands-on exercises that give you experience working with real data.

As you complete the module's online exercises you will:

- Configure a spreadsheet to gather and organize information that helps you and your audience answer specific questions.
- Use Excel to sort, filter and analyze data.
- Ask the audience questions in a way that yields useful data.
- Publish data online so news site users can get the information they want on demand.
- Experiment with data visualization tools.

ONLINE LEARNING

10 JOURNALISM AS PROCESS: BLOGS AND BREAKING NEWS

In this chapter, you will learn how to:

- Write a blog.
- Launch a blog using Wordpress.
- Make editorial decisions about how and when to publish information.
- Cover a live event.
- Alert readers to updates in traditional inverted pyramid stories.
- Stream live audio and video broadcasts from your phone.

A story. A headline. A photograph. A video. A database. Although the Internet has substantially changed the way these media are produced, edited and published, it hasn't changed their essence as discrete, static pieces of information. Journalists traditionally have taken the raw commodities of events, interviews and documents, chosen and highlighted details and added context to manufacture a product that has news value. The story gets done, the product gets delivered. And, like farmers at the end of the harvest, journalists who have completed their pieces pause briefly before starting all over again.

But online journalists are not farmers. They are more like gardeners—nurturing and pruning but never really harvesting. You've learned that the online audience likes to snack on news throughout the day. The more often your site rewards its grazing with something new—a story, a photograph, whatever—the happier it is and the more likely it will be to come back again soon and see what else you have to nibble on.

As a journalist, the need to feed an ever-snacking news audience puts you at risk of jumping onboard the hamster wheel. Run, run as fast as you can. You'll never catch up. The audience will always want more. If you're not careful, you'll always be publishing, never reporting.

The only way to avoid the hamster wheel is to think of your job as one that provides a service—like an investment adviser or a doctor or a hot air balloon pilot—rather than a product. This fundamental change in thinking will alter the way you view your work and your audience. It may also change the way your audience regards you. And, as an added bonus, it will keep you sane. Maybe.

Journalism has always been a service to the public, of course, but its value couldn't be realized until the product was delivered. True service providers charge their customers for verbs (cutting, inspecting, flying), not nouns (milk, box, car). Online journalism is a process, not a product.

This change in approach means new opportunities and new challenges for journalists. Suddenly, the reporting process—the messy task of assembling the sausage—is open to the audience. And the audience is naturally going to have suggestions. Will you see these suggestions as a help or a hindrance? They can be both.

As reporter Ryan Teague Beckwith wrote his Oct. 27, 2007, front-page story for The (Raleigh, N.C.) News & Observer, his process was open to the public. Beckwith started his day as so many beat reporters have always done—checking in with his sources. Like many beat reporters today, he included in those sources anyone blogging about his beat. In the Good Ol' Days, a reporter might have stopped in at the local coffee shop on his way to work to see what The Audience was talking about. Beat reporters do still make those rounds. But today, finding out what people are saying on the street means checking in with the word on the Web.

One of the blogs Beckwith checked was "Talk Politics," written by Leroy Towns, a University of North Carolina professor and the former chief of staff for Sen. Pat Roberts (R-Kansas). Towns had written a post the previous afternoon that said the presidential campaign of Democrat John Edwards had "used some pretty heavy-handed tactics" to get a journalism student to remove from YouTube a video story she had done about the candidate.

For a political reporter in the home state of a presidential candidate, that is a great tip. In product-oriented journalism, these tips don't get repeated until they are vetted through additional reporting that typically includes getting the story from at least two unrelated sources. Not so in this case. Beckwith's first post went up at 8:51 a.m., shortly after he'd seen the blog and nearly 24 hours before his final story would appear in the paper. (All of Beckwith's posts that day are archived at http://projects.newsobserver.com/tags/carla_babb?page=1.)

At this early stage, Beckwith had no firsthand knowledge of the events. He had only the secondhand information from the professor's blog. Three minutes later, at 8:54 a.m., Beckwith found the student's video news story on YouTube and embedded it into his own blog. He had begun the process of reporting. And he immediately let his readers in on it.

Seen through the lens of traditional product-oriented journalism, Beckwith's move might look reckless and misleading. But through the lens of process-oriented journalism, it is an act of courageous transparency that both respects the judgment of the audience and empowers the audience to interact in a public debate more quickly.

For the rest of the day, Beckwith continued with the process of reporting. And through the use of his blog, that process was completely transparent and open to the audience, some of whom weighed in with their opinions and talked with Beckwith as he was still reporting the story. Let's follow the timeline:

8:43 a.m.—Beckwith writes a brief, inverted pyramid news story for the newspaper's site.

1:26 p.m.—The blog post gets its first reader comment. The comment criticizes the report for being published before it is fully and fairly reported. The criticism comes from someone who uses the same pseudonym that is often used by a liberal blogger who is married to yet another journalism professor at UNC.

1:30 p.m.—Beckwith gets a quote from the professor who edited the student's story. We still don't have both sides of the story, but we have a more detailed account from one side.

2 p.m.—Beckwith responds to the first commenter, defusing the potential flame war with: "Thanks for asking. We've put in multiple calls to the staffers in question and will report more as this story unfolds." Fifteen minutes later, the commenter expresses his appreciation for the update.

3:53 p.m.—Beckwith updates the inverted pyramid story.

6:42 p.m.—Beckwith posts to the blog some quotes from the student.

The *process* detailed above is what Beckwith used to create the *product*—the news story—in the next day's paper. But here is the question on which you should reflect: When was the story finished? Was it done when Towns published his blog post, or when Beckwith published his? Or when the story went into the paper or was posted on the website?

Or was it done when the story was repeated in The New York Times' political blog? Maybe the story wasn't done until Beckwith did some more fact-checking on the student's piece—two days later. Or maybe the story was finally finished two *months* later, when the student won the MTV contest to which she had submitted her story.

The point is this: the morning newspaper and the evening news have always been arbitrary deadlines requiring editors to declare a story "done." But in reality, many news stories—and especially complex ones that are most likely to have great impact—deserve another phone call to a source, another visit to the scene of the crime, another perspective to be considered. The people and events in the story continue their dance, long after the journalist has turned away. That's the difference between a product and a process.

Journalism—and life—is as Kenneth Burke described it in "The Philosophy of Literary Form." You enter a room in which the conversation has already begun. "You listen for a while until you decide that you have caught the tenor of the argument; then you put in your oar." The conversation continues as others react to you and you react to them. "The hour grows late, you must depart. And you do depart, with the discussion still vigorously in progress."

The endless cycling of journalism today was conceived in the 24/7 environments of cable news channels and talk radio, but moved from audio-visual journalism to text with the advent of the Web. The post-centric, reverse-chronological order of blogs is just one of the relatively new formats that has moved journalism away from a product and into a process. But we'll also see in this chapter how the on-demand, always-on nature of the Web requires specific skills for present-tense storytelling, and specific techniques for correcting and updating information as the often messy and confusing process of searching for truth is opened up for all to watch, critique and contribute to.

BLOGGING

Before you can use a blog for journalistic purposes, it is important to understand what blogging is and what it is not. Traditional journalists and bloggers have spent the last 10 years arguing the wrong question about whether journalists can blog and whether blogging is journalism. It is the wrong question because it turns out that blogs are not defined by the content inside them. They are defined by the structure of their format, and that structure in turn affects how journalists write for a blog.

Like other narrative formats—a news story, a biographical book, a screenplay, a haiku—blogs follow rules that govern their structure. But there are really no rules regulating the content that goes inside them. Formatting rules impose both limits and mandates. A news story in the inverted pyramid format must start with the most important facts and progress to the least important. A haiku in English is three lines. But an inverted pyramid news story or a haiku can be about any topic. So too can a blog.

The reason that blogs have developed as a distinct format is due largely to their heritage as a simple software program. Starting in 1999 with the widespread adoption of the first Web-based, free publishing system called **Blogger,** the Web has exploded with sites that are laid out in the blog format. The **blog**—a condensed version of "Web log"—grew in popularity because its format made it easy for a person to create a website without any knowledge of computer coding. The programs' ease of use stemmed partly from the fact that blogging software published information in a standardized format, originally with little flexibility.

This ease of use made it possible for almost anyone to publish his or her own thoughts on the Web. There is a saying that freedom of the press belongs to those who own one, and with the birth of blogs suddenly everyone—from cabinet secretaries to lunatics to political dissidents—owned a press. The proliferation in amateur reporting and editing that has accompanied the rise of the blog format has had a profound effect on American journalism, raising a wide variety of questions about law, ethics and reporting strategy.

What Is a Blog?

All blogs have the following three characteristics in common:

1. A **blog** consists of "posts," which can be of varying length. A **post,** like a news story or article, is about a single topic or event. But unlike an article or news story, it does not necessarily follow an inverted pyramid structure.

2. Posts are laid out vertically on a blog's homepage in reverse chronological order. The most recent post appears at the top of the page and the oldest at the bottom.

3. Professional news blogs almost always focus on a single topic. In newsrooms these topics are called **"beats."** Music, schools, parenting, technology, politics, a certain sports team or a specific television show—all are common topics for a blog.

In addition to these basic similarities, there are some other features that are commonly found in blogs. For example, most blogs allow their readers to comment on each post. Most blogs are written by a single author, though some of the most popular technology news blogs have several reporters who post to them. And most bloggers make prolific use of links within their posts to footnote their commentary or to demonstrate transparency by allowing readers to view original source material.

There are four different types of blogs:

1. A personal blog is a diary written by a single author for a limited audience of friends and family. Most blogs are personal blogs.

2. An opinion blog is dedicated to advocating the opinion of the author on a range of topics as diverse as national politics and baby strollers. It is written for a broad range of readers, most of whom don't personally know the author.

3. A **beat blog** is written (typically) by a professional reporter who adheres to traditional journalistic ethics of full, fair and accurate original reporting. It is generally focused on a single topic. The beat blog is written for a broad range of readers, most of whom don't personally know the reporter.

4. A **breaking news blog** is written by one or more professional reporters and provides quick updates about live news events for consumption by a general audience.

The most common type of blog, the personal blog, shares little in common with news blogs. The audience for a personal blog is most often a small group of family and friends. Many personal blogs are even hidden from public view. These bloggers don't consider themselves journalists, and their posts do not exhibit traditional news values or emphasize traditional news elements.

In some cases, however, personal blogs are *very* public. Celebrities such as Glenn Beck or Kanye West write blogs as a way to speak directly to their fans. Some celebrities use their fame to promote their opinions about current events and public affairs on a blog. And many opinion bloggers have become minor celebrities in their own right. Opinion blogs are the second most common type of blog, albeit a distant second.

Opinion blogs combine various amounts of original reporting with commentary about current events and public affairs. The "Instapundit" blog authored by Glen Reynolds includes almost no original reporting. As he writes on the site, "As with anything else you read on the Internet, you should take what you read here as a starting point for your own research and investigation in the process of arriving at your own informed opinion (again, kind of like a card catalog) not as an ending point."

Reynolds does little original reporting, and his commentary is often minimal as well. But what Reynolds lacks in verbosity he makes up for in frequency, posting as many as 50 times a day starting before 7 a.m. and often going until past midnight.

On the other extreme, opinion blogger Joshua Micah Marshall does so much original reporting that he won the prestigious George Polk Award for Legal Reporting in 2007. According to the press release announcing the award, it was "Marshall's tenacious investigative reporting [that] sparked interest by the traditional news media and led to the resignation of Attorney General Alberto Gonzales." Marshall began writing his opinion blog at www.talkingpointsmemo.com in November 2000, during the recount of Florida's votes in the presidential election. The archive of the posts that won him the Polk award can be accessed at http://tpmmuckraker.talkingpointsmemo.com/us-attorneys/2007/03/.

While Reynolds and Marshall are opinion bloggers who tend to tackle national political issues from generally partisan perspectives, other opinion bloggers operate more like traditional newspaper columnists. For example, Marc Fisher, a former Metro columnist for The Washington Post, also wrote a blog called "Raw Fisher" (see http://blog.washingtonpost.com/rawfisher/). The subtitle of the blog was "The Cold Splash of Reality, With A Side of Sizzle." Most of the blog posts were heavily reported; they also contained Fisher's unique take on the subjects he was covering. In his farewell column for the newspaper, Fisher wrote about what he had learned about the new relationship between writers and audience in the online world:

> I loved the new battleground of ideas even as I lamented how opinion—the laziest form of journalism—was elbowing out the rigorous work of reporting. In this new world, it was so cheap to mouth off that the difficult and sometimes less-exciting work of ferreting out facts became too easy to discard or trim back.

While Fisher readily agreed with the view of columnist Mary McGrory—"the second you stop reporting, you're just one more pontificating, pusillanimous pundit"—he didn't shy away from making judgments about his subjects. As Fisher put it, he used both his column and his blog to "dig up the story, then say it straight."

In the same way a news columnist mixes reporting and commentary, many "super-users" who know a lot about a particular subject or product category have become influential bloggers by mixing advice and evidence. David Pogue of The New York Times is an example of this type of blogger. Pogue writes about consumer technology at http://pogue.blogs.nytimes.com/.

But consumer advice blogs aren't just the domain of large news outlets. There are hundreds, if not thousands, of amateur commentators who offer their opinions on just about every type of product. For example, if you're a "beauty addict" you might follow the opinion of "Vanessa" at http://nessasarymakeup.blogspot.com. If you're a World of Warcraft player, you might read or even contribute to www.wow.com. And if you want to use your Mac Mini to build a home theater system, well, don't miss Andrew Werhane's blog at http://www.macminihometheater.com/ or his **Twitter** feed at http://twitter.com/MacMiniHTPC.

These consumer-experts gain some of their authority from their laser-like and mile-deep focus on a single topic. This focus is a trait that is shared by beat blogs, which are most often written by professional reporters working in traditional newsrooms. The term "beat blog" was popularized by New York University journalism professor Jay Rosen, who described it as a blog that "presents a regular flow of reporting and commentary in a focused area the beat covers; it provides links and online resources in that area, and it tracks the subject over time. Beats can be topical (like dot.earth, which is about natural resources and the environment) or narrowly geographic (West Seattle blog) or both (Atlantic Yards Report) or activity-related (Family Life, which is about 'raising a family')."

Just as many opinion blogs produce at least some small bit of original reporting, many beat blogs are written in a conversational tone that can include commentary and analysis on the patterns and trends of news topics as well as original reporting on those topics. Beat bloggers open up their reporting process, which includes, among other things:

- Reading and assessing the work of other news sources
- Talking with sources
- Receiving tips
- Acquiring documents
- Forming hypothesis
- Making connections
- Developing analysis

Tool: Wordpress ────────────────────────────

Whether you're an entrepreneurial journalist looking to start your own website and blog or a reporter creating a beat blog for a larger news organization, it is important to understand the capabilities, limitations and general organizational structure of blogging software.

Most blogging platforms are collections of software that are installed on a Web server. If you have your own Web server, or rent space on one, you can download for free and install on your server one of the most popular blogging tools, **Wordpress.**

The process of setting up a Web server and installing several pieces of software is complicated and can be frustrating for people who do not have experience with computer programming and server administration. So the good news is, you don't have to go through the hassle. Subscribers to the website that accompanies this book have a Wordpress blog waiting for them, installed and ready to use.

Once you've claimed your blog, you can get started with Wordpress by following these 10 easy steps:

1. Choose an address for your blog. The URL of your blog should be as short and simple as possible so that it is easy for people to remember and type into their Web browsers. But it should also be descriptive of the subject your blog will cover. And it needs to be one word.

2. Choose a name for your blog. Keep in mind that the title and the URL should bear some similarity to one another. The screen on which you choose your title gives you an important choice about the privacy of your blog. As a journalist, you'll want to be read by as many people as possible, so you don't want to hide your blog from anyone. But if you are just getting started, it might be better to keep your blog private. This will allow you to practice—and make mistakes—out of the critical eye of the public. You can adjust your privacy setting at a later time.

3. While you wait for the registration of your blog to be confirmed and verified, craft a personal message about yourself. Remember, your profile isn't being written for family and friends but for people who have probably never met you before and want to know whether they should trust your reporting. They want to know why they should prefer your blog to any of the others out there that might be about the exact same topic.

4. Once your account is verified, your blog will be created. From this point forward you will be able to view your blog at http://[blogname].wordpress.com and log in to the administrative interface at http://[blogname].wordpress.com/wp-login.php. After you log in, you will see the main administrative Web page, called the Dashboard, at http://[blogname].wordpress.com/wp-admin/.

5. Now that your account is up and running, you are ready to start writing. But you will want to get the look and feel of your blog just right before making it public. Changes

to the layout or design of a blog can be disorienting for readers once they are accustomed to a certain way of doing things. You can preview and activate a **theme** for your blog by selecting from one of the many free themes that Wordpress makes available at http:// [blogname].wordpress.com/wp-admin/themes.php. Go ahead and try out several themes. You will discover how the content of your blog is separate from the design, and how the database works with the layout and display rules.

Once you've selected a theme, you may want to change the color of the header—also called a banner—at the top of your blog. To change header colors, go to http://[blogname] .wordpress.com/wp-admin/admin.php?page=functions.php. To create a custom header, go to http://[blogname].wordpress.com/wp-admin/admin.php?page=custom-header. You will find that it is easier to simply change the colors, because changing the header requires creating and uploading image files.

6. You might need to update some of your settings. For example, to change the blog post and the time format setting, go to http://[blogname].wordpress.com/wp-admin/ options-general.php. (Note that there is not an off-the-shelf option in Wordpress to display the timestamp in a format that matches the AP style format "a.m." and "p.m." This is the case with many templated Web content management systems.)

Settings that determine how many posts appear on your homepage and other rules about how posts are displayed can be accessed at http://[blogname].wordpress.com/ wp-admin/options-reading.php.

7. Before you make your blog public, it is important to set some ground rules covering the basics of author/audience interaction. The options for how you deal with comments on your blog posts can be changed by going to http://[blogname].wordpress.com/wp-admin/ options-discussion.php. You can read more about how these rules alter audience engagement patterns by reading Chapter 11, on social media.

8. Now that you've set up some of the basic preferences of your blog, you are ready to start adding words and multimedia to the site. You may have already created an "About" page. If you have, you can edit it now by going to the "Pages" link on the left-side menu of the Dashboard. If you don't have an "About" page, you can create one by going to the same place and then clicking on "Add New," which will take you to http://[blogname].wordpress .com/wp-admin/page-new.php.

Static pages are an excellent way to add evergreen resources to your blog. Perhaps you want to have a profile of all the key sources of your blog, or maybe you have an important document you want to post and use repeatedly. These pieces of content should be created as pages rather than posts. At the very least, you should create a static "About" page before you get started. You can always add other pages as they're needed.

9. Many of the coolest tricks you see other bloggers using are generated by extras and plugins. These features are created by third-party developers for use on the Wordpress

platform. In the free Wordpress.com platform, you can look at your options by going to the "Appearance" menu on the Dashboard and then selecting **"Widgets."**

You'll see a lot of options here, but use them only as you need. A good place to start is by activating the "Search," "Calendar," "Categories List," "Tag Cloud" and "Top Posts" options. These are all common features of news blogs.

Later you may want to use the "Widgets" option to start publishing directly to your blog your social bookmarks from the Delicious website. Or, perhaps you will want to distribute news photos via Flickr. Using the Flickr widget in Wordpress allows you to post selected photos automatically on your blog. The whole idea behind a syndication widget is to publish your content once online and then have it appear on the Web via many distribution channels without any additional effort on your part.

As you become more experienced as a blogger and move off of free services, you will have many more options when it comes to the bells and whistles you might want to add to your blog. New tools, many of which are available for free, are being released every month. It is wise to stay abreast of the latest add-ons available for the blog platform of your choice. Here are a few tools that have become popular on news blogs and can be useful for entrepreneurial journalists looking to build an audience:

- Sociable, at http://wordpress.org/extend/plugins/sociable/. Sociable provides your site visitors with an easy way to bookmark or share your posts with their social networks.

- Google Analytics, at http://wordpress.org/extend/plugins/google-analytics-for-word press/. Google Analytics is a free tool that can be used to measure the size of your audience.

- Google Sitemap, at http://wordpress.org/extend/plugins/google-sitemap-generator/. Google Sitemap makes it easier for Google to crawl your site and add your content to its index. This improves the chances that people will find your blog posts via a Web search.

- reCAPTCHA, at http://wordpress.org/extend/plugins/wp-recaptcha/. reCAPTCHA is a free tool that reduces "comment spam" by making it difficult for automated computer programs to post irrelevant comments on your blog.

- All in One SEO Pack, at http://wordpress.org/extend/plugins/all-in-one-seo-pack/. This tool makes it easier for you to edit the metadata on the posts and pages of your blog.

10. You're finally ready to create a post. The Dashboard offers several ways to navigate to the Web form where you write and edit posts, but they all end up at http://[blogname] .wordpress.com/wp-admin/post-new.php. Here, you write a headline, type the body of your post, write a summary (but only if you've chosen to use summaries in your blog's design) and

change the default comment setting if you'd like. You can also create a **tag** for the post and select one or more categories. Tags are like keywords. They are often nouns. You can read more about keywords in Chapter 5, on editing for searchers and scanners. Categories are broad and long-lasting sections of the site. There shouldn't be too many of them, and they shouldn't change very often. Finally, you will want to check your spelling. Then save, preview and publish. Congratulations. You are now a blogger!

Tutorials on using Wordpress

Screencasts on applying add-ons to your Wordpress blog

What Makes a Good Blog?

The best bloggers are a hybrid of two kinds of traditional journalists: the newspaper beat reporter and the television broadcast anchor. The beat reporter knows the ins and outs of the topic she is covering; she knows every source, procedure, document and detail. The anchor is a good host; he greets his audience using an informal tone and introduces the topics he thinks it should care about.

One of the ironies of online journalism is that, while blogging tools have made it much easier for anyone to publish a website, the rapid proliferation of blogs is making it increasingly difficult to be heard above the din. Competition for the attention of the online audience is fierce. The best ways to distinguish your blog from any others are to cover a unique beat and develop a unique voice.

High-quality news blogs share four fundamental qualities:

1. They have a well-defined and narrow topic.
2. They provide brief, incremental updates.
3. They are well reported.
4. Their authors are engaged with the audience.

At most newspapers, reporters are given "beats." Beats are subjects or topics that a reporter will cover regularly. Having a beat allows a reporter to develop an expertise on a subject. He knows the history of the issues and the personalities involved; he has followed the debates and can identify patterns that only reveal themselves over time.

At television and radio news outlets, general managers craft entire editorial strategies around the development of "anchors"—the people whose job is to host the news broadcast and introduce the audience to stories done by other reporters in the field. The most successful anchors develop their own unique style and voice; they essentially become the face of the entire newsroom. How powerful are anchors? In a 2002 poll, respondents deemed the anchors of the national nightly news programs on ABC, CBS and NBC more trustworthy than the news organizations that employed them.

Defining a Beat

In baseball, there is an old saying: "Hit 'em where they ain't." In other words, the best way for a batter to get a hit is to simply survey the field and hit the ball to a spot that is not occupied by a fielder. Before you start a blog, scour the Web and find the unoccupied spot. While you almost certainly will have a topic in mind, it is important to survey the field and familiarize yourself with the voices already covering the topic, or even one that is similar. Your blog will need to be different in some way from your competitors' blogs, both amateur and professional. You are going to need to offer the audience better reporting, both more focused and in-depth, or you might try to meet the needs of an audience that differs slightly from the audience of your competitors.

As a beginning blogger, it is better to start with a narrow topic and expand it later. Joshua Micah Marshall is a good example of this. His blog originally focused on the 2000 presidential vote recount in Florida, but it quickly grew into a wide-ranging blog about national politics. Starting small gave him an initial hook around which he was able to develop an audience.

The competitive landscape of blogging isn't necessarily a bad thing. It will force you to carve out a unique niche. And with so many people, so many interests, so many concerns—you are almost sure to find an audience whose needs are not being met. But keep in mind, it is the real needs of real people that you are seeking to fill. After all, no one is blogging about the airspeed velocity of unladen swallows for a perfectly predictable reason—there is no audience for such a thing. It is not enough to have a niche topic. You also have to have a niche audience.

Table 10.1 Blog Ideas and Better Blog Ideas

Blog Ideas	Better Blog Ideas
News	Breaking news
Education	Houston Independent School District
Hot-button issues	Immigration
The opinion of the editorial board members	The opinion of one editorial board member
Animals	Doggies
Marshmallows	Peeps

Blog ideas should be as specific as possible. Think you've found a niche that no one else is covering? Search for it and you may well be surprised by what you find—someone else out there already doing it.

Good target audiences are those that are already compact and discrete. For example, perhaps you feel that environmental issues are under-reported. You may decide to develop a blog for "people who care about the environment." But "the environment" is an awfully big topic. In this case, it would be better to target the blog to an audience of "people who are concerned about the placement of the county's new solid waste landfill." The people who are concerned about the landfill have likely already identified themselves in some way. Perhaps they live in neighborhoods that will potentially be affected. Or perhaps they've even organized a citizens' action committee with its own blog.

A niche audience can be conceptualized in a variety of ways. But its members must share traits in common as well as exhibit differences from nonmembers. Those differences can be psychographic, demographic or behavioral. Psychographic characteristics deal with a person's attitude, values, fears or aspirations. For example, a psychographic group might be people who always like to have the latest consumer electronics gadget. Demographic characteristics involve the kinds of data that we often associate with a census—age, gender, race and geographic location, for example. The residents of the Pine Oaks subdivision would be a demographic group. Teenage girls would be another.

Finally, behavioral characteristics describe what an audience actually does. A person's values would be part of a psychographic profile. But how a person acts out those values would be part of his or her behavioral profile. For example, commuting an hour to downtown on Interstate 70 in a single-occupancy vehicle is a behavioral characteristic. Having concern about the air quality in the Denver region is a psychographic characteristic. The two aren't always in sync.

Finding your niche as a blogger gives you a chance to develop your authority on a particular subject and increase the amount of trust your readers have in you. Authority will make it easier for people to find you via search engines, and trust will increase the number of people who will create links to your site. These people go from being readers to being something just as crucial: advocates for your reporting.

As you develop the topic for your blog, ask yourself these four questions:

1. Who is my typical visitor? Can I describe him in sufficient detail—in no less than 500 words? What are the psychographic, demographic or behavioral characteristics that separate my potential visitors from people who won't visit?

2. What problem do my visitors face? How can I help them solve it? What service can I provide?

3. Who else is blogging on this topic? (You don't want too many competitors—nor too few.)

4. How can I make mine the "go-to" blog? Why should visitors seek me out versus others writing about this or a similar topic?

The proliferation of hyper-niche topics and hyper-niche audiences has public affairs implications that deserve consideration here. How does a country—or even a community—carry on a robust debate and search for democratic solutions if everyone is living in his or her own narrow silo of interest? The role that journalists play in shaping public issues is changing. Today it is much more difficult to exert broad impact; it is, perhaps, easier to have a deep impact on a small group of people.

Making Posts the Unit of Composition

In "The Elements of Style," William Strunk and E. B. White said that writers should "make the paragraph the unit of composition: one paragraph to each topic." If they had been writing a style guide for blogs, they might have said bloggers should "make the post the unit of composition: one post to each new fact."

Like the posts of a fence, the posts of a blog work together to hold up a continuous narrative that ties one post to the next in sequence. Remove a single post from its context inside a blog, and both the post and the narrative of which it is a part will probably still make sense. But remove too many posts, or space the posts too far apart, and both a fence and a blog narrative will collapse.

Strunk and White recognized that most stories have more than one topic, and that each of these topics should be the subject of a single paragraph. But reporters working in the blog format are crafting posts before they can see the whole picture. So a blogger who attempts to make each post a comprehensive account of an entire topic may find herself imposing delays between posts that last days, or even weeks—not encouraging to an audience that likes to snack.

Blogs, like conversations, work better when information is delivered in short spurts rather than one long monologue. New facts should be reported as soon as they can be verified. Each blog post is dedicated to a single piece of information. This means that news bloggers make posts the unit of composition.

Limiting each post to a single fact also helps news bloggers keep posts brief. Remember, the online news audience snacks on small bits of information throughout the day rather than consuming it in one or two well-balanced meals. Chapter 3, on the online news audience, has more details about audience habits.

The inverted pyramid story that Beckwith eventually wrote for The News & Observer was crafted for an audience that consumes its news diet in a single sitting. The story had to be comprehensive. Beckwith had only one shot at telling it. The story was 687 words. But none of his blog posts detailing the process were more than 190 words. Taken all together, he wrote about 490 words on the topic for his blog the day the story broke. If you compare the blog and story versions side by side, you will see that there really isn't much difference in the information they contain. Quite simply, the two versions represent different formats that are used differently by different audiences.

Developing a Conversational Voice

Bloggers often describe their writing style as "conversational." It is less formal in its adherence to grammatically correct sentence structure and more likely to include subjective adjectives like "finally" or "only." That said, there is nothing about a casual writing style that gives you permission to be casual about your collecting and reporting of the facts. In fact, the right balance between being casual in tone but precise in reporting is the mark of an excellent journalist.

Finding your voice as a blogger is a highly personal endeavor. Individuality notwithstanding, frequent reading and analyzing of other bloggers whose voices you like can be very helpful in finding your own voice. The style employed by most good bloggers is personal without being self-centered. And it is casual without being careless. In a word, the voice of a good blogger is authentic.

Columnists and feature writers have always sought to develop a unique voice, and one piece of advice they've always heard is "write as you speak." Verbal conversations are much less formal than lectures or speeches. Good conversations are both impromptu and intelligent. In the best conversations people trade questions and answers, with both parties learning bits and pieces of new information during the process. Neither blurts out everything he or she has to say all at once. Blogging builds upon itself—just as good conversation does.

Broadcast journalists often use on-air conversation—sometimes to the point of gimmickry—to tell their stories. As a report ends, anchors will often ask additional questions of the reporter and engage in a brief, often scripted, conversation. Done poorly, this kind of banter can make journalists seem like play actors. But if done well, these conversations humanize the broadcasters and convey authenticity.

VIEW SOURCE

EDWARD R. MURROW, BLOGGER

One of the original—and still best—conversational tones in the history of U.S. media belonged to radio broadcast pioneer Edward R. Murrow. Murrow, reporting on the eve of World War II more than 60 years ago, is widely regarded as one of the most influential American journalists of the 20th century. He died long before blogs ever came on the scene, but the words he used and the way he reported would have fit well in a blog format.

Listen to Murrow's report on the first CBS World News Roundup at http://audio.cbsnews.com/2006/11/14/audio2181434.mp3. Before skipping ahead to Murrow's report, which begins 26 minutes and 48 seconds into the broadcast, listen first to the two speakers who precede him. Their style is formal. Now listen to Murrow. His is a noticeably less formal style, both in choice of words and manner of delivery.

As you listen keep in mind that his words were spoken on March 13, 1938, the very first time that a national anchor in New York linked field reporters in Europe in a radio broadcast. In fact, this was the very first time Murrow had ever spoken on air. He wasn't even hired to be a reporter. His job was to book and schedule other people to speak on air. None of the correspondents of the day had studied in college to be a correspondent, and obviously none of them had a long tradition to emulate. At this moment of journalistic innovation, Murrow set boldly off down a distinctly different path from that of his predecessors.

Murrow's report is both more detailed in its content and breezier in its delivery than that of the other correspondents. The other speakers offer their opinions or describe what they are seeing in cities from which they are reporting. But Murrow talks about his reporting process, and during his account of the process we learn about conditions in Vienna. He packs his sentences with first-person pronouns and with street-level intelligence. He inserts long pauses. In at least one place, he stumbles over words. His voice doesn't sound polished—it sounds authentic.

When you write a blog post, remember Murrow. Imagine that you are appearing on a radio show as an expert on your topic. Try writing the posts in the same voice you would use to respond to questions from the host and from listeners. Like Murrow, your word choice and delivery style can be casual, but your reporting can never be sloppy.

Live Blogging

Because the layout of blogs places the most recent post at the top of the page, blogs are good tools to use for covering breaking news. Wire editors for decades have been reading breaking news updates on the Associated Press and other wire services. When big news breaks, wires still move **"alerts"**—brief accounts of the newest information—that resemble the posts on a breaking news blog. But while AP breaking news alerts are available only to subscribers of this expensive service, news organizations are using breaking news blogs to create breaking news updates for retail distribution.

When a gunman killed 32 people and himself at Virginia Tech University in 2007, student journalists on the campus and professional reporters at the nearby Roanoke Times both turned to a blog format to publish breaking news updates to the Web.

Here, in chronological order, are the first four updates on the shooting from The Roanoke Times. Note how the newer posts avoid repeating information in older posts. This aspect of the blog format makes it different from the updates of breaking news stories written in a traditional inverted pyramid style.

Updated: 10:17 a.m.

Multiple shootings have occurred at Virginia Tech this morning involving multiple victims. The second shooting happened in Norris Hall, the engineering building near Burruss Hall. Police are on the scene and rescue workers have set up a temporary treatment facility. The campus is on lock down. All classes and activities have been cancelled for the day.

Montgomery County public schools are all on lock down. In Blacksburg, no one is being allowed in any school building without approval by the school administrators, said Superintendent Tiffany Anderson.

The university has posted a notice of the incident on its website and is urging the university community to be cautious and contact Virginia Tech police at 231–6411 if they notice anything suspicious. No further details were available. The Roanoke Times will update with new information as it become[s] available.

Updated: 11:06 a.m.

The Associated Press is reporting there [is] at least one person dead as a result of multiple shootings on the Virginia Tech campus this morning. Wounded have been removed from buildings. Tech student Steve Hanson was working in a lab in Norris Hall at 10:15 a.m. when he hears what he thought was loud banging from construction. Hanson was soon scrambling out of the building and he said he saw one person who was shot in the arm. At Pritchard Hall, a dormitory near one of the shooting sites, students were being pulled into the buildings and told to stay away from windows and off the phone.

11:49 a.m.

The Associated Press is reporting eight to nine casualties, attributing the information to an unnamed official source.

Virginia Tech's Newman Library became a shelter as university staff urged students and passersby to come in from the sidewalk. Library staff estimated that hundreds of people are in the building now, far more than would be usual at this time of day.

Sarah Ulmer, a freshman from Covington, sat on the floor and recounted how she'd been walking between buildings this morning when she saw police officers near McBryde and Norris halls.

"The police said, 'Get out of the way, get out of the way,' and then they said 'Run,' " Ulmer said. She couldn't return to her dorm room in East Ambler Johnson hall because it was near one of the shooting sites, so she headed toward Newman.

"I figured it was safe," she said. "It was the library."

Watching police from the library's fourth-floor windows, David Russell, a sophomore from Montgomery County, Md., echoed a common sentiment, comparing today's events to last year's manhunt for accused murderer William Morva.

"This year with Morva, the bomb threats and this now, it's crazy. It's not really what you'd expect from a small farm school."

11:53 a.m.

Scott Hendricks, an associate professor of engineering science and mechanics, said he was on Norris Hall's third floor this morning around 9:45. "I started hearing some banging and some shots, then I saw a student crawling on the ground."

Hendricks said he was not sure if he saw any of the casualties, but "I saw a bloody T-shirt."

Hendricks said he went into a classroom with students, closed the door and waited until things were quiet before leaving the building.

Source: "Governor closes gun purchase loophole" by The Roanoke Times. Copyright 2007 by The Roanoke Times. Reproduced with permission of Roanoke Times in the format Other Book via Copyright Clearance Center, www.roanoke.com/news/nrv/breaking/wb/113294.

NEWS JUDGMENT

BLOGGING BREAKING NEWS: MELANIE ASMAR

What do you do when you're just three months into your new reporting job in a new state and your editor taps you to do something you've never done before: sit in a courtroom and liveblog a murder trial?

"We just did trial and error and figured out what worked," says Melanie Asmar, with no pun intended. "I guess I thought about it as if I were retelling it to a friend who was sitting right next to me."

When she joined the weekly Westword in Denver, Asmar was six years out of college. She'd been a reporter at the Concord (N.H.) Monitor when the 2008 presidential campaign brought the periodic glare of the international media to New Hampshire, so she knew how important it was to get stories up on the Web as fast as possible. But liveblogging the trial of a man accused of killing a transgender teenager in Greeley, Colo., turned out to be very different.

Says Asmar, "Live blogging is definitely more blippy; you're not really giving context. In a news story you'd always have that nut graph that tells you so-and-so is accused of killing so-and-so."

When the trial first started, Asmar began posting to the blog every five minutes. "And then the editors were, like, 'Whoa.'" Asmar and her editors—who were instant messaging with her via Google—decided to slow the pace a bit. No need to burn out the reporter, editor, producer, publishing system *and* the audience all on the first day.

THE ALWAYS-ON NEWS CYCLE

Blogs—a wonderful format for providing a journalistic service—aren't for everyone. While online journalism is always available to the audience, the audience isn't always watching. For many busy people, journalists are valuable because they sort through quantities of information before presenting only the most important details. Many news consumers relate to journalists the same way they relate to a retirement investment adviser: they check in periodically to make sure everything is going OK, but they don't want or need to be bothered by the details of incremental change in the market.

The audience relies on you, the journalist, to provide the right information at the right time. The always-on nature of online news requires journalists to tell a story in real time. These two fundamentals of online journalism—timeliness and accuracy—together can

Sitting behind the cameras for truTV, Asmar was unable to provide all the detail of the physical action in the courtroom, so she had to exercise some news judgment about what her audience might be interested in. She presumed her audience was either people who stumbled on the blog and found it interesting to follow for a few minutes or people who were intensely interested in the play-by-play of the case. In either case, Asmar knew that her value was as a fast filter.

"I'm not going to live blog an expert explaining his or her credentials," Asmar says. "I don't think the audience is interested in that, but that's what takes up a lot of time at the trials. Readers don't want to know how you analyze the DNA of hair you found. They want to know whose hair it was."

The blog essentially became notes for the story Asmar would later write for the paper, she says. And because her note-taking process was open to the public, she had an incentive to pay much closer attention than she might have otherwise.

"It was pretty stressful, but not in a bad way," she notes. "You feel like you have to be on for six hours."

"At the end of the day it's all about being able to tell a story, and you can't forget that. Knowing how to use Twitter and knowing how to live blog doesn't replace knowing how to craft a story, and hook readers in, and be a good reporter. You may only be writing 140 characters, but they still have to be a good 140 characters."

present a challenge. This is one reason why accurate updates and transparent corrections to inaccurate information are crucial aspects of the online mix.

Alerts, Adds and Writethrus

Writing news stories for a website is more like writing for a wire service such as the Associated Press or Reuters than writing for a newspaper. In a newspaper, only one version of a story gets published. And that version, for the most part, is considered a "complete" accounting of whatever news it conveys. Wire services, which got their start as private suppliers of breaking news to news editors and reporters, are versed in relaying what is "incomplete"—that is, breaking news.

Wire reporters have always filed stories that they knew were incomplete—accurate, but probably lacking key information. Newspaper reporters traditionally would never dream of filing a report that lacked key information. Wire reporters knew that they would have another shot at updating the story. Newspaper reporters knew they would not.

But as the wire services began being published directly to the Web—on Yahoo News, Google News and almost every other news website—the general public increasingly had access to breaking news. All it needed was an Internet connection. In fact, the online audience got the news almost as soon as the news organizations that subscribed to the wires got it. For the online audience, breaking news *is* the news.

When it comes to breaking news, the goal of the online news reporter is to file the first piece of substantiated and accurate reporting that is complete enough so that it doesn't mislead or unnecessarily alarm readers. Following is a rundown of how the Associated Press reports and updates breaking news, according to its "Editor's Guide to AP News Services for Newspapers," published in 2001.

First, the AP files a "NewsAlert." This alert is "a one-line item that condenses the essence of the development." Alerts are the first version of a story. They typically contain the news elements "Who?" and "What?"

Websites also file news alerts when stories break. Often, news organizations will send out e-mails to subscribers containing breaking news headlines and summaries. For example, here are the breaking news e-mail alerts sent out by The Washington Post, The New York Times and CNN when Sen. Edward Kennedy died in 2009:

Mass. Sen. Edward M. Kennedy Dies After a Yearlong Battle With Cancer

Edward M. Kennedy, one of the most powerful and influential senators in American history and one of three brothers whose political triumphs and personal tragedies captivated the nation for decades, died at 77. (from The Washington Post at 2:22 a.m.)

Edward M. Kennedy, Senate Stalwart, Dies at 77

Senator Edward M. Kennedy of Massachusetts, a son of one of the most storied families in American politics, a man who knew triumph and tragedy in near-equal measure and who will be remembered as one of the most effective lawmakers in the history of the Senate, died late Tuesday night. He was 77. (from The New York Times at 1:32 a.m.)

Senator Ted Kennedy has died of brain cancer at age 77

(from CNN at 1:29 a.m.)

Most news websites allow visitors to subscribe to breaking news alerts sent to their e-mail accounts or as **SMS** text messages to their cell phones. Some are also posting breaking news alerts as **RSS** feed and to social media platforms such as Twitter and Facebook. In these cases, the alert provides basic information about the event—the "Who?" "What?" "Where?"—and links back to more detailed stories on an organization's website.

Crafting breaking news e-mails is an especially important task. In e-mail, the subject line should alert the audience to the main facts of the story. Many people—especially those who use Web-based e-mail—do not see the body of an e-mail unless they actively click to open it. The subject line should be enticing and informative enough that a recipient will be interested and make the decision to open it and read more. The body of the e-mail can then provide additional information about the breaking news, along with a link back to the site. Links from breaking news e-mail alerts should go directly to an article page on the site rather than to the homepage. If the link goes to the homepage, the visitor might have a difficult time finding the relevant article.

According to its "Editor's Guide," the next item the AP moves is "a short, publishable story" that "consists of no more than one or two paragraphs," with a promise of "MORE" to come. These second versions usually add to the "Who?" and "What?" news elements their "When?" and "Where?" counterparts.

Following these short stories of one or two paragraphs is one of two things: an add or a writethru. An **add** is an additional paragraph that is appended to the end of the first few graphs. As new information becomes available, it is simply added to the end of the story. Adds don't make any sense without the paragraphs that precede them. For example, later adds only use second-references to people who were introduced in earlier adds. So, a potential third add to the story about the death of Sen. Edward Kennedy would refer to him only as "Kennedy." Adds may also contain pronouns to antecedents in earlier adds.

A writethru of a story typically comes after several adds. A **writethru** essentially resets the story by taking all the information previously gathered and potentially re-ordering it for the sake of clarity and news judgment. A writethru is a complete story that begins with a lead and consists of several additional paragraphs. Another name for a writethru is a **"take."**

When a story arrives at its first writethru, additional news elements will be added to the "Who?" "What?" "When?" and "Where." Writethrus will usually provide at least some elementary mention of the "Why?" or "How?" news elements.

The life of a story after a first writethru can take several paths. It may receive additional adds that append information to the end of the writethru. Or, it may receive adds that insert information between existing paragraphs in the writethru. Or, it may be supplanted with yet another writethru of the entire story. When subsequent writethrus of a story get new leads to reflect changing news judgment and new information, the process is known as **re-topping.**

When writing a breaking news story for a website, you can follow the same process:

1. Write a one-sentence news alert. Be sure to include the "Who?" and the "What?"

2. Write a two- or three-paragraph bulletin that adds the "Where?" and "When?" news elements.

3. Write adds and append them to the bulletin.

4. Compose a complete writethru that organizes all the information you have to date in an inverted pyramid news story.

5. File additional adds as needed, either appended to the end or inserted between paragraphs.

6. File a second writethru; does the story need to be re-topped?

Telling Readers What Is New

As you update a news story, you have to consider two different news audiences. One audience will have already seen your earlier reports on the story and will be turning to you for updates. A second audience will be coming to the site and seeing your story for the first time. Visitors in the first news audience will be looking for new information—not what they've already read. The second news audience will need all of the information, ordered in an inverted pyramid style from most to least important.

While surveys of online news readers indicate that slightly more readers say they read news online for its immediacy than say they read online news for its depth or breadth, it is important to consider the needs of both audiences when updating stories. You can use techniques such as timestamping, persistent URLs and highlighted updates to do so.

Timestamping is the easiest way to convey the freshness of your story. Timestamps are typically placed at the top of the story and tell the audience at what time it was posted to the Web. News stories that are being updated should have two timestamps, one that tells the audience when it was first published and another that tells the audience when it was last updated.

A **persistent URL** allows a visitor to find a breaking news story at the same place each time she checks in with the site. Each update of a story should be published so that it replaces the earlier version of the story at the same URL. You don't want to clutter your site or its CMS database with multiple versions of the same story. If outdated versions of the story stay on the site, there is a chance that someone could find one of them and mistake it for the current version. By overwriting old versions with updated versions, you also ensure that someone who finds and bookmarks the first version will receive all subsequent updates.

There are a few cases in which online writers should deploy a new story at a new URL. For example, a new URL is warranted when the angle of a story changes significantly. Following are two examples:

Example 1: A news site has a story previewing an upcoming basketball game. The preview story talks about the strengths and weaknesses of each team and how these might affect the outcome. After the game takes place, the site will want to tell its visitors who won and what happened during the game. The postgame review should be published at a separate URL. Even though both stories concern the same event, the angle of the postgame story differs significantly from that of the preview story.

Example 2: A news site runs a story previewing an anticipated bill-signing at the White House. The bill will fund military activity overseas. The president had been a longtime supporter of the legislation as it moved through Congress, and he is expected to say a few words about it. At the signing ceremony the president signs the bill as expected (this event alone would necessitate a simple update of verb tenses in the original story). But the president also announces at the event a surprise reorganization of his military staff. This represents a completely new angle on the original story. As such, a separate story at a separate URL is now needed. Of course, the two stories should be linked to each other.

A highlighted update is exactly that: you draw your readers' attention to story updates through use of highlighting. This device serves the needs of both frequent and infrequent news audiences. For example, before the first paragraph you could summarize or create a list of bullet points of the new information. Then, even if this new

STORY HIGHLIGHTS

- NEW: Burning oil rig sinks in Gulf of Mexico, Coast Guard says

- NEW: Federal lawsuit alleges companies connected to oil rig explosion were negligent

- Search continues for 11 workers missing since explosion on rig

- Blast occurred Tuesday night with 126 aboard rig off Louisiana

(CNN) -- An oil rig that was burning in the Gulf of Mexico for more than a day after an explosion has sunk, the U.S. Coast Guard said Thursday.

Lt. Cmdr. Cheri Ben-Iesau of the Coast Guard announced this latest development as an aerial search resumed for 11 workers who have been missing since the explosion on the rig Tuesday night off the Louisiana coast.

Crude oil was leaking from the rig at the rate of about 8,000 barrels per day, Coast Guard Petty Officer Ashley Butler said. The Coast Guard also is preparing for possible leaks of up to 700,000 gallons of diesel fuel but can do little to protect the environment until the fire is out, Butler said.

CNN uses the word "NEW" in red, capital letters to tell readers what information is the most recent in the traditional inverted pyramid stories on its site.

information is buried in the third or fourth paragraph, it will be immediately available to people seeking quick updates without distracting readers who are coming to the story for the first time.

Correcting Errors

Sometimes a news site must be updated not with new information, but with a retraction of previously published information. This type of update, known as a correction, is critical to maintaining the audience's trust.

Daily newspapers print corrections of previously published stories almost every day. The corrections are usually published in a regular and prominent spot in the paper so that readers can efficiently find the corrected versions of stories they may have seen the day before. Print corrections refer back to the original story, often by date, page number and headline, so that the readers are clear about which article contained the incorrect information.

Corrections are even more important online than they are in print. Because of the important role that searches play in directing people to news stories, an article may get most of its visitors days or even weeks after it was originally published. Errors in the original article don't end up lining the birdcage or wrapping fish, as do errors in newspaper articles. Instead, they remain linked from blogs; as such, the error can get repeated over and over again.

There are three ways to correct a factual error on an online news article:

1. **Correct the text of the article itself.** If you wrote, "The mayor said Tuesday he was responsible for the city's budget crisis," but the mayor actually said he was *not* responsible for the budget crisis, then you need to rewrite the sentence so that it says, "The mayor said Tuesday he was not responsible for the city's budget crisis." You will also need to update the timestamp on the article so that readers will know it has changed from the original version. When you do correct the text of an article, be sure that you know how that correction will affect any archived versions of the story that may have been distributed to other databases or news organizations.

2. **Write a correction note and place it on the article itself.** A correction note should clarify the error without repeating it. Using our example from above, a correction note that reads, "An earlier version of this story incorrectly reported that the mayor said he was responsible for the city's budget crisis," does not in fact clarify anything. It just adds to the confusion. What *did* the mayor say then? Nothing? Here is how the correction note should be worded: "An earlier version of this story incorrectly reported the mayor's statement about his responsibility for the city's budget crisis. The mayor said he was not responsible." Okay. So, the mayor did make a statement about the city's budget crisis. He said he was not responsible for it. The difference is subtle—but oh-so-important.

Here are two versions of correction note placements on articles:

Retailer's Shake-Up Continues as Executive in Charge of Gap Resigns

Cynthia Harriss, the president of Gap and a longtime colleague of Paul S. Pressler, the former chief, retired Thursday. The move was viewed as sign that Gap was preparing a major overhaul of its brand.

By MICHAEL BARBARO
Published: February 2, 2007

Correction Appended

The Disney team is out at Gap.

A week after ousting the chief executive, Paul S. Pressler, a former

FACEBOOK
TWITTER
RECOMMEND
E-MAIL
SEND TO PHONE

The New York Times puts the words "Correction Appended" at the top of the article, and then links those words to the full text of the correction at the bottom.

---

washingtonpost.com > Metro > Special Reports > Virginia Politics

CORRECTION TO THIS ARTICLE
A Feb. 2 article about the collapse of a Republican transportation proposal before the Virginia General Assembly incorrectly said that state Sen. John H. Chichester (R-Northumberland) joined with three Republicans and five Democrats on the Senate Finance Committee to defeat the GOP deal. He joined with five Republicans and five Democrats to defeat the deal.

Va. Transportation Deal Withers in Senate Panel

By Amy Gardner and Tim Craig
Washington Post Staff Writers
Friday, February 2, 2007

RICHMOND, Feb. 1 -- A fragile Republican-brokered deal on transportation funding collapsed Thursday after a Virginia Senate committee endorsed a competing proposal with dim prospects in the House of Delegates, increasing the chances that the session's key issue could go unaddressed in an election year.

Sen. Thomas K. Norment Jr. presents a GOP-brokered transportation bill to the Senate Finance Committee. The committee rejected the plan and backed an alternative proposal with a statewide sales tax on gasoline. (By Bob Brown -- Associated Press)

The Senate Finance Committee voted 9 to 6 for a plan that would impose a statewide tax rather than divert money from other priorities, such as schools and social services. The plan would apply the state's 5 percent sales tax to gasoline to generate hundreds of millions of dollars for road and transit improvements. Like the competing plan, it also would allow Northern Virginia and Hampton Roads to raise local taxes to pay for transportation projects in those traffic-clogged regions.

TOOLBOX
Resize   Print
E-mail

COMMENT
0 Comments

COMMENTS ARE CLOSED

The Washington Post posts the full correction above the article.

3. **Create a page at a persistent URL that collects all correction notes you publish to the site.** These notes should link back to the original stories to make it clear which article is being corrected. Here are some examples of correction pages on major news sites:

- CNN Money: http://money.cnn.com/news/corrections/
- ESPN: http://sports.espn.go.com/espn/corrections

Sometimes it is not always clear whether a correction is actually needed. In 2009, for example, news organizations reported on their websites that a six-year-old boy in Colorado had climbed aboard an experimental balloon and taken off into the air. They based their stories on information from police, who based their information on a report from the boy's father. But, as it turned out, the boy had never been aboard the balloon. The local sheriff later called it an elaborate hoax put forth by the boy's family.

Clearly, the news organizations reported inaccurate information, but do they need to run a correction? Probably not. They based their reporting on reliable sourcing and followed professional standards. In a case like this, news organizations should simply update the story, indicating the new twist in the tale.

What about spelling or grammar errors? Do these require a correction or an update? In most cases, minor spelling or grammar errors can reasonably be changed without alerting readers. While such errors, if persistent, will erode reader trust over time, the occasional dropped article or misspelled verb isn't significant enough to warrant distracting readers with an update or correction. However, any spelling or grammar error that affects a reader's perception of reality must be corrected, and the correction noted as such. Name misspellings, misplaced commas in numbers and misspellings that change the meaning of a word are some examples of the types of spelling and grammar errors that can affect a reader's perception of reality.

Corrections need not always be formal. Some opinion columnists and bloggers use a more informal tone to alert readers to their errors. For example, U.S. News & World Report columnist Michael Barone posted this correction to his blog in 2005:

In my August 25 post I made a mistake.

Austin Bay, syndicated columnist, novelist, blogger, and reserve Army colonel who has served in Iraq, is always worth reading. Here, in response to a challenge by blogger Jeff Jarvis, he argues that the Bush administration should try to engage the mainstream media, despite its bias and hostility, rather than engage in what he and Jarvis agree is a policy of "rollback."

The blogger I cited was not Jeff Jarvis, of www.buzzmachine.com, but Jay Rosen, of New York University. Since I linked to the correct post, many readers may well have caught the error and therefore were not materially misled. Still, I'm sorry for the sloppiness, and I apologize to Jay Rosen and to Jeff Jarvis. In his courteous E-mail pointing out my mistake, Rosen notes that many people confuse him and Jarvis and wonders why. My reply was that both have first names starting with J and both seem (to me anyway) to specialize in intelligent press criticism not from a right-of-center perspective—a small category, I think.

Barone's blog correction can be accessed at http://politics.usnews.com/opinion/blogs/barone/2005/8/29/.

Regardless of the tone, placement or content of corrections, professional writers aim to make them rare. Errors of style, grammar or fact compromise the trust that a writer has established with the audience. Professional writers should never report information that has not been vetted and verified as fact. Unconfirmed rumors—even those from a usually reliable source—have no place in news writing in any medium.

Live Audio and Video

Before there was the 24-hour never-ending news hole of the Internet, there was the 24-hour never-ending news hole of cable television news networks. And even before the birth of CNN in 1980, broadcast news outlets would interrupt their regular programming to report breaking news. The newspaper wouldn't be out until the next morning, but television and radio could step up to the plate at a moment's notice. And they still can. For online news organizations, however, challenges abound.

Live broadcasting over the Internet is known as **streaming.** The word derives from the technology involved, which pushes packets of information over the Internet in a "stream" rather than a single, uninterrupted download. Many videos on the Web today don't require users to fully download them before they begin playing. These videos, which use a technology called **progressive download,** are not true live streaming multimedia, however.

Online services such as **Ustream.tv** and **LiveStream.com** provide users the ability to Web-cast live video directly from a computer that is connected to the Internet. But what is a reporter to do out in the field, away from her computer? One of news media's biggest challenges today is streaming live video from the field. Broadcast outlets typically send audio over phone lines to be retransmitted over the air from a studio, or they use trucks that send video back to the studio via satellite.

Since 2008, news organizations have been experimenting with technology that allows their reporters to Web-cast live video from certain makes and models of mobile phones. For example, The Huffington Post used a service called **Kyte** to transmit live video of a protest at the White House. MTV used similar technology to cover the 2008 presidential campaign. You can view The Huffington Post's **Web-cast** at http://www.huffingtonpost.com/2009/04/15/million-tea-bag-protest-i_n_187243.html.

Mobile video streaming services require reporters to have a compatible mobile phone and a data plan from its mobile services provider. These data plans allow mobile phones to connect directly to the Internet from anywhere the phone can receive a signal. The reach of these services is wider than that of **WiFi** mobile **hotspots,** where a reporter can connect a laptop computer to the Internet.

The higher the speed of the connection between a mobile device and the Internet, the higher quality the video will be. Phones that can connect to a **3G** network are able to upload data at about the same rate as a **DSL** line in a home. Not all phones are 3G-enabled, however, and not all areas of the country have 3G access. Without 3G access, it would be nearly impossible to stream video from a phone.

Whether you are reporting via video or text, operating as an online journalist is a bit like being a tightrope walker operating without a net. When you practice journalism as a process, everything you do is extremely public. This means that journalists today have to pay more attention than ever before to writing clearly, precisely and accurately. Get your spelling, your grammar and, most crucially, your facts right. And do it all without an editor to back you up. The audience is watching—and responding. That's online journalism today.

ONLINE LEARNING MODULE 10

ACTIVATE THIS MODULE: journalism.cqpress.com

The pace of news gathering and delivery is constantly increasing, and the number of people who engage with reporters and editors is increasing as well. To take advantage of these trends and not become overwhelmed by them, journalists must be able to present their reporting process in a way that provides facts and contexts—and even unanswered questions—that build toward a more complete understanding of the world we share.

On my blog, I am opening up the reporting I'm doing for future editions of this book—sharing the latest examples of social media and discussing with my readers how they might eventually be used to tell stronger stories.

When you buy or activate this chapter's online learning module, you will have access to:

- A digital version of this chapter's text.
- Interactive flashcards for the terms used in this chapter.
- Links to tools and tutorials for managing and presenting the reporting process.
- A printable step-by-step guide to writing news in a blog format.
- A quiz to test your mastery of the material in this chapter.
- A screencast that walks you through the creation of your first blog using Wordpress.
- Hands-on exercises that give you experience creating and maintaining your own practice blog.

As you complete the module's online exercises, you will:

- Analyze and critique professional news blogs.
- Write a proposal for a new news blog and have the opportunity to share your proposal with other readers of the book as well as professional reporters and editors.
- Live-blog a breaking news event.

ONLINE LEARNING

CHAPTER 11 JOURNALISM AS CONVERSATION: ENGAGING THE AUDIENCE

This chapter will teach you how to:

- Identify opportunities for engaging an audience.
- Behave professionally on social media.
- Moderate online discussions involving yourself, sources and the audience.
- Develop a structure for distributed reporting and crowd-sourced projects.

P oundman had a question:

> As I was outside enjoying nature yesterday, I got to thinking about the uproar the construction of the new steakhouse in Southern Pines caused. If you remember, the developer cut down one of the prettiest Deodora Cedars in the county to put up his "Ruth Chris." . . . My question to anyone is what has happened with the restaurant? I was hoping someone here would know the status.

"Here" was the website for The Pilot, a three-times-a-week newspaper in Southern Pines, N.C. In this 12,000-person town and surrounding Moore County, the site—after a redesign and relaunch—had become a meeting place for the people who worked at the paper, the people who read the paper and even people who didn't read the paper.

One of the first answers to Poundman's question came from the audience. "I Have Heard By A Close Freind [sic] Of Owner That Wife Decided To Leave And Asked For Part $$ Of Steakhouse," smith78 said.

Another contributor, Ricksarno, reminded the online discussion board, "There was an article in the Pilot not too long ago quoting the owner saying he would open in the spring."

That story had been written by Tom Embrey, one of the paper's reporters. And as he did regularly, he was eavesdropping on this online conversation. Embrey had been meaning to follow up on the steakhouse story, and now he knew it was time to move the piece off the back burner. He made a call to the developers and posted to the site.

"When I know more, you will too," he wrote. "For those interested, you can also find Southern Prime on Facebook."

Before anyone could say another word, Embrey came back with more.

"Another update: Just got off the phone with Phillip O'Connor, one of the owners of Southern Prime. He says things are moving forward, but the economy—which O'Connor thinks is improving—hasn't come back enough to justify opening a high-end steakhouse."

Forty-five minutes after the topic first came up, Tom had the story. And he knew exactly with whom he wanted to share it. Poundman was waiting to know.

"Here's a link to my story on the Southern Prime steakhouse www.thepilot.com/news/2009/nov/06/pri. . . ."

Because of their interaction, the audience and the reporter both benefited. The reporter knew exactly what kind of story would be relevant to his audience. The audience was able to turn to a professional reporter who had experience taking questions like this and delivering answers based on fact, not rumor.

"We feel like we have an obligation to listen to them and see what they have to say," Embrey says about the commenters on his site. "If they have a question, I can just go in there and answer it. And if I don't know, then it's on me to find out and let them know as soon as possible."

Engaging the audience requires not only a place for them to respond to you and talk among themselves. It also requires journalists to participate in the conversation—both by answering visitors' questions and asking questions of visitors. Meanwhile, the journalist must maintain that skeptical eye—the one that is always looking for proof and always wondering what *else* might be part of the story. A community's conversation needs someone to guide it, and journalists who engage their audience are proving their value to their communities by leading those conversations.

ENGAGING YOUR AUDIENCE

Traditional journalism flows in one direction: from source to reporter to audience. The reporter asks a question, the source answers the question, the audience reads or hears the answer. This description of the reporting process, albeit simplistic, has played out in newspaper and broadcast news organizations around the country for decades, and still does in most markets. But something else is going on now too. And that something is revolutionary.

The interactivity of the Web has brought an end to the one-way flow. Reporters are now answering questions from the audience. Politicians, businesspeople and celebrities are now speaking directly to the audience, without a reporter as an intermediary. And the audience is now demanding explanations, both from reporters and directly from sources. It is getting harder to tell who is the reporter, who is the source and who is in the audience.

In 2008, Mayhill Fowler, a volunteer reporter for The Huffington Post, broke a damaging story about then-candidate Barack Obama. Fowler was a member of the audience at a campaign event in Pennsylvania where Obama referred to "bitter" voters who "cling to guns or religion." Fowler was present in the audience not because she was a reporter, but because she was an Obama donor. Her support notwithstanding, Fowler reported on the candidate's choice of words, ultimately forcing the Obama campaign to swing into damage control mode.

Fowler's is an example of how roles are increasingly fluid. She was up front with her readers that she attended the event as an Obama supporter—as part of The Audience. And she remained an Obama supporter. But as a journalist who was responsible for giving her readers a complete and accurate picture, she went ahead and reported on the candidate's ill-advised characterization.

The new roles and relationships aren't always transparent, however. Wal-Mart in 2006 paid a public relations firm to create blogs promoting the company. Creating promotional blogs is good advertising—but neglecting to disclose that they are being paid for by the company being promoted is deceptive. In the 2004 presidential election, Howard Dean's campaign paid political bloggers largely to ensure that they posted positive commentary about the candidate.

Journalism as only a one-to-many mass medium is a relic. While people once turned to journalists to get an authoritative digest of the noteworthy changes and conflicts that had occurred over the previous 24 hours, today everyone is talking to everyone else, and all at the same time. But this doesn't mean that journalists too are relics. On the contrary. Journalists have never been more necessary.

Civil society today needs a group of dedicated professionals who will sort through the deluge of information, distinguishing fact from fiction and unmasking people who tell lies to gain and preserve their power. It needs professionals to elevate the voices of the powerless and to help people find common ground in an increasingly diverse nation that is part of an increasingly interconnected world. Journalists are no longer just reporters at the beginning of a one-way flow of information. Twenty-first century journalists are leaders of community conversation and facilitators of civic debate who are fully engaged with both their sources and their audience.

But how can journalists engage in conversation while still reporting the news "without fear or favor," as New York Times publisher Adolph Ochs put it way back in 1896? Connections can certainly help strengthen news reporting. But connections must be cultivated and maintained both ethically and effectively. Different situations call for different "conversations." It is up to the journalist to define the parameters.

Journalists still need to know how to ask interesting questions. But they also need to know how to listen to questions from the audience and to respond in a way that increases audience understanding and moves a story forward. Before journalists can take advantage of the distributed reporting power of the audience, they need to cultivate their community's ability to ask questions and think critically.

Reporters who wish to practice journalism as a conversation and not just a one-way lecture need to do two things: (1) go to where the audience is and respond to its questions, and (2) listen to the audience's comments and share the best ones with other people. The best place to do this is online. But once you've created a forum, be sure and attend. Setting up a place on a website where readers can discuss news and then ignoring them when they come there is a bit like throwing a party at your house and then going upstairs to take a nap. The guests will certainly help themselves to the drinks in your fridge, but they are likely to leave the place a mess.

Participating in conversations about news and public affairs helps strengthen your connection to your audience. You can model good behavior in online discussions at the same time that you show your audience that a powerful person—you, a public facilitator—is paying attention to what they have to say. Engaging your audience online also has benefits for your reporting:

- It alerts you to things you didn't know about the topic of your story.

- It lets you know when you've made a mistake.

- It alerts you to questions the audience has about your sourcing.

- It gives you the chance to share your vast knowledge of the topic—tidbits beyond what fits in your story.

- It gives you ideas for angles on additional stories.

Actively Listening

Journalists find themselves in confrontational situations almost every day. Somebody doesn't want them to know a piece of information they're trying to obtain for tomorrow's story. Somebody else doesn't like the way they presented the information in yesterday's story. Online discussions can seem at first like just another occasion for conflict, with people behaving in ways they'd never behave in person. Done badly, putting journalists in online discussion areas can be a lot like pouring gasoline onto a fire. Done well, it builds trust and understanding.

To lead a community conversation, journalists have to learn how to practice a technique called **active listening.** Active listening leads to deeper engagement with your audience because, just like traditional reporting, it requires you to detach yourself from your own personal frame of reference. It requires you to suspend judgment, even if the speaker is challenging your work.

When you scroll to the end of your story online and look at people's comments, you'll see statements that look belligerent, others that misstate the facts, others that misinterpret what you wrote or assign you nefarious motives. No matter how much you want to scream at these people, remember: most of them are really trying to ask a question. Your job as a journalist is to be an active listener so you can help visitors figure out the answers to the questions that they might not even know how to ask.

A key component of active listening is reframing the speaker's statement in your own words. This can be followed by a question that seeks clarification of the speaker's statement. You may also want to articulate your perception of what the statement is saying about the person's feeling on the subject. There's a popular notion in journalism that says that even if a comment someone makes is 90 percent crazy, there's at least 10 percent of truth to it. Your job is to figure out which 10 percent that is.

Meeting the Audience on Its Turf

Legend has it that bank robber Willie Sutton once told a reporter he robbed banks "because that's where the money is." Similarly, journalists need to learn how to engage in conversation on social media because that's where the audience is. According to the Web analytics service comScore, in 2010 Facebook had more than 572 million monthly unique visitors around the world, and Twitter had more than 93 million. Both dwarf the audience of any news site.

Conversations about your stories are—you hope—taking place all over the Web. The most engaged journalists venture out from the confines of their own websites and join the conversations that are under way elsewhere on the Web. In the sometimes unruly world of social media, reporters should take the time to understand how to behave as a guest at parties hosted by their readers—and at parties hosted by people who don't even know them.

Social media platforms are more than just digital newsstands—yet another place to distribute your story to an audience. Social media platforms are places where journalists can ask questions and find sources, as described in Chapter 6, on online research. They are also a place where journalists can use their reporting skills to answer questions.

Tool: Twitter for Sharing Your Stories

Twitter for journalists has become as much a tool for audience engagement as for news distribution. More and more Americans are following journalists on the microblogging service, and most of these expect to receive more than just breaking news headlines. Take the example of The Charlotte Observer. The news organization has two primary Twitter feeds, one for its reporters to engage with the audience and the other to distribute headlines.

In September 2010, 1,060 people were following the news feed. More than 7,600 were following the reporters. National news organizations like CNN or The New York Times have millions of followers on Twitter.

If you are just getting started with Twitter, here are some things you need to know about using it to practice interactive journalism. Consider these your "Twelve Twitter Tricks":

1. Don't start by talking. Start by listening—and then replying to someone. Use the @ symbol followed immediately by the user's name to send a response to your followers. Point them in the direction of interesting stuff.

2. You can also use the @ symbol to ask questions of sources in public. Using the @ symbol allows your followers to see the user name of your source. And when the source replies, if she uses the @ symbol followed by your user name she will be introducing her followers to you. See if you can get sources to engage with your readers.

3. Ask questions of your followers. Have them help guide your reporting.

4. Use the # symbol before a word to create a keyword, also known as a **hashtag.** Be consistent in your use of a hashtag over time. And be sure someone else isn't using the same hashtag for a similar purpose. For example, a reporter in Portland, Ore., another for Southern California Public Radio and the city manager in Rochester, N.H., are all using the #citycouncil hashtag to refer to very different city councils.

5. Retweet newsworthy comments. Or interesting questions.

6. When you find an interesting link, post it to Twitter. What is "interesting" on Twitter? Anything that people will click on. More interesting? Something people will retweet. But most interesting of all? Anything that spurs discussion.

7. Because you can use only 140 characters to write a post on Twitter, be sure to use a URL shortening service, such as http://bit.ly. These services allow you to take a long Web address and create a 13-character abbreviation for it.

8. Be sure to post your Twitter name on your news organization's website—and anywhere else you can post it. This makes it easier for people to find you and verify your identity. Also, be sure to include your organization's name in your ID, such as "KPCCmolly" if you work at KPCC Radio or "MelAntonenUSAT" if you work at USA Today.

9. Use the direct message tool to send a private message to one of your followers.

10. Tweet during primetime. Most people use Twitter during the middle of the work-day, so post your messages then. Messages posted at night or over the weekend

might be buried under later messages coming in from other people. Tweets older than about 10 days are often not archived and therefore become unavailable.

11. Maintain the same professional identity across all social media platforms. This means using the same company logo or photograph of yourself. You can change the background and colors of your Twitter page to match those of your organization. Finally, use **www.knowem.com** to reserve the same username on all social media sites.

12. Synchronize your activity across all social media so that when you post in one place, such as Twitter, it automatically shows up on other sites, such as Facebook.

Screencast introduction to Twitter

Tutorials on using Twitter for interactivity

Tutorials on Google keyword and search insight tools

Leaving your site and engaging in conversation elsewhere online does not mean that you can abandon your professional ethics or your responsibility to your audience. The way you behave on social media sites will affect the way people think about you as a journalist.

In September 2009, ABC News political reporter Terry Moran posted this controversial comment to Twitter: "Pres. Obama just called Kanye West a 'jackass' for his outburst at VMAs when Taylor Swift won. Now THAT'S presidential."

In less than 140 characters, Moran did two things he probably would not have done on any of his television reports: he had disclosed an off-the-record comment by Obama and he injected his personal opinion about the behavior of the president. Moran removed the posting later the same day, and ABC News issued an apology to the White House for "prematurely" tweeting Obama's comments.

The lesson we learn from Moran's lapse in judgment is that the rules of journalism follow reporters and editors wherever they go. Almost nothing you do online is private, so behave as if people are watching—because they are. Even if you restrict your online behavior to a limited group, anyone in that group can take a snapshot of his or her computer screen that reveals unprofessionalism. These so-called screen grabs can get you in trouble long after the moment has passed.

News organizations are struggling to balance free-flowing online conversation with the need to protect their brands and guard against inappropriate reportorial commentary that may eventually, albeit inadvertently, erode the audience's trust. At ESPN, for example, editors vet most of the staff's tweets before they're posted. And reporters are not permitted to post comments about any sports that they are not covering.

In many ways, answering questions on social media isn't much different than answering questions on a television or radio program—something that reporters have been doing for years in an effort to explain their reporting and extend both its reach and its depth. The journalist who writes news stories with a detached tone and strict adherence to AP style can and should take a more informal tone and relaxed style in conversational news settings, whether they are on-air or online.

Keep in mind, however, that whereas audio/video comments are fleeting, text comments are often archived and remain available to be scrutinized long after they are first posted. A small lapse in judgment on the radio will evaporate into the ether almost as soon as the words are uttered. In online social media a lapse in judgment, encapsulated in a post to Facebook or Twitter, will remain online and accessible—and potentially damaging to a journalist's reputation—for months or even years afterward. Even after Moran removed his comment about Obama, bloggers were briefly able to access it using Twitter's search engine.

Tool: Facebook

If you're like most Americans who use the Internet, you have an account on Facebook. But being a journalist on Facebook is a far cry from being a college student on Facebook. Journalists, like good football referees, should never make themselves part of the story. But journalists on social media should be advocates for their own content and get accustomed to being public figures as part of their professional obligation.

As you grow into your role as journalist in a community, you will want to extend your knowledge and use of Facebook.

Privacy settings. If you have a personal account on Facebook, you may still want to use it for personal social interactions. If you do, you'll want to put your professional "friends" in a different category from your real friends. Facebook's privacy settings have changed frequently, but in 2010 they allowed you to create different groups of people and manage in great detail the information about yourself that you share with members of each group. In any case, it will be important for you to follow news reports of the changes in Facebook policy so that they don't catch you by surprise.

Fan pages. While it stretches the imagination to believe that most people will want to be a "fan" of a journalist, Facebook's "pages" allow you to create a place where you can post information without having to be mutual friends with the people who read the information there. With fan pages, you'll also have access to a wealth of information about the demographics and behaviors of your audience. This information isn't available on the standard personal profiles.

Group pages. Group pages are much like fan pages, but you can share administration control with other members of the group.

Applications. If you want Facebook to be more than a place where you post content and share comments with other people, then you may want to create an application for the social network. To build an application you will have to know some computer programming. But even a little programming knowledge can go a long way in giving you control over the environment you create for your Facebook audience. You can, for example, create a trivia game based on your site's stories and then show Facebook members how their scores stack up against those of their friends.

Facebook Connect. A tool called Facebook Connect allows members of a social network to log on to your site with their Facebook account. The benefit for site visitors is they don't need to remember multiple logins. The benefit for the news site is that it can gather a lot of information about its visitors, including the relationships between visitors. Sites such as The Huffington Post allow Facebook members to easily see what their friends are reading on the site.

Online Module 11

Tutorials on using Facebook for journalism

Working Without a Script

For young reporters just getting started on a career in journalism, it can be tough to understand when the job is done each day. And that can mean not seeing clearly where your professional duties end and your personal life begins. For editors who are increasingly grappling with staff members who mix professional ethics and personal escapades on social networking sites, it can be tough to delineate between the two.

News organizations of all sizes are encouraging their reporters to "extend their brands" to new platforms such as Facebook and Twitter even as they rein in journalists whose behavior on those sites has reflected poorly on the organization. Here is an example of the type of language that was in a policy released for Wall Street Journal staffers in 2009, according to Editor & Publisher:

- "Consult your editor before 'connecting' to or 'friending' any reporting contacts who may need to be treated as confidential sources. Openly 'friending' sources is akin to publicly publishing your Rolodex.

- "Don't discuss articles that haven't been published, meetings you've attended or plan to attend with staff or sources, or interviews that you've conducted.

- "Business and pleasure should not be mixed on services like Twitter. Common sense should prevail, but if you are in doubt about the appropriateness of a Tweet or posting, discuss it with your editor before sending."

The guidelines at the BBC warn that staff

- "Should not engage in activities on the Internet which might bring the BBC into disrepute.

- "Should act in a transparent manner when altering online sources of information.

- "Should not use the Internet in any way to attack or abuse colleagues.

- "Should not post derogatory or offensive comments on the Internet."

You can keep track of the social media guidelines of various news organizations by following a newsgroup on **Publish2.com** at http://www.publish2.com/newsgroups/social-media-guidelines/ or by visiting http://socialmediagovernance.com/policies.php.

Engaging with the audience on its own turf can sometimes be a delicate task for journalists who want to maintain professional detachment while rolling up their sleeves and entering the fray of online conversation. This balancing act becomes more treacherous when you speed up the pace of conversation in live discussions on your own site.

Discussions that take place via article comments or **discussion boards** are asynchronous. The comments may have been made hours apart. But journalists can also hold online conversations in real time. During these conversations, journalists make themselves available to answer questions. This type of interactivity is similar to when reporters take questions from callers on a television or radio program. Live discussions have both advantages and limitations. For example, while they focus the audience's interactivity and attention, not everyone who is interested in a topic may be available at the time of the event. And while they limit the amount of time a reporter spends talking with the audience—they limit the amount of time a reporter spends talking with the audience. An advantage and a limitation rolled into one!

When journalists host a live online discussion, they and their news organizations work to promote it in advance of the actual event. The more infrequent such an event is at a news organization, the more lead-time is needed. Generally speaking, a week is too long but less than a day is too short.

Prior to a live event, journalists will open up the discussion forum for questions. Audience members can submit questions via e-mail or a Web link. These questions can either be published in advance or stored until the event gets under way. Collecting questions from the audience beforehand allows broader participation, offers insight into how the discussion might proceed and provides the added safeguard of having a reserve of questions "in the bank" before going live. Too many questions is never a problem: they can either be answered in advance or saved and then posted during the event. Quite often the same question or questions will show up again and again, so journalists must be prepared to address these common audience concerns.

The conversation during a live event should be spontaneous and not too rigidly stuck to a list of questions submitted beforehand. While typing fast can lead to spelling or grammar errors, this is not of great concern if they won't remain on the site for long and can be corrected on the archived transcript. Don't work so fast, though, that you don't provide thoughtful or accurate answers. Be sure to allow and encourage follow-up questions.

Afterward, journalists sometimes archive the event in some way. If the questions and answers are interesting and stay relevant for a long period of time, the audience for the archived version of a live discussion transcript can eventually be larger than the audience for the live event. While spelling and grammar errors can be corrected at this point, no change in the content of the questions or answers is ever permissible. If an error of fact during the discussion was made, then a note can be added to the body of the transcript directing readers to the correct information.

Managing Your Time

While audience engagement is part of the reporting process, every minute spent in conversation with the audience is a minute that isn't spent sitting inside a courtroom or digging through public records. There is never enough time to answer every question or interview every person on the street. So journalists have to "triage" their conversations. Here is how to decide which comments deserve your attention.

First, it is important to correct errors. Correcting reportorial errors has long been part of the journalistic tradition, but online it is also important to do your best to correct a visitor's misunderstanding of the facts that you present. Readers who miss careful phrasing in a news story may misinterpret the reporting and use it to arrive at conclusions contrary to those intended by the reporter. The more widely held the misunderstanding, the more urgent the need for you to clarify.

Next, polite inquiries almost always deserve a response. If you want your audience to behave civilly, then it is important to reward civil behavior. And if more than one person has asked the same question, then answering that question can be an efficient way to satisfy the specific information needs of a lot of people. Answer it once and put your answer at a permanent **URL.** As long as the Web page where you put your answer remains online, all you have to do is point people back to that one answer. For each person who asked the question, there are probably 10 more who want to know the answer and might turn to Google to find it. This is an easy way to build a list of "frequently asked questions" on your beat.

Questions about details in your reporting provide an opportunity to share the additional information that you gathered but were not able to insert into your story. Sharing this extra information can reward loyal and careful readers by giving them an "inside scoop" that is not available to your general audience.

While some questions about your reporting can help you understand the kinds of information your visitors need most from you, be careful not to get stuck in the trap of trying to report out every tiny detail. Stick to the big stories and the hard-to-get information. When possible, give your audience some tips on how they can do a little of their own legwork to find information that is specific to their individual needs. Of course, you should also encourage them to report back their findings to the rest of the community. This type of "report back" is known as distributed reporting, which will be covered later in this chapter.

Every now and again, you should explain to your audience how you see your role as a reporter—especially if you are being called upon to advocate for one side or another in a community debate. Explaining how the news gets made is a valuable public service, but be careful not to get embroiled in a protracted exchange about your political views or the behavior of other journalists. A good rule for interactive journalists is to make your point once and then let the topic lie. There is rarely much to be gained from re-arguing a point of perception.

And while it can be a painful confession for any hardworking journalist to make, it is certainly appropriate to tell your audience "I don't know" when that is in fact the case. Admitting that you don't know the answer to something is straightforward and honest, and it gives you a starting point to ask for your audience's help in finding answers—answers that can make you a better reporter.

VIEW SOURCE

CONCIERGE JOURNALISM

Anyone who has stayed in a budget hotel in an unfamiliar city has seen the racks of pamphlets in the lobby promoting nearby attractions and riffled the free visitor's guide laid out on the desk in the room. But only people lucky enough to have stayed in a luxury hotel have had a chance to interact with a well-versed concierge who knew exactly what it was you were looking for even when you didn't. Sushi at 10 p.m. on a Monday? While the guidebook might be able to direct you to a nearby Japanese restaurant, only the concierge can tell you that the new deli around the corner actually has really great sushi but you'd better head over pronto because it usually closes up by 10:30 p.m.

Every year, the Knight-Batten Awards honor innovation in journalism, and in 2009, one of the winners was a concierge service. The Star-News, in Wilmington, N.C., had created MyReporter.com, which offered readers the opportunity to ask questions directly of its reporters.

Using the Wordpress blogging platform and his programming know-how to customize it, Vaughn Hagerty, the company's Web development manager, built the service from scratch.

"For pretty much any project in which citizen participation is key, avoid launching with just an empty shell," Hagerty says. "We seeded the site with about 300 staff-originated items before we opened it to the public. I really believe that helped encourage people to ask questions, because no one likes being the first."

In the first few months after its launch, the feature was getting about 70,000 page views a month and was among the 10 most-viewed sections of StarNews Online.com. The audience was submitting 75 questions a week—that's more than 10 every day. The reporting staff made a commitment to at least acknowledge the receipt of every question within 24 hours, even if they couldn't as quickly come up with an answer.

"Dialog is important," Hagerty notes. "People want to know that someone's listening to them, and that's especially important in a project like this."

Two reporters, with the help of about a dozen beat reporters, researched and answered most of the questions. Spending a combined 60 hours a week on the project, the staff was able to answer about two-thirds of the questions that came in. On average, the staff was spending about 1 hour and 15 minutes reporting and writing the answer to a question.

"A number of questions have turned into news stories. And, in aggregate form, they give us a constantly updated snapshot of the types of things we should consider covering, based on the subject of the questions," Hagerty told the journalism.co.uk website. "So, reporters get a better idea of what is important to readers."

MyReporter.com from The Star-News in Wilmington, N.C.

PRO-AM JOURNALISM: COLLABORATING WITH THE AUDIENCE

Dan Gillmor, the director of the Knight Center for Digital Media Entrepreneurship at Arizona State University, has said, "My readers know more than I do, and that's a good thing." What Gillmor means is that a reporter's audience collectively knows more than the reporter himself. It is the job of the journalist to figure out how to capture some of that collective wisdom.

We know that some news consumers—the ones who are most engaged and interested in the news—already behave as reporters some of the time. But what standards do they uphold when they do report? Is their reporting ethical? Is it in-depth? Are they asking the right questions of the right people? Professional journalists have experience reporting difficult stories, and they adhere to a set of loosely agreed-upon professional ethics. They also often have privileged access to powerful people. These important aspects of the job are rarely part of the amateur reporters skill set.

Attempts to marry the focus and depth of professional reporting with the breadth of amateur reporting falls under a broad category known as **pro-am journalism.** In simple terms, pro-am journalism is the effort by professional journalists to help the audience understand professional standards and do a better job as amateur reporters. Pro-am journalism seeks to improve the news experience for the audience by facilitating amateur reporting and modeling a basic skill set.

Audience involvement in the reporting process is not without its precedents. Both community journalism and civic journalism have a history of audience participation. **Community journalism** is reporting, often by a small, professional staff, on a small community, one with which the staff is highly integrated. Community journalism, in effect, is the small-town newspaper. And most of the newspapers in America are small-town papers. Community news, when practiced online, is called **hyperlocal journalism.** Whatever it is called, the focus is on coverage of what is going on inside a small geographic area.

In community journalism there is a large overlap between the audience of the news and the subjects of the news. Community journalism offers stories that are "below the radar" of larger news organizations serving broader audiences. These stories focus on community events and milestones in readers' lives.

Civic journalism is another form of journalism with a tradition of audience participation. According to David K. Perry, in his book "The Roots of Civic Journalism," this type of reporting creates an overlap between the journalists and the audience by developing the news organization as a forum for the discussion of community issues, rather than as a detached spectator. Civic journalism seeks to foster debate and discussion among the audience and strives to use journalism to build social capital. The civic journalism movement was particularly strong in the 1990s, gaining momentum when The Pew Charitable Trusts launched the Center for Civic Journalism in 1993. In 2003, the center evolved into J-Lab: The Institute for Interactive Journalism, making clear the direct relationship between the philosophy of civic journalism and the mindset of online journalism.

Some online news organizations, like The Pilot introduced at the opening of this chapter, have given the audience its own place to interact by providing members of the community a site to create blogs or upload photos or videos of community events. Reporters sometimes mine this **user-generated content** for news or feature story ideas—and sometimes they don't. These sites, filled with the type of social capital a reporter is trained to exploit, exist parallel to the professional journalism on a site, and the two too often have little to do with each other.

A popular example of user-generated content is CNN's iReport, a site where the audience can upload "your story" and share it with visitors. CNN does not vet most of the photos or videos uploaded to the site for accuracy. But some do get fact-checked and are incorporated into the traditional broadcast of CNN television.

One prominent example of CNN's iReport derived from the April 2007 mass shooting at Virginia Tech. A graduate student at the university, Jamal Albarghouti, captured the sounds of the shooting in a video he recorded with his cell phone. Albarghouti sent the video to iReport, and it served as CNN's trademark audio and visual image during its wall-to-wall coverage of the event. It was the only live video of the shooting to appear anywhere.

When journalists ask their entire audience a specific question for a specific story, they are beginning to integrate the audience into the reporting. In some ways, this is no different from the time-proven **"man-on-the-street"** interview that sought out elusive pieces of ground-level intelligence by knocking on doors. While the process is still a bit like searching for a needle in a haystack, the ability of the online reporter to rapidly distribute a single question to a large group of people has made the hunt more efficient.

Distributed Reporting

From housing foreclosures to campaign finance reports to public health crises, many of the stories that journalists cover require reporters and editors to look for patterns in a large collection of small pieces of data. In many cases, it is not practical for a journalist to sift through raw data looking for a story. But if a journalist can distribute small, specific pieces of the assignment across a broad network of volunteers, then together they may be able to unveil a story that would otherwise remain hidden.

Distributed reporting is the technique of parceling out a single reporting effort among many people. Perhaps the first prominent distributed reporting effort was a 2007 collaboration between Wired magazine and New York University professor and civic-journalism enthusiast Jay Rosen. The project's goal was to "have a crowd of volunteers write the definitive report on how crowds of volunteers are upending established businesses," according to a recap of the project on Wired's website.

The plan was originally to have each volunteer report and write a feature story on a single topic within the subject area. But when that proved too unwieldy for Wired's small group of professional and volunteer editors to process, the request to the audience was scaled back. The contributors were asked to conduct interviews and take notes rather than file full-blown stories. The lesson, according to Rosen, was this: "Be *waaaay* clearer in what you ask contributors to do."

It is important to give your volunteers clear, specific and limited instructions so that the information that comes back to you is easily analyzed. Even after the questions have been distributed, journalists will still need to sort through the answers to find what is truly meaningful and therefore usable in the story.

If you were interviewing a source, you might want to start with a broad question, for example, "What do you know about this?" But if you are using a network of readers to quickly collect a lot of information about a particular story, it is better to ask about specific points of data. For example, ask how many potholes are on the block where the source lives rather than asking if he knows of any problems with city streets. Open-ended questions work better in interviews, but closed-ended questions with a limited set of valid responses work best for distributed reporting.

In 2009, the British Parliament became embroiled in a scandal over the lavish personal expenses its members were charging to taxpayers. When it dumped 700,000 documents on the public, The Guardian newspaper quickly set up a system that allowed its readers to help sift through the piles. The Guardian posted the documents to its website. But the key to the project was the way the editors gave interested visitors very specific instructions on what to do once the documents were in front of them. Rather than asking readers to "look for interesting information"—an open-ended directive that would have been very difficult for an experienced reporter, much less someone unfamiliar with the intricacies of parliamentary expense reporting requirements and the context of what constituted "normal" expenses for a member of Parliament, to carry through on—The Guardian asked readers to answer specific questions that would alert professional reporters to a potential need for further investigation.

Visitors to The Guardian's site got started by hitting a button that said "Start Reviewing." This delivered to their Web browser a randomly selected image of a page from The Guardian's database of documents. Visitors were then asked the following questions: "What kind of document is this?" and "Is this page interesting? Should we investigate further?"

Rather than allowing visitors to give open-ended and free-form answers that could potentially include as much opinion as fact, The Guardian gave visitors a limited set of choices. To answer the first question (what kind of document?), the reader could select from one of four choices:

- Claim—an expense form

- Proof—receipt, invoice or purchase order

- Blank—nothing to see here

- Other—something we haven't thought of

To answer the second question (is it interesting?), again, the reader was limited to four possible responses:

- Not interesting—e.g., a coversheet or stationery

- Interesting, but known—e.g., it's a duckhouse

- Interesting—it's significant expense data

- Investigate this!—I would like to know more

It was up to the staff reporters to figure out what to do with all the information they received from the audience. The Guardian met with some success—its editors posted some of the most interesting finds during the scandal. But its venture into distributed reporting also sounded a cautionary note: The Guardian had to run an embarrassing correction after one of its readers misread the handwriting on a form. As it turned out, MP Adrian Bailey had spent £160 at the Sandwell Training Association, not the "Solihull Tanning Center." Verification is still king.

Tool: Google Docs

Distributed reporting—asking your audience to help you collect and categorize a large amount of data in a relatively short time—requires you to provide your site's visitors a form to fill out. But what if you're not a Web programmer and don't have access to one? The Guardian's parliamentary expense project was built on a programming framework called **Django.** The (Wilmington, N.C.) Star-News' MyReporter was built using **PHP, MySQL** and **JavaScript.** And Wired magazine's Assignment Zero relied on a custom programmed version of the Drupal CMS.

The quick and easy way for nonprogrammers? Google Docs.

Google Docs is a service from Google that provides users with a Web-based spreadsheet similar to Microsoft's Excel program. These spreadsheets can be used to store data in fields, which simplifies the tasks of searching, sorting and analyzing. Chapter 9, on data-driven journalism, has more information about using spreadsheets.

The spreadsheet feature of Google Docs also comes with a function that allows you to create and publish to the Web a form on which your readers can add information.

Tutorials on using Google Docs for distributed reporting projects

Crowdsourcing

If distributed reporting works well when a reporter has a finite set of data that needs to be categorized or collected—that is, when you know what you don't know—then crowdsourcing works best when a story is unfolding quickly in many places all at once—that is, when you don't know what you don't know.

Crowdsourcing is a technique in which journalists ask the audience to report back information about a story that is happening in a lot of places all at once. Rather than using a few authoritative sources to prepare a story, crowd-sourced stories rely on many sources that are not authoritative.

Some crowd-sourcing projects call for a very restrictive and formulaic approach, similar to the approach of The Guardian when it sought to sort parliamentary expenses. An example is Ushahidi.com, a Web application that allows visitors to upload information about a political crisis or natural disaster that is unfolding in many places at once.

When postelection violence broke out across Kenya in January 2008, the government issued an order prohibiting news organizations from covering any of the events live. As a result, coverage of riots and other violence did not make it into print media until several days later. Faced with these restrictions, bloggers began to fill the void. One of Kenya's most prominent bloggers, Ory Okolloh, put out a call asking for help in building a Google Map highlighting locations where people were reporting violence. The challenge was that fewer than 10 percent of Kenyans—perhaps even as little as 5 percent—had access to the Internet. The solution, then, would need to leverage mobile phones, which were owned by about a third of the population.

Two programmers answered Okolloh's call and created Ushahidi.com, an online service that allowed anyone with a mobile phone to send an SMS text message to a central database that was tracking the locations and types of violence. As the messages came in, they were verified and posted to a live map that allowed both the media and individual citizens to track the violence and make decisions about their own safety. Voices that could not be heard in traditional media became sources for an online site that the government was unable to restrict.

To make the information useful, the site's builders had to create a form that asked for specific information and gave users limited choices. In situations of political violence, a crowd-sourced information site could easily become another battlefield—one that played out as information warfare. So the site's organizers focused on asking visitors *what they saw* rather than *how they felt*. They didn't use the site to answer the news questions "How?" and "Why?" but instead focused on "When?" "Where?" and "What?"

Crowd-sourcing techniques can also be used to gather qualitative information rapidly. In spring 2009, when North Dakota experienced its worst flooding in over a decade, people turned to Twitter and Flickr to report, read about and view conditions at specific locations. No single reporter—or even the entire collective reporting force of professional journalists in the state—could have covered the disaster as quickly and as broadly as a group of decentralized residents posting their reports to a central network.

In a breaking news situation, journalists rely on existing platforms to crowd-source information. Emergencies don't allow them enough time to build a database and Web interface on their own sites. Neither would such sites last long enough to build a meaning-ful cadre of contributors. By turning to existing, off-site social media platforms such as Twitter and Flickr, journalists can take advantage of a structure that is already built and a community that already uses that structure to share information. In such cases, journalists must organize the community around a common goal. It is up to journalists to lead and organize the amateur reporting corps.

To help them do this, journalists should attempt to quickly recognize which hashtag on Twitter is being used by contributors to report information related to a specific story. A hashtag is a keyword on Twitter that is preceded by the # symbol. The inclusion of a hashtag on a post to Twitter allows the person who posts the message to "telegraph" other members of the community that the post is related to a specific topic. In the case of the North Dakota floods in 2009, the most common hashtag was #Flood09, but people also used #fargoflood, #redriver, #flood and #ndfloods.

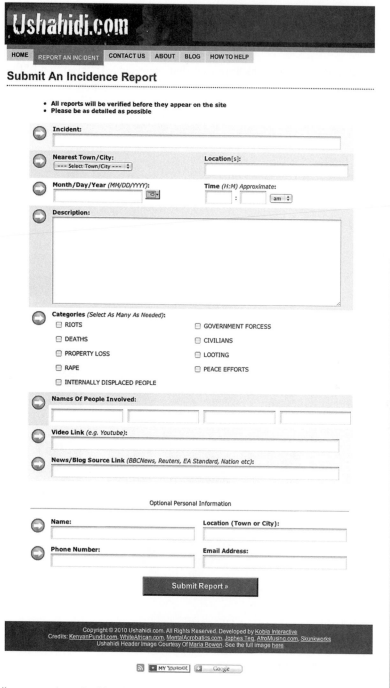

Ushahidi.com was launched in 2008 to track postelection violence in Kenya.

On Flickr, 825 photographs appeared that were tagged "fargo" and "flood" and "2009," and there were 223 photos tagged "fargoflood." By helping the community agree on a common set of tags, or keywords that each person uses to label a photo, journalists were organizing an effort to share information inside a community in a time of crisis.

Photos tagged with "fargoflood" on Flickr.com.

MANAGING A COMMUNITY

In mid-2009, the family of blogs owned by Gawker Media, including Gizmodo, Lifehacker and some of the other most popular blogs on the Web, was experiencing what might be called a champagne problem. "Over the past year (or more), the commenting communities on Gawker Media websites have literally exploded," wrote Anna Holmes, editor of Gawker's blog Jezebel. "But as with any massive increase in quantity, the quality of commenting threads on all of our sites have suffered." It was time to change the structure of the community. The best commenters would now be given special privileges. The rest would be hidden.

In the first two months after the new rules were put in place, the number of comments dropped by about 25 percent. But then the trend suddenly reversed itself, and five months into the new regime the network of sites was getting 10 percent more comments every month than it had before the change.

So what happened? What is the lesson to be learned from this change? The way a community is set up, from its user interface to its rules of engagement, affects the way that people behave in the community. While some online communities seem to develop organically purely by chance, most involve hard work. Site developers carefully cultivate an audience and manage their site's parameters. If journalists want to do more than just be visitors in the audience's communities—if they want to lead a community—then they have to build that community in the right way and then stay engaged with it. Or, as Ellyn Angelotti, an instructor at The Poynter Institute for Media Studies, puts it: "The teacher shows up in the room and people stop throwing pencils."

Writing a Code of Conduct

The first step in building an online community is to write a code of conduct. A code of conduct makes it easier for you to moderate the group and avoid the appearance that you are sanctioning offenders because you disagree with their opinions. To paraphrase a popular saying, America is a nation of laws, not moderators.

A code of conduct should be written like any good news story—simple and straightforward. It should address the issues that are most important to you, and it should be written in language the average visitor can understand. You may also want to include on your site an official (i.e., lawyer-generated) set of "Terms & Conditions" that deal with privacy and content ownership issues, but the code of conduct itself should be written by an editor or community manager.

Two topics should be covered by any code of conduct: content restriction and treatment of community members.

Content Restriction

The standards for user-generated content on any news site should be higher than those required by libel, copyright and other relevant laws. For example, while publishing vulgarity on a news site is not illegal, you will probably want to prohibit it or any other kind of content that will discourage visitors from participating in the conversation.

Commercial content should be restricted from the editorial content areas of your site, including discussion boards. A visit to an online community that allows commercial content can be like a walk down the midway at the state fair. It's tough to have a conversation if someone is always in your face trying to sell something.

Double-posted material can be a problem on community sites. This applies most explicitly to material that is posted more than once by the same person on the same website. Some visitors may think this is an effective way to make sure their opinion is heard, but the repetition can annoy other visitors.

Off-topic posts of any sort can be distracting to the community. Consider whether you want your site to play host to a free-for-all or to a narrowly tailored discussion around specific topics.

Copyrighted material should not be posted to your site. That said, two laws that govern online copyright issues, the Digital Millennium Copyright Act and **Section 230** of the Communications Decency Act, ensure that there is almost no circumstance in which you would be held responsible if someone else posts libelous or copyrighted material to your site. But this legal standard is the floor through which you should not fall. Journalists need to maintain the highest standards and make every reasonable effort to prevent the appearance of libel or illegally copied material on their sites.

Treatment of Community Members

Codes of conduct at the very least should prohibit hate speech, threats and impersonation. Hate speech is speech motivated by hostility to a person or group, often based on race, religion, gender or sexual orientation. It has no place on news sites. It is probably the most sensitive and difficult community regulation to enforce, which means that it is important to address front and center in a code of conduct. Threats of any sort have no place in online conversations about news. Threats are especially harmful to a community if they're leveled against another member, are aimed at children or are sexual in nature.

Impersonation of another community member—or even someone who is not part of the community—is different from using a pseudonym. There are valid reasons for allowing pseudonymity—for example, it permits the posting of unpopular opinions without opening the commenter up to repercussions. And while impersonation can sometimes be an effective parody, parody has no place in serious news. Bottom line, impersonation of any sort should never be allowed.

There might also be other areas you want to outline in your code of content, such as how you deal with participants under the age of 13. According to the federal Children's Online Privacy Protection Act **(COPPA),** most commercial sites are not allowed to collect any personally identifiable information from anyone who has explicitly identified himself or herself as being younger than 13. You can read more about COPPA at http://www.ftc.gov/coppa/.

Whatever you choose to include in your code, be sure to keep it simple. USA Today displays this brief message on each of its articles: "You share in the USA TODAY community, so please keep your comments smart and civil. Don't attack other readers personally, and keep your language decent." Its complete "Conversation Guidelines" is available at http://www.usatoday.com/community/conversation-guidelines.htm.

Appropriate conduct is a serious matter. But that doesn't mean that your code of content can't be a bit irreverent. This is how YouTube begins its code of conduct: "Respect the YouTube Community: We're not asking for the kind of respect reserved for nuns, the elderly, and brain surgeons. We mean don't abuse the site. Every cool new community feature on YouTube involves a certain level of trust. We trust you to be responsible, and millions of users respect that trust. Please be one of them." YouTube's full guidelines can be accessed at http://www.youtube.com/t/community_guidelines.

Identifying Participants

After you've written your code of conduct, you will need to decide whether you want to verify the identity of people who leave comments. If you decide you do, you can do one of two things. You can require visitors to fill out their names and e-mail addresses before posting each comment, or you can require visitors to first register on your site before they can leave comments.

The least restrictive approach is to require no verification of the identity of people who want to comment. This choice lowers the barrier to entry and potentially allows more voices to be heard—a vaunted goal of good journalism. But it doesn't provide for any accountability. And people do and will make outrageous claims. Accountability is also a hallmark of good journalism.

While journalists will in some instances offer anonymity to sources in order to encourage the source to speak openly without fear of retaliation, offers of anonymity should be made on a case-by-case basis and limited to those circumstances where there is really no other way to get the information. Writing an anonymity "blank check" is not reasonable in the face of such journalistic values as accountability and transparency.

Requiring visitors to fill out their names and e-mail addresses each time they post a comment represents the lowest level of verification, and it does not prevent visitors from using false names or false e-mail addresses. Usually sites do not publish the e-mail addresses of people who comment on articles; they publish only the names.

Many news sites require their visitors to register with the site before any comments may be posted. Once registered, however, the commenter is able to post comments regularly, without further verification, simply by using a logon. Of course, site registering doesn't prevent someone from using a false name, but with a verified e-mail address the site administrators can be more confident that they are dealing with one and only one real person.

Requiring visitors to register and wait while their e-mail address is being verified also has the benefit of giving people a chance to cool off before posting a first comment to a site. An impulse to rapid response is usually brought on by a certain degree of heated passion. The added wait time may encourage a commenter to reconsider the tone or content of his intended response. While he waits for a confirmation e-mail to arrive back in his inbox, he might take that opportunity "to count to 10." He might.

While even this tiny barrier to entry will prevent some people from commenting on stories, the visitor who is willing to wait a few moments while registration is completed is the kind who may well become your most loyal. People who never or rarely return to your site are less likely to take the time to register than people who come back regularly. Registration of site visitors tends to build a community of commenters that is most representative of your loyal audience.

Finally, having a registered e-mail address for each comment allows site administrators to track a visitor's behavior over time. If visitors repeatedly violate the terms of your community, they can be restricted from participating.

Approving and Editing Comments

Letters to the editor are usually read, vetted and verified by an editor before they go into the paper. Editors look for comments that are not just salient, but that are based on accurate facts and were written by someone whose identity can be verified.

With the automated publishing systems of most blogging platforms and content management systems, journalists have the option of allowing completely unmoderated comments to be posted immediately to their sites. But they also have the option of using traditional standards of vetting and moderation.

If you choose to conduct traditional vetting of visitor comments, you will have to approve every comment before it appears on the site. This is the most reliable way to ensure that comments you don't want on your site never appear there. However, keep in mind that conversation can be stifled when comments don't quickly appear on a site. Commenters who make good observations or ask good questions may get frustrated if it takes a long time for their comments to be approved. The topic may get stale in the meantime, which means that other readers who might add valuable responses to the original comment may never see it.

The issue of time should be part of your decision-making calculus about whether to moderate comments. How much time will it take to moderate them? First, multiply the volume of comments you are likely to receive on an average day by the number of minutes you expect it to take to vet each comment. A safe ratio is to estimate that you will have 10 comments for every 100 visitors to your site. You then need to weigh that investment of time against the risk of receiving a comment on your site that would hurt your reputation.

Community managers of online news organizations should be extremely cautious about editing a visitor's comment before publishing it. Changing a comment's meaning, either intentionally or inadvertently, can seriously damage the visitor's trust in you and your site. Editing comments may also put you at greater risk for libel. Just as journalists don't clean up quotes that appear in news stories, they should not clean up comments. It is better to make a decision to either publish the comment or not publish it. If in doubt, contact the visitor by phone or e-mail before you condense or clean up her comment. This allows her to verify that the change accurately reflects the original message of the comment.

Requiring prepublication approval is best suited for hot-button issues, which are typically issues about race, religion, immigration, gender, sexual orientation, sexual crimes, national politics and even sports. It is also a good idea to require prepublication approval if you rarely go back and read comments on your site after they've been published.

If you decide not to vet comments, then you will almost inevitably find yourself at some point in the position of needing to remove a post that does not comply with the code of conduct for the site. Many sites allow visitors to flag comments they think are inappropriate, bringing them to the attention of editors. This gives visitors a sense of control and investment in the community, while also reducing the amount of time you have to spend patrolling the site for violations.

Sanctioning a visitor for inappropriate behavior is done in stages. First, a user's offensive comment is removed from the site. The editor who removes it usually leaves a note saying that the content has been removed. This is done so that other members of the community don't think the Internet is randomly eating comments. The editor should also e-mail the person who posted the comment to let her know the reason it was removed. It is a good idea to copy the original comment in the e-mail to the person so she can see the actual words she typed. Often, people are shocked on Wednesday morning when they see the words they wrote on Tuesday night.

When crafting e-mails to people who posted inappropriate comments, remember that even good people sometimes do bad things. You're not trying to shame or anger people, but correct their behavior and encourage them to participate in a more appropriate way in the future.

Finally, one compromise measure between previewing all comments and previewing none is to preview *some* of the comments. Some community discussion platforms allow site moderators to require pre-approval for all first-time commenters. Other sites preview all comments except those from certain visitors who have developed a positive reputation either with site editors or with other members of the community.

Filtering Spam

Just as e-mail **spam** has become a rampant problem, comments that promote fraudulent activity or vandalize blogs with sexually explicit content are becoming commonplace. There are a few ways you can inoculate your site against spam. The most foolproof is to approve every comment before it is published. But there are also some automatic tools available that can provide substantial help without eating up much of your time.

One popular spam filter is **Akismet,** developed by the creators of the blogging platform **Wordpress.** It is available for use on any site, and is even free for small sites. Akismet works in much the same way as e-mail spam filters.

Inside the Wordpress blogging platform there is an option in the Discussion settings that allows you to hold a comment in the queue if it contains a certain number of links. As the Wordpress blogging interface helpfully notes, "a common characteristic of comment spam is a large number of hyperlinks." This feature is also available in most online community management tools.

Wordpress and other online community tools also allow you to create a "blacklist" of certain words that you might want to carefully monitor. The Discussion settings page in Wordpress has two form fields labeled "Comment Blacklist." One field allows the filtered words to trigger prepublication moderation. The other field allows filtered words to cause a post to be automatically marked as spam. With the right software, you can also block certain e-mail addresses, URLs or **IP addresses** if you find that your site is being targeted by a specific visitor.

Once you've set up a good foundation for your online community and built a system that will protect the people who want to listen and share their knowledge and opinions, you can focus on what is really important: developing stronger stories by building more connections with your audience and finding patterns in the great and growing mass of data that is the public conversation.

ONLINE LEARNING MODULE 11

ACTIVATE THIS MODULE: journalism.cqpress.com

Engaging the audience turns journalism from a lecture into an interactive conversation and turns the reporter from an investigator into a community guide and moderator. Undoubtedly, collaborating with the audience can make your stories more effective and increase your audience; however, it is always important to maintain independence from its influence.

My blog is the hub of conversation for students and others using this book. There you will be able to engage other readers and me in conversation about crowdsourcing, distributed reporting and conversational journalism.

When you buy or activate this chapter's online learning module, you will have access to:

- A digital version of this chapter's text.
- Interactive flashcards for the terms used in this chapter.
- Links to updated tutorials, social media tools and current examples of crowdsourcing and distributed reporting.
- A printable guide to the key points of using Twitter for journalism.
- A quiz to test your mastery of the material in this chapter.

- A screencast that guides you through the most widely used features of Twitter.
- Hands-on exercises that give you experience with interactive journalism.

As you complete the module's online exercises, you will:

- Critique professional journalists' use of social media.
- Examine the ethical dilemmas you may encounter with social media.
- Cover a live event using Twitter.
- Create a community engagement policy for a new site.

ONLINE LEARNING

12 REMIXING THE NEWS

In this chapter, you will learn how to:

- Coordinate your social media activity across multiple platforms simultaneously.
- Conceptualize and write nonlinear narratives.
- Use social bookmarking and collaborative filtering.
- Understand basic JavaScript.

This paragraph, for everyone who reads it, is the first paragraph of the chapter titled "Remixing the News" in the book called "Producing Online News: Digital Skills, Stronger Stories." But that may be where the common experience of my audience ends. For some of you, this is the 12th and final chapter you are reading as you wrap up a semester-long study of online journalism. For others of you, this may be one chapter of a few you have selected to read online. And still others have purchased only this specific chapter to read—to you, welcome.

I've interacted with some of you online, and many of you have participated in online discussions about this book with your fellow readers. Others have watched multimedia presentations that taught you how to use the new tools of journalism or see and hear directly from professionals in the field today as they reflect on changes in the way the world is getting information about itself.

Regardless of how each of you has come to this point, you've done it at your own pace and in your own place. And in an ideal world, I'd be using an advanced algorithm with hundreds of variables that would determine which, of many possible variations, is the sentence that is exactly right for you based on whether or not your behaviors, demographics and social interactions meet any of several conditions. I'd still have to write all of the sentences, but I'd be able to program them to suit the individual needs of my audience.

In an ideal world, you and I and all of the other people who are reading the introduction to this chapter would be sampling the words I wrote here in September 2010 and remixing them with additional, new information in ways that meet the specific needs and new challenges created by the context of your life at this precise moment.

To get to this ideal world, in which you see, when you most need to see it, the information relevant to you, journalists will need to start thinking like computer scientists; they will need to take a set of inputs and apply specific rules and conditions to those inputs to make something new. Computational thinking makes news stories dynamic, always changing as the inputs and conditions change. The police department posts its daily crime reports to the Web, and your news site's map of crime locations is automatically updated. So is your site's chart showing the frequency of different crimes at various times of day. Your news website is automatically analyzing and presenting trends because *you* have used computer languages to tell your site which trends have news value.

In an example like this—one already in place at dozens of news sites around the country—journalists break down the crime reports into small samples of data and then remix those samples so they can tell a larger story. The information from the police department gets mashed up against code from yet another website—Google Maps in this example—to give people an easy way to get into the story. One day each person who logs on to the site will be able to see the homes of his Facebook friends marked, allowing him to measure the impact of crime on the people he knows.

In a world where anyone can log on to the police department's website and read the kind of crime blotter that has long been a staple of print newspapers, this kind of dynamic analysis is one way that journalists will turn the raw materials of news into something that people will spend time exploring—and maybe even paying for. It is time to stop thinking of Web pages and to start thinking of Web programs that mix and mash information so that they tell stories that are timely, relevant, complete, accurate and transparent.

Remixing is becoming a part of our culture, not just in news but in almost every type of media. The music industry continues to struggle with declining CD sales as consumers turn to the Internet to buy one song at a time on iTunes. The television entertainment industry once relied on a popular show to carry its audience over into the next time slot and provide continuous viewing; today it is seeking new strategies to deal with an audience that uses DVRs and online videos to watch only a single, specific show. Increasingly, traditional packages of media are being broken into smaller parts before being consumed.

At the same time, content from a variety of different packages is being reaggregated into new groups that the content's creators never envisioned. For example, iTunes publishes "iTunes Essentials"—a one-stop remix of an artist's best songs pulled from multiple albums. TiVo has partnered with television critics at The Chicago Tribune, Miami Herald and other news organizations to create "Guru Guides," which are essentially customized channels with content remixed from many sources. Google allows its users to create automated searches of a topic across thousands of sources, with e-mail links to new articles on the topic sent directly to the user.

For content creators, the culture of remixing requires an understanding that the work they have created will live a life of its own once it leaves their hands. The process of content creation itself now involves the crafting of entirely new forms of information from pieces that have been disaggregated from their original containers. In fact, the rules of content remixing have themselves become content. An **algorithm**—a specific and finite set of rules that always gives the right answer to a question, regardless of the context in which the question is asked—is today as much a storytelling tool as a photograph or a paragraph.

Editing the daily news report is becoming a dispersed responsibility. Reporters and editors choose which information to report. Google News and other automated news aggregators gather stories from diverse sources. And bloggers and your Facebook friends mix their own commentary and anecdotes with these professional reports. Reporters and editors need to understand how to reach the audience in a distributed world. They also need to be familiar with the fundamental concepts of computer programming so that they can efficiently collect and remix for the benefit of their audience trusted information already on the Web.

TEAR IT APART

Throughout this book you have seen time and again that traditional news packages are being torn apart by an audience seeking to funnel a firehouse of online news and conversation. From a search results page or Facebook or a blog, a visitor clicks on a link to your site, visits just the content she wants to see and then leaves. Your headlines, once uniform in appearance to everyone who read them, are now being reformatted and sent to mobile phones, social networks and **RSS** readers. Crime reports are no longer published on 10 inches of newsprint in the paper but have been broken down into their atomic attributes and published in a database for your audience to search and browse. Conversations that once took place only when a reader sent to your office letters that were then reprinted in your paper are now being conducted on the audience's own turf via blogs, on Twitter and at hundreds of places other than your own site.

Samples of the content you have created are the building blocks that your audience, sources and even competitors are using to construct creative new ways to share the facts that you have uncovered. The economic, legal and ethical implications of this are tremendous. In fact, before you read any further you should ask yourself these questions: Can you stop the audience from tearing apart your content so that it better serves individual needs? Do you want to? If the answer to either of these is no, then read on.

Distributing Your Data

Chapter 6, on using the Internet for research, showed you how to use RSS feeds to track updates from trustworthy and relevant (to you) news sources. If you are interested in carbon emissions, perhaps you've since grabbed feeds from a national newspaper, a niche blog by an environmental sciences professor and a government agency. All of these feeds bump up alongside each other.

But perhaps you are also interested in keeping up with the Dallas Cowboys football team. From that same national newspaper, you've pulled its NFL news feed. You've commingled it with a feed from the team's website and a feed from the blog of an avid

Redskins fan (just because you enjoy succumbing to the guilty pleasure of hate). To keep those feeds separate from your carbon emissions stories, you've put them in a different place—either by tagging the football feeds with a separate keyword or putting them in a separate folder. (Of course, not in a real, tangible folder—you've put them in a virtual folder. Most computer users are already familiar with this kind of abstraction. And it is this type of abstraction that lies at the core of computational thinking.)

RSS feeds make it easy to remix the news. To you, the headlines and article summaries are written in a natural language—English. But to the RSS reader in your computer, the feeds can be mixed and mashed because they are in a machine-readable format—**XML**. A computer program takes this machine-readable input, tests to see whether it meets certain conditions and applies rules based on those conditions. The output to you is a customized news service: The Daily Me.

If The Daily Me is the customized output that is seen by the audience, then you as a journalist are creating The Daily You—a machine-readable feed of all your comments, thoughts, photographs, videos and interactions that might be of interest to your audience. If you are using Twitter and Facebook and writing news for a site that publishes RSS feeds, then you are already producing those feeds. Those feeds become The Daily You when journalists connect them in a meaningful way.

With the constant birth—and occasional death—of various social media platforms, a journalist could easily spend his whole day posting individual but nearly identical updates to each platform. That wouldn't leave much time for actual reporting and editing, though. It would be sort of like visiting every church in your town to tell people the news instead of just printing it in the Sunday paper.

When you post on Twitter, you want the information to go to your Facebook fan page. And when you update the wall on your Facebook fan page, you want to be sure that visitors to your website get the news at the same time. Usually. Because sometimes your visit to Cold Stone makes sense for your Foursquare followers but not your pals on Publish2. And you don't want your Facebook friends to see your Tweets twice. What you would really like to do is create a single piece of content—an input—and have it go through some sort of computer program that determines where and when it should get spit out.

The good news is you can. This is because social media sites are, in essence, programs. If you provide Facebook with your Twitter user name and password at http://apps.facebook.com/twitter, Facebook will read the data you publish with Twitter and output it to your Facebook page.

But that's not very discriminating—or at least, Andy Young didn't think it was. So Young, a Facebook user, went to Facebook's API (at http://developers.facebook.com/docs/reference/api/) to create a new algorithm for Facebook's program. Young's algorithm, which he makes available for free at http://apps.facebook.com/selectivetwitter, includes a rule that tells Facebook to publish Twitter posts only if they contain a #fb hashtag. The algorithm—like all algorithms—works the same every time. Your tweets should be published to Facebook if and only if they contain #fb. *My* tweets should be published to *my* account if and only if they contain #fb.

Publishing your news once and having it appear simultaneously on various sites requires the use of good editorial judgment. When is information on one network appropriate for the audience on another? It also exemplifies one of the essential principles of computer programming—**Don't Repeat Yourself,** or **DRY.** This principle, as described by Andrew Hunt and David Thomas in their book "The Pragmatic Programmer," maintains that "every piece of knowledge must have a single, unambiguous, authoritative representation within a system." In other words, create something in a single place, but then use it in many different places. This is both efficient and easily controllable. In the case of journalists, the "system" is the community you cover—your audience, your sources, your competitors. This community lives in a lot of different places online. You need to be in all of them.

VIEW SOURCE

"WHY JUST READ THE NEWS WHEN YOU CAN HACK IT?"

Don't Repeat Yourself isn't a mantra restricted to social media. It also applies to information sharing between journalists and news organizations that each wish to create value for their communities.

In October 2008, The New York Times followed in the footsteps of The Guardian when it began giving Web programmers the ability to re-use information gathered by New York Times reporters and edited by New York Times editors. It did this by creating an **application programming interface,** or **API.** More and more prominent news organizations, including NPR and the BBC, are creating application programming interfaces.

Programmers use APIs to retrieve data from a publisher's site and then manipulate that data. For example, you can use the Facebook API to access information about your friends' activities and searches and sort, filter and display that information in ways that you can't on Facebook.com. Using The New York Times' API allows you to find and display information and data on everything from book reviews to the New York legislature. With NPR's API, you can retrieve transcripts that meet the criteria you specify, such as the original air date.

News organizations publish their APIs for two reasons. First, APIs make it efficient for programmers at the news sites themselves to re-use data they've already gathered. Second, they get new ideas by watching the way the audience remixes the data that the news organization has made available.

On its site for developers, http://developer.nytimes.com/, The New York Times programmers say the news organization's APIs "help us fulfill the newspaper's journalistic mission by putting more information in the hands of the

VIEW SOURCE

public—and they also expand that mission by giving users the ability to find and tell their own stories."

Derek Willis, one of the Web developers for the Times, notes that news organizations today have to see the data that flows through their editorial process not just as an input—something that can be analyzed for trends that tell a story beyond anecdotes—but as one of the products that they create. "It all comes back to treating data as a first-class citizen in the newsroom," he notes.

In addition to making its own stories and metadata available via API, the Times is also using APIs from other Web services to help it tell stories more efficiently and effectively. For example, YouTube's API has changed the way news organizations can analyze political video advertisements. While there has always been a way to get political ads, it was tedious. Now, many political candidates put up their ads via a YouTube channel. The journalists are notified by YouTube's API that new ads are available. The reporters can then watch the ads, store the URLs and other metadata that YouTube publishes about the videos and then add their own metadata about the contents or context of the ad. This additional context allows the reporters to automatically display on their site, for example, all videos about a particular issue.

"Now, just the act of posting something on the Web can turn things into data," Willis says. "So, for example, status updates on Facebook or Twitter are now individual datapoints."

And sites such as Legistalker.org, which mashes up data from the Congressional Record with feeds from Twitter to create a tool that tracks legislators across a variety of media, are using these social media datapoints to help the audience better understand national politics, government and public sentiment.

Without the ability to mix and mash social media as pieces of atomic data, they would just be "blobs of text, like a diary," says Willis. You could still read through every post and look for patterns, but that's not putting news judgment and algorithmic thinking to their best uses.

"If you're doing anything with a computer and you're doing repetitive tasks over and over again, you're doing it wrong," says Willis.

Unwriting Your Stories: Nonlinear Narratives

When an editor at The New York Times says he wants to produce everything as organized data, he is trying to achieve both a business goal—ubiquity of The New York Times' information and influence, and a social goal—efficient use of information. If one person has a piece of information and can share it at no cost to everyone else, other people shouldn't have to repeat the work that went into acquiring that information. The DRY principal of programming when applied to news creates a sustainable news ecology. The energy that is used to gather a fact needs to be expended only once. After finding information from a trustworthy source, journalists can spend all of their energy on analyzing and providing relevant context that adds value to the piece of information. Within a news organization, journalists can also reduce, re-use and recycle content. Consider the way that hyperlinks in a story make news consumption and news production both more efficient.

Often in news stories the audience wants to know more about specific people or organizations than just their names. In print journalism, reporters provide this information in an appositive immediately after the name of the person or organization. For example: "Irwin Collier, an economy expert for North American at the John F. Kennedy Institute at the Free University, pointed out that [German Chancellor Angela] Merkel, who has backed the package, holds a majority in parliament." Online, by linking the words "Irwin Collier" to a biographical page about the expert—a page that would not be limited to the cursory information presented in the appositive example—the sentence would be almost half its original size.

Once you begin thinking of facts as pieces of organized data, you are ready to start thinking about how you might "program" information as a nonlinear narrative, one that doesn't proceed in the usual order from top to bottom, but instead might update or rearrange pieces of information dynamically depending on the conditions and context of the audience.

The **inverted pyramid** has long been used in journalism as a metaphor to describe the traditional structure of a basic news story—the most important information is summarized in the lead, with details of decreasing importance following in each subsequent paragraph or section. For an audience that skims articles rather than reads them, the inverted pyramid remains one of the best ways to construct a news story for the Web. But by using links, online journalists can turn a news story built as an inverted pyramid into a story presented as *several* inverted pyramids. While printed inverted pyramids are linear, online inverted pyramids can be nonlinear.

In a linear inverted pyramid, every reader starts in the same place—the first paragraph—and ends at the last paragraph, taking the only logical path between those two points. This is a perfectly acceptable way to write news stories both online and off.

But some news events lend themselves to a nonlinear story structure, which breaks apart the traditional news narrative and creates several paths of links the audience can choose to follow. By establishing links from the lead to various elements of the story, and also links among those story elements, journalists can craft a nonlinear narrative that helps each reader more quickly find the specific information he or she wants.

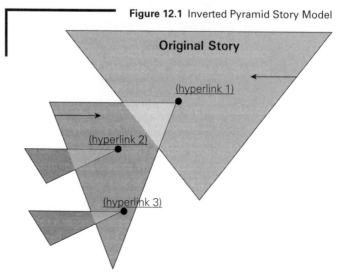

Figure 12.1 Inverted Pyramid Story Model

Original Story

(hyperlink 1)

(hyperlink 2)

(hyperlink 3)

Adrian Holovaty, a pioneer of online news, wrote in 2006 that for journalists to take full advantage of the Web's hypermedia, they first needed to abandon what he calls "the story-centric world view." Using as his example a newspaper story about a local fire, Holovaty wrote on his blog:

> [W]hat I really want to be able to do is explore the raw facts of that story, one by one, with layers of attribution, and an infrastructure for comparing the details of the fire—date, time, place, victims, fire station number, distance from fire department, names and years experience of firemen on the scene, time it took for firemen to arrive—with the details of previous fires. And subsequent fires, whenever they happen.

By breaking down a story into its atomic pieces and using hyperlinks to reconnect those pieces, readers can explore different aspects of the story, each at a level of detail chosen by the visitor. In nonlinear storytelling, journalists gather the input and information as usual, but then tell the story using links that allow the audience to drive the experience.

Deciding When to Use a Nonlinear Narrative

Not every story should be told in a nonlinear narrative. Knowing *when* to use it is as important as knowing how. Nonlinear structures are particularly good for news stories that have any of the following characteristics:

- Many different people that the reader must track
- Many different audiences, each of which might be interested in a different element of the story
- Multiple subjects of equal importance, such as votes on two resolutions
- A long shelf-life, a likelihood that the story will be used as a reference long after it is published

Perhaps the most common—and most daunting—examples of multiple-element stories are pieces about federal, state or local budgets. Government budgets, even in the smallest towns, can run page upon page, all filled with numbers. With a traditional linear story, a reporter must choose one thing—either one element of the budget or a broader trend that risks being a sweeping, imprecise generalization—to serve as the lead. With a nonlinear structure, journalists can simply direct attention to each item that different audience members might consider important and want a link to additional information.

Creating Chunks

The first step in creating a nonlinear narrative is breaking the story into "chunks." Each **chunk** is a piece that can stand on its own. Sometimes these chunks are as short as a paragraph; sometimes they are as long as several paragraphs. There is no right size for a chunk as long as it is about one and only one subject.

The process of creating chunks begins as soon as you start taking notes for your story. Typically, as you begin to report a story, you already have an idea about the different angles you want to include. For example, a story on a new robotic medical device used in delicate surgeries might include information on the surgeons who developed the device, the patients who have benefited, the science of medical innovation, the business of the company that manufactures it and any regulatory hurdles faced during its development. Each of these topics is a chunk in your story.

Once you know your chunks, keep them in mind as you collect information during the reporting process. You may do an interview with a hospital administrator and touch on the subject of each chunk. Immediately after the interview, go back through your notes and separate the different subjects of the interview into different word-processing documents. Or label each subject in your notes with a different color. Then, when it comes time to build each chunk, you will be able to readily access the raw material for each since you have already separated it out in the note-taking process.

In dealing with chunks, the **rule of thirds** is particularly useful. If it is going to be written in nonlinear form, a story should have at least three chunks. And you should avoid putting more than three facts in each chunk. For chunks with fewer than three facts, see if you can put the orphaned facts in other chunks. If it appears that a chunk is going to need more than three facts, consider breaking it up. This rule of thirds is more of a guideline, but it is a good place to start. All of your chunks should be of relatively equal size and importance.

Nonlinear thinking can also help you work on the focus of your story—the hardest task for journalists producing any kind of news. If you are faced with a fact that doesn't seem to fit with any chunk, it may not warrant inclusion in your story and you should consider discarding it.

At the early reporting and drafting stages, some of the best pieces of journalism can appear to be large and unwieldy. Stories that illuminate trends or patterns in the news often touch on many, many subjects and seem to resist being chunked into neat little buckets, just as a complex story can resist sorting into a linear narrative. When faced with a story that doesn't seem to divide into clearly defined chunks, try these techniques:

- Create a separate chunk for each question you're attempting to answer for your audience. For example, when snack food companies in 2009 began recalling products made with contaminated peanut butter, the audience had numerous concerns: "Am I in danger?" "What are the symptoms?" "What do I do if I have contaminated products?" "What is the science behind the cause of this health hazard?" "How widespread is the problem?" "Are there any potential legal remedies being considered?" "What will be the effect on the businesses involved?"

- Think about the search engine keywords for your story. Create a chunk for each search term. For example, with the peanut butter story the word list might include "peanut butter," "products," "stores," "lawsuit" and "symptoms."

- Create a separate chunk for each news element (who, what, when, where, why, how).

Linking Chunks

In linear stories, writers trying to figure out how the pieces of the narrative should be ordered will often make an outline. Outlines are hierarchical—that is, they are designed to create a story that flows clearly from top to bottom in one direction. Since a nonlinear story doesn't proceed in this way, a traditional outline is no help. Instead, for nonlinear stories, reporters build a **storyboard,** or a flow chart that shows the different chunks of a story and how they relate to each other.

At this point in the construction of your nonlinear narrative, the path, or flow, will depend almost entirely on the choices made by your audience. At various points in the narrative, the user will have one or more choices about which path to follow. But the path is not *entirely* determined by the user because you, as the content creator, still play a role in defining those paths. You are choosing the size of the chunks, how they connect and what finite and specific set of choices will be available to the user in each context. You tell your narrative by the information you choose to reveal to the reader at any given point, and you devise the rules that must be followed as the user moves from one chunk of information to the next.

Just as the inverted pyramid is not the only way to construct a linear news story, there are several templates you can use for constructing a nonlinear story. The template you use will depend on the story you are trying to tell.

The hub-and-spoke model is the simplest storyboard template for a nonlinear narrative. With this model, writers create one central chunk (the hub) and then link from that hub to several chunks that are connected to the hub like the spokes of a wheel. You can think of the spoke as a lead, with each connected chunk a separate fact. Each spoke—and therefore each chunk—rates a similar degree of importance in the story. This type of structure works best with stories with a strong central element, such as a story about four local students that each have been named an All-State Scholar Athlete. The storyboard of a hub-and-spoke story looks like this:

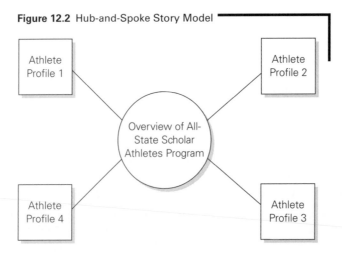

Figure 12.2 Hub-and-Spoke Story Model

A more complex variation of nonlinear storytelling is the multinodal model, a template in which each spoke also serves as a hub for secondary, less important spokes.

Figure 12.3 Multinodal Story Model

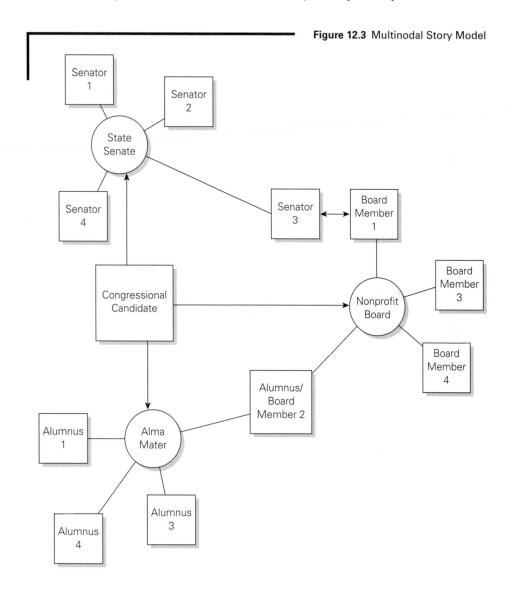

An example of a story that might work well as a multinodal story would be a piece about political alliances on either side of some piece of impending legislation. A story about people involved in a business corruption scandal might also make a good multinodal story. These stories are all about complex connections.

Both the hub-and-spoke and multinodal structures offer the reader many entry points. Scanners can quickly find the element of the story most important to them and go directly there via hyperlink. Searchers who are looking for a particular piece of information will have an easier time finding it if it isn't buried in a longer story. But these story structures also have their weaknesses. For example, they are not good at telling stories that involve a lot of action or a sequence of events.

A journalist's job isn't only to describe to the audience events that have already happened. Part of his or her job is to serve as an early warning system that helps the audience consider and take action on debates that are under way or events that might occur in the future. Stories that tell about the things that might happen if certain conditions are met—for example, what cuts in services might result if the proposed state budget passes, or how the area might deal if hit by a hurricane—can be structured in a nonlinear format called a decision tree.

Decision trees start with a problem or conflict that could have at least two different outcomes. Of course, journalists can't predict the future, but they can explain what social or natural laws indicate would happen, or what experts in the field say is likely to happen. This structure is called the decision tree model because it is used to help people make a decision.

A decision tree storyboard looks like this:

Figure 12.4 Decision Tree Story Model

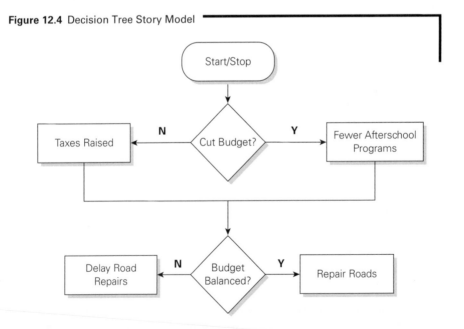

Decision trees can have an infinite number of levels. The simplest decision tree has a single starting point and two potential outcomes. A simple decision tree story—and one that probably doesn't require a nonlinear structure—would be a story about the potential outcomes of a sporting event. Two outcomes are possible: winning and losing. (OK . . . I guess a tie is also possible, but who wants that?)

As you begin to put together a decision tree story, you may not realize it but you're mimicking one of the most basic and important elements of computer programming: you are creating **conditional statements.** Conditional statements describe what would happen if a certain condition is met. As a student you are familiar with a real-life application of conditional statements: *if* you do well on this quiz, *then* you will get a good grade.

The basic format of a conditional statement is:

IF ["X" is true]

THEN

[do "Y"];

OTHERWISE

[do "Z"].

In the peanut butter story, a conditional statement might look like this:

IF [you live in Ohio, an affected state]

THEN

[show the reader a list of contaminated brands]

OTHERWISE

[tell the reader that no cases have been reported in her state].

MASH IT UP

When you distribute your content to a variety of social media platforms, and when you break up your stories into nonlinear narratives, you are making it easier for the audience to remix the news. But in a world in which traditional news media packages have been disaggregated, it's not just the audience that's remixing. Journalists, too, have an opportunity to reaggregate content in new ways to tell stronger stories. Sometimes you'll do this by actively choosing content from around the Web, and sometimes you'll use computational thinking to create rules that automatically pull content from the crowd.

Collaborative Filtering

As news programmers gather information from around the Web and mash it up with the reporting that is being generated by their own organizations, they are practicing a form of collaborative filtering. **Collaborative filtering** occurs when multiple filtering agents—people, computer programs or a combination of the two—decide to hide some pieces of information while illuminating others.

An example of collaborative filtering is **social bookmarking,** a process in which members of the online news audience, working independently of one another, extract news articles from websites and dynamically recategorize them based on **keywords,** or **tags,** that are not created or controlled by the original publisher. This form of collaborative filtering looks at the past actions of a large group of people and creates predictions about the future preferences of individuals in the group.

The idea that a large and diverse group of human beings acting independently of one another would do a better job than either computer algorithms or a small group of experts at finding the most important and useful websites is the concept on which social bookmarking is based. As individual Web users bookmark sites and create the metadata to go with them, other users can then search the collection of public bookmarks and benefit from the efforts of social bookmarkers who collectively have already found the "best" sources on a topic. Examples of social bookmarking sites include **Delicious** and Publish2.

If you bookmark a Web page and tag it with the keyword "tax-cuts" (tags on Delicious and other platforms cannot have spaces, so hyphens often substitute for spaces in connecting two words that are part of the same idea), then another person who is interested in finding information about tax cuts can browse or search a list of tags, one of which will be the "tax-cut" keyword you created. That person might find another Web page that is related to the topic, so she can save it and also tag it with the "tax-cuts" keyword.

Now, assume that a third person who is browsing or searching the list of tags finds the "tax-cut" tag and sees links both to the page that you tagged with "tax-cuts" and to the page that she tagged with "tax-cuts." He might then access one or both of the pages. But let's say that he has a different perspective on the topic discussed on your Web page. He can take the page you bookmarked and add his own tag, perhaps something like "budget-deficit." When he saves the link, his tag and your tag will both be pieces of metadata attached to the same Web page. As a result, when yet another browser is searching the list of tags, she might access that single Web page via one of two paths: by following the "tax-cuts" tag pathway you created or by following the "budget-deficit" tag pathway that he created.

Journalists, too, are using social bookmarking to curate lists of relevant, trustworthy and current links to news and information on sites other than their own. In traditional news organizations, editors select the best articles from their own staffs each day and aggregate them into a news product. In online news, editors can select and link to the best articles written by journalists—or anyone, for that matter—whether they are on staff or part of the staff of another news organization.

Because the social tagging technique is dynamic and democratic, it stands in contrast to traditional techniques of content categorization. These traditional methods of classifying items, known as **taxonomies,** are typically hierarchical and controlled by a few experts.

An example of traditional content categorizing might be the Dewey Decimal System that is used in libraries. Three experts at the U.S. Library of Congress, advised by a 10-person board at the Online Computer Library Center, are in charge of adding a Dewey decimal number to more than 60,000 items every year.

Dewey decimal organization is hierarchical. It has 10 classes, each divided into 10 divisions, which are each further divided into 10 sections. Each item in the Dewey decimal taxonomy must fit into one and only one section that lies within one and only one division that lies within one and only one class.

Tagging, on the other hand, has no hierarchy and is infinitely open. In 2004, information architect Thomas Vander Wal coined the term **"folksonomy"** to describe the democratic, dynamic and flat system of categorizing information. Vander Wal notes that folksonomy

> is the result of personal free tagging of information and objects (anything with a URL) for one's own retrieval. The tagging is done in a social environment (usually shared and open to others). Folksonomy is created from the act of tagging by the person consuming the information.
>
> The value in this external tagging is derived from people using their own vocabulary and adding explicit meaning, which may come from inferred understanding of the information/object. People are not so much categorizing, as providing a means to connect items (placing hooks) to provide their meaning in their own understanding.

For more on Vander Wal's definition, go to http://vanderwal.net/folksonomy.html.

So we have information that is being disaggregated from its original packaging and then reaggregated into entirely new packages, both by journalists and by members of the audience. And in many cases those newly remixed packages are themselves being redistributed across the Web.

For every tag on Delicious, users can subscribe to an RSS feed of all the pages to which Delicious users have assigned that tag. For example, if you wanted to follow what pages people were saving and sharing during the national health care debate in 2010, you could subscribe to an RSS feed that supplied all the pages that were tagged "hcr," which stands for health care reform, at http://delicious.com/tag/hcr. In effect, this was the "health care news and information section" of the social bookmarking site that was created by the crowd remixing news and information from other sites. But that remix could itself be mashed up against a package of Twitter posts about the same topic. On Twitter, you could subscribe to the #hcr hashtag at http://search.twitter.com/search?q=&tag=hcr. In Google Reader or another RSS feed reader, subscriptions to those two remixes would merge into their own remix.

Tool: Dipity

Talk long enough to people who grew up reading the newspaper and you will hear a frequent lament: in a world of microtargeted, grazed and friend-fed news, people are missing out on the serendipity of picking up the morning edition and finding a story they would never have thought to ask for but that turned out to be an engaging, thought-provoking read. In today's mashed-up news world, Dipity aims to bring back to news readers that unique pleasure.

Screencast of how to use Dipity

Dipity is a tool that allows you to select data and feeds from around the Web and mash them up into a visually appealing and dynamically updated timeline. Rather than using advanced programming languages like **PHP**, Java or **Django**, Dipity employs a graphical user interface that is easily manipulated.

PROGRAMMING JOURNALISM

Presuming, reader, that you are consuming this book—or at least this chapter—linearly, I know I don't have much time left with you. So I have no choice but to be blunt. It is time to act like a computer scientist—after all, whether you realize it or not, you are already thinking like one.

I don't mean to scare you with this pronouncement. I am simply being straightforward and honest about something that I've been skirting for a while now. Consider the facts. As a journalist you do your best to do the following:

- Explain to your audience the world's people and processes with clarity and precision—key traits of an algorithm
- Follow arcane rules of **syntax**—just like a computer programmer
- See in the world around you interesting questions that you seek to answer with overarching explanations that will, in some measure, illuminate universal truths

And so your (perhaps unwitting) ability to think like a computer scientist now leads of necessity to the next—incredibly empowering—step. It is time to learn to use the tools of a computer scientist to efficiently and effectively answer complex questions.

It is time to supplement your use of the incredibly imprecise, beautifully ambiguous, redundant and metaphor-filled English language and learn to speak in JavaScript. It is time to learn about variables, conditional statements and functions so that you can put your ideas into action and express yourself in a way that is increasingly valuable to society and to newsroom managers who value stories that challenge the conventional wisdom.

You Down With OPP? (Other People's Programming)

Programming skills allow you to create robust and interesting remixes of the news and information you find on the Web. And more and more Web services are giving you the training wheels you need to remix by providing readily accessible pages on their site's APIs. These pages give you a peek under the hood at the actual code. They offer examples to examine and eventually mimic, in much the same way that first-time HTML coders benefit from their browser's "view source" feature.

Beginners can use the APIs to create Web widgets. A **widget** is "an interactive single purpose application for displaying and/or updating local data or data on the Web, packaged in a way to allow a single download and installation on a user's machine or mobile device." This definition comes from the World Wide Web consortium, the most prominent standards-making body for Web development. Wikipedia defines a widget this way: "a portable chunk of code that can be installed and executed within any separate HTML-based web page by an end user without requiring additional compilation. They are derived from the idea of code reuse."

YouTube is one of numerous sites that offer an API with which to build widgets. You can create a customized feed of videos to place on your website by going to http://www .google.com/uds/solutions/wizards/videobar.html. You can create a feed of whatever videos on YouTube you choose—all video from ABC News and the Associated Press, for example, or all the video about "Obama." Once you've used the Web form to build your widget, you can see the JavaScript code that is used to access the API.

Similarly, you can generate XML and **JSON** (JavaScript Object Notation) from The New York Times by visiting http://prototype.nytimes.com/gst/apitool/index.html. Twitter's widget-builder page also gives you a peek at the JavaScript used to access its API. You can take a look at http://twitter.com/goodies/widget_search.

Google Maps provides two easy ways to access the API and customize maps for your site, but neither makes it easy to see the underlying code. Both use Google Spreadsheets to manipulate the API. These sites are accessed at http://gmaps-samples.googlecode.com/svn/trunk/spreadsheetsmapwizard/makecustommap.htm and http://earth.google.com/outreach/tutorial_spreadsheet.html.

All of these sneak peeks give you the general idea about how you can create rules that dynamically update and generate content on your site from data that is produced elsewhere on the Web. But to truly be creative with mashups, you will need to know some basic programming. In the following section, we will look at the most basic concepts of a computer scripting language called JavaScript.

JavaScript is a good language to use to learn programming because it is at once powerful and accessible—it requires no special tools to learn. JavaScript code is written using a plain text editor (though—take note—not Microsoft Word); it can be placed directly inside the body of an HTML document. When you put JavaScript inside an HTML document, it can be read by any Web browser.

(When JavaScript is used in a Web widget, the actual JavaScript code is written in a file that sits on the host's Web server. The embedding site simply links to the JavaScript file.)

Here is an example of the JavaScript widget for links curated on Publish2.com by technology reporters for The New York Times:

```
<script type="text/javascript" src="http://www.publish2.com/syndicate/
widget/?feed=newsgroups/nyt-technology-journalists.js"></script>
```

Variables

Programming looks a lot less intimidating once you learn the basic terms. The term "variable" is one you've no doubt heard before in other contexts, and it shows up again in computer programming. Lawrence Snyder, a computer science professor at the University of Washington who was chairman of the National Research Council's report "Being Fluent With Information Technology," explains variables in a way that will make a lot of sense to a student of journalism—think of a variable as the name of a public office and the name of the current officeholder as the value of that variable. For example, there is a mayor of Chino, a U.S. president and a principal of King High School. Over time, the people who hold these offices change. Right now, Dennis Yates is the Chino mayor, Barack Obama is president and Dan Brooks is the principal. Those men are the current values for our variables.

When you start programming in JavaScript, one of the first things you need to do is "**declare**" your variables. To declare a variable in your JavaScript program you type in "var" followed by the name you wish to give the variable. For example:

```
var ChinoMayor

var USPresident

var KHSPrincipal
```

In JavaScript, "var" is the declaration command. Declaring variables at the start of your program is sort of like deciding which news elements are going to be in your story. (Note that the syntax and terms used in JavaScript programming are not the same as in other programming languages. Even though you declare variables in every programming language, the *way* you declare them depends on the language you use.)

If you want, you can also go ahead and set an initial value for each variable. You initialize variables by using the "**assignment symbol**" in JavaScript. (You can call it the equals sign if you want.)

```
var ChinoMayor = "Dennis Yates"

var USPresident = "Barack Obama"

var KHSPrincipal = "Dan Brooks"
```

You've probably noticed that the values for each variable are contained within double quotation marks. If you have read this book's previous lessons on HTML coding, those quotation marks will look familiar in their purpose. They are used to denote the beginning and the end of a specific string of letters. You can also assign numbers and **Boolean values** (*true* or *false*) as values for variables in JavaScript.

Objects, Properties and Methods

Variables on their own don't do anything. So let's look at a little piece of JavaScript that will actually make your browser do something, namely display the words "Hello, World!"

```
<script type="text/javascript">
document.write("Hello, World!");
</script>
```

You can place JavaScript code in a separate file, in the header of an HTML page or in the body of an HTML page. For this example, we will be working with JavaScript code that is placed inside the body of an HTML document.

Any JavaScript that appears on a Web page must be placed within a pair of <script> tags. The open script tag must also tell the browser what type of script is between the tags. You do this by adding the "type" attribute to the open script tag. Anything inside the script tags will not be displayed to the user. This means, however, that if you forget to open or close your script tags properly, then your JavaScript code will be displayed right in the middle of your page and look like gobbledy-gook to your audience. So be sure to close your tags properly. You can also see some other pieces of the code. In this example, there are the following:

- An **object** called "document"
- A **method** called "write"
- An **expression**, which is "Hello, World!"

JavaScript is an **object-oriented** scripting language. Most everything that you will do in JavaScript is centered on an object. An **object** in JavaScript is a "thing" that typically represents its real-world equivalent. You can create your own objects, or you can use some of JavaScript's built-in objects. The most basic built-in object is the one we are working with here—the "document" object. The real-world equivalent of the document object is the HTML page on which your JavaScript code has been placed.

Just as entities in a database have **attributes** (as Chapter 9, on data-driven journalism, explains), objects in object-oriented programs have **properties.** For example, the object properties include the title of the page, the URL of the page and the body of the page.

Objects can also do things. It is the **method** that tells them what to do. The method is connected to the object on which it is acting by a period. In our example the "write" method has to tell the document object what exactly it is supposed to write. We wanted it to write an **expression** that in this example consists of the string "Hello, World!" A **string,** you might recall from earlier chapters, is a sequence of characters. The syntax rules of JavaScript require us to put the element inside parentheses and the string inside quotes. You could also put HTML code inside the quotes so that the JavaScript would write out a more properly formatted piece of text, and even, if you like, make it boldfaced by adding the <strong> tag—"<p><strong>Hello, World!</strong></p>" . This string would be written to the HTML document, but the HTML would then be parsed by the Web browser and not displayed as text to the user. The text on the page would look like this: Hello, World!

Finally, we end our JavaScript **statement** by punctuating it with a semicolon.

Now that we have some variables, and know how to use the write method to change our document object, let's get back to our values:

```
<script type="text/javascript">
var ChinoMayor = "Dennis Yates"
var USPresident = "Barack Obama"
var KHSPrincipal = "Dan Brooks"
document.write("Hello," + ChinoMayor + "," + USPresident + " and" +
KHSPrincipal + "." );
</script>
```

After typing this JavaScript code in the body of the HTML document you are editing on your computer, save the file as an HTML document (named "3people.html," for example). If you then open it in your browser, you should see this:

Hello, Dennis Yates, Barack Obama and Dan Brooks.

(An important note about this example is that the plus sign was used to combine strings of text and variable values to print the sentence we got as our result. The programming word for "combine" is **concatenate**. Concatenation differs from addition. For example, in programming, the plus sign can tell the computer to *add* two numbers together—"5 + 2" would yield a value of seven—or concatenate two strings—"'5' + '2'" would yield "52.")

Functions

We could handcode static Web pages using JavaScript all day long, but there is really no point. We want to make our Web pages dynamic and customizable, and we want to follow the DRY philosophy—that is, we want to save ourselves effort by writing a piece of code that does something and then use it over and over again. In order to do this, you will need to learn to write a function.

A **function** is just an algorithm that can be reused inside a computing language. An algorithm, as you learned earlier in this chapter, is a finite and specific set of instructions used for solving a problem. An algorithm for making your sister a peanut butter and jelly sandwich might be written in English like this:

- First, look in the cupboards to see whether you have bread, peanut butter and jelly.
- If you have more than one kind of jelly, tell your sister what kinds there are.
- Ask your sister what kind of jelly she prefers, and remember that.
- Get out two slices of bread.
- Spread the peanut butter on one slice of bread.
- If your sister wanted strawberry jelly, then spread that kind of jelly on the other slice of bread. Otherwise, spread grape jelly on the other slice of bread.
- Put the two pieces together.

Web browsers don't understand English. But they do understand JavaScript, so let's learn how to write a function in JavaScript.

The first thing we want to do is declare the function, which is basically just creating it and giving it a name. It is best to declare functions inside the header of an HTML page, because you can't use a function until after it has been declared. It is a good idea to declare functions as high in a document as possible.

Let's make a function called "greeting" that would write "Hello, World!" to our Web page. Here is what that code looks like:

```
<script type="text/javascript">

function greeting()
{
document.write("<p><strong>Hello, World!</strong></p>");
}
</script>
```

The first step in declaring any function is to type "function" on a new line. The next thing to do is give it a name—in this case, "greeting"—and follow that name immediately with a set of open and closed parentheses. The parentheses are sometimes used to store **parameters** of the function, something that we won't be doing here. Keep in mind, however, that regardless of whether or not you are going to use them, you will still need to include these parentheses in your code.

The next thing we see in our code is a bracket symbol, { . The bracket symbol tells JavaScript that we're going to write a new block of code that is separate from other blocks of code. Since we only have one block here, it may seem extraneous. But using these brackets is a good habit to develop, and placing them on a line of their own is also a good habit because it will later make it easier for you to read long lines of code.

On the next line, we see our familiar document object and method, which tell the browser to write Hello, World! inside itself. Finally, we close the JavaScript block with the closed bracket symbol, }.

But declaring this function in the header of your HTML document isn't going to be enough. This code just creates and defines the function. We also need to **"call"** the function and put it to work. We call the function from inside the body of the HTML document. The code looks like this:

```
<script type="text/javascript">
greeting();
</script>
```

This code calls the function named "greeting" that is inside the document's header. It looks a bit like a method because it has those parentheses after the name, but this function call is not specific to an object.

You can think of declaring a function as similar to creating a variable in algebra and then assigning a value to it. After a value has been assigned to the variable, it can be used over and over again. So every time you call the function named "greeting" in your HTML page, it will execute the same algorithm, thus sparing you the work of doing it yourself.

Now it is time to show off. Go ahead. Display your programming prowess in a new HTML document. Can you execute the Hello, World! trick three times in a row?

Conditions and Instances

By writing instructions that we can store as a function and then reuse, we don't have to type out a complete command over and over again. We can just reference the function greeting() any time we want to print Hello, World! on the Web page. While possessing these skills is certainly exciting, our end product—Hello, World!—is not exactly earth-shaking. The goal of computer programming, of course, is to find answers to interesting questions. To do this, we need to go a step further. We need to start writing conditional statements.

Let's look at our variables and values again:

```
var USPresident = "Barack Obama"
```

This is great—as long as Obama is president. But maybe we want to go back in time and say hello to the man who was president before Obama, George W. Bush. I don't know about you, but sometimes I have a difficult time remembering trivial things like the name of the president, so let's write some code—once—that will automatically help us make the proper introduction.

Remember, when talking to a computer we have to be very literal. We need to tell the computer program that it is going to need to know what year it is. Luckily, there is an object called Date() that is prebuilt into JavaScript. When you use it in your program, it retrieves the current date and time. To use this object, we need to create an "instance"—essentially, a copy of it. We do this by creating a variable and initializing it with the value of Date() like this:

```
var now = new Date();
```

In English, this tells our program to create a variable called "now" (it can be called anything) and assign to it a new instance of the Date() object.

We still need to get one specific piece of information from this new instance of the Date() object. Or, as Derek Willis of The New York Times might say, "We need to interview the data." Luckily, we're in charge here, so we don't have to ask. We can command the Date() instance to tell us what year it is and to forget all the other stuff like the current month and minute. To do this, we can use a prebuilt JavaScript method called getYear(). We connect the getYear() method to the now object with a period—called "dot notation"—just as we connected the write() method to the document object earlier. We'll create a new variable and give it an initial value of the current year:

```
var year = now.getYear();
```

Finally, it is time to set the value of the USPresident variable based on the context of the current year. To do this, we need to write a conditional statement that says if the year is greater than or equal to 2009, we should say hello to Obama. Otherwise we should say hello to Bush.

```
if (year >= 2009) {
USPresident = "Barack Obama;
}
else {
USPresident = "George W. Bush";
```

We start by writing the word "if," and then we put inside parentheses the condition that must be true for the operation to be performed. In our example, the condition that must be true is that the value of the "year" variable must be greater than or equal to 2009, which we write as "year>=2009." The sign ">=" is an **operator** just like "=". (You can read more about all the JavaScript operators at http://www.w3schools.com/js/js_operators.asp.)

But you're a reporter, right? Steeped in logic and an understanding of the American political process? So you can look at that conditional statement and see that it has some problems. First, Barack Obama did not become president at midnight on Jan. 1, 2009. He became president at noon on January 20. And Bush was not actually president for the entirety of American history before Obama became president.

For much the same reason it is important for copy editors to have some knowledge about the names, places, histories, rules and traditions of the community in which they are editing stories, news programmers must know how the world really works so they don't write code that gives an answer that is computationally valid, but not effective—or, as the rest of the folks in your newsroom might say, "dead wrong."

The example we've been using here is silly and simple, one meant to get you started on JavaScript programming. If you really want to put programming to work to achieve your journalistic goals—and trust me, you do—think about how you'd go about creating an algorithm in JavaScript code that allows users to calculate potential Electoral College outcomes in the next presidential race, or explain all the different ways a bill might move through Congress. Not quite as simple as Hello, World!, but oh, so much more useful. And, I hope, within reach as you go forward and practice with and utilize computer programming tools.

Tool: JavaScript and the Google Maps API

Exercises on creating a simple Google Map using API and JavaScript

Online tutorials on using API and JavaScript

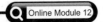

Screencast on building Google Maps

The text in this book has given you just enough JavaScript vocabulary to introduce you to the most basic and most widely used concepts in computer programming. But there is so much more you can do. For example, you can use loops—repeating instructions until a condition is met—and event handlers—the pieces of JavaScript that allow the audience to interact with the algorithms.

A good place to get started with some of these advanced concepts is by creating a simple Google Map using the API and JavaScript.

By one path or another, you have reached what we have arbitrarily decided will be the end of the book. But it is not the end of the service this book provides. Updates and new examples are posted regularly on the book's website. Some of these new ideas and examples are coming from you, the audience. And presumably, you will re-use what you learned here in situations and circumstances I probably can't even begin to imagine.

Maybe you have decided to circle back and read over what you missed, or wish to review. Or, perhaps you are ready to try some exercises that you didn't try before. Upon reflection, you will see that first you learned how to produce the raw materials of journalism—that is, you learned how to take text, audio, video, photographs and other media and post it to a website in a way that is appealing to the audience. Following this, you took a peek at what it takes to program that content. You have discovered that to be an online journalist today means to be both a content producer and a content programmer.

From the news values and news elements introduced in the first chapters of the book, to an understanding of the three pillars of online news—multimedia, interactivity and on-demand delivery—to a fundamental understanding of how the audience engages with news online, you have now arrived at a starting point. You know that programming the news calls for a clear vision of journalism online as a networked, interactive and dynamic process. You are ready to get started on your career producing online news.

Remember at the start of this chapter that I said I wasn't sure how you got there? Well, neither do I know for certain where you, or any other journalist—veteran or novice—will go from here. But this uncertainty about *how* journalism will work in the future does not mean it will not work. All it takes is a new commitment from experienced and young journalists alike to look for opportunities to use new tools to tell stronger stories. Go forward with these skills and strategies to forge your own vision of how journalism will continue to play a special role in our democracy—holding powerful people accountable, shining light in dark places and explaining an increasingly complex and interconnected world to your audience.

Remixing the news is one of the most creative aspects of online journalism. Providing others with the raw material for telling news stories truly empowers your audience. Re-using reliable tools and information in new ways can help you find and present patterns that might have remained unclear otherwise.

ONLINE LEARNING MODULE 12

ACTIVATE THIS MODULE: journalism.cqpress.com

On my blog, you will find an ongoing discussion about news mashups, complete with links to examples, tools and tutorials.

When you buy or activate this chapter's online learning module, you will have access to:

- A digital version of this chapter's text.
- Interactive flashcards for the terms used in this chapter.
- A printable guide to writing nonlinear narratives.
- A quiz to test your mastery of the material in this chapter.
- Links to tutorials from across the Web where you can learn advanced programming techniques.

ONLINE LEARNING

- Video screencasts that show you how to build news mashups.
- Hands-on exercises that give you experience remixing the news.

As you complete the module's online exercises, you will:

- Use social bookmarking to aggregate news stories.
- Identify and describe uses of APIs by news organizations.
- Create a nonlinear text narrative.
- Create dynamic news mashups.
- Develop a simple algorithm using JavaScript.

GLOSSARY

3G. The "third generation" of mobile phone standards. Phones that use 3G technology usually download data at a rate of about 800 kbps to 1.4 Mbps and upload data at a rate of 300 kbps to 800 kbps. (This compares to home DSL and cable broadband speeds that range anywhere from 768 kbps to 20 Mbps.) Chapter: 10

AAC (.aac). The file extension for compressed audio files using the Advanced Audio Coding codec. AAC is also used as the audio compression codec in video formats such as MP4. Most songs downloaded from iTunes are in AAC format. Windows Media Player did not support AAC files prior to version 12. Users of earlier versions of WMP need to download additional software if they wish to use AAC files. AAC files are generally of higher quality at lower bit rates than MP3 compressed files. Chapter: 8

absolute link. A link to another Web page that is written in such a way that it always points to the same unique location. An absolute link includes the protocol, the domain name, complete file path and file name of the link destination. Chapter: 7

Access. A relational database management system created by Microsoft for use on personal computers using the Windows operating system. New versions are released about every three years. Chapter: 9

ActionScript. A scripting language developed by Adobe for use in programming Flash applications. ActionScript has the same syntax and semantics as JavaScript. Chapter: 8

active listening. A communication technique whereby listeners suspend their own frame of reference and judgment, repeat statements made by the speaker and reflect on those statements. Chapter: 11

actuality. The audio recording of an interview. Chapter: 8

add. Used as a noun in breaking news situations to refer to a short update—usually about three or four paragraphs—that "adds" additional information to the end of previous versions of the story. Chapter: 10

administrative interface. The part of a content management system that editors, producers and reporters use to add content, organize it or remove it from the site. The administrative interface is usually protected by a password and not publicly available. Chapter: 4

Adobe. Adobe Systems Incorporated is a computer software company headquartered in San Jose, Calif. It was founded in 1982 and acquired Macromedia in 2005. It makes many of today's most popular software programs for digital content creation. Chapter: 8

AIFF (.aiff).   The file extension for uncompressed audio using the Audio Interchange File Format. This file format was developed by Apple but also plays in Windows Media Player 7 and later versions. Chapter: 8

AJAX.   Acronym for Asynchronous JavaScript and XML. A method of creating dynamic Web pages that change content without reloading new HTML files. AJAX became popular after 2004 when Google used it to deploy GMail and Google Maps. Chapter: 8

Akismet.   A Web service that filters blog comments for spam. It was originally developed by the company that created the blogging platform Wordpress. Now available as a free tool for personal use and as a paid tool for commercial use. It works by collecting comments that are submitted to a site, taking those comments to its Web servers where tests are run on them and then flagging those suspected of being spam before returning them to the original site. Chapter: 11

alert.   The first information that is published in a breaking news situation. Alerts are often only one sentence or sometimes only a headline. Chapter: 10

algorithm.   A problem-solving process that involves a finite number of precise instructions that are followed in a specific order to yield a correct answer. Chapter: 12

anchor link.   Used to mark the beginning and end of hyperlinks in an HTML document; also known as an "anchor element," "a tag" or "anchor tag." Chapter: 7

aperture.   A setting on a camera that determines the amount of light that reaches the image sensors. The aperture setting is usually expressed in terms of "f-stop," with a larger number indicating that less light is reaching the sensors. Larger f-stop values also contribute to a wider depth of field. Wider depths of field allow objects at a wide variety of distances to be in focus. Chapter: 8

API.   Acronym for Application Programming Interface. An interface that allows desktop software or Web applications to share information with other applications. Web APIs typically consist of requests sent via HTTP and responses that return information structured as XML, JSON or another similar standard format. Chapters: 9, 12

article summary.   In an article, a brief sentence or two that, in conjunction with the article's headline on an index page, provides information about the article and creates in the audience a desire to read further. Chapter: 5

aspect ratio.   The ratio of an image's width to its height, expressed as two numbers— reduced to their lowest common denominator—separated by a colon. For example, an image that is 600 pixels wide and 400 pixels high has an aspect ratio of 3:2. Chapter: 8

assignment symbol.   In mathematics and computer programing, a symbol that assigns a specific value to a specific variable. For example, in the phrase "X = pickles" X is the variable, *pickles* is the value and = is the assignment symbol. The equal sign is the most common assignment symbol. The variable is always on the left side of the assignment symbol and the value is always on the right side. Chapter: 12

attribute. A descriptive that provides additional information about an HTML element when it is given a specific value. Also called a "property." Chapters: 7, 9, 12

Audacity. A free and open-source audio-editing/audio-recording application available for Mac OS X, Microsoft Windows and Linux operating systems. Available at http://audacity .sourceforge.net/. Chapter: 8

Audio Hijack. An application for Mac OS X operating system that allows users to record audio from any application onto their computers. It is useful for recording interviews using VoIP software such as Skype. A free trial version of the software allows users to record up to 10 minutes of audio. A paid version allows unlimited recording. Available at http://www.rogueamoeba.com/audiohijackpro/. Chapter: 8

backpack journalist. A reporter who carries a variety of multimedia reporting and editing hardware in a backpack. Chapter: 8

Backtweets.com. A Web service that shows posts on Twitter that link to a specific URL. Chapter: 6

beat. A geographic area or group of related subjects that a reporter covers regularly. Chapter: 10

beat blog. A blog that covers a well-defined subject area. Chapter: 10

bit depth. In digital audio compression, the number of bits of information that are recorded each time the program takes a sample of sound. Chapter: 8

bit rate. In digital audio and video, the amount of information that is stored per unit of time of a recording; typically expressed in kilobits per second, or kbps. CD quality sound is 128 kbps, and many podcasts are recorded at 96 kbps. Chapter: 8

blog. Short for Web log, a format of digital content that is crafted by placing posts on a Web page in reverse chronological order so that the most recent is at the top. Popular blogging platforms include Wordpress and Blogger. Chapter: 10

Blogger. Google's blogging service, hosted at blogspot.com. It was launched in 1999 by Pyra Labs and was the first widely popular blogging tool. Chapter: 10

body. The content of an article. The body of an article begins with the first paragraph and ends with the last paragraph; headlines, bylines, datestamps and other metadata are not part of the body. Chapter: 7

Boolean logic. A system of solving problems by representing relationships among entities in terms of logical operators such as AND, OR and NOT. Used in search engine queries, among many other uses. Chapter: 4

Boolean value.   A type of data that has one and only one of two and only two possible values—"true" or "false." Chapter: 12

breaking news blog.   A blog that emphasizes the news value of timeliness above other news values. Topics are typically wide ranging and posts are created by multiple authors. Chapter: 10

Brightcove.   A company that many news organizations use to host and manage video assets. For more information, go to www.brightcove.com. Chapter: 8

B-roll.   Supplemental or environmental footage used to illustrate the words being used by a subject in an interview. B-roll video is recorded in the field and used to create cutaways. Chapter: 8

call.   In JavaScript and other programming languages, the act of executing a previously described function. Chapter: 12

capture.   In video editing applications, the act of transferring video images from their original tape source into a video project where they can be manipulated by the application. Chapter: 8

card reader.   A computer hardware component that allows users to view the contents of removable memory cards. Chapter: 8

cardioid microphone.   A microphone that is sensitive to a relatively wide area of sound in front of it and a smaller area of sound to the rear right and left. It is called a cardioid mic because the sound pattern looks like a heart (Latin root *cardi*). These microphones are good for recording the speech of a single subject. Chapter: 8

Caspio.   A subscription Web service that provides a graphical user interface that makes it easy for online news producers to manage data and build Web search forms that can be used by a news organization's site visitors. Chapter: 9

CCD.   Acronym for Charge-Coupled Device. A type of sensor used in digital cameras; high-end cameras usually have three CCDs. Chapter: 8

cell.   In a spreadsheet, the intersection between a specific row and a specific column. Cells are identified by the letter of the row followed by the number of the column. For example, the first cell in a spreadsheet—the one in the upper-left corner—is cell A1. Chapter: 9

child directory.   A directory that is inside another directory. Also called a "subdirectory." Chapter: 7

chunk.   In nonlinear narratives, a piece of the story that can stand on its own. Usually consists of all the details related to a single subject, verb or object. Chapter: 12

civic journalism. An approach to journalism, popular in the 1990s, in which the journalists are highly engaged with the audience rather than positioned as detached spectators. Chapter: 11

CMOS. Acronym for Complementary Metal-Oxide-Semiconductor. A type of digital camera sensor that is gaining in popularity over CCD sensors. Chapter: 8

codec. A piece of computer software used to convert (and often compress) audio or video signals into digital information and then back again to audio signals and video images. Chapter: 8

collaborative filtering. The process of using multiple filtering agents—people, computer programs or a combination of the two—to hide some pieces of information while illuminating others. Chapter: 12

column. In a spreadsheet, a vertically aligned sequence of cells that contains values for a single type of data field or attribute. Each column is identified by a unique number that starts with "1" for the left-most column and increases by an increment of one for each subsequent column to the right. Chapter: 9

comments. User-generated content describing the reaction of the audience member/writer to a specific news article. Comments are often displayed below the body of the original news article on a website. Chapter: 1

community journalism. Journalism that provides comprehensive coverage of events occurring in a narrowly defined, often geographically contiguous community. Community newspapers are typically weekly publications with a circulation of fewer than 50,000 copies. Chapter: 11

CompactFlash (CF) card. A type of portable memory card that is used in digital cameras. Chapter: 8

complete uptime. When referring to a website or other information medium, the state of being entirely available at any time a user requests information. Chapter: 1

compression. The practice of reducing the bit rate and/or file size of digital audio and visual files. Compression will decrease the quality of the audio or image. Chapter: 8

concatenate. The process of combining two or more strings of characters, one right after the other, without a space between. Chapter: 12

conditional statement. In computer programming, an instruction to perform different actions based on whether a certain condition is met. Chapters: 4, 9, 12

container format. A specification that describes how different pieces of audio and video data and metadata are stored in a single file. Container formats may include a variety of audio or video codec formats. Chapter: 8

content. The collective term for news articles, videos, animations, audio interviews, photographs, discussion forums and any other tool for transmitting information. Chapter: 4

content management system (CMS). The human and computerized processes used to create, organize and publish content, especially to a website or other digital platform. Chapter: 4

convergence. The degree to which different media are integrated at a specific layer of information. For example, converged newsrooms may produce a variety of different media formats, but the stories themselves are converged only if multiple media are integrated in the telling of a common story. Chapter: 1

COPPA. Acronym for Children's Online Privacy Protection Act. Act passed by Congress in 1998 requiring commercial websites to obtain parents' informed consent when collecting personal information about children under age 13. The act is enforced by the Federal Trade Commission. Chapter: 11

crawler. The component of a search engine that automatically visits Web pages in a methodical fashion searching for new or updated content. Chapter: 6

Creative Commons license. A license issued free of charge by a nonprofit corporation that aims to encourage the sharing of content between content creator(s) and those interested in using/re-using it. Creative Commons issues several types of license, each of which provides permissions related to attribution, redistribution, the creation of derivative works and commercial use. Chapter: 8

cropping. In photography, the process of removing an area along at least one edge of the image. Chapter: 8

crowdsourcing. A reporting technique in which journalists ask the audience to report back information about a story that is happening in different places at the same time. Chapters: 1, 11

CSS. Acronym for Cascading Style Sheets. A standardized computer language that is used to describe the presentation of a structured HTML (or XML) document. CSS is used to separate the display of a document from its content. If more than one style rule applies to more than one section of a document, CSS determines which rule takes priority. This creates the "cascade" effect of style rules. Chapter: 4

cutaway. In video storytelling, a technique that interrupts some piece of continuously recorded action with the insertion of another visual element. Cutaways use B-roll recorded in the field, often to illustrate the words of an interview subject or to avoid displaying some distracting visual element recorded as part of the interview. Chapter: 8

data element. Representation of a real-world object that is being recorded and analyzed for information. Found in spreadsheets and databases, data elements consist of precisely and narrowly defined attributes. Each data element must be described in a way that makes it distinct from every other data element. Chapter: 9

dataset. A collection of data, usually in a fielded or delimited format organized so that each row is a unique entity that shares attributes with all other entities in the table. Chapter: 9

data structure. A definition of a specific set of data elements and the relationships among them. Chapter: 9

data tier. The set of data that is on a server in a relational database management system. Chapter: 9

database normalization. The process of re-organizing data so that there is no redundancy. Chapter: 9

datapoint. A single measurement of a single attribute of a single data element. Chapter: 9

declare. In JavaScript and other programming languages, the process of writing a set of specific instructions that is mostly independent from the rest of the program (a function) and then giving those instructions a concise, descriptive and unique name so that they can be re-used without being rewritten. Chapter: 12

Deep Web. Documents on the World Wide Web that are not accessible to search engine crawlers. Chapter: 6

de-interlace. To convert interlaced video (commonly used in broadcast television) to progressive scan video (used on the Web). Chapter: 8

Delicious. A Web-based social bookmarking serviced owned by Yahoo. Launched in 2003. Chapters: 6, 12

destination. In a hyperlink, the value of the href attribute of the HTML anchor element. The destination is the specific page that a browser opens when a user clicks on a specific link. Chapter: 7

Digg. A collaborative filtering website that allows users to submit news stories and then allows other users to vote those stories up or down. Launched in 2004. Chapter: 6

digital zoom. A technique used in digital cameras that is achieved by cropping equal amounts from all edges of the image. Chapter: 8

dimension. The width and height of a digital image, usually measured in pixels. Dimension is expressed as the width multiplied by the height. For example, an image that is 200 pixels wide and 150 pixels high is 200x150. Chapter: 8

Dipity. A Web application that combines information from different sources and displays that information as a single timeline. Chapter: 12

directory. A virtual container holding files and folders. Directories on personal computers and Web servers are used to keep files organized. Also called a "folder." Chapter: 7

discussion board. Web application that displays comments written by site visitors. Discussion boards are typically independent of other content and are directed at a single topic. Comments are usually asynchronous, meaning that there is a delay between the time a message is written and when it is read by other people. Also called a "discussion forum." Chapters: 1, 11

distributed reporting. The technique of parceling out a single reporting effort among many people. Chapters: 1, 11

Django. A free and open-source Web application framework that was developed at The Journal-World newspaper in Lawrence, Kan. Its purpose is to make it easier to build dynamic websites. Django is written in the Python programming language and works in conjunction with Web server software such as Apache and a relational database management system such as PostgreSQL, MySQL, SQLite and Oracle. Chapters: 9, 11, 12

domain name. The part of a Web page address that usually ends with ".com" ".org" ".net" or "edu"; the domain name indicates a unique set of computers and data that are controlled by a single entity. Chapters: 4, 7

Drupal. A free and open-source content management system. Chapters: 6, 7

DRY. Acronym for Don't Repeat Yourself. A principle of software development first described by Andrew Hunt and David Thomas in their book "The Pragmatic Programmer." In the words of Hunt and Thomas, "every piece of knowledge must have a single, unambiguous, authoritative representation within a system." Put more simply, create something in a single place, but then use it in many different places. Chapter: 12

DSL. Acronym for Digital Subscriber Line. A technology that enables the sending of digital data over standard telephone lines. DSL data rates typically range between 384 kbps and 10 Mbps. Chapter: 10

Electronic Frontier Foundation. A nonprofit civil liberties organization founded in 1990 and based in San Francisco that advocates for free speech rights, personal privacy and other issues as they relate to the Internet and other digital media. Chapter: 8

element. In HTML, any individual component of an HTML page. Elements are usually defined by a start tag and a corresponding end tag. Chapter: 7

embed element or tag. A nonstandard HTML element that is used to help some browsers display multimedia content such as Flash SWF files and QuickTime MOV files; also provides additional variable settings that are unique to Flash or QuickTime files. Will be standardized in HTML5. For more information go to http://kb2.adobe.com/cps/127/tn_12701.html, http://support.apple.com/kb/TA26486?viewlocale=en_US and http://www.w3schools.com/htm15/tag_embed.asp. Chapter: 8

entity.   In a database, a representation of a distinct and unique real-world object. An entity is defined by the values of its various attributes. Chapter: 9

environmental video.   Video that is used primarily to capture and communicate the sights and sounds of a particular place at a particular time. It may or may not include narration or dialogue. Chapter: 8

establishing shot.   In video reporting, a wide shot that allows the audience to establish the location of the story. It is used at the beginning of a video sequence. Chapter: 8

evergreen.   Attribute of a news story containing information that retains relevance to the audience for longer than the week, or so that is typical of information in an event-based story. Chapter: 1

EveryBlock.   A website that provides a user interface for locating specific events and public records by type or by narrowly defined geographic parameters. Developed by Adrian Holovaty and launched with funding from the John S. & James L. Knight foundation, it is now owned by MSNBC. The source code is available free at http://code.google .com/p/ebcode/. Chapter: 9

Excel.   A desktop spreadsheet application made by Microsoft for use on Windows or Apple OS X operating systems. Chapter: 9

exclusion statement.   In programming, a statement that provides instructions about what to do when a specific condition is not met. Chapter: 4

expression.   In JavaScript and other programming languages, a constant string of characters that is treated literally and not given any programmatic meaning. Chapter: 12

F4V (.f4v).   The newer of two file extensions commonly called "Flash Video" (the other is FLV). These files may contain audio and video that use one of several codecs, often H.264 for video and AAC for audio. F4V files can be played with the popular Flash Player plug-in that is installed on almost all Web browsers. It can also be played with several desktop applications, and it can be incorporated into Flash projects. YouTube and other major Web video services use Flash video for their videos. Chapter: 8

Facebook Connect.   A set of APIs created and hosted by Facebook that makes it possible for developers of third-party websites to allow their site visitors to log in to those sites using their Facebook ID and password. Chapter: 11

fading.   In audio editing, a gradual change in volume. In video editing, the gradual appearance or disappearance of the visual image. Chapter: 8

failover.   The process of automatically switching from one broken or failed computer system, such as a Web server or database, to an identical computer system. The goal of a failover is to keep a site running without users noticing a change in the computer system. Chapter: 4

Fan Page (Facebook).   A semicustomizable template in the Facebook social network that allows organizations and public figures to broadcast official, nonpersonal information to an audience. Fan pages also allow organizations to track audience use of different features on the page. Chapter: 11

FAQ.   Acronym for Frequently Asked Questions. A list of question-and-answer pairs intended to anticipate an audience's information needs and proactively respond to them. Chapter: 7

feature story.   In news, a story that does not rely on the news value of timeliness to be relevant to the audience. Typically longer and more complex than hard news stories. Chapter: 1

field.   The attribute of a data element; in databases, fields are represented visually as columns of datapoints. Chapters: 4, 9

file name.   The string of characters that identifies a unique and specific collection of digital data; usually ends with a three-letter file extension. The name of a file can be changed without altering the data inside the file itself. A file can also be moved from one location to another without changing the file name. Chapter: 7

file (or directory) path.   The hierarchical location of a specific file. The file path includes the names of the file's parent (or "home") directory, as well as the names of all the ancestor directories. Chapter: 7

file suffix.   The letters and numbers—usually three or four—that follow the period at the end of a file name. File extensions are a type of metadata that tells humans and computers what type of digital information is contained within the file. Also called the "file extension" or "file format." Chapter: 8

Final Cut.   A digital video editing software application created by Apple for use on the Mac OS X operating system. Chapter: 8

FireWire.   A hardware interface that is typically used to connect a computer to an audio or video recording device. FireWire is an industry standard for controlling these devices from the computer software interface. Also known as "IEEE 1394" and "i.Link." Chapter: 8

FLA (.fla).   The file extension for files that contain source material for multimedia projects created with Adobe's Flash program. These files can only be opened with the Flash program. They are used to distribute completed projects. Chapter: 8

Flash.   A multimedia authoring software application developed by Adobe. Chapter: 8

flash memory. A technology for storing digital data. Flash memory can be erased and re-used. It is popular in portable audio/video recording devices, memory cards and portable drives that connect to a PC via a USB port. Also called "solid state memory" because it has no moving parts. Chapter: 8

Flickr. A Web-based photo and video storage and sharing service available at Flickr.com. It was originally created by Ludicorp in 2004 to support an online game and was acquired by Yahoo in 2005. Chapters: 6, 8

Flip4Mac. A software application that allows Macintosh users to play Windows Media Video files with the QuickTime application. Developed by Telestream, it is free to download at http://www.telestream.net/flip4mac-wmv/features.htm. Purchased versions of the software include the ability to import and export WMV files from video editing applications on the Macintosh. Chapter: 8

FLV (.flv). The file extension for videos that use the Flash Video container file format. These files may contain audio and video that use one of several codecs, often Sorenson Spark or VP6 for video and MP3 for audio. FLV files can be played with the popular Flash Player plug-in that is installed on almost all Web browsers. It can also be played with several desktop applications, and it can be incorporated into Flash projects. YouTube and other major Web video services use Flash video for their videos. (FLV files are one of two types of files commonly referred to as "Flash Video" files. FLV files are very different than the newer "Flash Video" files that use the F4V file extension.) Chapter: 8

folksonomy. A democratic, dynamic and flat system of categorizing information. The term was coined by information architect Thomas Vander Wal in 2004. Chapter: 12

foreign key. A field in a database table that contains values that match—and thus create a relationship with—the values of a field in another table. Chapter: 9

forum. See *discussion board*.

frame rate. In video production, the number of times per second that a new image is displayed to the viewer. The frame rate of NTSC television (used in the United States) is 29.97 frames per second (fps). Movie cameras record 24 fps. Chapter: 8

framework. A tool used to build a Web application. Frameworks are a standardized set of commonly used functionality—such as connecting a program to a database and displaying the results in HTML—that make it easier to build dynamic websites. Two popular frameworks for building news applications are Django (written in the Python programming language) and Ruby on Rails (written in the Ruby programming language). Chapter: 9

FTP. Acronym for File Transfer Protocol. An Internet protocol used for transferring files between a client computer and a Web server, or between two Web servers. Chapter: 8

function. In spreadsheets, a re-usable mathematical formula that creates a specific output value when given one or more specific input values. In JavaScript and other programming languages, a function is a re-usable algorithm that is largely independent of other portions of the program in which it exists. Chapters: 9, 12

gain. The magnitude of change in the sound signal after it is received by the microphone and output to a digital file. Chapter: 8

GarageBand. An audio editing application developed by Apple for use on the Macintosh OS X operating system. It is available as part of Apple's iLife software package. Chapter: 8

gigabyte. A unit of measurement of digital data storage. A gigabyte (GB) equals 1,024 megabytes (MB) and 1,048,576 kilobytes (kB). Chapter: 8

GIGO. Acronym for Garbage In Garbage Out. A truism in computer programming that says the end result of an algorithm is only as valid and accurate as the data that is put into the algorithm. Chapter: 4

GIMP. Acronym for GNU Image Manipulation Platform. A free and open-source digital image editing application for use on Windows, Macintosh and Linux operating systems. A version of GIMP, called GimpShop, has a user interface intended to replicate the user interface of Photoshop. It is available to download at http://www.gimpshop.com/download.shtml. Chapter: 8

Google Analytics. A free proprietary Web-based service that helps website administrators better understand audience behavior on their site. Available at www.google.com/analytics/. Chapter: 3

GPS. Acronym for Global Positioning System. Application developed by the U.S. Department of Defense and maintained by the U.S. government that uses space satellites to provide the specific time and location of a client device. Chapter: 2

Group Page (Facebook). A semicustomizable template in the Facebook social network that allows Facebook users to quickly establish a place for online conversation and easily invite their contacts to join. Chapter: 11

H.264. A group of standards for video compression; its uses range from Internet video to HDTV broadcasts. Also called "AVC (Advanced Video Coding)" or "MPEG-4, Part 10" or "MPEG-4 AVC." Chapter: 8

Handbrake. A free and open-source desktop application that is used to change video from one digital format into another. It is available for Windows, Mac OS X and Linux operating systems. Chapter: 8

hashtag. On Twitter, a word that is used to identify a message related to a specific topic; a "keyword" on Twitter. Hashtags are designated by the # symbol immediately preceding any string of characters. There is no governing body for hashtags—they are a folksonomy. Chapters: 6, 11

HD. Acronym for High Definition. In the context of video, HD is an image that has a pixel density of at least 720 vertical pixels. Chapter: 8

header. In an HTML document, the portion of the file marked by the <head> and </head> tags. Information in the header includes metadata about the file but is not displayed within the browser window. Chapter: 5

homepage. The page retrieved by a Web browser when a user points the browser to a domain name without any additional file path or directory name. Although the user may type only the domain name, such as "cnn.com," the homepage of most domains is actually a specific file that is named "index.html" or "index.php" or something similar. Chapter: 7

homepage package. A collection of related information that is placed together on a news site's homepage and functions as single piece of content that may point to several different resources on the site. Chapter: 7

hotspot. A location where a device can receive a WiFi signal. Chapter: 10

HTML. Acronym for HyperText Markup Language. The dominant technique used for describing the structure of a Web page. Chapters: 4, 5, 7

HTML5. A draft standard for marking up Web documents. It is being developed by the World Wide Web Consortium as a major revision to HTML4 and XHTML, the current standards for marking up Web documents. Chapter: 8

HTTP. Acronym for HyperText Transfer Protocol. The set of standards that governs how data flows from a server to a client computer over the World Wide Web. Chapter: 7

hypercardioid microphone. Microphone with a pickup pattern similar to cardioid microphones but more sensitive to sound at the sides and less sensitive to sound at the rear. Chapter: 8

hyperlink. A specific area on a Web page that, when activated in a Web browser, takes the audience to another specific location on the World Wide Web. Chapters: 1, 7

hyperlocal journalism. Journalism carried out in a very narrowly defined geographic community, typically small cities within a metropolitan area or even neighborhoods within a town. The term tends to be relative to the coverage area of mainstream media in the same locality. Chapters: 2, 11

ICANN. Acronym for Internet Company for Assigned Names and Numbers. A California not-for-profit corporation that is contracted by the U.S. Department of Commerce to assign top-level domain names and allocate IP address space. It was created in 1998 as the successor to InterNIC, run by Network Solutions and AT&T under the auspices of the National Science Foundation, and the Internet Assigned Numbers Authority, run by the University of Southern California for the U.S. Department of Defense. Chapter: 6

IEEE 1394. See *FireWire*.

i.Link. See *FireWire*.

iMovie. A digital video editing software application created by Apple for use on the Mac OS X operating system. It comes with the iLife software package, but does not offer as many features as Final Cut or Premiere. Chapter: 8

importing. The process of making a digital media file available to a multimedia editing software tool, such as Final Cut, Soundslides or Flash. Chapter: 8

in point. The place the user of an audio or video editing application has designated as the start of a clip. Chapter: 8

index page. A page on a news site that serves primarily as a pointer to other pages of a related type or subject. Index pages are often named "index.html" or "index.php" and are automatically displayed when a user points a Web browser to a specific directory path without providing a specific file name. Chapter: 7

inline link. An HTML link that is inside the body of an article. Chapter: 7

interactivity. A quality of media that is described in terms of (1) how much people control the content they consume; (2) how easy it is for people to create, publish and share their own content; and (3) the degree to which content creation is shared. Chapter: 1

interlaced video. Video that is painted on the screen in alternating sets of horizontal lines. First the odd-numbered lines of pixels are displayed on the screen and then the even-numbered lines are displayed. This is how broadcast television is displayed in the United States, but not how computers display video. Chapter: 8

interview video. A piece of video content that is intended primarily to convey the words of one or more people. Chapter: 8

inverted pyramid. A style of news writing that begins with a brief summary of the most important facts and then presents details of the story in order of decreasing importance. Chapters: 5, 12

IP address. A four-number address that describes a piece of hardware's unique location on any computer network that uses the TCP/IP protocols. In the traditional version of IP addresses (IPV4), each number is separated by a period. Each number is given a value between 0 and 255, so that a complete IP address might look like this: 192.168.0.255. IP addresses do not need to be globally unique. On a private network—one not connected to the Internet—an IP address just needs to be unique relative to the other devices on the same network. The world is running out of globally unique IP addresses. The solution has been to create a new nomenclature for IP addresses (IPV6). Addresses in this format might look like this: 2001:0db8:85a3:0000:0000:8a2e:0370:7334. Chapters: 6, 11

iPhoto. A digital image editing software application made by Apple for use on the Macintosh OS X operating system. It comes packaged with the iLife suite of software. Chapter: 8

JavaScript. An object-oriented computer programming language that typically runs inside the Web browser of a personal computer. Among other uses, it makes Web pages dynamic and interactive. Chapters: 9, 11, 12

JPEG or JPG format. Acronym for Joint Photographic Experts Group. A compression standard for digital images. Chapter: 8

JSON. Acronym for JavaScript Object Notation. A standard of defining and exchanging pieces of fielded data between computers, JSON was originally written to be used with JavaScript. It is an alternative to XML. Chapter: 12

jumpcut. In video editing, a transition that shows the same person in adjacent shots, but in a different position. Chapter: 8

kbps. Abbreviation for kilobytes per second. A measurement of data rate; can be used in the context of the amount of data per second of audio or video footage, or as the amount of data that is transmitted over a network. Chapter: 8

keyword. A word that is used to identify a piece of content related to a specific topic. Chapters: 5, 12

kHz. Abbreviation for kilohertz. In digital audio, a measurement of sample rate. Chapter: 8

knowem.com. A Web service that checks for the existence of a single user name across several social networks. Chapter: 11

Kyte. An online video distribution service that provides, among other things, the ability to display on the Web live video recorded from a mobile phone or other device. Chapter: 10

lavaliere microphone. A small microphone that clips to the clothing of an interviewee. Excellent for use in single-person interviews because of its unobtrusive size and its narrow pickup pattern. Chapter: 8

lead. The first paragraph of a news story. Chapter: 5

link. See *hyperlink*.

linkset. A collection of hyperlinks that share some common trait and appear adjacent to each other on a Web. Chapter: 7

live chat. An online conversation between one or more people that is conducted in real time, meaning that the typing of one participant is almost instantaneously seen by all other participants. Chapter: 1

LiveStream.com. A Web platform for live streaming of audio and video. Chapter: 10

load balancing. The technique of distributing workload across several computers. Chapter: 4

logging. In video editing, the process of setting in and out points on a piece of raw footage in order to mark the location of clips to be captured and/or transferred into a digital video editing project. Chapter: 8

logic tier. The logic, or rules, written in a computer programming language that governs the conditions under which different pieces of data should be pulled from the database and sent to the HTML pages. Chapter: 9

logical operator. A symbol or word used to connect two statements in a computer programming language. Chapter: 6

loop. In computer programming, a piece of code that runs over and over until a specific event occurs or condition is met. Chapter: 4

lower thirds. On videos, graphics and words that are placed in the lower third of the frame so that they do not obstruct the primary subject. Chapter: 8

lux. A measurement of light in a given area. Chapter: 8

M4V (.m4v). A nonstandard file extension for MP4 video files. It is a video file in the MPEG-4 container format. Although the M4V file is not standard, it is popular because it is used by iTunes. These files contain video compressed with the H.264 codec and audio compressed with the AAC codec. Chapter: 8

man on the street. A person, of either gender, who is interviewed for a news article for the purpose of representing popular opinion rather than providing expert knowledge. Chapters: 7, 11

ManyEyes. A Web service for creating data visualizations by pairing templates against existing datasets. It is run by IBM's Collaborative User Experience research group. Chapter: 9

matched action. The technique of showing the same action from different distances or slightly different angles. Chapter: 8

media/medium. Anything on or through which information is stored or transmitted. Depending on the context, it can refer to physical devices that store digital information, the news and entertainment content-creation industry, or newspaper, among other things. Medium is the singular form of media. Chapter: 1

MediaWiki. A free and open-source software application for hosting a wiki on a Web server. MediaWiki is the software that runs Wikipedia. Both are developed by the Wikimedia Foundation. MediaWiki is written in the PHP computer language and must be connected to either a MySQL or PostgreSQL relational database management system. Chapter: 4

megapixel. A measurement of the number of image sensors (pixels) in a digital camera. The equivalent of 1 million pixels. Chapter: 8

meta description tag. An HTML "meta" element that has some value for the "description" attribute. It appears in the header of an HTML document and is in search engine optimization. Chapter: 5

meta keywords tag. An HTML "meta" element that has some value for the "keyword" attribute. It appears in the header of an HTML document and is in search engine optimization. Chapter: 5

metadata. A description—usually fielded—of the content contained inside any kind of digital media file; essentially, "data about the data." Chapter: 5

method. In JavaScript and other programming languages, a portion of code that performs a specific action (usually on a specific object). Chapter: 12

MiniDV tape. A format of digital videotape most often used to record standard definition video. Chapter: 8

MiniHD tape. A version of MiniDV digital videotape used to record high-definition video. Chapter: 8

mini-plug. A single-pronged plug that is commonly used to connect headphones to a variety of consumer audio equipment. It has a diameter of 1/8-inch. Chapter: 8

mixdown. Both the name of an audio file that combines and flattens several tracks into one file and the process of creating such a file. This is typically the last step when working with a multitrack audio project. Chapter: 8

mixing. In audio editing, the process of combining two or more sounds into a single file. Chapter: 8

MOV (.mov). A file extension indicating that a file uses the QuickTime container format. This format is essentially an older version of the MPEG-4 container format. This proprietary format was developed by Apple but can be used with a wide variety of editing and playback software. Chapter: 8

MP3 (.mp3). The file extension for compressed audio files using the MPEG-3 codec. MP3 is used as the audio compression codec in video formats such as FLV. MP3 is the most universally used compression codec; however, it generally produces a lower-quality audio than files using the AAC codec. Chapter: 8

MP4 (.mp4). The file extension for files that use the MPEG-4 container format. These files usually contain video compressed with the H.264 codec and audio compressed with the AAC codec. MPEG-4 files sometimes use a wide variety of nonstandard file extensions, including M4V for video and M4A (.m4a) for audio. Chapter: 8

MPEG-4. See *MP4*.

multichannel distribution. Distribution of the same piece of content via multiple channels. For example, putting a newspaper story on paper and on a website without making any changes between the versions. Chapter: 8

multimedia reporting. The use of more than one technique—text, audio, still images, or moving images—to tell a single story. Chapter: 8

MySQL. A relational database management system that is used on Web servers as the back end of many content management systems and other dynamic Web applications. It comes in a free, open-source version and a paid version. It was launched in 1995 and is now wholly owned by Oracle Corporation. The free version is available for download at http://www.mysql.com/downloads/mysql/. Chapters: 9, 11

name attribute. Used to designate a specific HTML anchor element as a unique location on a Web page. Chapter: 7

naming convention. Rules for naming digital media files in such a way that a casual observer could infer useful information about the content of the file simply by reading the file name. Chapter: 8

National Institute for Computer-Assisted Reporting. A program of Investigative Reporters and Editors, Inc., and the Missouri School of Journalism aimed at helping reporters find and use digital information. Chapter: 9

National Press Photographers Association. A 7,000-member nonprofit organization founded in 1946 and based in Durham, N.C., whose mission is to provide resources for professional news photographers. Chapter: 8

nesting. The inclusion of one rule or function completely inside another rule or function. Chapter: 5

Network Solutions. The for-profit company that controlled the assignment of Internet domain names from 1991 until 1998. It remains one of the largest registries of domain names. Chapter: 6

news element. One of the following categories of facts in a news story: Who? What? When? Where? Why? How? Chapter: 2

news hole. The space or time available for news in a given setting. Chapter: 5

news peg. A recent event that provides the value of timeliness to a news story. Chapter: 2

normal form. A component of database theory aimed at determining and eliminating logical inconsistencies in the way data is organized. Chapter: 9

normalization. The process of determining and eliminating logical inconsistencies in the way data is organized. Chapter: 9

object. In JavaScript and other object-oriented programming languages, a particular entity that is defined by specific attributes (or elements) that have specific values. Once they are defined, programmers can manipulate objects to achieve specific results. Chapter: 12

object element or tag. An HTML tag used for the purpose of displaying audio and visual files inside HTML documents. While standard, it is not supported the same way in all browsers. See also *embed element*. Chapter: 8

object-oriented. A type of programming language that is based on the paradigm of using virtual representations of real-world things—or objects. Many of today's most popular computer programming languages incorporate at least some elements of object-oriented programming. Chapters: 9, 12

omni-directional microphone. A microphone that picks up sound in an equal pattern in all directions. Chapter: 8

Omniture. A company that provides products and services to help content creators acquire, track and analyze their audiences. It is owned by Adobe. Chapter: 3

on-demand delivery. The ability of a news organization to deliver specific information to a specific user at the moment he or she requests it. Chapter: 1

operating system. Software that governs the interaction between software programs and computer hardware. Microsoft's Windows operating systems are by far the most popular in the world. Apple's OS X operating system and varieties of the Linux operating system are also widely used. Chapter: 7

operator. In JavaScript and other programming languages, symbols that perform arithmetic on or define the relationship between two or more values or variables. See http://www.w3schools.com/JS/js_operators.asp. Chapter: 12

optical zoom. The process of magnifying an image in a digital camera by physically moving the lens. Chapter: 8

Oracle. Both the name of a server-based relational database management system and the company that makes it. The Oracle company also controls the MySQL relational database management system. Chapter: 9

out point. The place the user of an audio or video editing application has designated as the end of a clip. Chapter: 8

PageRank. The proprietary algorithm invented and used by Google to determine the relative value of different Web documents based on an analysis of links to and from the document. See http://infolab.stanford.edu/~backrub/google.html. Chapter: 5

page scraping. The process of downloading and storing information that is displayed on a screen (or contained in a Web document). Also called "data scraping" or "screen scraping." Chapter: 9

page view. A unit that counts each time a server sends out a new Web page. Chapter: 3

pan. In video recording, the movement of the camera along a (typically horizontal) plane. Chapter: 8

parallel presentation. The side-by-side presentation of two or more versions of the same set of facts, each version created for a distinct medium and standing independent of the other versions. Chapter: 1

parallel reporting. The process by which two or more reporters use different techniques to simultaneously gather information for two or more versions of the same story. Chapters: 1, 8

parameters. In JavaScript and other programming languages, the values or variables that determine the specific outcome of a given function. Chapter: 12

parent directory. The directory that is immediately one step higher than the current directory or file. Chapter: 7

parsing. The process of analyzing a digital document or file to determine the structure of information contained within it. Chapter: 4

pattern matching. The process of checking to see whether a string of characters in a document matches a given template pattern. Chapter: 9

PDF (.pdf). Acronym for Portable Document File. A file extension created by Adobe Systems in 1993 that became open standard in 2008. It is used to ensure that a document's layout is preserved regardless of the application, operating system or hardware on which it is viewed. Chapters: 4, 7

persistent URL. A URL that does not change, even as the content of the resource changes. Chapter: 10

photo gallery. A collection of photos used to tell a story. Chapter: 1

Photo Gallery. A free photo-editing application developed by Microsoft that can be used on Windows operating systems. Available at http://explore.live.com/windows-live-photo-gallery. Chapter: 8

Photobucket. A Web-based photo and video storage and sharing service at photobucket.com. It was launched in 2003 and is often used in conjunction with pure-play social networks such as MySpace, Facebook and LiveJournal. Chapter: 6

Photoshop. The most widely used professional photo-editing software application. It is made by Adobe and is available in a variety of feature levels for both Windows and Mac OS X operating systems. Chapter: 8

PHP. A scripting language that has been widely used to develop content management systems and other Web applications. For more information go to http://www.w3schools .com/php/default.asp and http://php.net/index.php. Chapters: 9, 11, 12

Picasa. The name of both a photo-sharing website and a photo editing and management application for Windows, Mac OS X and Linux operating systems. It was created by Idealabs in 2002 and purchased by Google in 2004. For more information go to http:// picasa.google.com and http://picasaweb.google.com. Chapter: 8

pipe. A text character represented by a vertical line and used to separate one string of text from another on the same line. On most keyboards it is [Shift-\]. Chapter: 7

pixel. The smallest independent piece of visual information in a digital image. The shapes and sizes of pixels are determined by, among other things, the size of the computer monitor on which they are displayed, the density of pixels in the display's resolution and the aspect ratio of the screen. Chapter: 8

pixelation. The "mosaic" effect that occurs when a bitmap image is increased beyond its original size and individual pixels can be distinguished by the audience. Chapter: 8

plug-in. A piece of software that adds a specific functionality to a larger stand-alone software application. Plug-ins cannot be used without the application for which they are written. Chapter: 8

podcast. A series of recorded audio to which the audience can subscribe and request delivery of new episodes. Chapter: 1

post. The dominant content type of a blog; a post consists of a body, a headline, a time-stamp and often a byline, tags and a collection of associated comments. Chapter: 10

PPI. Abbreviation for pixels per inch. A measurement of pixel density in a printed image or a computer display. Also called DPI, or "dots per inch." Chapter: 8

Premiere. A professional video-editing application made by Adobe for the Windows and Mac OS X operating systems. Chapter: 8

presentation tier. The HTML and CSS formats that display data to the audience. Chapter: 9

primary key. In relational databases, the field in a data table that contains a unique and permanent value for each record. Chapter: 9

Pro-am journalism. A collaboration between professional and amateur journalists in which the amateurs are directly publishing a portion of the content. Chapter: 11

progressive download. A method of delivering recorded video content over the Internet. The viewer can begin to watch the video before the file is completely downloaded to the viewer's machine. Chapter: 10

progressive scan video. Video that is painted on the screen in horizontal lines that appear sequentially. This is how most computers and some high-definition televisions display video. Chapter: 8

property. In JavaScript and other programming languages, any characteristic of a specific object. Chapter: 12

protocol. A standardized definition of message formats and the rules for exchanging messages. Computers can talk to one another by using a common protocol such as FTP or HTTP. Chapter: 7

ProTools. A collection of digital audio editing hardware and software made by Avid for use on Windows or Mac OS X operating systems. Chapter: 8

Publish2. A site that provides collaboration and content curation tools for online journalists. Chapter: 11

Python. A server-side programming language that is used to create Web applications as well as the Django Web application framework. Chapter: 9

query processor. The part of a search engine that attempts to find documents and other resources that are relevant to a user's search terms. Chapter: 6

QuickTime. Both the name of a software application that plays audio and video files as well as a broad multimedia framework developed by Apple. The QuickTime applications are available for Windows and Mac OS X operating systems. The framework supports a wide variety of file types and compression codecs. Chapter: 8

radio button. In a Web form, a round interactive element that allows users to select only one option from a list. Chapter: 9

RDBMS. Acronym for Relational Database Management System. A program that is used to define datasets, define relationships between datapoints and perform a variety of tasks including record creation, reading, updating and deletion. Chapter: 9

record. In a database table, one horizontal row of datapoints that, together, define the attributes of a particular entity. Chapter: 4

registrar. Any company that manages the creation and allocation of Internet domain names. Chapter: 6

relative link. A link to another Web page that is written in such a way that it defines the location of the destination file only in terms of its relationship to the departure point. If only one of either the destination or departure point changes, then the relationship is altered and the link is broken. Chapter: 7

resolution. Describes the number of pixels that can either be recorded or displayed in a given physical area. Chapter: 8

re-topping. In a breaking news situation, the process of writing a new lead for a story that reflects the changing importance of various news elements. Chapter: 10

root directory. The directory that contains all other directories. Chapter: 7

row. In a spreadsheet, a horizontally aligned sequence of cells that contains values for all the attributes of a single entity. Each row is identified by a unique letter that starts with "A" for the top-most row and increases by an increment of one letter for each subsequent row below the first. Chapter: 9

RSS. Acronym for Really Simple Syndication. A standardized format for describing news articles and blog posts in a fielded data format that can be read by a computer. The field structure, field names and their content are stored in a document called an RSS feed or RSS channel. Chapters: 6, 9, 10, 12

Ruby on Rails. A free and open-source Web application framework that is widely used to build dynamic websites. It is written in the Ruby programming language and works in conjunction with Web server software such as Apache and a relational database management system, especially SQLite. Chapter: 9

rule of thirds. The standard in photojournalism of keeping an image's primary subject aligned along horizontal and vertical axes that divide the frame into equal thirds. Chapters: 8, 2

sample rate. In digital audio recording, the number of times in one second that sound is recorded. It is measured in kilohertz (kHz). A sample rate of 44.1 kHz is considered CD quality for a stereo recording. Chapter: 8

sampling. Any number of methods of using portions of an audio or video source to represent the original visual or audio source. This is often performed in order to reduce the size of a digital media file while limiting reduction in quality. Chapter: 8

Screen-Scraper.com. A software application that automatically accesses and records information stored on one or more Web documents. It is available for Windows, Mac OS X and Linux operating systems. Chapter: 9

search query. The words a user submits when conducting a search in a search engine. Chapter: 6

Section 230. The section of the Communications Decency Act of 1996 that says providers of "an interactive computer service" cannot usually be held liable for content posted on the service by users. Chapter: 11

section titles. Short phrases, typically displayed with bold text, that mark the start of different sections of text in an online news story. Chapter: 5

Secure Digital (SD) card. A type of portable memory card that is used in digital cameras. Chapter: 8

sensor chip. The hardware in a digital camera that detects light coming through the lens and converts it to digital data. Chapter: 8

SEO. Acronym for Search Engine Optimization. Chapters: 3, 5

shotgun microphone. A long microphone that picks up sound almost directly in front of it. Chapter: 8

shutter speed. The amount of time that a digital camera exposes its sensor chips to light. Chapter: 8

Shutterfly. An online photo storage and printing service. Available at http://www.shutterfly.com. Chapter: 6

sidebar link. A link that is placed outside the body of a news article. Chapter: 7

SiteCatalyst. Software from Adobe's Omniture division that tracks users on a website. Chapter: 3

smart phone. A mobile phone that can access the Internet. Chapter: 3

SMS. Acronym for Short Messaging Service. A protocol for transmitting 160-character text messages between mobile phones. Chapter: 10

social bookmarking. A form of collaborative filtering in which members of the online news audience, working independently of one another, extract news articles from websites and dynamically recategorize them based on keywords, or tags, that are not created or controlled by the original publisher. Chapter: 12

solid state memory. See *flash memory.*

Sound Forge. A digital audio editing application made by Sony for use on Windows operating systems. Chapter: 8

spam. Any type of unsolicited bulk message that is sent over a digital communication network. Chapter: 11

spreadsheet. A computer application that arranges information in cells that are arranged in a grid of horizontal rows and vertical columns. Chapter: 9

SQL. Acronym for Structured Query Language. Language for managing data stored in relational database management systems. Pronounced either "S-Q-L" or "sequel." Chapter: 6

SQL Server. A relational database management system created by Microsoft as a server from which users can deploy database-driven Web applications. Chapter: 9

statement. The smallest independent element of a computer program. Chapter: 12

storage media. Any physical object that stores digital information. Examples include CD-ROMs, USB flash memory drives, hard disk drives and CompactFlash memory cards. Chapter: 8

storyboard. A series of illustrations that demonstrates the flow of a linear visual story or nonlinear interactive application. Chapter: 12

streaming. A technique for delivering digital audio or video content to an end-user without first storing the digital data on a disk. Chapter: 10

string. A sequence of text characters that is meant to be interpreted literally and not as a programming instruction. Chapters: 6, 12

subdirectory. See *child directory.*

subhead. An extension of the headline of a news story; additional information that provides further description of the story. Chapter: 5

SWF (.swf). The file extension for complete and self-contained Flash projects. They can be played with the Flash Media Player, one of the most popular browser plug-ins. They cannot be re-edited in Flash (editing of the FLA file from which the SWF project was created is possible, however). SWF files often go by the confusing term "Flash movie" (as opposed to "Flash video," which are files with FLV or F4V extensions). SWF files are also sometimes called "Swiff" files. Chapter: 8

Switch. A software application for converting digital audio files from one codec to another. It is made by NCH Software and available for both Windows and Mac OS X operating systems. A free version of the software is available for noncommercial use at http://www.nch.com.au/switch/index.html. Chapter: 8

syntax. The rules governing the way words and symbols are used to construct statements. Chapter: 12

table. In a database, a collection of unique records that all share a common set of attributes. Chapter: 9

Tableizer. A Web-based tool for converting spreadsheets into HTML tables. It was created by Danny Sanchez, the digital platform manager for Courant.com and CTnow.com. Available at http://tableizer.journalistopia.com/. Chapter: 10

tag (HTML). The symbols and letters that are used to define the start and end points of an element in HTML. Tags include an opening angle bracket < and a closed angle bracket >, with the name of the HTML element in between the brackets. Closed tags also include a slash immediately after the open angle bracket </. Chapters: 7, 8

tag (organizational).   A keyword or term used to describe a piece of content, commonly used in social bookmarking and blogging platforms. Chapters: 10, 12

take.   Another word for writethru.

target attribute.   Component of an HTML anchor element that describes in which browser window a link should open. Chapter: 7

taxonomy.   A collection of rules governing the hierarchical classification of related objects. Chapter: 12

theme.   A collection of programming logic and display rules that governs the visual appearance and user interface of a blog. Chapter: 10

third-party social site. A website to which members can post content, but that is controlled by neither the journalist's news organization nor an individual in the journalist's audience.

three-tiered architecture.   A structure of Web applications in which the presentation rules are stored in one place and controlled by one system, the "logic" or programming rules are controlled by another system and the data is stored and controlled in a third system. Chapter: 9

thumbnail.   A small, tightly cropped image. Often a square. About the size of the nail on your thumb. Chapter: 8

timestamping.   A visible indication of the time at which a piece of content was created or updated. Chapters: 4, 10

tip line.   Traditionally, a phone number that people could call to provide news editors with information. Chapter: 1

title.   In videos, text that describes the content or provides additional information about the images. Chapter: 8

title tag.   An HTML element that defines the name of the document. Chapter: 5

Total Recorder.   A software application that can be used for recording phone interviews and VoIP interviews directly onto a Windows PC. Available at http://www.totalrecorder .com/. Chapter: 8

Twitter.   A Web-based application used to send and receive 140-character messages among defined social networks known as "followers." The application's Web page is at http://www.twitter.com. Chapters: 7, 10

UID.   Acronym for Unique Identifier. Chapters: 6, 9

unique visitor. The number of people who visit a website during a given time, usually a month. Chapter: 3

URL. Acronym for Uniform Resource Locator. The address of the location where an HTML document or other object lives on the Web; technically, a URL must begin with a protocol. Chapters: 7, 11

usability. The ease with which humans can use a tool, specifically an interactive application or website. Chapter: 5

USB. Acronym for Universal Serial Bus. A widely used specification for connecting two pieces of hardware and allowing them to exchange data. Chapter: 8

user interface. Any part of a website or software application that the audience sees. Chapter: 9

user-generated content. Any type of text, audio or visual material that is created and displayed on a website by someone other than the person or organization that built and controls the website. Chapters: 1, 11

UStream.tv. A platform for streaming live video over the Web. Chapter: 10

value (of data). The variable that at a specific time describes a specific attribute for a specific record. Chapter: 9

value (of HTML attribute). Used to give a specific quality to a specific attribute of a specific HTML element. Chapter: 7

Vimeo. An online video storage and distribution service. Available at http://www.vimeo.com. Chapter: 6

visit. A unit counted each time a unique visitor accesses a website. Also called "session." Chapter: 3

vodcast. A series of recorded video to which the audience can subscribe and request delivery of new episodes. Chapter: 1

VoIP. Acronym for Voice-Over-Internet Protocol. The term covers any method of transmitting voices or other sounds over the Internet. Chapter: 8

WAV (.wav). The file extension for uncompressed audio using the Waveform Audio File Format. It can be used on the Windows, Mac OS X and Linux platform and is often the original format for professional news audio interviews. Chapter: 8

Web Developer Toolbar. An add-on for the Firefox Web browser; provides insight about how a Web page was constructed. It was built by Chris Pederick, the lead front-end developer at Bleacher Report. It can be downloaded at https://addons.mozilla.org/en-US/firefox/addon/60/. Chapter: 8

Web page.   Another name for an HTML document, usually available on the Web. Chapters: All

Web-cast.   Audio or video content that is distributed via the Web to multiple people at the same time. Chapter: 10

website.   A set of related Web documents, usually all at the same domain name. Chapters: All

WhoIs.   Distributed database that matches domain names with computers and their owners. Chapter: 6

widget.   Interactive single-purpose application for displaying and updating local data or data on the Web that requires only a single download and installation on a user's machine or mobile device. Chapters: 10, 12

widow.   A single word at the end of a headline that appears on a line by itself. Chapter: 4

WiFi.   Although a trademark of the Wi-Fi Alliance, the term generally refers to any use of the IEEE 802.11 standard for creating or accessing a wireless network. Chapters: 3, 10

wildcard operator.   Symbol used to represent one or more characters. The asterisk character is often used as a wildcard operator representing one character and the exclamation point is often used to represent several characters. Chapter: 6

Windows Media Player.   Software application for playing audio and video files made by Microsoft for use with the Windows operating system. Some older versions do not natively support all the codecs supported by Version 12 for Windows 7. Chapter: 8

Windows Movie Maker.   A free video-editing application made by Microsoft for use with the Windows operating system. It cannot open FLV, MP4 or MOV files. It saves files as WMV, WMA or AVI files. Chapter: 8

WMA (.wma).   The file extension for audio files using the Windows Media Audio formats. WMA can refer to both a container format and one of several related codecs. WMA files are usually compressed audio but can also sometimes be uncompressed audio. Windows Media files use a proprietary format developed by Microsoft; as such, they often must be converted to another file format before they can be opened with non-Microsoft editing software. Chapter: 8

WMV (.wmv).   The file extension for video files using the Windows Media Video formats. WMV can refer to both a container format and one of several related codecs. Windows Media files use a proprietary format developed by Microsoft; as such, they often must be converted to another file format before they can be opened with non-Microsoft editing software. Chapter: 8

Wordpress. A free and open-source blogging platform found at http://www.wordpress.com and http://www.wordpress.org. Chapters: 7, 10, 11

writethru. In a breaking news situation, a complete rewrite of the facts aimed at improving the organization of information. Chapter: 10

XLR. A type of microphone connector used on professional mics. XLR connectors have three pins and may need to first plug into an adapter before being used on audio and video recording equipment. Chapter: 8

XML. Stands for eXtensible Markup Language. Set of rules for describing and storing data in fields that can be read by other computers. Chapters: 4, 6, 9, 12

YouTube. A Web-based video distribution system to which registered users can upload their own videos. Owned by Google. Chapter: 7

INDEX

Figures and tables are indicated by f and t following the page number.